Edna Joseph Fund

A PEPYSIAN GARLAND

A PEPYSIAN GARLAND

BLACK-LETTER BROADSIDE BALLADS
OF THE YEARS 1595–1639

CHIEFLY FROM THE COLLECTION
OF SAMUEL PEPYS

EDITED BY

HYDER E. ROLLINS

HARVARD UNIVERSITY PRESS
CAMBRIDGE, MASSACHUSETTS

1971

First published 1922
Reprinted by permission of Cambridge University Press

Publication of this book has been aided by a grant from the
Hyder Edward Rollins Fund

Library of Congress Catalog Card Number 74–176041
SBN 674–66185–0

Printed in the United States of America

TO

O. F. MORSHEAD

PREFACE

PERHAPS the most important of all the treasures—
apart from the inimitable *Diary*—in the library be-
queathed by Samuel Pepys to Magdalene College, Cambridge, is his collection of broadside ballads. These were
grouped loosely according to subject-matter and provided
with title-pages and descriptive headings in Pepys's own
hand before being bound into five large folio volumes.
The first title-page runs:

My Collection of Ballads. Vol. I. Begun by Mr Selden; Im-
prov'd by ye addition of many Pieces elder thereto in Time; and
the whole continued to the year 1700. When the Form, till then
peculiar thereto, vizt. of the Black Letter with Picturs, seems (for
cheapness sake) wholly laid aside, for that of the White Letter
without Pictures.

Nearly every broadside in the first four volumes is printed
in black-letter type, while in the fifth volume appear only
broadsides in roman and italic type. Ballads of a comparatively early date—almost none later than 1640—are
found in the first volume, those in the other volumes being,
for the most part, printed during the years 1660–1700.
It seems likely that the majority of the older ballads came
from John Selden's collection. A careful study of the old
numbering on the separate sheets and of Pepys's new
pagination would no doubt partially reveal the extent of
the Selden nucleus on which the collection was built.

A manuscript catalogue of the collection shows 1797
entries of first lines. This number, however, not only in-
cludes printed duplicates as well as manuscript ballads
that Pepys copied but also fails to indicate when more than
one ballad is printed on a single sheet. J. W. Ebsworth[1],
after a painstaking examination of the collection, stated
that it contains 1738 individual printed sheets, 67 of

---

[1] *Roxburghe Ballads*, VIII, 740.

vii

which are duplicates, and that of the 1671 distinct ballads in the five volumes 964 are unique.

No edition of Pepysian ballads has hitherto been published: for the present edition students are indebted to the good offices of Mr Stephen Gaselee and Mr O. F. Morshead, past and present Librarians of the Bibliotheca Pepysiana. The Ballad Society, founded by Dr Furnivall in 1868, announced its intention of printing the Pepys collection as an initial effort, but, failing to obtain the necessary authorization, turned instead to the huge collections in the British Museum. The Roxburghe and Bagford collections, have, as a result, long been accessible in the eleven volumes published by the Ballad Society under the titles of the *Roxburghe Ballads* (1871–1897) and the *Bagford Ballads* (1878). Among the eight volumes of these publications that appeared under his riotous, if learned, editorship, Ebsworth[1] estimated that he had reprinted, in one form or another, at least five hundred ballads that occur in Pepys's collection. From the collection, too, long before Ebsworth's time, distinguished students had drawn heavily. Bishop Percy made a thorough study of it before beginning the publication of his epoch-making *Reliques of Ancient English Poetry* (1765), in that work reproduced a number of Pepysian ballads, and had many others copied for him. These copies, by the way, are now preserved in the Percy Papers owned by the Harvard College Library. Others were reprinted by Thomas Evans and R. H. Evans in various editions of their *Old Ballads, Historical and Narrative* (1777–1810). Macaulay gleaned from the ballads some picturesque facts for his *History of England*; and within the last few years many other broadsides from the collection have been here and there reprinted[2], often in unexpected places. Many of Pepys's ballads, then, are accessible if one searches diligently. The bulk of the collection, however, is still generally unknown,

[1] *Roxburghe Ballads*, VIII, 740.
[2] Noteworthy are the photographic reproductions in Professor C. H. Firth's six volume illustrated edition of Macaulay's *History*.

PREFACE

and is likely to remain so until a trustworthy printed catalogue is published. Such a catalogue I hope to make some day. Meanwhile, this *Garland* reprints the most interesting seventeenth century ballads in Pepys's first volume, none of a later date than 1639, and to them adds from other sources six or seven early ballads in which Pepys himself would have revelled.

Undeniably the golden age of the ballad, like the golden age of the theatre, ended with the outbreak of the Great Rebellion. During the Commonwealth period (1649–1659) ballad-singing was prohibited by law, and offending street singers were flogged out of the trade. To be sure, ballads continued to be printed, but in not so large numbers as in the years before 1642 and after 1660. For this decay repressive laws were but partly to blame: more important is the fact that the chief writers turned from ballads to chapbooks and news-pamphlets. Martin Parker, the greatest of them all, is known to have written many pamphlets but only five or six ballads after 1642, and with his death in 1652 the best part of balladry came to an end. Laurence Price, almost the last of the distinguished line of ballad-writers that began in 1559 with William Elderton (or in 1512 with John Skelton), wrote for only a brief time after the Restoration. In authorship, in typography, and in subject-matter, Restoration ballads can seldom compare in interest with those of the reigns of the Tudors and early Stuarts.

It may be well to explain the use of the word *ballad*. Modern critics very often think of a ballad only as a traditional song that, like "Sir Patrick Spens," "Barbara Allen," or "Johnny Armstrong," has decided merits as poetry. This unhistoric restriction of the term to the English and Scottish "popular" ballads is a development of the nineteenth century. To quarrel with it would be out of place; but at least readers may be reminded that to Shakespeare, Jonson, Beaumont, Fletcher, Dryden, and Pepys the word *ballad* had in general one meaning only: namely, a song (usually written by a hack-poet) that was

ix

printed on a broadside and sold in the streets by professional singers. If "Johnny Armstrong," "Chevy Chase," or Sir Edward Dyer's "My Mind to Me a Kingdom Is" got into the hands of the John Trundles of London, it, too, became a ballad. Elizabethans and Jacobeans recognized no difference whatever in type between what are now called traditional (or popular) ballads and broadside (or stall) ballads: some of them no doubt thought "Chevy Chase" a better ballad than, say, "The Famous Rat-catcher" (No. 10). But, if so, they were judging each by its manner and matter, not discriminating between traditional and stall songs. In this book the word *ballad*, when otherwise unqualified, refers to the printed broadside type only.

To judge the ballad as poetry is altogether unfair. A few ballads, to be sure, do appear in *Tottel's Miscellany*, the *Paradise of Dainty Devises*, and the *Gorgeous Gallery of Gallant Inventions* without reeking of their humble origin; while the *Handfull of Pleasant Delights* (1584), which contains nothing but ballads, has been absurdly overpraised by critics (who, apparently, do not know that all of its songs had before collection been printed as broadside ballads) as "a work of considerable merit, containing some notable songs," or as "one of the most prized of the poetical book gems of the Elizabethan period," or as "lyric poems[1]." If such criticism of the *Handfull* were sound, an editor need have no fear in introducing the eighty ballads in this book as a very notable collection indeed of Elizabethan and Stuart lyrics. But sound it is not.

Ballads worthy to be called real poetry can almost be counted on the fingers of both hands. Among them might be placed the old ballad of "Love Will Find Out the Way," which Palgrave included in his *Golden Treasury* and which Thomas Hardy and Alfred Noyes quote with

---

[1] See a discussion of *A Handfull of Pleasant Delights* by the present writer in the *Journal of English and Germanic Philology*, January, 1919.

evident gusto; or "A Farewell to Love," from Thomas Deloney's *Garland of Good Will*, that is also included in the *Passionate Pilgrim* as the work of Shakespeare; or "Mary Ambree," a stirring song beloved by literary men from Ben Jonson to George Meredith; or, possibly, "The Babes in the Woods," so highly praised in Wordsworth's preface to the *Lyrical Ballads*.

From the point of view of sheer melody and rhythm, ballads often answer more than fairly to the test. It is a fact too often forgotten that, whatever their subject, ballads were written to be sung to certain definite and well-known tunes. Hence it often happens that the most doleful subject-matter is embodied in a measure that is decidedly musical and attractive. Cases in point are the refrains to the lugubrious ditty of Mrs Francis (No. 52) and the history of Jonah (No. 11). The matter and the diction of ballads are often contemptible while the measure is very good indeed. For this reason, or simply from the fact that a naïve news-story is told, ballads may at times pardonably be described as "remarkable" or "splendid" or even "delicious."

Ballads were not written for poetry. They were, in the main, the equivalent of modern newspapers, and it cannot well be denied that customarily they performed their function as creditably in verse as the average newspaper does in prose. Journalistic ballads outnumbered all other types. Others were sermons, or romances, or ditties of love and jealousy, of tricks and "jests," comparable to the ragtime, or music hall, songs of the present time. As such they may be beyond praise, however woefully lacking in high seriousness and criticism of life. The ballad has interest and value quite independent of its defects or its merits as poetry; and many of the most delightful and most valuable ballads are those which as poetry are worthless or even contemptible. Written for the common people by professional rhymesters—journalists of the earth earthy—ballads made no claims to poetry and art. They have always interested educated men, not as poems but as popular songs or as mirrors held up to the life of the people. In them are clearly reflected the lives and thoughts, the hopes and fears, the beliefs and amusements, of sixteenth and seventeenth century Englishmen. In them history becomes animated.

Shakespeare knew dozens of ballads by heart: he and his fellow-dramatists quote from ballads in nearly every play; and if occasionally they quote in ridicule, then their ridicule applies also to "John Dory," "George Aloe," "Little Musgrave," and "Mussleborough Field,"—traditional ballads now enshrined in Professor Child's *English and Scottish Popular Ballads*. The great Elizabethans did not dream of judging ballads as poetry—though indisputably they enjoyed reading and singing them—and lost no opportunity of denouncing their authors. Ben Jonson, for example, flatly declared that "a poet should detest a ballad-maker," echoing Thomas Nashe's grave remark that if a man would "love good poets he must not countenance ballad-makers." The Parkers and Prices of balladry were butts of never-ceasing ridicule: their very names were odious to poets, though many of their ballads rang pleasingly on the ear, sounded trippingly on the tongue. Nothing else brings one so close to the mass of people for whom Shakespeare wrote as do these songs of the street. Produced solely for the common people, in them are presented topics often of real value and interest. It is doubtful if a more remarkable group of ballads has ever been brought together in one volume than those here reprinted; but he would be a bold man who should characterize them as poetry.

The *Pepysian Garland* contains eighty ballads. Seventy-three of them come from the Pepys collection, six from the Wood and Rawlinson collections at the Bodleian Library, and one from the Manchester Free Reference Library. The earliest is dated 1595, the latest (except for No. 26, which is included only to illustrate another ballad) 1639. For obvious reasons a chronological arrangement has been adopted, with the result that great variety of subjects

greets the eye of a reader as he turns through the pages,
—a variety characteristic of the wares offered daily in the
streets of seventeenth century London. A ballad-monger,
said Thomas Middleton, never lacked "a subject to
write of: one hangs himself today, another drowns himself tomorrow, a sergeant stabbed next day; here a petti-
fogger a' the pillory; a bawd in the cart's nose, and a
pander in the tail; *hic mulier*, *haec vir*, fashions, fictions,
felonies, fooleries;—a hundred havens has the ballad-
monger to traffic at, and new ones still daily discovered[1]."
Middleton's comment reads like a description of the
Pepysian Garland!

Among the eighty ballads are historical accounts, more
or less trustworthy,—a few derived from news-books,
others from actual observation,—of the assassination of
Henry IV of France, the execution of Sir Walter Raleigh,
the activities of three Northamptonshire witches against
the Earl of Rutland, the fall of Oldenbarneveldt and of
Sir Francis Michell, prodigies above Cork and the burning
of that city in 1622, the Amboyna Massacre, the murder
of Dr John Lamb, and a battle between the Dutch and
Spanish fleets in 1639. Journalistic, too, are the "hanging
ballads" and doleful "good-nights" of criminals who
atoned for their crimes at the stake or on the gallows—
illustrating a curiosity for news, often mistakenly called
morbid, that is quite as eager to-day as then. As journalism
some of these ballads are admirable.

Sermonizing ballads full of dire warnings and moraliz-
ing also have a place, and we are asked to shudder at a
"passing bell" that tolled from heaven in 1582, at Caleb
Shillock's prophecies for the year 1607, and at a prophecy
of the Judgment Day found in France in 1618. In a
curiously modern tone "The Goodfellow's Complaint"
and "The Back's Complaint" present the woes attendant
on drunkenness and plead for total abstinence; while for
the edification of the unread other ballads paraphrase the
Biblical account of Solomon's judgment and of Jonah.

[1] *The World Tost at Tennis*, 1620 (*Works*, ed. A. H. Bullen, VII, 154).

PREFACE

A number deal with marvellous events or persons,— with the "admirable" teeth and stomach of Nicholas Wood, with a "monstrous strange" fish caught in Cheshire, with a sprightly "pig-faced gentlewoman" who was called Miss Tannakin Skinker, or with the too severely punished Lamenting Lady who bore 365 children at one burden. Fewer demands on one's credulity are made by the romances of Hero and Leander, of a conventionally cruel Western Knight and a Bristol maid, of a Wiltshire Cressid and a doting old dad. Pictures of manners and customs as valuable as those in the comedies of Dekker and Middleton,—coming as they do from another angle of observation,—are given in "Whipping Cheer," "The Rat-catcher," "A Banquet for Sovereign Husbands," and "Turner's Dish of Lenten Stuff." Satires of the foibles of the people abound. Lovers and their ladies are laughed at in "Ten Shillings for a Kiss," "A Proverb Old," and "The Wiving Age"; husbands are depicted as "He-Devils," wives as incorrigible scolds; and all trades and professions are held up to scorn for their dishonest actions. In contrast to these tirades, however, are a number of pleasing ballads written to glorify certain low trades and honest manual labour.

The most important single ballad in the volume is "Francis' New Jig" (No. 1), of the date 1595. This is apparently the only printed Elizabethan jig that has been preserved. Of hardly less interest is the "Country New Jig between Simon and Susan" (No. 21), and there are at least two other ballads (Nos. 29, 36; cf. also No. 38) that perhaps were jigs. A jig may be defined as a miniature comedy or farce, written in ballad-measure, which, at the end of a play, was sung and danced on the stage to ballad-tunes. Thanks to the mystifications of J. P. Collier[1] the

---

[1] In his *New Facts Regarding the Life of Shakespeare* (1835), pp. 18–20, Collier gave an erroneous definition and a specimen jig from a spurious MS. that have deceived his followers. Fleay (*Biographical Chronicle of the English Drama*, ii, 258), Furness (*New Variorum Hamlet*, i, 190), A. W. Ward (*History of English Dramatic Literature*, i, 454, 476), and

jig has received scanty and inadequate treatment from historians of the English drama. A number of other genuine jigs are extant. First in importance is that preserved in MS. Rawlinson Poet. 185 under the title of "A proper new ballett, intituled Rowland's god-sonne. To the tune of *Loth to departe*." There is a reference to this jig in the prologue to Nashe's play *Summer's Last Will*, and a two-part moralization was registered on April 28 and 29, 1592[1]. Almost as interesting is an unnamed jig preserved among the Henslowe papers at Dulwich College, which Collier misled scholars into believing to be a fragment of a play by Christopher Marlowe[2]. Still other jigs occur among the *Roxburghe Ballads*[3], in Robert Cox's drolls[4], and, from lost originals, in German translations[5].

By 1590 jigs were thoroughly established in London theatres as the usual conclusions to plays. In his *Pierce Penilesse* (1592) Thomas Nashe sneered at

the queint comedians of our time,
That when their Play is donne do fal to ryme[6];

and he threatened Gabriel Harvey that "Comedie vpon Comedie he shall haue, a Morall, a Historie, a Tragedie, or what hee will...with a Iigge at the latter ende in English Hexameters of *O neighbour Gabriell, and his wooing of Kate Cotton*[7]." Comparatively few jigs were registered at

others accept Collier's definition and his specimen as genuine. W. W. Greg (*Henslowe's Diary*, II, 189) says that "no undoubtedly genuine specimen [of a jig] is extant."

[1] Andrew Clark's *Shirburn Ballads*, p. 354; *Herrig's Archiv*, 1904, CXIV, 326 ff.; R. B. McKerrow's *Nashe*, III, 235; Arber's *Transcript of the Stationers' Registers*, II, 609 f.

[2] Collier's *Alleyn Papers*, pp. 8–11; G. F. Warner's *Catalogue of the MSS. and Muniments of Alleyn's College at Dulwich*, pp. 60 f.; A. Dyce's *Marlowe*, Appendix.

[3] *E.g.* I, 125, 201, 249.

[4] *Actaeon and Diana*, etc., 1656.

[5] *E.g.* "Roland und Margareth, Ein Lied, von Englischen Comedianten albie gemacht" (F. M. Boehme's *Altdeutsches Liederbuch*, 1877, pp. 174 ff.), which appears to be a translation of the "gigge betwene Rowland and the Sexton" that was licensed on December 16, 1591.

[6] R. B. McKerrow's *Nashe*, I, 244.   [7] *Ibid.* III, 114.

Stationers' Hall, all during the years 1591-1595. The
reason for the small number lies, no doubt, in the unwill-
ingness of the dramatic companies to have their jigs
"staled" by the press: they protected the jigs in their
repertory more successfully than their plays. Uncertainty
about printers' rights to the copies caused the Clerk of
the Stationers' Company to license, in December, 1591,
two jigs with the proviso, so often met with in entries of
plays, "so that they appertain not to any other[1]." But
jigs did not die out in 1595; far from it.

On December 12, 1597, Philip Henslowe bought two
jigs for the use of a company of actors, paying for the
two six shillings and eight pence[2],—proof that jigs had
received the approval of the box-office. In 1598, Ben
Jonson tells us, jigs came "ordinarily after a play[3]." He
loathed "the concupiscence of jigs and dances," and believed that they prevented audiences from appreciating
plays[4]. "Your only jig-maker," Hamlet calls himself after
he has carried on a vulgar dialogue with the bewildered
Ophelia. As for Polonius, who is bored by the long tragic
speech of the Player, Hamlet sarcastically remarks: "He's
for a jig or a tale of bawdry, or he sleeps[5]."

Customarily when a play was finished and the epilogue
spoken, the musicians struck up a tune and the comedians
came dancing out for the jig. "I haue often seene,"
wrote Thomas Dekker in 1613, "after the finishing of
some worthy Tragedy, or Catastrophe in the open Thea-
ters, that the Sceane after the Epilogue hath beene more
blacke (about a nasty bawdy Iigge) then the most horrid
Sceane in the Play was[6]." There can be no doubt that
some people went to the theatres to see the jig no less

---

[1] Arber's *Transcript*, II, 600.
[2] *Henslowe's Diary*, ed. W. W. Greg, I, 70, 82.
[3] *Every Man out of His Humour*, II, i.
[4] Induction to *Bartholomew Fair*.
[5] *Hamlet*, III, ii, 132; II, ii, 522.
[6] *A Strange Horse Race* (*Works*, ed. Grosart, III, 340). Cf. Edmund
Gayton's *Pleasant Notes upon Don Quixot*, 1654, pp. 108, 187, 271-272.

than the play. Says Thrift, in Thomas Goffe's *Careless Shepherdess* [1] (about 1620):

> I will hasten to the money Box,
> And take my shilling out again, for now
> I have considered that it is too much;
> I'le go to th' Bull, or Fortune, and there see
> A Play for two pense, with a Jig to boot.

A document of the highest importance,—not quoted, I believe, in any work on the drama,—that shows the attitude both of the common people and of the civil authorities towards jigs is printed in J. C. Jeaffreson's *Middlesex County Records* (ii, 83). It is "An Order for suppressinge of Jigges att the ende of Playes" passed at the General Sessions of the Peace on October 1, 1612, which runs as follows:

> Whereas Complaynte have [*sic*] beene made at this last Generall Sessions that by reason of certayne lewde Jigges songes and daunces vsed and accustomed at the play-house called the Fortune in Gouldinglane divers cutt-purses and other lewde and ill disposed persons in greate multitudes doe resorte thither at th' end of euerye playe many tymes causinge tumultes and outrages... Itt was hereuppon expresselye commaunded and ordered by the Justices of the said benche That all Actors of euerye playehouse within this cittye and liberties thereof and in the Countye of Middlesex that they and euerie of them utterlye abolishe all Jigges Rymes and Daunces after their playes And not to tollerate permitt or suffer anye of them to be used vpon payne of ymprisonment and puttinge downe and suppressinge of theire playes, And such further punishment to be inflicted upon them as their offences shall deserve...

As a result of this order, the comedian John Shank ceased "to sing his rhymes," as William Turner (cf. p. 35) phrased it: no doubt other jig-dancers suffered a like eclipse; but the effect of the order was temporary, and jigs continued to be sung regularly down to 1642.

At least two characters were required in all jigs for the sake of dialogue, and the number often, perhaps usually, was three or four. Jigs were never improvised: instead they were composed by professional ballad-writers or jig-

---

[1] 1654 ed., sig. B 4ᵛ (*Praeludium*).

makers, and were performed with fairly elaborate costumes and stage-properties. "Francis' New Jig" has rôles for two women, both of whom were at times masked, and for two men, whose costumes indicate which was the gentleman, which the farmer. Furthermore, the gentleman was provided with ten pounds in stage money and a ring to give his supposed mistress. One scene in "Rowland's Godson" is represented as taking place in an orchard, where the servant beats his master, who is disguised in a woman's clothes. One of Robert Cox's jigs required a bedroom set and a chest big enough to hold a man. Stage-directions, too, were as explicit as in the majority of plays and, with the action itself, show that jigs were written with the peculiar conventions of the Elizabethan stage in mind. Notice, for example, the principle of alternating scenes and the lapse of an entire night's time in "Francis' New Jig."

There is reason to believe that educated and ignorant people alike delighted in jigs. Good jig-makers invariably aimed at making their work "both witty to the wise, and pleasing to the ignorant[1]." That they succeeded the continual protests of the great dramatists show. Shortly before his death John Fletcher declared with some bitterness that a good play

> Meets oftentimes with the sweet commendation
> Of "Hang't!" "'tis scurvy": when for approbation
> A jig shall be clapt at, and every rhyme
> Prais'd and applauded by a clamorous chime[2].

In jigs Elizabethan comedians won much of their fame. William Kemp, in particular, gained enormous popularity during the years 1591–1595 with his jigs of "The Broomman," "The Kitchen-Stuff Woman," "A Soldier, a Miser, and Sym the Clown," and the three parts of "Kemp's Jig[3]." That his reputation for jigs had not declined in 1599 is attested by striking allusions to

---

[1] *Hog Hath Lost His Pearl* (Dodsley-Hazlitt's *Old Plays*, xi, 435).
[2] Prologue to *The Fair Maid of the Inn*.
[3] Cf. Arber's *Transcript*, ii, 297, 600, 669; iii, 50.

them in the satires of John Marston and Edward Guilpin [1]. Hardly less popular, perhaps, were Augustine Phillips— an actor in Shakespeare's plays—whose "Jig of the Slippers [2]" was licensed in May, 1595; George Attowell, who danced "Francis' New Jig" in 1595; John Shank, who is mentioned in "Turner's Dish" (No. 5); and, much later, Robert Cox.

Of the widespread influence of the jigs a bare mention must suffice. Through the visits of English comedians to the Continent after 1585, a lively imitation of English ballad-tunes and jigs grew up, especially in the Netherlands, Scandinavia, and Germany. A particularly notable result in Germany was the *Singspiele* of Jacob Ayrer and his successors [3]. In England itself, until the closing of the theatres by the Long Parliament, jigs lost none of their popularity. In 1633 Lupton wrote that "most commonly when the play is done, you shal haue a Iige or dance of all trads, they mean to put their legs to it, as well as their tongs [4]." After the severe anti-stage laws of 1642 and 1649, jigs continued to be performed regularly, though the term usually applied to them nowaday is *droll*. "The incomparable Robert Cox, who," as Francis Kirkman [5] wrote, "was not only the principal actor, but also the contriver and author of most of these farces," did not flatter himself on inventing a new type of amusement. He merely substituted jigs for the plays themselves; his performances were called jigs by some of his contemporaries [6]; and in several of them, like "Singing Simpkin," he merely

[1] Marston's *Works*, ed. A. H. Bullen, iii, 372; Guilpin's *Skialethia*, Satire V.

[2] Arber's *Transcript*, ii, 298.

[3] Cf. J. Bolte's *Die Singspiele der englischen Komoedianten und ihrer Nachfolger in Deutschland, Holland, und Skandinavien*, 1893, and a review by B. Hoenig in *Anzeiger für Deutsches Altertum*, xxii, 296–319.

[4] *London and Country Carbonadoed*, p. 81.

[5] Preface to *The Wits, or Sport upon Sport*, 1672.

[6] Thus *Mercurius Democritus* for June 22–29, 1653, tells of how soldiers raided the Red Bull playhouse and arrested Cox who was performing "a modest and ha[r]mless jigge, calle[d] *Swobber*"—one of the drolls on which Kirkman lavished praise.

revived old jigs that years before had been carried abroad by English comedians and that survive in Swedish, Dutch, and German versions far earlier than his own[1].

But by an extension of the drolls to include farces in prose as well as comic scenes cut from the plays of Shakespeare, Fletcher, and other playwrights, the jig may have been partially forgotten. After the Restoration, however, it was immediately revived. Typical early examples are "A Dialogue Betwixt Tom and Dick, The former a Country-man, The other a Citizen, Presented to his Excellency and the Council of State, at Drapers-Hall in London, March 28. 1660[2]," and Thomas Jordan's "The Cheaters Cheated. A Representation in four parts to be Sung by Nim, Filcher, Wat, and Moll, made for the Sheriffs of London[3]." Jigs and drolls long survived in the provincial towns after they had been displaced from the London theatres[4]; and possibly their influence can be traced in the farces with which plays even in the first half of the nineteenth century customarily ended. Certainly their influence is seen in the dances and dialogue songs[5] so common in Restoration plays. Few minor forms of literature have had so great an influence, and none has been so neglected by students.

The *Garland* introduces a number of ballad-writers who have for three centuries been forgotten, in spite of the belief they once must have shared with other members of their tribe that

> Who makes a ballad for an ale-house door
> Shall live in future times for evermore[6]!

[1] See especially Cox's own edition, *Actaeon and Diana*, etc., and cf. the work of Bolte previously cited.

[2] Luttrell Collection, II, 63 (British Museum); *The Rump*, 1662, II, 188 ff.

[3] Thomas Jordan's *A Royal Arbor of Loyal Poesie*, 1664, pp. 34–55.

[4] At Norwich licenses were granted to players of drolls on October 21, 1671, and March 9, 1687 (Walter Rye, *Depositions taken before the Mayor and Aldermen of Norwich*, 1905, pp. 143, 180).

[5] Many of them are printed with the music in *Wit and Mirth, or Pills to Purge Melancholy* (*e.g.* 1719 ed., I, 46, 91, 236).

[6] *Parnassus Plays*, ed. Macray, p. 83.

PREFACE

The most important of these old ballad-poets is undoubtedly Thomas Brewer. His ballad of the year 1605 on the Society of Porters, and another, dated 1609, on two monstrous births (cf. No. 2) clearly indicate that he flourished rather in 1605–10 than, as all writers interested in the history of the drama have said, in "1620?" The 1605 ballad is the earliest work of Brewer's yet brought to light. Interesting also is the signature of George Attowell, a well-known Elizabethan actor, though the authenticity of it is open to grave suspicion. William Turner, a figure who has mystified earlier commentators, is the author of No. 5, and is shown to have been actively writing ballads in 1613. Other new ballad-authors, about whom no biographical details are obtainable, are William Meash, T. Platte, Edward Culter, William Cooke, Thomas Dickerson, Ll. Morgan, and T.F.

Many well-known writers, too, are represented here by ballads that have not before been reprinted,—among them John Cart, Richard Climsal, and Robert Guy. Sixteen of the ballads are signed by Martin Parker, most of them new additions to his bibliography. Only one ballad by him now remains in the Pepys collection (1, 410) unreproduced: "The Married-womans Case. Or, Good Counsell to Mayds, to be carefull of hastie Marriage, by the example of other Married-women. To the tune of *The Married-mans Case.*" It was printed by H[enry]. G[osson]. and begins "You Maidens all, that are willing to wed," but almost the entire first column is torn away. Laurence Price is the author of five of the ballads, and one in the Pepys collection (1, 218) still remains to be reprinted: "Oh Gramercy Penny. To the tune of *Its better late thriue then neuer.*"

As to editorial methods: The original texts are reproduced diplomatically save for two slight exceptions: the statement of titles and tunes has been normalized by the printer, and unmistakable typographical errors, such as *bnt* for *but*, *nad* for *and*, are corrected in the text but indicated in the foot-notes. The long *s* (*ſ*), too, is disregarded.

PREFACE

Words and letters torn off the original sheets have been supplied within square brackets; but no attempt has been made to smooth away or omit the three or four objectionable words that occur. Bowdlerizing is out of the question in a work of this kind.

The separate introductions purpose to give the necessary bibliographical details, to establish the date, to indicate where the tune can be found, and to present appropriate facts about the author and the general situation of the ballad. It has not been possible to realize this aim for all the ballads, but perhaps it is permissible to call attention to the large number here first identified with entries in the Stationers' Registers, to the sources found for most of them, and to the identification of tunes heretofore wrongly assigned or unknown. As the texts themselves present few difficulties to any one versed in Elizabethan literature, annotations have been reduced to the minimum, and such explanation of archaic words and of names as seems desirable has been put for the most part in the glossarial index.

Grateful acknowledgment must be made to the authorities of the Pepysian, Bodleian, and Manchester Free Reference Libraries for permission to reproduce ballads from their collections, especially to Mr Morshead, of Magdalene College, whose interest and aid have been unceasing; to Mr S. C. Roberts, of the Cambridge University Press, for help in securing rotographs of all the ballads contained in this book and for many valuable suggestions as the book was passing through the press; to Mr Alfred Rogers, of the Cambridge University Library, for a transcript of the fourth ballad; to Miss Addie F. Rowe, of the Harvard College Library, for verifying a number of references and quotations; to my colleague, Dr Albert S. Borgman, for his help in the proof-reading; and to Professor C. H. Firth, whose essay on "The Ballad History of the Reign of James I" (Royal Historical Society *Transactions*, 3rd Series, v, 21–61) has been frequently consulted. It would be churlish to fail to mention the

xxii

PREFACE

consideration and courtesy shown me by the officials of the British Museum and the Harvard College Library, two noble libraries from whose treasures I have drawn heavily.

Above all, I am indebted to Professor George Lyman Kittredge, who read the text in manuscript and to whose great erudition (the despair of his students) and equally great kindness this book owes very much indeed. In the separate introductions to the ballads I have tried specifically to indicate his aid. Such an acknowledgment, however, is at best misleading: it was my delightful years as a student at Harvard under Professor Kittredge that gave me an interest in ballads, and only my training under him has made this book—whatever its faults—possible.

H. E. R.

New York City.

CONTENTS

CONTENTS

CONTENTS

CONTENTS

CONTENTS

xxix

CONTENTS

LIST OF ILLUSTRATIONS

FROM BLACK-LETTER BALLADS

LIST OF ILLUSTRATIONS

A NOTE ON BROADSIDE TUNES
By Claude M. Simpson, Jr.

Hyder Rollins' chief source for information on tunes to which broadside ballads were sung was William Chappell's *Popular Music of the Olden Time* (1855–1859). That pioneering work was authoritative for its day and, thanks to Chappell's extensive research, most of the associations and interrelations between texts and tunes remain as he described them. His treatment of the music, however, suffered from a scholasticism that led him to square up irregularities of form and modernize modal details. Moreover, a good deal of evidence bearing on the origin and currency of broadside tunes was unavailable to Chappell but has come to light in the intervening years.

The following notes, supplementing and occasionally correcting Rollins' commentary, direct the reader to my book, *The British Broadside Ballad and Its Music* (1966), where authentic tune transcriptions may be found, together with information on tune sources and on the often complex relationships to be traced when an air is called by different names derived from associations with refrains, first lines, or titles of broadsides to which it is attached.

A B C: Unknown
Angel Gabriel, The: Unknown
As I went to Walsingham: See *Walsingham*
Bessy Bell: Cf. BBBM 298; an independent tune now lost, not an
   alternate name for *A health to Betty*
Blazing torch, The: Unknown
Bonny Nell: BBBM 57
Bragandary (down): Unknown

BROADSIDE TUNES

Brave Lord Willoughby: See *Lord Willoughby*

Bugle bow: BBBM 74

Cannons are roaring: See *When cannons are roaring*

Carman's whistle, The: BBBM 85; this and *O neighbour Robert* (i.e. *Lord Willoughby*) are independent tunes, not identical as Rollins stated

Charles Rickets his lamentation: Unknown

Clean contrary way, The: Cf. BBBM 109, 778 n.

Codlings: Unknown; cf. BBBM 352

Crimson velvet: BBBM 141

Dainty come thou to me: Unknown

Day will come shall pay for all, A: Unknown

Did you see Nan to-day: Unknown

Drive the cold winter away: BBBM 197

Dulcina: BBBM 201

Falero lero lo: Unknown

Flora farewell: Unknown

Fly brass: Cf. BBBM 713

Flying fame: Cf. BBBM 96

Fortune my foe: BBBM 225

Gallants come away: Unknown

Go from my window: BBBM 257

Golden age, The: BBBM 777

Health to Betty, A: BBBM 298

Hemp and flax: Unknown

How shall we good husband live: Unknown

Humming of the drone, The: Unknown

I can nor will no longer lie alone: Unknown

I have for all good wives a song: Unknown

I will give thee kisses one two or three: Unknown

I'll beat my wife no more: Unknown

I'll never love thee more: BBBM 355

In Edinburgh behold: Unknown

In peascod time: BBBM 368

In slumbering sleep: See *Rogero*

In summer time: Cf. BBBM 373

In the days of old: See *Crimson velvet*

Jasper Coningham: See *Lord Willoughby*

Jewish dance, The: Unknown

Joan's ale is new: Cf. BBBM 387

Jovial tinker, The: Cf. BBBM 713

BROADSIDE TUNES

Keep a good tongue in your head: See *The milkmaids*

Lady's fall, The: See *In peascod time*

Last Christmas 'twas my chance: BBBM 427

Let us to the wars again: Cf. BBBM 486; this lost tune is interchangeable with *Maying time* but the two are not equivalent, as Rollins asserted

Lord Willoughby: BBBM 467

Love's tide: Cf. BBBM 751

Lover's dream, The: Unknown

Maid's A B C, The: Unknown

Martin Parker's medley: See *Tarlton's medley*

Maunding soldier, The: Unknown

Maying time: BBBM 486

Merchant of Emden, The: BBBM 602

Merchantman, The: BBBM 602

Milkmaids, The: BBBM 490

Mother beguiled the daughter, The: Unknown

My bleeding heart: Unknown

My husband is a carpenter: Unknown

Ned Smith: See *Dainty come thou to me*

North-country lass, The: Unknown

O folly desperate folly: See *Bragandary*

O neighbour Robert: See *Lord Willoughby*; although Rollins equated *O neighbour Robert* with *The carman's whistle*, they are independent tunes

O no no no not yet: Cf. BBBM 356; probably an independent tune now lost, rather than a secondary name for *I'll never love thee more*, as Rollins assumed

O Roundheads desperate Roundheads: See *Bragandary*

Oil of care, The: Unknown

Old Simon the king: BBBM 545

Over and under: BBBM 722

Pagginton's round (Packington's Pound): BBBM 564

Permit me friends: Unknown

Philliday: BBBM 576

Ragged and torn and true: See *Old Simon the king*

Rock the cradle John: See *Over and under*

Rock the cradle sweet John: Unknown

Rogero: BBBM 612

Shackley hay: BBBM 647

Shall I wrestle in despair: BBBM 653

She-devil, The: Unknown

Shore's wife: Cf. BBBM 121

Sir Andrew Barton: Cf. BBBM 589; the ballad of that title was sung to *Come follow my love*, a tune which has not survived; see B. H. Bronson, *The Traditional Tunes of the Child Ballads*, III (1966), 133 for "Sir Andrew Barton" in modern tradition

Southampton: Unknown

Spanish pavin, The: BBBM 678

Tarlton's medley: Cf. BBBM 680; Rollins' identification with *The Spanish pavin* is unsubstantiated though possible

There was a ewe had three lambs: See *Rock the cradle sweet John*

Thomas you cannot: BBBM 703

Tom of Bedlam: BBBM 710

Triumph and joy: Cf. BBBM 270; apparently an independent tune now lost, not another name for *Greensleeves*, as Rollins implied, following Chappell

Twenty pound a year: Unknown

Two lovely lovers, The: Unknown

Two slips for a tester: Unknown

Virginia: Unknown

Walsingham: BBBM 741

Wanton wife of Westminster, The: Unknown

Watton Town's end: BBBM 460

Welladay: BBBM 747

When cannons are roaring: BBBM 757

Who list to lead a soldier's life: BBBM 773

Whoop do me no harm good man: BBBM 777

Wigmore's galliard: BBBM 783

Wiving age, The: BBBM 777

Woman to the plough and the man to the hen-roost: See *I have for all good wives a song*

June 1971

I

Francis' new jig

Pepys, I, 226, B.L., two woodcuts, five columns.

This ballad is of the very highest importance, for it is the only printed copy extant, so far as is known, of a genuine Elizabethan dramatic jig (cf. pp. xiv ff.). It belongs to the original edition that was licensed for publication to Thomas Gosson on October 14, 1595 (Arber's *Transcript*, III, 49), as "A pretie newe J[i]gge betwene ffrancis the gentleman Richard the farmer and theire wyves." Another version is preserved in manuscript (Clark's *Shirburn Ballads*, pp. 244–254) under the title, "Mr. Attowel's Jigge: betweene Francis, a Gentleman; Richard, a farmer; and their wives." The printed sheet has a number of misprints, and is occasionally inaccurate in its attribution of lines to the speakers, but is far superior to the Shirburn copy (*S.*). It differs from *S.* in many details, corrects it in others, and is three stanzas longer. A collation of the two versions is made in the notes. A few stage directions have been inserted in the text between square brackets.

George Attowell, or Atwell, was himself a prominent Elizabethan actor. He is mentioned in Henslowe's *Diary* (ed. W. W. Greg, I, 6, II, 240; cf. Murray's *English Dramatic Companies*, I, 15) three times: on December 27, 1590, and February 16, 1591, when he received payment on behalf of the combined Lord Strange's and Lord Admiral's players for performances at the Court; and on June 1, 1595, when he was probably a member of the Queen's Company. It may well be doubted whether Atwell did anything more than dance in the jig; his name was probably signed to it from that fact alone—not because he was the author—just as the authorship of the jigs in which William Kemp danced was foisted on that famous comedian (see his *Nine Days' Wonder*, 1600). It is strange, however, that for more than three hundred years the jig itself and Atwell's connection with it have remained unknown.

The tune of *As I went to Walsingham* is given both in the *Shirburn Ballads* and in William Chappell's *Popular Music of the Olden Time*, I 121. It applies only to the first division of the ballad. *Bugle Bow* and the *Jewish Dance* are apparently unknown: with the latter Clark suggests a comparison with the ballad of eighteen-line stanzas in the *Roxburghe Ballads*, VI, 490; with the former may be compared a ballad of "The Bugle Bow, or A Merry Match of Shooting. The Tune is, *My Husband is a Carpenter; or, The Oil of Care*" (Pepys, III, 118; Crawford, No. 1231; British Museum, C. 22. f. 14(90)). With the plot itself compare *Measure for Measure* and the analogues of the story cited by various Shakespearean scholars.

ffrauncis new Jigge, betweene ffrauncis a Gentleman, and Richard a ffarmer.

To the tune of *Walsingham*.

Besse.

1 AS I went to Walsingham,
    to the shrine with speed,
Met I with a iolly Palmer,
    in a Pilgrims weede.   [*Enter Francis*]
Now God you[1] saue you iolly Palmer.
    Fran. Welcome Lady gay,
Oft haue I sued to thee for loue.
    B. Oft haue I said you nay.

2 *F.* My loue is fixed. *B.* And so is mine,
    but not on you:
For to my husband whilst I liue,
    I will euer be true.
    F. Ile giue thee gold and rich array.
    B. Which I shall buy too deare.
    F. Nought shalt thou want: then say not nay.
    B. Naught would you make mee I feare.

3 What though you be a Gentleman,
    and haue lands great[2] store?
I will be chaste doe what you can,
    though I liue ne're[3] so poore.
    F. Thy beauty rare hath wounded mee,
    and pierst my heart.
    B. Your foolish loue doth trouble mee,
    pray you Sir depart.

4 *F.* Then tel mee sweet wilt thou consent
    vnto my desire:
    B. And if I should, then tel me sir,
    what is it you require?

---

[1] *S. omits.*   [2] lands great: land and good *S.*   [3] never *S.*

   F. For to inioy thee as my loue.
      B. Sir you haue a wife:
   Therefore let your sute haue an end.
      F. First will I lose my life.

5 All that I haue thou shalt commaund.
      B. Then my loue you haue.
     F. Your meaning I well[1] vnderstand.
      B. I yeeld to what you craue.
     F. But tel mee sweet when shall I enioy
     my hearts delight.
      B. I prethee[2] sweete heart be not coy,
     euen soone at night.

6 My husband is rid ten miles from home,
     money to receiue:
   In the euening see you come.
      F. Til then I take my leaue.   (*Exit:*
      B. Thus haue I rid my hands[3] full well
     of my amorous loue,
   And my sweet husband wil I tell,
     how hee doth me moue.

       Enter Richard Besses husband.
        To the tune of *the Iewish dance.*

7 *Rich.* Hey doune a doune,
     hey doune, a doune a doune,
   There is neuer a lusty Farmer,
     in all our towne:
   That hath more cause,
     to lead a merry life,
   Then I that am married
     to an honest faithfull[4] wife.
     B. I thanke you gentle husband,
     you praise mee to my face.
     R. I cry thee mercy, Bessee,
     I knew thee not in place.

[1] well I *S.*   [2] praye the *S.*   [3] husband *S.*   [4] *S. omits.*

8 *B.* Beleeue me gentle husband,
      if you knew as much as I,
The words that you haue spoken,
      you quickly would deny:
For since you went from home,
      A sutor I haue had,
Who is so farre in loue with mee,
      that he is almost madde.
Heele giue me gold and siluer[1] store,
      and money for to spend,
And I haue promis'd him therefore,
      to be his louing friend.

9 *R.* Beleeue me, gentle wife,
      but this makes mee to frowne,
There is no gentleman nor[2] knight,
      nor Lord of high renowne:
That shall enioy thy loue, gyrle,
      though he were ne're so good:
Before he wrong my Bessee so,
      Ile spend on him my blood.
And therefore tell me who it is
      that doth desire thy loue.
B. Our neighbour master Francis[3],
      that often did me moue.

10 To whom I gaue consent,
      his mind for to fulfill,
And promis'd him this night,
      that he should haue his will:
Nay doe not frowne, good Dickie,
      but heare me speake my minde:
For thou shalt see Ile warrant thee,
      Ile vse him in his kind.
For vnto thee I will be true,
      so long as I doe liue,
Ile neuer change thee for a new,
      nor once my mind so giue.

[1] Jewels *S.*   [2] or *S.*   [3] *S. adds* 'tis.

11 Goe you to mistrisse Frauncis,
  and this to her declare:
And will her with all speed,
  to my house to repaire:
Where shee and ile deuise
  some pretty knauish wile:
For I haue layd the plot,
  her husband to beguile.
Make hast I pray and[1] tarry not,
  for long he will not stay.
 R. Feare not, ile tell her such a tale,
  shall make her come away.   [*Exit*]

12 B. Now Besse bethinke thee,[2]
  what thou hast to doe.
Thy louer will come presently,
  and hardly will he woo:
I will teach my Gentleman,
  a tricke that he may know,
I am too craftie and too wise,
  to be ore-reached so:
But heere he comes now: not a word,
  but fall to worke againe. *she sowes* [*Enter F.*]
 F. How now sweetheart, at worke so hard.
  B. I sir[3], I must take paines[4].

13 F. But say, my louely sweeting,
  thy promise wilt thou keepe?
Shall I enioy thy loue,
  this night with me to sleepe?
 B. My husband rid[5] from home,
  heere safely may you[6] stay.
 F. And I haue made my wife beleeue
  I rid another way.

---

[1] yow *S.*
[2] *This line in S. runs,* Make hast sweet Francis, *which Clark amends to* Make haste, then, my sweet Richard.
[3] *I.e.* aye, sir.   [4] *Read* paine *S.*   [5] is rid *S.*   [6] yow may *S.*

B. Goe in good sir, what ere betide,
   this night and lodge with mee.
F. The happiest night that euer I had,
   thy friend still will I bee. [*Exit F. Bess retires*]

Enter Mistris Frauncis with Richard.

To the tune of *Bugle Boe.*

Imprinted at London for I.W.[1]

The Second part of *Attowels* **new Jigge.**

To the tune of *as I went to Walsingham*[1].

14 *W.* I Thanke you neighbour Richard,
      for bringing me this newes:
R. Nay, thanke my wife that loues me so[2],
   and will not you[3] abuse.
W. But see whereas shee stands,
   and waiteth our return.
R. You must goe coole your husbands heate,
   that so in loue doth burne.
B. Now Dickie welcome home,
   and Mistris welcome hither:
Grieue not although you finde
   your husband and I together.
For you shall haue your right,
   nor will I wrong you so:
Then change apparrell with me straight[4],
   and vnto him doe goe.
W. For this your kind goodwill[5],
   a thousand thankes I giue:
And make account I will requite
   this kindnesse, if I liue.

---

[1] These are printer's insertions due to the fact that the first part and the third column ended here. Both should be omitted.
[2] *S. omits.*   [3] me *S.*   [4] *S. omits.*
[5] This line and the following seven lines are not in *S.*

6

B. I hope it shall not need,
    Dick will not serue me so:
I know he loues me not so ill,
    a ranging for to goe.
R. No faith, my louely Besse,
    first will I[1] lose my life:
Before Ile[2] breake my wedlock bonds,
    or[3] seeke to wrong my wife.   [*Exit W.*]
Now thinks good Master Frauncis,
    he hath thee in his bed:
And makes account he is grafting
    of hornes vpon my head.
But softly stand aside,
    now shall wee know his minde,
And how hee would haue vsed thee,
    if thou hadst beene so kind.

*Enter Master Francis with his owne wife, hauing a
maske before her face, supposing her to be Besse.*

To the tune of *goe from my window.*

15 *F.* Farewell my ioy and hearts delight,
    til next wee meete againe:
Thy kindnes to requite, for lodging me al night,
    heeres ten pound for thy paine:
And more to shew my loue to thee,
    weare this ring for my sake.
W. Without your gold or fee you shal haue more of
    mee.
    F. No doubt of that I make.
W.[4] Then let your loue continue still.
    F. It shall[5] til life doth end.
W. Your wife I greatly feare. *F.* for her thou needst
    not care,
    so I remaine thy freind[6].

---

[1] I will *S.*   [2] I *S.*   [3] to *S.*
[4] Really a new stanza.   [5] shall be *S.*   [6] *S. omits this line.*

W. But youle suspect me without cause,
    that I am false to you:
And then youle cast mee off, and make mee but a
    scoffe,
    since that I proue vntrue.

16 *F.* Then neuer trust man for my sake,
    if I proue so vnkind:
[*W.*] So often haue you sworn, sir, since that you
    were borne,
    and soone haue[1] changde your minde.
[*F.*] Nor wife nor life, nor goods nor lands,
    shall make me leaue my loue,
Nor any worldly treasure make me forgoe[2] my pleasure,
    nor once my mind remoue.

17 *W.* But soft a while, who is yonder? doe you see
    my husband? out alasse.
F. And yonder is my wife, now shal we haue alife
    how commeth this to passe?
R. Com hither gentle Besse I charge thee do confesse
    what makes Master Francis heere.
B.[3] Good husband pardon me, Ile tel the troth to thee.
R. Then speake and doe not feare.

18 *F.* Nay, neighbour Richard harke to mee,
    Ile tel the troth to you.
W.[4] Nay tell it vnto me, good sir[5], that I may[6] see,
    what you haue here to doe.
But[7] you can make no scuse to colour this abuse,
    this wrong is too too great.
R. Good sir I take great scorne you should profer me
    the horne.
    W. Now must I coole this[8] heate.
                   [Wife unmasks]

---

[1] haue soone *S.*   [2] forget *S.*   [3] *So S., but read* W.
[4] *Read* B. (*S.* gives these two lines to Francis, but they are undoubtedly intended for Bess, who is still disguised as Mrs Francis.)
[5] *S. omits* good sir.   [6] may quickly *S.*
[7] In *S.* Bess begins to speak here.   [8] his *S.*

19 *F.*[1] Nay neighbour Richard be content,
  thou hast no wrong at all:
Thy wife hath done thee right, and pleasurde me this
    night.
  F. This frets mee to the gall.
Good wife forgiue me this offence,
  I doe repent mine ill.
W. I thank you with mine hart, for playing this kind
    part,
  though sore against your[2] will.

20 Nay gentle husband frowne not so,
  for you haue made amends:
I thinke it is good gaine, to haue ten pound for my
    paine[3]:
  then let vs both be friends.
F. Ashamed I am and know not what to say,
  good wife forgiue this crime[4]:
Alasse I doe repent. *W.* Tut I could be content,
  to be serucd so many a time.

21 *F.* Good neighbour Richard be content,
  ile woo thy wife no more:
I haue enough of this. *W.* Then all forgiuen is.
  I thanke thee Dick therefore.
And to thy wife ile giue this gold,
  I hope youle not say no:
Since I haue had the pleasure, let her enioy the treasure.
  F. Good wife let it be so[5].

22 *B.* I thank you gentle Mistris. *R.* Faith & so do I.
  sir, learne your owne wife to know:
And shoote not in the darke, for feare you mis the
    marke.
  B. He hath paid for this I trow.

---

[1] *Read* W. The wife addresses Richard in the first two lines and her
husband in the last line.
  [2] my *S.*   [3] paynes *S.*
  [4] me this tyme *S.*   [5] *S. ends here.*

9

All women learn of me. *F.* All men by me take heed
   how you a woman trust.
W. Nay women trust no men. *F.* And if they do:
   how then?
W. Ther's few of them prooue iust.

23 Farewell neighbour Richard, farewell honest Besse
   I hope wee are all friends.
W.[1] And if you stay at home, and vse not thus to
   come,
   heere all our quarrell ends.

𝔉inis.

George Attowell.[2]

At London Printed for I.W.[2]

[1] *Read* R.   [2] *Not in* S.

2

Commendation of porters

Pepys, 1, 196, B.L., three columns. There is one large cut (here reproduced) in which a porter is first depicted as standing idle with an empty basket, next as walking with a heavy load in his basket, and finally as setting out in holiday costume for a meeting of his society. Above the figures are printed the headings, "At the first went we, as here you see," "But since our Corporation, on this fashion," "And to our Hall, thus we goe all."

Nobody will deny the interest of this account of how the 1041 porters in London formed a corporation and secured a Hall for meetings. Here we see a worshipful company in the making! More interesting, however, is the author. Thomas Brewer is now remembered because of his prose tract *The Merry Devil of Edmonton*, which was registered for publication on April 5, 1608. The ballad, which is omitted in the list of Brewer's publications given in the *Dictionary of National Biography*, was registered on June 15, 1605 (Arber's *Transcript*, III, 292). No early copy of *The Merry Devil* is extant; but from the ballad it is evident that in 1605–1608 Brewer was "flourishing." He appears, further, to have been a common person who applauded manual labour; and the entry at Stationers' Hall on January 14, 1609 (*ibid.* p. 399) of "A ballad made by Thomas Brew[er]. of the Twoo monstruous births in Devon and Plymmouth in November last" indicates that he was, like Antony Munday, more or less a professional ballad-writer. Like Munday, too, he wrote a number of dramatic compositions. His *A knot of Fooles*, preserved in editions of 1624 and 1658, was almost certainly, I think, *the Knott of Fooles* that, along with Shakespeare's *Tempest* and twelve other court entertainments (see the list in H. H. Furness's *New Variorum Tempest*, p. 275), was performed before the Princess Elizabeth and Frederick, the Elector Palatine, in 1613. His ideals of poetry are sufficiently revealed by the fact that in 1630 he contributed highly laudatory verses to the folio edition of the works of John Taylor, the Water Poet. Possibly he was the "Thom: Brewer, my Mus: Servant, [who] through his proneness to goodfellowshippe...attained to a very rich and rubicund nose," mentioned by Sir Nicholas Lestrange (1603–1655) (*Anecdotes and Traditions*, ed. W. J. Thoms, Camden Society, 1839, p. 76).

The tune is unknown.

A nevve Ballad, composed in commendation of the Societie, or Companie of the Porters.

To the tune of, *In Edenbrugh, behold.*

As the first went'st vs, as here you see.   But since our Corporation, on this fashion.   And to our Hall: thus we get all.

1   THrise blessed is that Land
    where King and Rulers bee,
and men of great Command
that carefull are to see,
that carefull are to see,
the Commons good mantainde
by friendly vnitie,
the proppe of any land.

2   Then blessed is this Land
by our dread soueraignes raigne,
whose prudence in command,
doth all estates maintaine:
[his helpe]¹ to comfort all
is vnto all extended:
rich, poore, both great and small,
are by his care defended.

¹ Torn off.

12

3 As plainly doth appeare,
by that was lately done,
for them that burthens beare,
and doe on businesse runne:
the Porters of this Cittie,
some being men of Trade,
but now the more, the more the pitty
by crosses are decayde.

4 Yet bearing honest mindes,
their charge for to maintaine,
as Gods command them bindes,
with trauell and with paine:
they all haue wisely ioynd,
for that they haue effected,
their company to binde
and make it more respected.

5 Now they that were before
of meanest estimation,
by suite haue salude that sore,
and gainde a Corporation:
excludes, and shuts out many
that were of base esteeme,
and will not suffer any
such person bide with them.

6 But such as well are knowen,
and honest Acts imbrace:
among them theile haue none
that haue no biding place:
among them theile haue none
(as neare as they can finde)
but such as well are knowen
to beare an honest minde.

7 For now vnto their hall
they pay their quarteridge downe,
attending maisters call,
and fearing maisters frowne,

there seeking for redresse
and right if they haue wrong,
there, they that doe transgresse
haue that to them doth long.

8   If there be any one
of them, a burthen takes,
and with the same be gone:
their hall, the owner makes
sufficient satisfaction
for that that he hath lost:
the theefe without redemption,
out of their numbers crost.

9   It is a better order
then that they had before,
when as the malefactor
was on a coultstaffe bore:
for th' owner tis much better,
but for th' offender worse,
to taste this newe made order,
then ride a wooden horse.

10   That shame was soone slipt ouer,
soone in obliuion drownde,
and then againe, another
would in like fault be found:
not caring for their credit,
and trust another time,
this orders therefore as a bit
to hold them from that crime.

11   They that are rash, and rude,
and obstinately runne
as their owne willes conclude,
and cannot well be wonne
to condescend, and stand
to orders they haue made,
by the Rulers out of hand,
haue fines vppon them laide.

12 All iarres and braules are bard
that mongst them might arise,
first commer, first is serude,
where as a burthen lyes,
if one be ready there
he must his profite take:
all other must forbeare
and no resistance make.

13 Such as haue long bin knowen
to vse this bearing trade,
and into yeares are growen,
(so that their strengths decayde)
they can no longer labour
as they haue done before,
the Companie doth succour
and maintaine euermore.

14 These and a many moe
good orders they haue, sure,
to make rude fellowes know
their stoutnesse, doth procure
but their owne detriment
and losse, if they could see't:
and likewise to augment
their generall good, there meete.

15 For great is the number
of this Societie:
and many without order
can neuer setled bee;
but things will be amisse,
as oft it hath bin knowen,
the number of them is,
a thousand fortie one.

16 They all mette together,
most hansomely arayde,
at *Christ church*, to heare there
a sermon, for them made.

There markes of Admittaince
made out of tinne, they bare
about their neckes in ribbons:
the chiefe, of siluer weare.

17   To haue seene them so, you'd wonder,
so many should maintaine
themselues, by such a labour,
but that, thats got with paine,
God doth increase and blesse:
for God[1] himselfe hath sed,
with paine and wearinesse,
we all should get our bread.

18   Thus therefore I conclude,
more happie men are they,
then many that delude
the world, and beare away
the sweete of poore mens labour
their chests to cram and stuffe,
not caring for Gods fauour,
so they haue golde enough.

19   Our royall King and Queene
thou King of Kings defend,
as thou to them hast beene
most mercifull and kinde:
thy loue to them increase,
blesse all they vndertake:
His Counsels counsell, blesse,
euen for thy deare sons sake.

Finis.

Tho. Brewer.

Imprinted at London by *Thomas Creed*, and are to be
solde at the signe *of the Eagle and childe, in
the olde Chaunge.* 1605.

[1] *Text* good.

16

3

Caleb Shillock's prophecy

Pepys, 1, 38, B.L., one woodcut, three columns.

The ballad is a poetical rendering of part of a prose pamphlet called *Newes from Rome... Also certaine prophecies of a Iew seruing to that Armie, called Caleb Shil[ock]*, which was "Translated out of Italian into English, by W. W." in 1607. From the slightly mutilated copy in the British Museum (C. 32. d. 26), sigs. B 3ᵛ–B 4, the prophecy is quoted. Square brackets indicate, as in the title quoted above, tears in the text.

Caleb Shilock his prophesie, for the yeere, 1607.

Be it knowne vnto all men, that in the yeere 1607. when as the Moone is in the watrie signe, the world is like to bee in great danger: for a learned Jew, named *Caleb Shilock*, doth write, that in the foresaid yeere, the Sun shall be couered with the Dragon in the morning, from fiue of the clocke vntill nine, and will appeare like fire: therefore it is not good that any man doe behold the same, for by beholding thereof he may lose his sight.

Secondly, there shall come in the same yeere a meruailous great flood of water, to the great terror and amasement of many people.

Thirdly, there shall arise a meruailous great wind, and for feare thereof many people shall be consumed, or distraughted of their wits.

Fourthlie the same yeere, about the month of May, will arise another wonderfull great flood, and so great as no man hath seene since *Noyes* flood, which wil continue three daies and three nights, whereby many Citties and Town[es] which standeth vppon sandie ground will be in [gre]at danger.

Fiftly, Infidels and Hereticks, through great feare and dread, will flie and gather together, and asmuch as in them lies, make war against Christian princes.

Sixtlie, in the same yeere after the great waters be past, about the end of the yeere will be very great and fearefull Sicknesses: so that many people are like to die by the infection of strange diseases.

Seauenthly, there will be throughout the Worlde great trouble and contention about matters of Religion, and wonderfull strange newes vnto all people, as concerning the same.

Eightly, the Turke with his God Mahomet shall bee in danger to lose his Septer, through the great change and alteration in his Regiment, by reason of famine and warres, so that the most part of his people will rather seeke reliefe from the Christian, then from him.

17

CALEB SHILLOCK'S PROPHECY

Ninthlie, there will also arise great Earth-quakes, whereby diuers goodly buildings & high houses, are like to be ouerthrowne and ruinated.

Lastlie, there will be great remoouings of the earth in diuers places, so that for feare thereof, many people will be in a strange amazement and terror.

These punishments are prognosticated by this learned Jew, to fall vppon the whole world by reason of sinne, wherefore it behooueth all Christian [*sic*] to amend their euill liues, and to pray earnestly vnto GOD to withhold these calamities from vs, and to conuart our harts wholy to him, whereby we may find fauour in our time of neede, through Jesus Christ our Lord. Amen.

Certain scholars have suggested that from this pamphlet Shakespeare got the name *Shylock* for his *Merchant of Venice* (Sir A. W. Ward, *History of English Dramatic Literature*, II, 107). For the tune cf. the notes to No. 49.

Calebbe Shillocke, his Prophesie: or, the Iewes Prediction.

To the tune of *Bragandarie*.

1 TO *Caleb Shillocks* Prophesies,
  VVho list to lend an eare,
Of griefe, and great calamities[1],
A sad Discourse shall heare:
  Of Plagues (for sinne) shall soone ensew
  Prognosticated by this Iew:
  O Lord, Lord in thy mercy,
  Hold thy heauy hand.

2 And first, within this present yeere,
  Beeing Sixteene hundreth seau'n:
The Prince of Planets shall appeare,
Like flaming Fire in heau'n,
  Like flaming Fire his radiant rayes
  To all shall seeme (old *Shillock* sayes.)
  O Lord, Lord in thy mercie,
  Hold thy heauie hand.

---

[1] *Text* calamitie.

18

3 No mortall man shall able bee,
  (As he affirmes) to looke
  Upon this fearefull Progedie,
  This sinners bloody Booke:
    this booke, by which he soone may know
    the cause of all our griefe and woe.
    O Lord, Lord in thy mercie, &c.

4 For he that dares to gaze vpon
  The Sunne, so dreadfull-bright,
  Shall neuer after gaze vpon
  An obiect sad, or light:
    But suddainly be striken blind,
    As leaues are shaken with the wind.
    O Lord, Lord in thy mercie, &c.

5 And next to this, old *Shillock* sayes,
  The waters shall arise,
  And set a period to the dayes
  Of many fond, and wise:
    And all that know't by eye, or eare,
    shal stand (almost) distraught with feare.
    O Lord, Lord in thy mercie, &c.

6 And after this hath playde his part,
  In *Calebs* Scrowle I finde,
  Another woe to wound the heart,
  And terrifie the minde:
    The winds (he sayes) shall strangly blow
    And strong-built Houses ouerthrow.
    O Lord, Lord in thy mercie, &c.

7 VVith greater Waters after this,
  The Earth shall plagued bee,
  So sore our God incensed is,
  By our impietie:
    So sore a Flood since godly *Noe*,
    As is to come, neare man did know.
    O Lord, Lord in thy mercie, &c.

8 Three dayes this Flood the Land shal hide
This learned *Caleb* writes,
VVithin her watry mantle, wide:
And iust as many nights.
   O then imagine you the rest,
   the sodaine death of man and beast.
    O Lord, Lord in thy mercie,
    hold thy heauie hand.

9 For to imagine the euent,
(VVith searching care and heed)
Of such a wofull accident,
VVould make the heart to bleed:
   For vnder such a wofull worke,
   full many wofull sights do lurke.
    O Lord, Lord in thy mercie, &c.

10 Of Heretickes and Infidels,
A multitude shall flocke
Together, (learned *Shillocke* telles)
VVith hope, like strongest Rocke,
   to stand and fight against all those,
   that power, against their power oppose.
    O Lord[1]*, Lord in thy mercie, &c.*

11 Next, Deaths Ambassadour shall come,
To act his fatall part,
To summon to receiue a doome,
According to desart:
   But, to desart, O gracious Lord,
   Let not thy Iudgement then accord.
    O Lord, Lord in &c.

12 VVhole Families at once, shall lie
Sore sicke vpon their beddes:
From house to house shall Sicknesse flie,
When his infection spreddes:

---

[1] *Text* Lard.

when he has paind them, mauger death,
shall step, to stop their vitall breath.
O Lord, Lord in. &c.

13 Through all the world, Great trouble, next
(He sayth) there shall be seene,
As strife about the Holy text,
The meaning altering cleene.
About Religion strife shall rise:
Enlighten Lord, our heartes and eyes.
O Lord, Lord in thy mercie, &c.

14 The Turke lyes next in dangers way,
VVith *Mahomet* his God,
(His Diuell rather, I should say)
to loose his Regall rod:
For in his Land a ciuill strife
shall many men bereaue of life.
O Lord, Lord in thy mercie,
hold thy heauie hand.

15 From Ciuill warres, shall Famine rise,
And all that Land oppresse:
In *Mahomet* no comfort lies,
when men are in distresse.
To Christians, shall his people flie
for succour in their miserie.
O Lord, Lord in thy mercie, &c.

16 When time, has borne these plagues away,
More greeuous shall succeede,
More heauie Judgements of the Lord,
Against vs shall proceede.
The Earth (with wind inclosd therein)
Shall quake and tremble, for our sinne.
O Lord, Lord in thy mercie,
Hold thy heauie hand.

17 Braue high-buylt Houses, on the earth,
The quaking earth shall lay,
When many at their Feastes and mirth,
Their iocund sports and play
(Mistrusting no such thing) are set,
Our sinnes desart we still forget.
O Lord. &c.

18 Then (for a time) the Seas grow calme,
The Skies are cleere, and still:
Which time of stilnesse (like to Balme)
Cures many, greefe would kill:
But when our hopes stand faire for peace
Our sorrowes shall againe increase.
O Lord. &c.

19 An other Earthquake presently,
Heart-wounding sorrow brings,
Remoouing Houses, Churches, hie
Hils, Trees, and other things.
Our sinnes, like *Hidras* heads, increase,
How should our plagues and torments cease?
O Lord. &c.

20 It is the part (*Boetius* sayes)
Of men discreete and wise,
Of wonderous thinges to search the cause:
For tis the Simples guise,
To gaze vpon the thing that's done,
and nere looke how, or why't begun.
O Lord. &c.

21 Then let vs search into the cause
Of these, with Plagues are past,
That to repentance they may drawe's
And to amend at last.
The cause is Sin, our Sinn's the cause:
Neclect of Gods decrees, and lawes.
O Lord, &c.

22 O let vs turne vnto the Lord,
   For he (alone) is hee,
   That can from water, fire, and sword
   At's pleasure set vs free.
     If we by grace, cast Sin away,
     By mercy he his hand will stay.
     O Lord, &c.

23 O Let vs flie those deadly sinnes
   The Conscience ouercloyes,
   The Conscience, Souls Saluation wins
   Or else the Soule destroyes,
     Let's labour then to keepe it free,
     That God, in glory, wee may see.
     O Lord, &c.

24 O Lord, with thy all sauing hand
   Our King and Queene defend:
   The Heire[1] to this vnited Land
   And all their isshue tend.
     The Honorable Counsell blesse
     With many dayes, and happines.
     O Lord, Lord in &c.

Finis.

At London printed for T.P.

[1] *I.e.* Henry, Prince of Wales († 1612).

4

The lamentable complaint of France

Pepys, 1, 112, B.L., two woodcuts, three columns.

William Barley registered this ballad on May 15, 1610 (Arber's *Transcript*, III, 433), as "The wofull complaynt of Ffraunce for the deathe of the late kinge Henry the Ffowrth." François Ravaillac (born in the town of Angoulême) killed Henry IV on May 14, 1610 (new style), and was executed with dreadful tortures on May 27. His crime and punishment aroused enormous interest in England: books on the subject were registered for publication on May 10, May 14, May 30 (three entries), 1610, January 12, 1611, and October 10, 1611. (I give these dates, except for the year, in English, or old, style.) A number of the books are extant, and from one of them—which is reprinted in the *Harleian Miscellany*, 1810, VI, 607 ff.—the account in the ballad appears to have been summarized. The spirit of Ravaillac appears at the end of Dekker's *If It Be Not Good, The Devil Is In It*, 1612, to remark that "were my tongue torne out with burning flesh-hookes, Fames 1000. tonges shall thunder out *Rauillacs* name, extoll it, eternise it, Cronicle it, Canonise it!" In the third stanza there is a description of the coronation of Henry IV's second wife, Maria de' Medici. Their son, the Dauphin of the last three or four stanzas (Louis XIII), was born on September 27, 1601.

For a transcript of this ballad I am indebted to Alfred Rogers, Esq., of the Cambridge University Library.

𝕿𝖍𝖊 lamentable[1] complaint of 𝕵𝖗𝖆𝖚𝖓𝖈𝖊, for the death
of the late 𝕶𝖎𝖓𝖌 𝕳𝖊𝖓𝖗𝖞 the 4., who was lately mur=
dred by one[2] 𝕵𝖗𝖆𝖚𝖓𝖈𝖊𝖘 𝕽𝖆𝖚𝖎𝖑𝖑𝖎𝖆𝖈𝖐𝖊, borne in the towne
of 𝕬𝖓𝖌𝖔𝖑𝖘𝖊𝖒, shewing the manner of his death, and
of the election and 𝕻𝖗𝖔𝖈𝖑𝖆𝖞𝖒𝖎𝖓𝖌 of the new 𝕶𝖎𝖓𝖌
𝕷𝖊𝖜𝖎𝖘, the 13. of that name, being a childe
of 9. peeres of age.

To a new tune.

---

[1] *Text* lamentabe.   [2] *n* upside down in the text.

THE LAMENTABLE COMPLAINT OF FRANCE

1 FRaunce that is so famous,
    and late in ioyes abounded,
May now lament the losse of him:
    that mischiefe hath confounded.
Their thrice renowned King,
    that Souldier braue and bolde,
In peace and wars so well belou'de,
    lyes clad in earthly molde.
All Kingdomes come and mourne,
    for this same sad mischaunce:
For wee haue lost our Countries King
    and flower of famous fraunce.

2 The bloudy hand that wrought
    and hart that gaue consent:
Now makes more eies in France to weep:
    then euer did lament.
More sighes [an]d[1] sobes was neuer heard,
    then be in Fraunce this day,
For euery one now mourning sits:
    this pleasant month of May.
No ioye, no hearts delight,
    but death and bloudy deedes,
In euery Coast of famous Fraunce:
    much griefe and sorrow breedes.

3 In May the thirteenth day,
    it pleased this royall King:
To make his Wife a Crowned Queene,
    which was a princely thing
Who then in Triumph rode
    along fayre Paris streets,
Whom all the Lordes & peeres of Fraunce
    in ioyfull manner greetes.
And all the streetes along,
    whereas the Queene did ride.
Were like the walles of Paradice,
    bedeckt on euery side:

[1] Text torn.

4 The royall King himselfe,
    the Dolphin his young sonne:
The lordly Prelates of that land,
    and Barrons many one.
With all the states of Fraunce:
    there honored Henries Queene,
More stately triumphes neuer was,
    within that Countrie seene.
But soone thiese glories vanish't,
    for death put in his hand,
And in lesse time then forty houres
    made Fraunce a wofull land.

5 This noble King god wot,
    supposing all good friends:
The following day for pleasures sake:
    a iourney foorth intends.
Wherein his Coatch he rides,
    some of his lordes with him,
Along renowned Paris streetes,
    being then deckt out most trim.
The people cryed with ioy:
    God saue our Royall King,
The presence of your Maiestie:
    reioycing loue doth bring.

6 The People throngd so fast,
    about him in the streetes,
That hardly he could passe along:
    such numbers did he meete.
Amongst so many friends,
    a Judas hand there was,
That turnd the cheereful flower of france
    to fading withered grasse,
Two Coatches by hard chance,
    his graces Passage stayde,
A time wherein his gentle life,
    by murder was betrayde.

7 The Traytour that three times,
 before had mist his ayme,
And could not in his royall bloud:
 his cursed fingers stayne.
Now desperatly thrust foorth:
 vnto his coatches side,
And gaue him there, 2 mortall wounds,
 by which, the King soone dyed,
A cursed knife it was,
 which did this bloudy deede,
But ten times cursed be the cause,
 that did this mischiefe breed.

8 The wounded King cryed out,
 then with a fainting breath:
Oh, saue his life till hee reueale[1],
 the plotters of my death.
The Traytour being stayed,
 was so offence bereauen,
That presently for this vilde deede:
 he thought to purchase heauen.
Some led this villaine thence,
 and some, the King conuaide:
Unto his Pallace mournfully,
 in bloudy Robes arrayde.

9 A natiue frenchman borne,
 this wretch is knowne to be:
Bred in the Towne of Angolsem,
 a Courtier in degree.
Fraunces Ravilliacke namde,
 in passed time a Fryer,
Maynteyned long about this court,
 to accomplish his desire.
But who the causers be:
 and chiefest in this crime,
By wisedome of the peeres of Fraunce:
 wilbe found out in time.

   [1] Text has a period here.

10   Meanewhile the villanes teeth,
    are pulde out euery one:
Least he should bite cleane out his tongue,
    and so no trueth be showen,
His nayles likewise pincht off,
    least he should teare it out,
And speachles thus should lose his life:
    and no wayes cleare this doubt[1].
But let vs speake againe,
    of this the bleeding King,
Who entring at his pallace gate:
    death broke his life heart string.

11   Euen in a Bushops Armes,
    he yeelded vp his breath,
And said I die true Christian King,
    sweete lordes reuenge my death.
His Queene, his sonne, and peeres,
    with wringing handes made mone,
And sayde, if God be not our friende,
    our states be ouerthrowne.
The heauiest day in Fraunce,
    this is that euer was seene,
His death now makes an orphant Prince,
    and eke a widdowed Queene.

12   Yet wisdome so preuailde,
    amongst the lordes of Fraunce,
That by the gracious helpe of God,
    they salued this mischaunce.
The next day in the morne:
    fower Cardinalls of estate,
And Princes of the Kings owne bloud,
    this buisines did debate.
To establish loue and peace:
    within this mournefull land,
They there proclaym'd the Dolphin King
    in Paris out of hand.

[1] No period in the text.

13 A childe of nine yeeres olde,
   being true and lawfull heyre,
The onely hope the Kingdome hath,
   to rid them from all feare.
Up to his fathers throne,
   the Dolphin straight was led,
In Purple Robes most gorgeously:
   with sumptuous Iewells spread.
Whome, in the peoples hearts,
   did moue such present ioy,
That euery one in gladsome sort,
   did cry vi, va, le roy.

14 Yea euery one doth pray,
   now dwelling in the land,
That like his father he may proue,
   an Impe of Mars his band.
But three such dayes in Fraunce,
   no age hath euer knowne,
Where present ioy gayn'd sudden woe,
   yet woe to ioy is growne.
One day a Crowned Queene,
   the next a murdred King,
The third a Prince in ioy proclaymde,
   a setled peace to bring.

15 But God defend each Land,
   from such a suddaine chaunce,
As lately hath befalne the King,
   of fayre renowned Fraunce.

Finis.

At London printed for William Barley, and are to be sould
at his shop in Gratious Streete 1610.

5

Turner's dish of Lenten stuff

Pepys, 1, 206, B.L., one woodcut, five columns.
There is another copy of this ballad, later by fifty years, in the collection of the Earl of Crawford (*Bibliotheca Lindesiana, Catalogue of English Ballads*, No. 841). It is entitled

The Common Cries of London Town,
Some go up street, some go down.
With Turners Dish of Stuff, or a Gallymaufery,

is signed "Finis. W. Turner," and has the imprint, "London, Printed for F. C[oles]. T. V[ere]. and W. G[ilbertson]. 1662." Lord Crawford's copy was formerly in the possession of J. P. Collier, who commented on it in his *Bibliographical and Critical Account of the Rarest Books in the English Language* (1, 163) and, later, reprinted it in his *Book of Roxburghe Ballads* (pp. 207–216). Collations with this reprint (*C.*) are given in the notes. It is curious that the existence of the Pepysian ballad has remained unnoticed, for Collier's reprint has attracted a considerable amount of attention from students of the Elizabethan drama. One of them, F. G. Fleay (*Chronicle History of the London Stage*, New York, 1909, p. 375), correctly argued that the ballad had originally appeared in 1612, and added the following important note: "The 'lean fool' is Thomas Greene, the Queen Anne's player at the Bull. The 'fat fool' is William Rowley, the player in Prince Henry's company at the Curtain who acted Plum Porridge in the Inner Temple Mask, and in it 'moved like one of the great porridge tubs going to the Counter.' Shank's rhymes were acted as 'Shank's Ordinary' after he moved to the King's Company, c. 1623." John Shank (cf. p. xix) and his jigs are mentioned, also, in a poem in *Choyce Drollery*, 1656 (ed. J. W. Ebsworth, p. 7).

Apart from its interesting comments on stage-players, the ballad preserves a curious lot of old street-cries; among them the cry of "Cherry Ripe" so often used by Elizabethan lyricists. Nothing else of Turner's seems to be extant, but evidently he was prominent among Jacobean balladists. Three ballads by him were licensed to Thomas Pavier on November 19, 1612 (Arber's *Transcript*, III, 503): "Turners disshe of wagtayles," "Turners Dreame of Sym Subtill and Susan the brokers Daughter," and "Turners Pylgrymage to the land of Iniquitye." He is again mentioned in the Stationers' Register when, on August 25, 1613

(*ibid.* p. 532), Charlton and Blackwell secured a license for a ballad called
"Wycked Wylles sawce to Turners sawce to Turners Dysshe of Wag-
tayles Sent to Turner for A fayringe."
The tune is given in Chappell's *Popular Music*, 1, 219.

Turners dish of Lentten stuffe, or a Galymaufery.

To the tune of *Watton Townes end.*

1 MY Maisters all attend you,
    if mirth you loue to heare:
And I will tell you what they cry,
    in London all the yeare.
Ile please you if I can,
    I will not be too long,
I pray you all attend a while,
    and lissen to my song.

2 The fish-wife first begins,
        nye[1] Musckles lylly white:
Hearings, Sprats, or Pleace,
        or Cockles for delight.
Nye[1] welflet Oysters:
        then she doth change her note,
She had need to hane her tongue by grease[2]
    for she rattles in the throat.

3 For why they are but Kentish,
        to tell you out of doubt:
Her measure is to little,
        go beate the bottom out.
Halfe a Pecke for two pence,
        I doubt it is a bodge,
Thus all the citty ouer,
        the people they do dodge.

---

[1] Anye *C.*
[2] She had need to have her tongue be greas'd *C.*

4　The wench that cries the Kitchin stuffe,
　　　I maruell what she ayles[1]:
　　She sings her note so merry,
　　　but she has a dragle taile,
　　An empty Car came running,
　　　and hit her on the bum,
　　Downe she threw her greasie tub,
　　　and away that[2] she did run.

5　But she did giue a[3] blessing,
　　　to some but not to all:
　　To beare a loade to Tyburne,
　　　and there to let it fall,
　　The miller with[4] his golden thumbe,
　　　and his dusty[5] necke:
　　If that he grind but two bushels,
　　　he needs must[6] steale a peck.

6　The Weauer and the Tayler,
　　　cozens they be sure:
　　They cannot worke but they must steale,
　　　to keepe their hands in vre,
　　For it is a common prouerbe,
　　　throughout all[7] the towne,
　　The Taylor he must cut three sleeues,
　　　for euery womans gowne.

7　Marke but the Water man,
　　　attending for his fare:
　　Of hot and could, of wet and dry,
　　　he alwaies takes a[8] share.
　　He carrieth bony lasses,
　　　ouer to the plaies,
　　And here and there he gets a bit,
　　　and that his stomake staies.

---

[1] *Read with C.* ayle.	[2] straight *C.*	[3] her *C.*
[4] and *C.*	[5] dirty *C.*	[6] must needs *C.*
[7] *C. omits.*	[8] his *C.*	

8　There was a slinging[1] boy,
　　　did write to[2] ride to Rumford:
　　When I go to my close stoole[3],
　　　I will put[4] him in a comfort:
　　But what I leaue behind,
　　　shall be no priuate gaine:
　　But all is one when I am gone,
　　　let him take it for his paine.

9　Ould shoes for new Broomes,
　　　the broome man he doth sing:
　　For hats or caps or buskins,
　　　or any ould Pooch rings.
　　[Buy[5]] a Mat, a bed Mat,
　　　[a pad]lock or a Pas[6],
　　A couer for a close stoole,
　　　a bigger or a lesse.

10　Ripe Chery ripe,
　　　the Coster-monger cries,
　　Pipins fine, or Peares,
　　　another after hies,
　　With basket on his head,
　　　his liuing to aduance,
　　And in his purse a paire of Dice,
　　　for to play at Mumchance.

11　Hot Pippin pies,
　　　to sell vnto my friends:
　　Or puding pies in pans,
　　　well stuft with Candles ends,
　　Will you buy any Milke,
　　　I heare a wench to cry[7],
　　With a paile of fresh Cheese and creame,
　　　another after hies.

---

[1] singing *C.*　　　[2] did write to: who did *C.*　　　[3] own school *C.*
[4] take *C.*　　　[5] *Text torn. C. has* Buy.
[6] a hassock or a presse *C.*　　　[7] to cry: that cries *C.*

12 Oh the wench went neately,
    my thought it did me good:
To see her cheery cheekes,
    so dimpled ore with blood,
Her wastecoate washed white:
    as any lilly flower,
would I had time to talke with her
    the space of halfe an houre.

13 Buy blacke, saith the blacking man
    the best that ere was seene:
Tis good for poore men[1] Cittizens
    to make their shooes to shine,
Oh tis a rare comodity,
    it must not be for-got,
It wil make them[2] glister gallantly
    and quickly make them rot.

14 the world is ful of thredbare poets,
    that liue vpon their pen:
But they will write too eloquent,
    they are such witty men.
But the Tinker with his budget,
    the begger with his wallet[3],
And *Turners* turnd a gallant man,
    at making of a Ballet.

Finis.

Imprinted at London for I.W.

---

[1] *C. omits.*   [2] them to *C.*
    [3] *Text* walled.

The second part, or you are welcome my guest to your Lentten fare if you come when Lent is gone, you shall haue better cheere[1]. To the same tune.

15 THat's the fat foole of the Curtin,
      and the leane foole of the Bull:
    Since *Shanke* did leaue to sing his rimes,
      he is counted but a gull.
    The players of[2] the Banke side,
      the round Globe and the Swan,
    Will teach you idle trickes of loue,
      but the Bull will play the man.

16 But what do I stand tattling,
      of such Idle toyes:
    I had better go to Smith-field,
      to play among the Boyes,
    But you cheating and decoying[3] Lads,
      with your base Art-tillery:
    I would wish you shun[4] Newgate,
      and withall the Pillery.

17 And some there be in patcht gownes,
      I know not what they be:
    They pinch the simple[5] Contry men,
      with nimming of a fee.
    For where they get a booty,
      theyle make him pay so deere,
    Theyle entertaine more in a day,
      then he shall in a yeere.

18 Which makes them trimme vp houses,
      made of brick, and stone:
    And poore men goe a begging,
      when house and land is gone.

---

[1] None of this title is in *C.* Text has a comma after *cheere* and *tune.*
[2] on *C.*   [3] deceiving *C.*   [4] to shun *C.*   [5] *C. omits.*

Some there be with both hands[1]
will sweare they will not dally,
Till they haue turnd all vpside[2] downe,
as many[3] vse to salley.

19 You Pedlers giue good measure,
    when as your wares you sell:
though your yard be short your thum wil slip,
    your trickes I know full wel,
And you that sel your wares by waight,
    and liue vpon the trade:
Some beames be false, som waits to light
    such trikes there haue bin plaid.

20 Buy smale Coles, or great Coles,
    I haue them one my backe:
The Goose lies in the bottom,
    you may heere the Ducke cry quacke,
Thus grim the blacke Colyer,
    whose liuing is so loose,
As he doth walke the comans ore,
    sometimes he steales a goose.

21 Thou Usurer with thy money bags,
    that liueth so at ease:
By gaping after gould thou doest,
    thy mighty God displease,
And for thy greedy vsur[ie][4]
    and thy great extortion:
Except[5] thou doest repent thy sinnes,
    hel fire wilbe thy portion.

22 For first I came to Hounds-dich,
    then round about I crept[6]:
Where cruelty is[7] crowned chiefe,
    and pitty fast a sleepe,

<hr />

[1] *Text* handsl?   [2] *Text* vpsie.   [3] *Text* mnay.
[4] Text blurred.   [5] *Text* Exdept.   [6] *Read* creep *with* C.
[7] was C.

Where Usury gets profit,
and brokers beare the bel,
Oh fie vpon this deadly sinne,
it sinkes the house[1] to hel.

23 The man that sweepes the chimneys,
with the bunsh[2] of thornes:
And one his necke a trusse of poles,
tipped al with hornes.
With care he is not cumbred,
he liueth not in dread:
For though he weares them on his pole,
some weare them one there head.

24 The Landlord with his racking rents,
turne poore men out of doore:
There children goe a begging,
where they haue spent their store,
I hope none is affended:
at[3] that which is indited,
If any be, let him go home,
and take a pen and write it.

25 Buy a trap a Mouse trap,
a tormentor[4] for the fleas:
The hang-man workes but halfe the day,
he liues too much at ease.
Come let vs leaue this boyes play,
and idle prittle prat,
And let vs goe to nine holes,
to spurne point or to cat.

26 Oh you nimble fingured lads,
that liues vpon your wits:
Take heed of Tyburne Ague,
for they be daungerous fits.

[1] soul C.   [2] bush C.   [3] with C.   [4] torment C.

For many a proper man,
　　for to supply his lacke:
Doth leape a leape at Tyburne,
　　which makes his neck to crack.

27 And to him that writ this song,
　　I giue this simple lot:
Let euery one be ready,
　　to giue him halfe a pot.
And thus I doe conclude,
　　wishing both health and peace,
To those that are laid in their bed,
　　and cannot sleepe for fleas.

Finis.

W. Turner.

At London printed for I.W.

6

Whipping cheer

Pepys, I, 208, B.L., two woodcuts, four columns.

Bridewell stood near Fleet Ditch. Originally a handsome house built by Henry VIII, it was turned over to the city of London in 1553, by Edward VI, to be used as a house of correction for rogues and loose women. "*Bridewel,*" says Antony Munday, in his *Briefe Chronicle of the Successe of Times* (1611, p. 522), was "appointed for the Vagabond, ydle strumpet, and vnthrift." It was formally opened in 1555 and was destroyed, more than a century later, in the Great Fire.

The author of the ballad had—what is so rare among ballad-writers—a real sense of humour. In the first part he represents three *filles de joie* —three "fatal sisters"—as moaning and complaining for departed pleasures while they are beating hemp with beetles or spinning flax at Bridewell under the vigilant eye and ever-ready lash of Matron and Beadle. In the second part, the roaring boys,—the gulls, coney-catchers, and panders of London,—are seen sending a comforting letter to the Sisters: "comfort" is supposed to come from the news that the roaring boys themselves are soon to be sent to Bridewell, and as misery loves company, the Sisters should cease their laments. That neither the roaring boys nor the fatal sisters exaggerated their punishment is evident from the sentence passed on one Henry Skyte (July 10, 1609), whom the court ordered "forthwith sent to Bridewell and there soundlye whipped for speakinge contemptuous wordes against Sir Robert Leighe, sittinge upon the Benche, and to be kepte to beatinge of hempe" (J. C. Jeaffreson, *Middlesex County Records*, II, 54).

The ballad was printed about 1612. It is a valuable commentary on the fifth act of Dekker's *Honest Whore, Part II*, where a constable with "two Beadles, one with hemp, the other with a beetle," and with various inmates of Bridewell play important rôles. The phrase *whipping-cheer* occurs often in the works of Thomas Nashe (*Works*, ed. R. B. McKerrow, II, 291) and in *Henry IV*, Part II, v, iv, 5. The refrain of the ballad is very attractive indeed, and it is a pity that the tune it demands, *Hemp and Flax*, is not known.

𝖂𝖍𝖎𝖕𝖕𝖎𝖓𝖌 𝕮𝖍𝖊𝖆𝖗𝖊.
𝕺𝖗 𝖙𝖍𝖊 𝖜𝖔𝖋𝖚𝖑𝖑 𝖑𝖆𝖒𝖊𝖓𝖙𝖆𝖙𝖎𝖔𝖓𝖘 𝖔𝖋 𝖙𝖍𝖊[1] 𝖙𝖍𝖗𝖊𝖊 𝕾𝖎𝖘𝖙𝖊𝖗𝖘 𝖎𝖓
𝖙𝖍𝖊 𝕾𝖕𝖎𝖙𝖙𝖑𝖊 𝖜𝖍𝖊𝖓 𝖙𝖍𝖊𝖞 𝖜𝖊𝖗𝖊 𝖎𝖓 𝖓𝖊𝖜 𝕭𝖗𝖎𝖉𝖊=𝖜𝖊𝖑𝖑[2].

To the tune of *hempe and flax.*

1   Come you fatall Sisters three,
        whose exercise is spinning:
And helpe vs to pull out these thrids,
    for heer's[3] but a harsh begining.
        Oh hemp, and flax, and tow to to to,
        Tow to to to, tow tero.
        Oh hempe, &c.

2   The blinded whipper hee attends vs,
        if the wheele leaue turning,
    And then the very Matrons lookes,
        turnes all our mirth to mourning.
            Oh hempe and flax and Tow to to to,
            tow to to to to to tero,
            Oh hempe &c.

3   Now for a Cup of bottle Ale,
        some suger-plummes and Cakes a,
    But neuer a client must come in,
        to giu's a poore pinte of Sacke[4].
            Heer's hemp and flax and tow to to to
            tow tow to to to to tero.
            Heer's hempe and &c.

4   *Besse* the eldest Sister, shee
        is slayned much with honour[5],
    And one cannot endure the labour,
        which is thrust vpon her.
            O hemp and flax and tow to to to,
            Tow to to, to to tero.
            O hemp &c.

[1] *Text* the the.   [2] No period in text.   [3] *Text* hee'rs.
[4] *Read* Sacke a.   [5] The *n* is upside down in the text.

5 Garden-allies cleare are swept,
  Hog-laine laments a little:
  Our tinder boxes ouer our heades,
  were broken at the Spittle:
>   *Heer's hemp and flax and tow to to to,*
>   *tow to to to to to tero.*
>   *Heer's hempe &c.*

6 If the London Prentises,
  And other good men of fashion:
  Would but refraine our companies,
  Then woe to our occupation.
>   *Then hempe and flaxe and tow to to to*
>   *Tow to to to to tero.*
>   *Then hempe, &c.*

7 O you lusty Roring Boyes,
  Come shew your brazen faces:
  Let your weapons turne to beetles,
  And shoulder out some of these lashes.
>   *At hemp and flaxe and tow to to to,*
>   *Tow to to to to to tero,*
>   *At hemp, &c.*

8 Gold and siluer hath forsaken,
  Our acquaintance cleerely:
  Twined whipcord takes the place,
  And strikes t'our shoulders neerely.
>   *Heer's hempe and flax and tow to to to,*
>   *Tow to to to to tero[1].*
>   *Heere's hemp, &c.*

9 You Punkes and Panders euery one,
  Come follow your louing sisters:
  In new Bridewell there is a mill,
  Fills all our hands with blisters.
>   *And hempe and flax and, tow to to to to tero.[2]*

10 If the Millers art you like not,
   to the hempe blocke packe yee:

---

[1] *Text* telo?   [2] Text has a comma.

Thumpe, and thumpe, and thump apace,
for feare the whipper take yee.
Ther's hemp, & flax and tow to to to,
Tow to to to to tero.

Finis.

**The Second Part of the Whipping Cheere. With the
Roring L[ads']¹ comfortable answere to three fatall Sisters.
To the same tune.**

11 SIsters wee haue receiu'd your letters,
And lament your² cases:
Worke but apace a little while,
Wee will possesse your places.
At hempe and flaxe and tow, to, to, to.
At hempe and flaxe, &c.

12 You haue plaid your parts wee see,
And well maintaind the battle:
Now to giue the Counterblow,
Weele make the beetles rattle.
At hempe and flaxe and tow, to to to,
At hempe &c.

13 Dice and cards and mony store,
Which euery foole disburses:
Commands vs all to sing and roare,
With full impleated purses.
Now to the hempe and Tow to to to,
Now to the, &c.

14 Clownes shall not escape our hands,
But still we will be nipping;
Weele ventures gentry state and lands,
Because weele haue some whipping.
At hempe and flaxe and Tow to to to,
At hempe, &c.

15 Sommons shall be sent abroad,
To call home country brothers:

¹ *Torn.*   ² *Text* yours.

42

Panders, Foysters, and roring boyes,
The Pimps and all such others.
> *To the hemp and flaxe & Tow to to to,*
> *To the hempe, &c.*

16 Cutpurse boyes shall grow to strength,
For labours best befitting:
Play the beetles out at length,
Unlesse youle goe to whipping.
> *To the hemp and flax and Tow to to to,*
> *To the hempe, &c.*

17 Pads and Prancers run and ride,
Decoyes come shew your cunning:
Make hast to bring the cards and dice,
Your labours worth the running.
> *Heer's hemp and flaxe and tow to to to,*
> *Heer's hemp, &c.*

18 Worke apace for Wine and Capon,
And good cheere growes scanty:
Now the beetles grow the weapon,
Our fares not halfe so dainty.
> *Heer's hemp and flaxe and tow to to to,*
> *Heere's hemp.*

19 Sisters what thinke you that we,
Do second out your labours,
When we meet abroad againe,
I display the double coulours.
> *O hempe and flaxe and tow to to to,*
> *O hempe, &c.*

20 Lastly to amend the matter,
Shew your shoulders printed:
Weele shew as faire and if not better,
For so it is appointed.
> *At hempe and flaxe and to to to to,*
> *At hemp and flaxe and tow to to to, &c.*

Finis.

Printed at London for H.G.

7

The peace between Denmark and Sweden

Pepys, 1, 100, B.L., four woodcuts, four columns.

Charles IX of Sweden imprudently assumed the title of "King of the Lapps of Nordland," which belonged to the Danish Crown, and the so-called War of Kalmar between him and Christian IV of Norway and Denmark (James I's brother-in-law) followed. Most of the fighting centered around Kalmar ("Calman"), the eastern fortress of Sweden, which the Danes finally captured. Charles IX's son, Gustavus Adolphus, concluded with Christian IV the disastrous peace of Knäred, celebrated in the ballad, on January 20, 1613. So onerous were the terms, however, that instead of the brotherly love mentioned by the balladist, for many decades hatred existed between the two countries. The peace terms—summarized from a pamphlet "translated out of the Dutche copy printed at Hamburgh" that Gosson registered on April 8, 1613 (Arber's *Transcript*, III, 518)—are accurately enough enumerated in the ballad.

The tune will be found in Chappell's *Popular Music*, 1, 144.

44

PEACE BETWEEN DENMARK AND SWEDEN

The Joyfull Peace, concluded betweene the King of
Denmarke and the King of Sweden, by the meanes
of our most worthy Soueraigne, Iames, by the
grace of God, King of great Brittaine
France and Ireland, &c.

To the tune of *who list to lead a Soldiers life*.

1 THe Lord of Hosts hath blest no Land
   As he hath blessed ours:
Whom neither famine, sword nor fire
Nor myserie deuoures.
But in his mercy alwayes still
He giues vs blessings store:
And doth the hungry euer fill,
And feeds both rich and poore.

45

2 For wee that know not woes of war
Forget the Ioyes of peace:
But if we once should feele wars stroak
Then would our Ioyes decreace,
Let men of Iudgement, ponder well
The dangerous State of Armes
And they will iudge a happy peace
More good then feirce allarmes.

3 How many kingdomes hath bin spoyld?
How many Cittyes sackt?
How many valliant men byn foyld
How many ships byn wrackt?
What bloody massakers and Rapes
What dismall horride deeds?
The wars hath both vndon and don
Whilst thousand thousands bleeds.

4 And true report to Britaines brings
What warlike cruell strife
'Twixt *Denmarke* & the *Sweauian* kings
Where thousands lost their life
Till mighty *Iames* our Royall Leidge
Did cause the wars to end,
And both these foes gaue or'e their seidge
And each is others freind.

5 For what the one demanded still
The other still denyed:
And Kings contention was the cause
That many subiects dyed.
What Princes speake in heate of blood
Is feirce consuming wrath
And seldome can it be withstood
Without their subiects scath.

6 The Royall King of *Denmarke* layd
Iust clayme to certaine Land
The which the *Sweauian* King denay'd
And did his force withstand

But after many myseries
And deadly dints of wars
Our gracious Soueraigne Lord King *Iames*
Did end these bloody Iars.

The second part of the Joyfull Peace, concluded betweene
the King of *Denmarke* and the King of *Sweden*, by
the meanes of our most worthy Soueraigne,
Iames, by the grace of God, King of great
Britaine France and *Ireland*, &c.

To the tune of *who list to lead a Soldiers life.*

7 SIxe Articles of consequence,
        betweene them is agreed:
    With oathes confirm'd betweene each Prince,
        to be performed indeed.
    The which conditions of the peace,
        in order follow heere:
    Whereby the cause of all those broyles,
        to all men may appeare.

8 First that the King of Sweden should,
        The City *Calman* yeald:
    Into the King of Denmarkes hands,
        (e're further blood be spil'd.)
    VVith all the profits of the same:
        If he the same would hold
    Or else to his commodity,
        The Citty must be sold.

9 That *Elsbach*, *Otland*, two great townes,
        and *Mensborch*, with the land:
    And Forces must be all deliuer'd,
        to mighty Denmarks hand.
    For twelue yeares space he must inioy,
        Those Castles Townes and Forts,
    And now in rest these Princes great,
        do florish in their Courts.

10 Besides the King of Sweden must,
   to end the mighty quarrels:
Unto the King of Denmarke pay,
   of gold full fifteene barrells.
For charges of the foresaid warres,
   and that their shippes at seas,
May passe through one anothers bounds,
   and no man them displease.

11 That *Layland* euer shall be free,
   without all contribution:
That *Greeneland* is the Danish Kings,
   and giue no restitution.
That Denmarks King without all let,
   foure golden Crownes may beare,
Which was the great and greatest cause,
   he first these warres did reare.

12 Besides some things of smaller note,
   betwixt them is decreed:
And so those mighty Christian Kings,
   like brothers are agreed.
Thus after many bloody fights,
   and many people slaine:
The deadly stroake of dangerous armes,
   brings blessed peace againe.

Finis.

Those which are desirous to see this matter more at large:
I referre to the booke newly come forth according to the Dutch
Coppie.

Printed for *Henry Gosson,* and are to be sold at his shop
on London Bridge. 1613.

8

Leander's love to loyal Hero

Pepys, I, 344, B.L., four woodcuts, four columns.

William Meash[1] is another writer quite forgotten by balladry and literature, though he professes an intention of immortalizing the names of Hero and Leander by this ballad. His choice of a tune seems inadvertently to add a touch of burlesque to the story of Hero and Leander. Burlesque, indeed, was not unusual: the story had long been a favourite for puppet-shows, as the parody in Jonson's *Bartholomew Fair* forcibly reminds us. There is a copy of this ballad—minus title, tune, and signature—in the Percy Folio MS. (ed. Hales and Furnivall, III, 295). Except for some unimportant variations in spelling, the scribe followed the printed broadside carefully: most of the other variants in his work (*P.*) are indicated in the foot-notes. Later ballads on "The Tragedy of Hero and Leander; Or, The Two Unfortunate Lovers" and "An Excellent Sonnet of the Unfortunate Loves of Hero and Leander," both dating about 1650, are preserved in the *Roxburghe Ballads* (VI, 558, 560).

The tune of *Shackley Hay* dates from March 16, 1613, but is given in Chappell's *Popular Music* (I, 367) only from a MS. of Charles I's reign. There is, however, a copy of the first stanza and the music in Additional MS. 38,599, fol. 140, that was made from the 1613 issue of the ballad of "Shackley Hay."

John White registered "Hero and Leander" for publication on July 2, 1614 (Arber's *Transcript*, III, 549).

𝕷𝖊𝖆𝖓𝖉𝖊𝖗𝖘 𝖑𝖔𝖚𝖊 𝖙𝖔 𝖑𝖔𝖞𝖆𝖑𝖑 𝕳𝖊𝖗𝖔.

To the tune of *Shackley hay.*

1   TWo famous Louers once there was,
    whom Fame hath quite forgott.
Who loued long most constantly,
    without all enuious blott;

[1] Possibly he was the "William" whose last name is torn off the Pepysian ballad (I, 306) of "Loues up to the Elbowes." To the tune of *Codlings,*" or the "W.M." who wrote "The Lamentation of Englande," 1584 (J. P. Collier's *Book of Roxburghe Ballads*, p. 127; Lord Crawford's *Catalogue of English Ballads*, No. 1361).

Shee was most faire, and hee as[1] true:
    which caused that which[2] did ensue; fa la,[3]
Whose storie I doe meane to write,
    and tytle it, True Loues delight, fa la.

2 *Leander* was this young-mans name,
    right Noble by dessent:
And *Hero*, she whose beautie rare,
    might giue great *Ioue*[4] content,
He at *Abidos* kept his Court,
    and she at *Sestos* liued in sport, fa la,
A Riuer great did part these twaine,
    which caus'd them oft poore soules complaine, fa la.

3 Euen *Hellespont*, whose Current streames,
    like lightninges swift did glide,
Accursed Riuer that two hearts,
    so faythfull must deuide.
And more, which did augment their woe,
    their[5] parents weare each others foe, fa la,
So that no Ship durst him conuey,
    unto the place whereas[6] his *Hero* lay, fa la.

4 Long time these Louers did complaine,
    the misse of their desire.
Not knowing how they might obtaine,
    the thing they did require.
Though they[7] were parted with rough seas,
    no waters could Loues flames appease, fa la,
Leander ventured to[8] Swim
    to *Hero*, who well welcomed him, fa la.

5 Euen in the midst of darkesome night,
    when all thinges silent were,
Would young *Leander* take his flight,
    through *Hellospont* so cleare;

[1] most *P.*   [2] that *P.*   [3] *P. throughout usually has* fa la la.
[4] Loue great *P.*   [5] the *P.*   [6] where *P.*   [7] hee *P.*
[8] for to *P.*

Where at the shore, *Hero* would bee,
　　to welcome him most louingly, fa la,
And so *Leander* would conuey,
　　vnto the chamber where she lay, fa la.

6 Thus many dayes they did enioy,
　　the fruits of their delight,
For he oft to his *Hero* came,
　　and backe againe[1] same night.
And she for to encourage him,
　　through *Hellospont* more bold to[2] swim, fa la,
In her Tower top[3] a Lampe did place,
　　whereby he might behold her face, fa la.

7 And by this Lampe would *Hero* sit,
　　still praying for her loue,
That the rough waters to *Leander*[4],
　　would[5] not offensiue proue.
Be mild quoth she, till[6] he doth swim,
　　and that I haue well welcomed him, fa la;
And then euer rage and rore amaine,
　　that he may neuer goe hence againe, fa la.

8 Now Boistrous Winter hasted on,
　　when windes and Waters rage:
Yet could it not the lustfull heate,
　　of this young Youth asswage:
Though windes and waters raged so,
　　no Ship durst venture for to goe, fa la;
Leander would goe see his Loue,
　　his manly Armes in Floodes to proue, fa la.

[1] *Text* aganie.　　[2] boldlye *P.*　　[3] tap tower *P.*
[4] vnto him *P.*　　[5] might *P.*　　[6] while *P.*

𝕿𝖍𝖊 𝖘𝖊𝖈𝖔𝖓𝖉 𝖕𝖆𝖗𝖙 𝖔𝖋 𝕷𝖊𝖆𝖓𝖉𝖊𝖗𝖘 𝖑𝖔𝖚𝖊 𝖙𝖔 𝕷𝖔𝖞𝖆𝖑𝖑 𝕳𝖊𝖗𝖔 : 𝕿𝖔 𝖙𝖍𝖊 𝖘𝖆𝖒𝖊 𝖙𝖚𝖓𝖊[1].

9 THen lept he into *Hellospont*
    desirous for to goe,
Unto the place of his delight,
    which he affected so.
But windes and waues did him withstand,
    so that he could attaine no land, fa la;
For his loues Lampe looking about,
    faire *Hero* slept, and it gone out, fa la.

10 Then all in vaine *Leander* stroue;
    till Armes could doe no more,
For naked he depriu'd of life,
    was cast vpon the shore:
Oh had the Lampe still stayed in,
    Leander liuelesse had not been, fa la.
Which being gone, he knew no ground,
    because thicke darknesse did abound, fa la;

11 When *Hero* faire awakt from sleepe,
    and saw her Lampe was gone,
Her senses all be nummed weare
    and she like to a stone.
Oh from her Eyes then Pearles more cleare,
    proceeded many a dolefull teare, fa la,
Presaging[2] that the angry Flood,
    had drunke *Leanders* Louely[3] blood, fa la.

12 Then to the top of highest Tower,[4]
    faire *Hero*, did ascend:
To see how windes did with the waues,
    for maistership contend:

---

[1] Not in *P*.
[2] perswading *P*.
[3] guiltlesse *P*.
[4] Text has a period.

And on the Sandes she did espie
    a naked body Liuelesse lye, fa la;
And looking more vpont, she knew,
    it was *Leanders* bloodlesse[1] hue, fa la.

13 Then did she teare her golden haire,
    and in her griefe thus sayd,
Accursed Riuer that art still
    a foe to euery Mayde,
Since *Hellen* faire, in thee was dround,
    nam'd *Hellospont* tha'rt[2] euer found, fa la;
And now to see what thou canst doe,
    thou hast made me a mourner too, fa la.[3]

14 But though thou didst attach my Loue,
    and tooke him for thine owne:
That he was only *Heroes* deare,
    hencefoorth it shalbe knowne.
Then from the Tower faire *Hero* fell,
    whose woefull death I sigh to tell, fa la:
And on his body there did die,
    that loued her most tenderly fa la;

15 Thus ended they both[4] life and loue,
    in prime of their young yeares:
Since whose vntimelie funeralls
    no such true loue appeares:
Untill more Constant loue arise,
    their names I will immortalize[5], fa la.
And heauens send[6] such as haue true friends,
    as faithful hearts, but better ends, fa la.

Finis. *quoth William Meash.*

Imprinted at London for *I.W.*

---

[1] bloudlye *P.*   [2] *I.e.* th'art = thou art.   [3] *Text omits* fa la.
[4] both they *P.*   [5] imupetelasze *P!*   [6] *P. omits.*

9

The arraignment of John Flodder

Pepys, 1, 130, B.L., five woodcuts, four columns.

"The arraignement of John Ffloder for burneing the towne of Windham in Norfolke" was registered at Stationers' Hall by John Trundle on September 26, 1615 (Arber's *Transcript*, III, 573).

The following passage, dealing with Flodder's crime, occurs in Francis Blomefield's *History of Norfolk*, 1805, II, 533:

On *June* 11th, 1615, this town [of Wymondham] was damaged by fire to above 40,000 *l.* value, there being above 300 dwelling-houses consumed...it appears it was fired on purpose; I have the original confession of one *Margaret Bix*, alias *Elvyn*, then under sentence of death, made before the under-sheriff, &c. in which she acknowledges that she was privy to the fact, and that it was committed by *Ellen Pendleton*, who was also under condemnation for it, and that the said *Ellen* lighted a match, and she placed it in the stable where the fire first began; *Will. Flodder* was not condemned, but his brother *John*, and others, were condemned also: it appears that they were *Scots*, but went under the name of *Egyptians*, all but this *Bix*, whom they promised to carry with them into their own country, and maintain well, and procure a pardon from the Pope, for committing the fact.

Ellen Pendleton (or "Helen Pendleton alias Floder," as she is called in the *Calendar of State Papers, Domestic*, 1611–18, p. 304) was the wife of John Flodder, and her examination is preserved in the Public Record Office. From the summary given in the *Calendar* it appears that she attempted to place the blame on "certain maimed soldiers, sailors, &c. whom she found on the road near Howlbruck, Derbyshire, who said they were employed by Lord Stanley beyond the seas in plots," and that her attempt was not successful because these men carried no "powder or match whereby they could be suspected of such a crime." On August 9, 1615, one Humphrey Clesby, talking with an acquaintance (who promptly reported his words to the Government) about a sermon against Popery at Paul's Cross, remarked that the burning of Wymondham, though falsely imputed to Roman Catholic fanatics, "was done by two sailors" (*Calendar of State Papers, Domestic*, 1611–18, p. 301).

The tune is given in Chappell's *Popular Music*, 1, 162.

THE ARRAIGNMENT OF JOHN FLODDER

𝕿𝖍𝖊 𝕬𝖗𝖆𝖎𝖌𝖓𝖊𝖒𝖊𝖓𝖙 𝖔𝖋 𝕵𝖔𝖍𝖓 𝕱𝖑𝖔𝖉𝖉𝖊𝖗 𝖆𝖓𝖉 𝖍𝖎𝖘 𝖜𝖎𝖋𝖊, 𝖆𝖙 𝕹𝖔𝖗𝖜𝖎𝖉𝖌𝖊, 𝖜𝖎𝖙𝖍 𝖙𝖍𝖊 𝖜𝖎𝖋𝖊 𝖔𝖋 𝖔𝖓𝖊 𝕭𝖎𝖈𝖐𝖘, 𝖋𝖔𝖗 𝖇𝖚𝖗𝖓𝖎𝖓𝖌 𝖙𝖍𝖊 𝕿𝖔𝖜𝖓𝖊 𝖔𝖋 𝖂𝖎𝖓𝖉𝖍𝖆𝖒 𝖎𝖓 𝕹𝖔𝖗𝖋𝖔𝖑𝖐𝖊, 𝖚𝖕𝖔𝖓 𝖙𝖍𝖊 𝖝𝖎. 𝖉𝖆𝖞 𝖔𝖋 𝕵𝖚𝖓𝖊 𝖑𝖆𝖘𝖙 1615. 𝖂𝖍𝖊𝖗𝖊 𝖙𝖜𝖔 𝖔𝖋 𝖙𝖍𝖊𝖒 𝖆𝖗𝖊 𝖓𝖔𝖜 𝖊𝖝𝖊= 𝖈𝖚𝖙𝖊𝖉, 𝖆𝖓𝖉 𝖙𝖍𝖊 𝖙𝖍𝖎𝖗𝖉 𝖗𝖊𝖕𝖗𝖎𝖚𝖊𝖉 𝖚𝖕𝖔𝖓 𝖋𝖚𝖗𝖙𝖍𝖊𝖗 𝖈𝖔𝖓𝖋𝖊𝖘𝖘𝖎𝖔𝖓.

To the tune of *Fortune my foe*.

1 B Raue *Windham* late, whom Fortune did adorne,
   With Buildings fayre, & fresh as Sommers morne:
   To coale-blacke Ashes now, quite burned downe,
   May sorrowing say, I was a gallant Towne.

2 Yea all my state and glory is put by,
   For mourning on the ground my Buildings lye:
   My Goods consum'd, my Dwellers brought full low,
   Which now goe wandring vp and downe in woe.

3 Three hundred dwelling Houses of account,
   Which did to fourtie thousand pounds amount,
   Are all consumd and wasted quite away,
   And nothing left, but ruine and decay.

4 Woe worth the causers of this blacke misdeed,
   That makes a thousand hearts with sorrow bleed:
   A thousand hearts with wringing hands may say,
   In *Windham* towne this was a wofull day.

5 The deed was done by such vnhallowed hands,
   Whose rigour card not for a thousand Lands,
   The Earth it selfe, if that it flam'd with fier,
   Were as these damned varlets did desier.

6 One *Flodder* and his cursed wife, were those,
   Which wrought this famous towne these sodaine woes:
   Confederate with one *Bickes* wife; which three,
   Unto this cursed action did agree.

7 As Rogues and Beggars wandring vp and downe,
They went to seeke reliefe from towne to towne:
And liued by the vsage of bace sinne,
As custome trayneth all such liuers in.

8 [But] sure the Diuell, or else some Feend of his,
[Persu]aded[1] them vnto this foule amisse,
With Fire to wast so braue a Market towne,
That florisht faire, with Riches and Renowne.

9 A Fier that was deuised of the Diuell,
A Fier of all the worst, and worse then euill:
Wilde fier it was, that could not quenched bee,
A Ball thereof lay kindling secretly,

10 Within an Eaues, not seene of any man,
A Match gaue fier, and so it first began:
In Seruice time, when people were at Prayers,
As God required, and not on worldly cares.

11 A time that such a chaunce could hardly bee
Preuented by mans helpe, as man might see:
For on a sodaine kindled so the flame,
That mazed people could not quench the same.

12 Within two howers the towne was burned quite,
And much good Wealth therin consumd outright:
The Free-schoole house, with many a gallant Hall
With Aged people, and poore Children small.

13 Such woes were neuer seene in any place,
Nor neuer men remaind in heauier case:
Strange doubts were made how first the fire begun
That hath so many good mens states vndone.

14 At last this *Flodder*, with his wandring Mates,
Which daily beg'd for food at rich mens Gates,
Examined were, where soone their guiltie tongues
Confest the chiefe occasions of these wronges.

[1] Margin torn.

15　And so with hearts bespotted with blacke shame,
　　They were araigned, and iudged for the same,
　　To suffer death, a recompence to make,
　　For this offence, they thus did vndertake.

The Second part of the Araignement of Flodder and his wife &c. To the same tune.

16　ANd when their day of death drew neere at hand,
　　　　According to the Judges iust commaund,
　　Before ten thousand peoples wondring eyes,
　　This *Flodder* like a damned monster dyes,

17　A selfe-wild *Papist*, of a stubborne heart,
　　That would but small submission from him part:
　　But boldly died as though he had done well,
　　And not been guiltie of the fact of Hell.

18　His hated body still on Earth remaines,
　　(A shame vnto his kin) hangd vp in Chaines:
　　And must at all no other Buriall haue,
　　But Crowes & Rauens mawes to make his graue.[1]

19　But *Bicks* his wife in signe of penitence,
　　With weeping teares bewayled her offence:
　　And at her death, confest with grieued minde,
　　This deed beyond the reach of Woman-kind.

20　And how most leawdly she had liued long,
　　A shamefull life, in doing deeds of wrong:
　　And trode the steps of Whoredome day by day,
　　Accounting sinne and shame, the better way.

21　And how that shee, was will'd to put her hope
　　At last, to haue a Pardone from the *Pope*
　　For all her sinnes: for which, she did repent,
　　And sayd, no *Pope*, but Christ was her content.

---

[1] No period in the text.

22 And as for *Flodders* wife, the chiefe herein,
And damded leader to this wilfull sinne,
Being bigg with child, repriued was therefore,
To giue that life, which in her Wombe she bore.

23 But hauing now deliuerance of her Child,
All further hopes of life are quite exild.
Yet hope of life, hath made her now confesse,
The Townes proceeding dangers and distresse.

24 And how the rest should all haue burned beene,
So with a second Fire to waste it cleane:
And how the Husband of the woman dead,
Had giuen consent to haue this mischiefe spread.

25 Likewise one *Hicks*, a fellow of good age,
She sayd, his credite and his word did gage,
To be a furtherer to this damned deed,
That now hath made a thousand hearts to bleed.

26 But let no such accursed wretch as this,
The course of Law and Iustice looke to misse:
But with repentance true prepare for death,
As most vnworthy of a minuts breath.

27 And now let *Englands* Townes both farre & neere
With wisedome still preuent like chance, & feare,
And weed away from euery place and Cittie,
Such idle Drones, you cherish with your pittie.

28 Yet in your hearts let Charitie remaine,
And freely giue, to buyld this Towne againe.
And in your Prayers desire the Lord of heauen,
That bountious guiftes may thereunto be giuen.

29 Our royall King, with good and gracious hand,
  Haue graunted them, the bounties of our Land:
  In euery Church that gathering there may bee,
  As by his Letterpatents we may see.

finis.

Imprinted at London for *Iohn Trundle*, dwelling
in Barbican at the signe of the No body.

The names in the Kings Letters Pattents, to
gather vp the mony, are these following.

Iohn Moore.	*William Horsnell.*
Steuen Agas.	*Esa Freeman.*
Robert Carre.	*Robert Agas.*
Iohn Doffeelde.	*William Rowse.*

The Countries and Cities, graunted for these
men to gather in, are these following.

London and *Westminster: Middlesex, Essex, Kent,
Hartford, Surry,* and *Sussex:* with the Cities of
Canterburie, Rochester, and the *Cinque Ports,*
with the Citie of *Chester.*

10

The famous rat-catcher

Pepys, i, 458, B.L., three woodcuts, four columns.

The date of this ballad is about 1615. Part I is preserved also in a MS. at Shirburn Castle, Oxfordshire, from which it is printed in Clark's *Shirburn Ballads*, pp. 94–95. The copyist (*S.*) followed the printed copy carefully, but the second part has been torn out of the MS.

The ballad is a highly interesting, if coarse, song. The rat-catcher specialized in the treatment of the so-called social diseases no less than in exterminating rats and mice by means of his "painful bag" of poisons. The ensign of his trade, a flag of several colours, is shown in the fine woodcut here reproduced from the ballad (cf. also Ebsworth's comment in the *Roxburghe Ballads*, viii, xxxvii***, and see a ballad dating about 1855, "The Ratcatcher's Daughter," in John Ashton's *Modern Street Ballads*, 1888, p. 142). King James I himself, by the way, had an official rat-catcher, to whom in 1623 he was paying 8*d.* a day (*Calendar of State Papers, Domestic,* 1623–25, p. 135).

The tune of *The Jovial Tinker, or Joan's Ale is new,* given in Chappell's *Popular Music,* i, 187, does not apply here. The correct tune is, instead, derived from "A pleasant new Songe of a jovial Tinker. To a pleasant new tune called *Fly Brasse*" (Pepys, i, 460), printed by John Trundle[1]. *Fly Brass,* identical with *Tom of Bedlam,* is in *Popular Music,* i, 333, ii, 779.

---

[1] Later versions of this ballad, beginning "Here sits [*or* There was] a jovial tinker, dwelt in the town of Turvey," are printed in the pamphlet of *The Tinker of Turvey* (1630, pp. 2–3) and in *Merry Drollery,* 1661, i, 17–18. There are many imitations of it: *e.g.* "Encomium of Tobacco" in *Sportive Wit,* 1656, sigs. F. 6ᵛ–F. 7, and "The Vagabond" in *Merry Drollery,* ii, 16–18.

**The famous Ratketcher, with his trauels into France,
and of his returne to London.**

To the tune of *the iouiall Tinker.*

1 THere was a rare Rat-catcher,
   Did about the Country wander,
The soundest blade of all his trade,
   Or I should him deepely slaunder:
     For still would he cry, a Ratt tat tat[1],
     tara rat, euer:
     To catch a Mouse, or to carouse,
     such a Ratter I saw neuer.

[1] tat tat: rat rat *throughout in S.*

2 Upon a Poale he carryed
    Full fourty fulsome Vermine:
    Whose cursed liues without any Kniues,
      To take he did determine.
        And still would he cry, a Rat tat tat,
        tara Rat, euer, &c.

3 His talke was all of *India*,
    The Voyage and the Nauie:
    What Mise or Rattes, or wild Polcats:
    What Stoates or Weesels haue yee:
      And still would he cry, a Rat, &c.

4 He knew the Nut of *India*,
    That makes the Magpie stagger:
    The *Mercuries*, and *Cantharies*,
    With *Arsnicke*, and *Roseaker*.
      And still would he cry, a Rat, &c.

5 Full often with a *Negro*,
    The Iuice of Poppies drunke hee:
    Eate Poyson franke[1] with a Mountebanke,
    And Spiders with a Monkie.
      And still would he cry, a Rat, &c.

6 In *London* he was well knowne:
    In many a stately House
    He layd a Bayte; whose deadly fate,
    Did kill both Ratte and Mouse.
      And still would he cry, a Rat, &c.

7 But on a time, a Damosell,
    did him so farre intice,
    That for her, a Baite he layd straight,
    would kill no Rats nor Mice.
      And still would he cry, a Rat, &c.

[1] ranke *S.*

8 And on the Baite she nibled,
 so pleasing in her taste,
She lickt so[1] long, that the Poyson strong,
 did make her swell i'th waste.
  And still would he cry, a Rat, &c.

9 H[e su]btilely[2] this perceiuing,
 to the Country straight doth hie him:
Where by his skill, he poysoneth still,
 such Vermine as come nie him.
  And still would he cry, a Rat, &c.

10 He neuer careth whether
 he be sober, lame, or tipsie:
He can Collogue with any Rogue,
 and Cant with any Gipsie.
  And still would he cry, a Rat, &c.

11 He was so braue a bowzer,
 that it was doubtful whether
He taught the Rats, or the Rats taught him
 to be druncke as Rats, togeather.
  And still would he cry, a Rat, &c.

12 When he had tript this Iland,
 from *Bristow* vnto *Douer*,
With painefull Bagge and painted Flagge,
 to *France* he sayled ouer.
  Yet still would he cry, a Rat tat tat,
  Tara rat, euer, &c.

Finis.

---

[1] to *S*.   [2] *Text* H ebtilely.

THE FAMOUS RAT-CATCHER

The Ratketchers returne out of France to London. To the same tune.

13 IN *France* when he ariued,
　　the heat so much perplext him,
That all his Pouch did swell so much,
　　and Poyson so had vext him.
　　　　That scarce could he cry, a Rat tat tat.
　　　　tara Rat, euer:
　　　　To catch a Mouse, or to carouse,
　　　　Such a Ratter I saw neuer.

14 At last, as Witches common,
　　must vse anothers ayding:
So did this Ratter, tell the matter
　　to another of's owne trading.
　　　　And then did he cry, a Rat tat tat. &c.

15 Who vsing many Simples,
　　to quench his fiery burning:
Did make him daunce cleane out of *France*,
　　And home hee's now returning.
　　　　And still doth he cry, a Rat, &c.

16 At *Douer* he ariued,
　　and *Kent* hath had his cunning:
The Maydens Lappes like poysoned Rattes
　　repent his backe-home comming.
　　　　For still doth he cry, a Rat, &c.

17 At *Grauesend* 'mongst the Maydens,
　　Greene sicknesse reign'd so briefly,
None could haue cure, but such as sure
　　would take his Potions chiefly.
　　　　And still doth he cry, a Rat, &c.

18 The Shippe wherein he sayled,
　　ere he on shore ariued,
Reports him that he kild a Ratte,
　　that nere will be reuiued.
　　　　And still doth he cry, a Rat, &c.

19 And to the Fayre in *Smithfield*,
  he now is gon and paced:
To search with Pole for the Rat-knawne hole
  that him so much outfaced.
  And still doth he cry, a Rat, &c.

20 Now to the Tipling houses,
  to kill the Vermine featly:
French Rats and Mice all in a trice,
  he will destroy full neatly.
  And still doth he cry, a Rat, &c.

21 An vgly Wench to see-to,
  whose Nose was knawne with Vermin,
The Ratte to kill, that vsd her ill,
  to vse him doth determine.
  And still doth he cry, a Rat. &c.

22 If any other Maydens,
  or Female kinds, will vse him,
Come call him quicke, for with a tricke
  hee's gone, if you refuse him.
  And still doth he cry, a Rat, &c.

23 To *Sturbridge* Fayre his iourny
  is plotted, and appoynted:
Approch with speed, you that haue need
  with Poyson to be noynted.
  And still doth he cry, a Rat, &c.

24 When backe he commeth home-ward,
  obserue his Flagge bepainted
With Mice and Rattes, and with Poulcats,
  if you will be acquainted,
  And heare him to cry, a Rat tat tat,
    tara Rat, euer:
  To catch a Mouse, or to carouse,
    such a Ratter I saw neuer.

Finis.

Imprinted at London for *Iohn Trundle*, and are to be sold
at the signe of the No-body in *Barbican*.

II

The history of Jonas

Pepys, I, 28, B.L., three woodcuts, four columns.

This may have been the ballad of "Jonas" that was licensed to William Griffith in 1562–63, or "ye story of Jonas" licensed to Alexander Lacy in 1567–68. Evidently similar in nature were ballads called "the mysse Deades of Jonas &c" (1569–70) and "nowe haue with ye to Ninive being a sonnet of Repentance" (September 5, 1586: Arber's *Transcript*, I, 205, 355, 410; II, 457). Edward Allde, the printer of the Pepysian ballad, printed ballads during the years 1584–1628: as a mere guess his "Jonah" may be dated 1615. It is a fairly close metrical paraphrase of the four chapters of the Book of Jonah. Possibly this is the ballad of "Jonas his Crying-out against Coventry" that the Fiddler in Fletcher's *Monsieur Thomas* (III, iii) says he can sing.

The story of Jonah was, like that of Hero and Leander, a favourite for puppet-shows. The great dramatists took especial delight in ridiculing them. "There's a new motion of the city of Nineveh, with Jonas and the whale, to be seen at Fleet-bridge," says Fungoso, in Jonson's *Every Man out of His Humour*, 1599, II, i. In Greene and Peele's *Looking-Glass for London and England*, 1594, a remarkable stage-direction runs: "Jonas is cast out of the whale's belly upon the stage."

The tune of *Paggington's* (or *Packington's*) *Pound* (or *Round*), a tune (used by Ben Jonson for a ballad of his own composition in *Bartholomew Fair*) that always entails a very attractive metrical and stanzaic form, is given in Chappell's *Popular Music*, I, 123.

The historie of the Prophet *Ionas*.

The repentance of *Niniuie* **that great Citie, which was 48. miles in compasse, hauing a thousand and fiue hundred Towers about the same, and at the time of his preaching there was a hundred and twenty thousand Children therein.**

To the tune of *Paggingtons round*.

66

THE HISTORY OF JONAS

1 VNto the Prophet *Ionas* I read,
   The word of the Lord secretly came,
Saying to Niniuy passe thou with speed,
To that mightie Citie of wondrous fame.
          Against it quoth he
          cry out and be free.
Their wickednesse great is come vp to me.
Sinne is the cause of great sorrow and care,
But God through repentance his vengeance doth spare.

2 Then *Ionas* rose vp immediatly,
And from the presence of the Lord God,
He sought by sea away to flie,
And went downe to *Ioppa* where many ships rode,
          The fare he did pay,
          and so got away.
And thus the Lords word he did disobey.
Sinn is the cause of great sorrow and care,
But God through repentance, &c.

3 But God sent out such a mighty great winde,
That a sore tempest vpon the sea came:
Which greatly tormented the Marriners minde
Their ship being like to be broke by the same.
          And being afraid,
          no time they delaide:
But each vnto his God earnestly praide.
Sinne is the cause of great sorrow and care.
But God through repentance, &c.

4 Yet seeing the tempest continue so sore
To lighten their ship they thought it the best,
Into the rough sea, therefore they cast ore,
All their rich marchandize ere they did rest,
          but while they did weepe,
          Ionas did sleepe,
And vnder the hatches himselfe he did keepe.
Sinne is the cause of great sorrow and care,
But God through repentance, &c.

5 Then came the Shipmaster to *Ionas* in hast,
　Saying thou sluggard why sleepest thou so?
　We being in danger away to be cast,
　Rise, pray to thy God to release our great woe.
　　　　for well you may see,
　　　　that likely we be,
　Each one to be drowned without remedy,
　Sinne is the cause of sorrow and care:
　But God through repentance, &c.

6 Then each vnto his fellow did say,
　Come let vs cast lots betweene vs each one,
　To know for which of our sinnes this day,
　This grieuous tempest vpon vs is blowne.
　　　　Then truth for to tell,
　　　　when wisely and well,
　The lots were all cast, vpon *Ionas* it fell.
　Sinne is the cause of great sorrow and care,
　But God through repentance, &c.

7 When they perceiued the lot to fall so,
　They asked of *Ionas* immediatly:
　from whence he did come and where he would goe,
　Where he was borne and in what countrie.
　　　　then *Ionas* replide,
　　　　and neuer denide,
　But all the whole truth vnto them discride,
　Sinne is the cause of great sorrow and care,
　But God through repentance, &c.

8 I am an Hebrew you shall vnderstand,
　And the Lord God of heauen I onely serue:
　Which made the sea and eke the dry land,
　But from his commandement late I did swarue.
　　　　In seeking to flie,
　　　　from his maiestie,
　He hath laid vpon me this great misery.
　Sinne is the cause of sorrow and care,
　But God through repentance, &c.

9 Then said the Mariners tell vs with speed,
What shall we doe with thee in this case:
That this great tempest may cease in our need,
Which rageth extreamly in euery place.
     Cast mee in the sea.
     thus *Ionas* did say,
For 'tis for my sake you are plagued this day,
Sinne is the causer of sorrow and care,
But God through repentance, &c.

10 Neuerthelesse the men were afraid,
And sought for to row the ship vnto Land:
But could not preuaile the tempest so plaid,
That they in great perrill of life still did stand.
     O Lord then quoth they,
     we humbly pray,
For this man let vs not perish this day,
sinne is the cause of great sorrow and care, &c.
But God through repentance, &c.

11 Then tooke they vp *Ionas* in place where he stood,
And threw him out of the ship in the sea:
And presently the fierce raging flood,
With the great tempest the Lord did alay.
     and then presently,
     they all did espie,
That the sea most calme and most quiet did lie.
Sinne is the cause of great sorrow and care,
But God through repentance, &c.

The second part. To the same tune.

12 A Great Whale fish the Lord sent that way,
Which swallowed vp *Ionas* immediatly.
Three daies and three nights in his belly he lay,
And there full oft to the Lord he did cry.
     Then God did command,
     The Whale out of hand,
To cast vp the Prophet vpon the dry land,
Sinne is the causer of sorrow and care, &c.

13 The word of the Lord came to *Ionas* againe,
Saying goe to *Niniuies* mighty Citie:
And preach vnto that people most plaine,
The words which I before shewed thee,
      then *Ionas* arose,
      to the Citie he goes,
And daily to them Gods iudgement he shewes,
Fortie[1] daies after yet remaineth quoth he,
And *Niniuie* then destroyed shall be.

14 The King and the people of *Niniuy* then,
At *Ionas* preaching repented full sore:
They proclaimed a fast both to beastes and to men,
And sackcloth and ashes most humbly they wore,
      and most bitterly,
      to God they did cry,
Asking forgiuenesse and crauing mercy.
For forty daies yet remaineth quoth he,
And *Niniuy* then destroyed shall be.

15 Their great repentance the Lord did behold,
Their true humble hearts in euery degree:
To them his mercy he did then vnfold
And turned his punishment from their Citie.
      his fauour and grace,
      he sent to that place,
And all their offences he cleane did deface.
Sinne is the causer of sorrow and care, &c.

16 At this was *Ionas* greatly displeasd,
And thus to the Lord in anger he said:
Now well I see thy wrath is appeas'd,
Whereby all falshood to me will be laid.
      and therefore quoth he,
      most blest should I be,
If my hatefull life thou shouldst take now from me.
Sinne is the causer of sorrow and care, &c.

[1] *Text* Footie.

17 So *Ionas* went out of the Citie with speed,
And on the east a boothe he did make:
There to behold, to marke and take heed,
what course with the city the Lord God would take,
  where God in one night,
  brought vp in his sight,
A wilde vine to shadow him from the Suns heate.
Sinne is the causer of sorrow and care, &c.

18 *Ionas* of this was wondrous glad,
For great was the force of the Sun in that place.
And he by that meanes a good couering had,
But God the next day the vine did deface.
  so then the Suns heate:
  on him did so beat,
That for this vine *Ionas* his anger was great.
Sin is the causer of sorrow and care, &c.

19 Then said the Lord God to *Ionas* againe,
And dost thou well to be angry for this?
He said I doe well to be angry certaine,
Seeing my comfort so soone I doe misse.
  and better quoth he,
  it is now for me,
To die then to liue in this miserie,
Sinne is the causer of sorrow and care, &c.

20 And hast thou such pitty the Lord God did say,
On this wilde Vine which sprung in one night:
And in a night likewise did wither away,
Which thou neuer plantedst, nor cost thee a mite.
  then why should not I,
  in tender mercy,
Pitty this great repenting Citie?
Sinne is the cause of great sorrow and care,
But God by repentance his vengeance doth spare.

Finis.

Printed at London by *E.A.*

1 2

The cucking of a scold

Pepys, 1, 454, B.L., one woodcut, three columns.

An amusing and a highly interesting description of how scolds were, after due process of law, ducked is given in this ballad. The cucking was no tame affair, but was instead an elaborate ceremonial involving a parade in which a hundred archers, a hundred armed men, and fifty parrots took part. There are ballads out of number on scolds, but most of them tell of the desperate remedies applied in more or less privacy by the martyred husbands, and none, I believe, deals with a public cucking such as befell this "dainty scold in grain." That her type still lingers would appear from the case of a woman who was tried and convicted of being a "common scold" by the Criminal Court of Pittsburgh, Pennsylvania, on February 18, 1921. There seventeen families testified that they were scandalized "when they left their houses for a minute and that such epithets as 'poor fish,' 'mountain of flesh' and 'dirty long legs' were hurled at them" by the scold in question. This scold was sentenced to pay the costs of the case and to move from the neighbourhood.

The printer G.P. could have been either George Purslowe or George Potter, who printed during the years 1614–1632 and 1599–1616 respectively. I suspect that the ballad dates at least as early as 1615. Its first appearance was probably at an earlier date even than 1615. The tune, usually referred to as *The Merchantman*, comes from a ballad of Thomas Deloney's of the date March 22, 1594. The music is given in Chappell's *Popular Music*, 1, 381.

The Cucking of a Scould.

To the tune of, *The Merchant of Emden.*

1   A Wedded wife there was,
     I wis of yeeres but yong,
But if you thinke she wanted wit,
Ile sweare she lackt no tongue.
Iust seventeene yeeres of age,
This woman[1] was no more,

    [1] *Text* women.

72

THE CUCKING OF A SCOLD

Yet she would scold with any one,
From twenty to threescore.
The cucking of a Scold,
The cucking of a Scold,
Which if you will but stay to heare
The cucking of a Scold.

2 As nimble as an Eele,
This womans tongue did wag,
And faster you shall haue it runne,
Then any ambling Nag.
But without mighty wrong,
She would not shew her skill.
But if that she were moued once
The sport[1] was not so ill.
The cucking &c.

3 Each man might quickly know,[2]
When as the game begun,[2]
But none could tell you for his life,
What time she would haue done.
She was a famous Scould,
A dainty Scould in graine,
A stouter Scould was neuer bred
Nor borne in Turne-gaine Lane.
The cucking &c.

4 Upon a time it chanc'd,
And she did thus alledge,
A neighbours maid had taken halfe
Her dish-clout from the hedge:
For which great trespasse done,
This wrong for to requite,
She scolded very hansomely,
Two daies and one whole night.
The cucking &c.

[1] sport: *word indecipherable.*   [2] Text has a period.

5 Which something did molest
   The neighbours round about:
   But this was nothing to the fits
   That she would thunder out.
   But once, the truth to tell,
   Worse scolding did she keepe,
   For waking of her little Dog,
   That in the Sun did sleepe.
       The cucking, &c.

6 Six winter dayes together,
   From morning eight a clocke,
   Until the euening that each one
   Their doores began to lock:
   She scolded for this wrong,
   Which she accounted great,
   And vnto peace and quietnesse
   No man could her intreat.
       The cucking &c.

7 So that this little Deuill,
   With her vnquiet tongue,
   Continually both far and neere,
   Molested old and yong.
   But yet soone after this,
   She made a greater brawle,
   Against the Constable, that did
   But pisse against her wall.
       The cucking, &c.

8 She cal'd him beastly knaue,
   And filthy Iacke for this,
   And said that euery Cuckold now
   Against her wall must pisse:
   And in most raging sort,
   She rail'd at him so long.
   He made a vow he would reuenge
   This most outragious wrong[1].
       The cucking, &c.

[1] *Text* worng.

74

9 And first of all behold,
   He clapt her in the Cage,
   Thinking thereby her deuillish tongue,
   He would full well asswage.
   But now worse then before,
   She did to brawling fall.
   The Constable and all the rest
   She vildly did miscall.
       The cucking, &c.

10 Thus night and day she sent
   Such brawling from her brest,
   That ner a neighbour in the towne
   Could take one houres rest.
   Which when the Iustice knew,
   This Iudgement than gaue he,
   That she vpon a cucking stoole
   Should iustly punisht be.
       The cucking, &c.

11 Vpon three market dayes,
   This penance she should bide,
   And euery thing fit for the same,[1]
   The Officers did prouide:
   An hundred Archers good,
   Did first before her goe,
   A hundred and fiue nimble shot
   Went next vnto the Roe.
       The cucking &c.

12 An hundred armed men
   Did also follow there:
   The which did guard the gallant Scould
   With piercing Pikes and Speare:
   And trumpets[2] sounding sweet.
   In order with them comes
   A company most orderly,
   With pleasant Phifes and Drums.
       The cucking, &c.

[1] Text has a period.   [2] *Text* trumptes.

75

13 And forty Parrats then,
   On sundry pearches hie,
Were carried eke before the scould,
   Most fine and orderly
And last of all a mighty wispe
   Was borne before her face.
The perfect token of a Scould
   Well knowne in euery place.
        The cucking, &c.

14 Then was the Scould her selfe,[1]
   In a wheele-barrow brought,[1]
Stripped naked to the smocke,
   As in that case she ought:
Neats tongues about her necke
   Were hung in open show;
And thus vnto the cucking stoole
   This famous Scould did goe.
        The cucking, &c.

15 Then fast within the chaire
   She was most finely bound,
Which made her scold excessiuely,
   And said she should be drown'd.
But euery time that she
   Was in the water dipt,
The drums & trumpets sounded braue,
   For ioy the people skipt.
        The cucking, &c.

16 Six times when she was duckt
   Within the water cleare,[1]
That like vnto a drowned Rat,
   She did in sight appeare.
The Iustice thinking then
   To send her straight away,

[1] Text has a period.

76

The Constable she called knaue,
And knau'd him all the day.
The cucking &c.

17 Upon which words, I wot,
They duckt her straight againe
A dozen times ore head and eares:
Yet she would not refraine,
But still reuil'd them all.
Then to 't againe they goe,
Till she at last held vp her hands,
Saying, I'le no more doe so.
The cucking &c.

18 Then was she brought away,
And after for her life,
She neuer durst begin to scould
With either man or wife.
And if that euery Scould
Might haue so good a diet,
Then should their neighbours euery day
Be sure to liue in quiet,
    The cucking of a Scould,
    The cucking of a Scould
    Which if you will but stay to heare
    The cucking of a Scould.

𝔉inis.[1]

Printed at London by *G.P.*

[1] No period in the text.

13

Ten shillings for a kiss

Pepys, 1, 316, B.L., three woodcuts, four columns.

The date is probably about 1615: John White printed during the years 1613–1625. The ballad is unusual in having a second part in a different measure and to a different tune from the first part. Rare indeed is this procedure[1]. When, towards the end of the sixteenth century, printers began to divide ballads into two parts, they felt that each part was an entity, and sometimes, as in the case of the well-known "Widow of Watling Street," actually printed each part on a separate broadside. Two tunes and different measures were then appropriate. In a few years, however, every ballad came to have two parts, but the division was a purely mechanical device due to the *forme*; as a result, only one tune could be used, and the formula, "The second part. To the same tune," became stereotyped.

The ballad is unique in manner and contents, and is rather clever. The maid bids an astonishingly high price for a kiss, for, as her lover tells her, other maidens are offering for a husband only five shillings. In stanzas 19–21 there is a general allusion to other ballads made by love-lorn damsels and a specific reference to "A Maiden's Lamentation for a Bedfellow. Or, I can, nor will no longer lye alone. As it hath been often sung at the Court. To the tune of *I will give thee kisses, one, two, or three*" (Pepys, 1, 246, 286).

The first tune is given in Chappell's *Popular Music*, 1, 315; the second, equivalent to *I will give thee kisses, one, two, or three*, is unknown; it seems to involve a refrain of "sweeter than the honey" and "sweeter than the blossoms," both of which are used throughout in No. 21.

---

[1] There are other examples in the Pepys collection, *e.g.* the ballads of "Nobody loves mee," with its first part to the tune of *Philliday*, its second to *Dainty, come thou to me*, and "The Lover's Lamentation to his Love Nancy," with its first part to the tune of *Did you see Nan today?* its second to *Virginia* (Pepys, 1, 430, and 332).

TEN SHILLINGS FOR A KISS

This Maide would giue tenne Shillings for a Kisse:

To the Tune of *Shall I wrastle in despaire.*

1   YOu young men all take pitty on me,
      the haplessest Maid you euer did see:
   Refus'd of all, of all neglected,
      hated of all and by none affected:
   The cause I know not: well I know,
      their fond neglect procures my woe.
   Then since their hopefull loues I misse,
      come, here's ten shillings for a kisse.

2   I doe as much as a Maide can doe,
      for gainst my nature I doe woe:
   I vse all meanes that ere I can,
      to get the loue of a proper man:
   Yet let me vse the best of skill,
      they still deny, and crosse my will:
   Then since their hopefull loues I misse:
      come here's ten shillings for a kisse.

3   With Sieuet sweet I make me fine,
      with sweet complection I doe shine:
   With beautious colours passing deere,
      I paint and prune, yet nere the neere.
   My cost is vaine, so well it proues:
      for all my cost there's no man loues:
   Then since their hopefull loues I misse,
      come here's ten shillings for a kisse.

4   I haue a face as fayre as any,
      my nose and lip surpasseth many,
   I haue an eye that rowling lies,
      though theies are better to intice:
   Why should all men disdaining proue?
      and worser beauties dearely loue?
   But since their hopefull loues I misse:
      come here's ten shillings for a kisse.

79

TEN SHILLINGS FOR A KISS

5 My armes are nimble to each poynt,
  actiue I am in euery ioynt:
I am not as some maidens are,
  so coy, for young men not to care,
Why should I then disdained be?
  when those are lou'd be worse then me?
But since their hopefull loues I misse:
  come here's ten shillings for a kisse.

6 My waste is small, and likewise long,
  my leg well calft, and boned strong,
My pretty foote you all may feele,
  is not in bredth an inch in th' heele.
From head to foote in euery part,
  I seeme a building fram'd by Art:
Yet since their hopefull loues I misse,
  come here's ten shillings for a kisse.

7 Yet man's obdurate to my mones,
  they all stand senslesse of my grones,
They nere regard a proper maide:
  great heyres are tane and she denaid,
Yet by all meanes I will assay,
  to gaine mens loues as well as they:
For since their hopefull loues I misse,
  come here's ten shillings for a kisse.

8 Is *Cupid* dead, will he not strike,
  and make some man perforce to like:
Or is he angry with a creature,
  making me liue the scorne of nature:
Or is his dart in 's Quiuer fast:
  oh no, I hope heele strike at last:
Since I their hopefull loues do misse,
  come here's ten shillings for a kisse.

9 To the Daucing schoole I vsuall goe,
  and learne farre more then many doe
Oft I resort to weddings for this,
  onely to gayne a young mans kisse.

Yet though my dauncing be so good,[1]
    by all youth there I am withstood:
Then since their hopefull loues I misse,
    come here's ten shillings for a kisse.

10 Let *Venus* guide some young mans hart,
    or *Anthropos* strike here thy Dart:
Let young men pitty my hard state,
    or proue like me vnfortunate.
Come gentle young men ease my griefe,
    nought but a kisse can giue reliefe,
For since their hopefull loues I misse:
    come here's ten shillings for a kisse.

Finis[2].

Printed at *London* by *I. White*.

The Second Part shewheth shee may haue them Cheape I wis:

To the Tune *I can nor will no longer lye alone.*

11 A Lack fayre Maide, why dost thou grone,
    Is it for a kisse, alack but for one?
Nay thou shalt haue a hundred one two or three,
More sweeter then the hunny that comes from the Bee.

12 Doe not thinke we men are vnkind,
    For a Kisse or two to stay behinde:
Nay thou shalt haue a hundred one two or three,
More sweter then the blossomes from the Tree.

13 All Maydes they say, not as you say,
    For if that we pray, they will say nay:
The more that we seeke they still will reply,
Alack they cannot loue, yet know not why.

[1] Text has a period.   [2] *Text* FIINS.

14 I doe not condem all of your kind,
    But such that beare a froward faithles minde:
    The good I doe protest, I loue with my heart,
    And with the euill I, will not take part.

15 Wee men are constant and Women to blame
    To be vnconstant, to their loues a shame:
    Yet tell them of their faults, they still will reply,
    They will haue their wills,[1] yet know not why.

16 I would all Maides were of thy minde,
    Then should we Men to woemen be kinde:
    And in loue and Amitie agree,
    More sweter then[2] the hunny that comes from the Bee.

17 Many examples I could procure,
    Shewing men constant in their loue:
    Which thou shalt finde in mee I tell thee plaine,
    Come kisse me gentle Sweeting O Kisse againe.

18 There dwels a Mayd in our Towne greene,
    With whome many Louers, I haue seene:
    Yet shee's so coy, God wot she will haue none,
    But lead a single life all alone.

19 But how it falles I doe not know,
    A Ballet they say, now doth it show:
    That sighing and protesting, she makes her mone,
    She can nor will no longer lye alone.

20 An other lately as I heare,
    That vow'd to liue a Mayden forty yeere:
    Fiue shillings for a Husband now doth cry,
    If that she be not holpen, alack shee'l die.

21 Come[3] *Ginny* come an other cryes,
    With the trickling teares in her eyes:
    My Mayden head alacke it troubles me,
    O *Ginny Ginny* I, may say to thee.

[1] *Text* wiles.   [2] *Text* uhen.   [3] *Text* Cowe.

22 Doe not blush at this I speake,
   For alacke I know your Sex is weake:
   Let coy Dames passe away, refusing their blisse,
   Upon thy sweet lipes I doe seale this Kisse.

23 And now to conclud this my Songe.
   Alacke for a Kisse thou hast stayd too long:
   Nay thou deseru'st a thousand one two or three,
   More sweeter then the blossomes of the Tree.

Finis.

Printed at *London* by *I. White.*

14

Anne Wallen's lamentation

Pepys, 1, 124, B.L., two woodcuts, four columns.

A "good-night" by T. Platte, an author known only by this one production. For the tune see Chappell's *Popular Music*, 1, 162.

Professor Kittredge points out the following passage in a letter written by John Chamberlain to Sir Dudley Carleton on July 6, 1616 (*The Court and Times of James I*, 1, 418):

> There was a seminary priest hanged at Tyburn on Monday...That morning early, there was a joiner's wife burnt in Smithfield for killing her husband. If the case were no otherwise than I can learn it, she had *summum jus*[!]; for her husband having brawled and beaten her, she took up a chisal, or some such other instrument, and flung at him, which cut him into the belly, whereof he died.

As July 6 came on Saturday, July 1 was Monday. On July 1, according to the ballad, Anne Wallen was burned, so that to her execution Chamberlain's comment seems applicable. For comments on burning women as a punishment for petty treason see the introduction to No. 52.

84

ANNE WALLEN'S LAMENTATION

𝕬nne 𝔚𝔞llens 𝕷amentation,
𝕱or 𝔱𝔥e 𝕸urt𝔥ering of 𝔥er 𝔥usband *Iohn Wallen* 𝔞
𝕿urner in 𝕮o𝔴-lane neere 𝔖mit𝔥field; done b𝔶 𝔥is o𝔴ne
𝔴ife, on 𝔰atterda𝔶 𝔱𝔥e 22. of 𝕵une. 1616. 𝔴𝔥o 𝔴as burnt
in 𝔖mit𝔥field 𝔱𝔥e first of 𝕵ul𝔶 follo𝔴ing.

To the tune of *Fortune my foe.*

1 Great God that sees al things that here are don
   Keeping thy Court with thy celestiall Son;
   Heere her complaint that hath so sore offended,
   Forgiue my fact before my life is ended.

2 Ah me the shame vnto all women kinde,
   To harbour such a thought within my minde:
   That now hath made me to the world a scorne,
   And makes me curse the time that I was borne.

3 O would to God my mothers haples wombe,
   Before my birth had beene my happy tombe:
   Or would to God when first I did take breath,
   That I had suffered any painefull death.

4 If euer dyed a true repentant soule,
   Then I am she, whose deedes are blacke and foule:
   Then take heed wiues be to your husbands kinde,
   And beare this lesson truely in your minde,

5 Let not your tongus oresway true reasons bounds,
   Which in your rage your vtmost rancour sounds:
   A woman that is wise should seldome speake,
   Unlesse discreetly she her words repeat.[1]

6 Oh, would that I had thought of this before,
   Which now to thinke on makes my heart full sore:
   Then should I not haue done this deed so foule,
   The which hath stained my immortall soule.

[1] No period in the text.

85

7 Tis not to dye that thus doth cause me grieue,
I am more willing far to die then liue;
But tis for blood which mounteth to the skies,
And to the Lord reuenge, reuenge, it cries.

8 My dearest husband did I wound to death,
And was the cause he lost his sweetest breath,
But yet I trust his soule in heauen doth dwell,
And mine without Gods mercy sinkes to hell.

9 In London neere to smithfield did I dwell,
And mongst my neighbours was beloued well:
Till that the Deuill wrought me this same spight,
That all their loues are turnd to hatred quight.

10 *Iohn Wallen* was my louing husbands name,
Which long hath liu'd in London in good fame.
His trade a Turner, as was knowne full well,
My name *An Wallen*, dolefull tale to tell.

Anne wallens Lamentation,
Or the second part of the murther of one *Iohn Wallen*
a Turner in Cow-lane neere Smithfield; done by his
owne wife, on saterday the 22 of June 1616. who was
burnt in Smithfield the first of July following.

To the tune of *Fortune my foe.*

11 MY husband hauing beene about the towne,
And comming home, he on his bed lay down:
To rest himselfe, which when I did espie,
I fell to rayling most outragiously.

12 I cald him Rogue, and slaue, and all to naught,
Repeating the worst language might be thought
Thou drunken knaue I said, and arrant sot,
Thy minde is set on nothing but the pot.

13 Sweet heart he said I pray thee hold thy tongue,
   And if thou dost not, I shall[1] doe thee wrong,
   At which, straight way I grew in worser rage,
   That he by no meanes could my tongue asswage.

14 He then arose and strooke me on the eare,
   I did at him begin to curse and sweare:
   Then presently one of his tooles I got,
   And on his body gaue a wicked stroake.[2]

15 Amongst his intrailes I this Chissell threw,
   Where as his Caule came out, for which I rue,
   What hast thou don, I prethee looke quoth he,
   Thou hast thy wish, for thou hast killed me.

16 When this was done the neighbours they ran in,
   And to his bed they streight conueyed him:
   Where he was drest and liu'd till morne next day,
   Yet he forgaue me and for me did pray.

17 No sooner was his breath from body fled,
   But vnto Newgate straight way they me led:
   Where I did lie vntill the Sizes came,
   Which was before I there three daies had laine.

18 Mother in lawe, forgiue me I you pray,
   For I haue made your onely childe away,
   Euen all you had; my selfe made husbandlesse,
   My life and all, cause I did so transgresse.

19 He nere did wrong to any in his life,
   But he too much was wronged by his wife;
   Then wiues be warn'd, example take by me.
   Heauens graunt no more that such a one may be.

---

[1] *Text* shall shall.   [2] No period in the text.

20 My iudgement then it was pronounced plaine,
Because my dearest husband I had slaine:
In burning flames of fire I should fry,
Receiue my soule sweet Jesus now I die.

T: Platte.

Finis.

Printed for *Henry Gosson,* and are to be solde
at his shop on London bridge.

15

Sir Walter Raleigh's lamentation

Pepys, 1, 110, B.L., one poor woodcut of a ship, four columns. A facsimile reproduction of this ballad, with a brief introductory note by Professor C. H. Firth, of Oxford, was issued in 1919.

The ballad is correct enough in dates and places, but misrepresents Raleigh's words and actions on the scaffold. For this misrepresentation, censorship of the press rather than personal animosity of the author is, no doubt, responsible. For although in 1601 Raleigh's supposed responsibility for the execution of the Earl of Essex aroused much hostile feeling against him, by 1618 this feeling had largely changed to sympathy for his own misfortunes. No ballads on Raleigh were entered in the Stationers' Register for 1618, but many were in fact printed. On November 21, 1618, John Chamberlain wrote: "We are so full still of Sir Walter Raleigh that almost every day brings forth somewhat in this kind, besides divers ballets, wherof some are called in, and the rest such poore stuffe as are not worth the overlooking" (*Calendar of State Papers, Domestic,* 1611–18, p. 597; C. H. Firth, Royal Historical Society *Transactions,* 3rd Series, v, 40). Of this "poore stuffe" the Pepysian ballad is the sole surviving printed specimen. Years later (in 1644) appeared a prose and verse pamphlet called *To day a man, To morrow none: Or, Sir Walter Rawleighs Farewell to his Lady, The night before hee was beheaded: Together with his advice concerning HER, and her SONNE* (reprinted in Charles Hindley's *Old Book Collector's Miscellany,* vol. III).

For the tune see Chappell's *Popular Music,* 1, 174.

Sir Walter Rauleigh his lamentation: Who was beheaded in the old Pallace at Westminster the 29. of October. 1618.

To the tune of *Weiladay.*

1   COurteous kind Gallants all,
      pittie me, pittie me,
  My time is now but small,
  here to continue:

Thousands of people stay,
To see my dying day,
Sing I then welladay,
   wofully mourning.

2 Once in a gallant sort
    liued I, liued I,
Belou'd in Englands court
    graced with honours:
Sir *Walter Rauleighs*[1] name
Had then a noble fame:
Though turned now to shame
    through my misdoing.

3 In youth I was too free
    of my will, of my will,
Which now deceiueth me
    of my best fortunes:
All that same gallant traine
Which I did then maintaine,
Holds me now in disdaine
    for my vaine folly.

4 When as Queene *Elizabeth*
    ruld this land, ruld this land,
I trode the honord path
    of a braue Courtier;
Offices I had store,
Heapt on me more and more,
And my selfe I in them bore
    proud and commanding.

5 Gone are those golden dayes,
    woe is me woe is me:
Offences many waies
    brought vnto triall,

[1] Text *Ranleighs*.

Shewes that disloyaltie
Done to his Maiestie,
Iudgeth me thus to dye;
    Lord for thy pitie.

6 But the good graces heere
      of my King, of my King,
  Shewd to me many a yeere
      makes my soule happie
  In that his royall Grace
  Gaue me both time and space
  Repentance to embrace:
      now heauen be praised.

7 Thirteene yeare in the tower
      haue I lien, haue I lien,
  Before this appoynted houre
      of my liues ending:
  Likewise such libertie
  Had I vnluckily,
  To be sent gallantly
      out on a voyage.

8 But that same voyage then
      prou'd amis prou'd amis,
  Many good gentlemen
      lost their good fortunes:
  All that with me did goe
  Had sudden ouerthrowe
  My wicked will to shew
      gainst my deere Countrey.

9 When I returned backe,
      hoping grace, hoping grace,
  The tower againe alacke
      was my abiding:
  Where for offences past,
  My life againe was cast
  Woe on woe followed fast
      to my confusion.

10 It pleas'd[1] my royall King
  thus to doe, thus to doe,
That his peeres should me bring
  to my liues iudgement.
The Lieutenant of the tower
Kept me fast in his power,
Till the appointed houre
  of my remoouing.

The Second Part.

11 TO Westminster then was I
  garded strong, garded strong
Where many a wandring eye
  saw me conuayed
Where I a Iudgment had,
  for my offences bad,
Which was to loose my head,
  there the next morning.

12 So to the Gatehouse there,
  was I sent, was I sent,
By knights and gentlemen,
  guarding me safely,
Where all that wofull night,
My heart tooke no delight:
Such is the heauie plight
  of a poore prisoner.

13 Calling then to my mind,
  all my ioyes, all my ioyes,
Whereto I was inclind,
  liuing in pleasures:
All those dayes past and gon,
Brings me now care and mone,[2]
Being thus ouerthrowne,
  by mine owne folly.

1 *Text* plea'sd.   2 *Text* moue.

14 When the sad morning came
  I should die, I should die:
 O what a fright of shame:
  fild vp my bosome:
 My heart did almost breake,
 when I heard people speake,
 I shold my ending make
  as a vile traitor.

15 I thought my fortunes hard,
  when I saw, when I saw
 In the faire pallace yard
  a scaffold prepared:
 My loathed life to end:
 On which I did ascend,
 Hauing at all no friend
  there to grant mercy.

16 Kneeling downe on my knee,
  willingly, willingly,
 Prayed for his Maiestie[1]
  long to continue:
 And for his Nobles all,[2]
 With subiects great and small,
 Let this my wofull fall
  be a fit warning.

17 And you that hither come
  thus to see, thus to see
 My most vnhappy doome:
  pittie my ending.
 A Christian true I die:
 Papistrie I defie,
 Nor neuer Atheist I
  as is reported.

---

[1] *Text* Maiustie.   [2] Text has a period.

18 You Lords & knights also
   in this place, in this place
Some gentle loue bestow
   pity my falling:
As I rose suddenly
Vp to great dignitie,
So I deseruedly
   die for my folly.

19 Farewell my louing wife
   woe is me, woe is me:
Mournefull wil bee thy life,
   Left a sad widdow.
Farewell my children sweet,
VVe neuer more shall meet
Till we each other greet,
   blessed in heauen.

20 With this my dying knell
   willingly, willingly,
Bid I the world farewell
   full of vaine shadowes
All her deluding showes
brings my heart naught but woes
Who rightly feeles and knowes,
   all her deceiuings.

21 Thus with my dying breath
   doe I kis, doe I kis,
This axe that for my death
   here is prouided:
May I feele little paine,
when as it cuts in twaine,
what my life must sustaine,
   all her deceiuings.

22 My head on block is laid,
   And my last part is plaid:
Fortune hath me betraid,
   sweet Iesus grant mercy.

SIR WALTER RALEIGH'S LAMENTATION

Thou that my headsman art,
when thou list, when thou list,
VVithout feare doe thy part
I am prepared:

23 Thus here my end I take
farewel world, farewel world,
And my last will I make,
climing to heauen:
For this my offence,
I die with true penitence,
Iesus receiue me hence:
farewell sweet England.

London Printed for Philip Birch and are to be sold at
his shop at the Guyld-hall.

16

Damnable practises

Pepys, 1, 132, B.L., two woodcuts, five columns. The left margin is mutilated, so that missing letters and words in the first column (stanzas 1–5) are restored within square brackets.

The book referred to at the end of the ballad is *The Wonderful discoverie of the Witchcrafts of Margaret and Phillippa Flower*, 1619, of which a reprint was issued in 1838 (British Museum, C. 27. b. 35 and 8630. g. 16). Similar books are *The Witches Of Northampton-Shire... Who were all executed at Northampton the 22. of Iuly last.* 1612 (Bodleian, Malone 709) and Thomas Potts's *The Wonderfvll Discoverie Of Witches in The Covn-tie of Lan-caster* (Bodleian, Wood B 18(2); *Somers' Tracts*, 1810, III, 95 ff.). The nobleman of the ballad was Francis Manners, sixth Earl of Rutland. His two sons died in infancy, supposedly from witchcraft, as the ballad describes; but his daughter Catherine survived to marry George Villiers, Duke of Buckingham. The inscription on the monument of the Earl of Rutland at Bottesford, Leicestershire (which is given in full in Nichols's *History and Antiquities of the County of Leicester*, II, 102; cf. William Hone's *Every-Day Book*, 1889, II, 185–187) mentions the death of his two sons "by wicked practice and sorcerye"; the "two boys kneel at his feet holding sculls, and one a rose. At the head a daughter in a coronet," and so forth. Cf. Notestein's *History of Witchcraft*, pp. 132 ff.

The spells which the witches are represented as making against young Lord Ross are, of course, conventional in witchcraft and folk-lore (see, *e.g.*, Jacob Grimm's *Teutonic Mythology*, translated by J. S. Stallybrass, 1888, IV, 1629, and W. J. Thoms, *Anecdotes and Traditions*, Camden Society, 1839, p. 101); they may even be found practised by fairly modern heroines in Mr Thomas Hardy's *Return of the Native* and in D. G. Rossetti's *Sister Helen*. The apparent judgment of God that caused Joan Flower's death could not do otherwise than convince Jacobeans of the truth of the charges made against her. Dozens of similar cases are vouched for by historians as well as by balladists. A somewhat remarkable judgment is chronicled in *The Weekly Intelligencer* for January 9, 1655:

One *Pilson*, a Bum Bayliff in *Oldstreet* came to arrest a Gentleman, who being secure in his Chamber, where the Bayliff could not arrest him, the Bayliff swore to him that if he would come to him, he would not arrest him, who opened the door, (yet the Bayliff contrary to his Oath) did arrest him, and was presently by the hand of God struck dumb and stil continues, and cannot speak a word.

For the tune see Chappell's *Popular Music*, 1, 196.

96

DAMNABLE PRACTISES

𝕯amnable 𝕻ractises 𝕺f three 𝕃incoln-shire 𝖂itches, *Joane Flower*, and her two 𝕯aughters, *Margret* and *Phillip Flower*, against *Henry* 𝕷ord *Rosse*, with others the 𝕮hildren of the 𝕽ight 𝕳onourable the 𝕰arle of 𝕽utland, at 𝕭eauer[1] 𝕮astle, who for the same were executed at 𝕃incolne the 11. of *March* last.

To the tune of *the Ladies fall.*

1 O F damned deeds, and deadly dole,
     I make my mournfull song,
By Witches done in *Lincolne-shire*,
    where they haue liued long:
And practisd many a wicked deed,
    within that Country there,
Which fills my brest and bosome full,
    of sobs, and trembling feare.

[1] *I.e.* Belvoir.

2 [F]ine *Beauer* Castle is a place,
    that welcome giues to all,
[B]y which the Earle of *Rutland* gaines
    the loues of great and small:
[His] Countesse of like friendlinesse,
    [d]oth beare as free a mind:
[And] so from them both rich and poore,
    [do] helps and succour find.

3 [Amo]ngst the rest were Witches three,
    [th]at to this Castle came,
[Call'd] *Margaret* and *Phillip Flower*,
    [ol]d *Ioane* their Mothers name:
[Wh]ich Women dayly found reliefe,
    [an]d were contented well:
[And] at the last this *Margret* was,
    [invit]ed there to dwell.

4 [She to]oke vnto such houshold charge,
    [as] vnto her belongd,
[Yet s]he possest with fraud and guile,
    [her] place and office wrongd;
[She s]ecretly purloyned things
    [vnt]o her mother home:
[And at] vnlawfull howers from thence,
    [wou]ld nightly goe and com.

5 [And wh]en the Earle & Countesse heard,
    [and all h]er dealings knew,
[They grie]ued much that she should proue,
    [vnto them] so vntrue.
And so discharg'd her of the house,
    therein to come no more:
For of heer lewd and filching prankes,
    of proofes there were some store.

6 And likewise that her Mother was,
    a woman full of wrath,
A swearing and blaspheming wretch,
    forespeaking sodaine death:

98

And how that neighbours in her lookes,
    malitious signes did see:
And some affirm'd she dealt with Sprits,
    and so a Witch might be.

7 And that her Sister *Phillip* was
    well knowne a Strumpet lewd,
And how she had a young mans loue,
    bewitched and subdued,
Which made the young man often say,
    he had no power to leaue
Her curst inticing company,
    that did him so deceaue.

8 When to the Earle and Countesse thus,
    these iust complaints were made,
Their hearts began to breed dislike,
    and greatly grew affraid:
Commanding that she neuer should,
    returne vnto their sight,
Nor back into the Castle come,
    but be excluded quite.

9 Whereat the old malitious feend,
    with these her darlings thought:
The Earle and Countesse them disgrac't,
    and their discredits wrought:
In turning thus despightfully,
    her daughter out of dores,
For which reuengement in her mind
    she many a mischiefe stores.

10 Heereat the Diuell made entraunce in,
    his Kingdome to inlarge.
And puts his executing wrath,
    vnto these womens charge:
Not caring whom it lighted on,
    the Innocent or no,
And offered them his diligence,
    to flye, to run, and goe.

11 And to attend in pretty formes,
  of Dog, of Cat, or Rat,
To which they freely gaue consent,
  and much reioyc't thereat:
And as it seemd they sould their soules,
  for seruice of such Spirits,
And sealing it with drops of blood,
  damnation so inherits.

12 These Women thus being Diuels growne
  most cunning in their Arts:
With charmes and with inchanting spells
  they plaid most damned parts:
They did forespeake, and Cattle kild,
  that neighbours could not thriue,
And oftentimes their Children young,
  of life they would depriue.

13 At length the Countesse and her Lord,
  to fits of sicknesse grew:
The which they deemd the hand of God,
  and their corrections due:
Which crosses patiently they bore,
  misdoubting no such deeds,
As from these wicked Witches heere,
  malitiously proceeds.

14 Yet so their mallice more increast,
  that mischiefe set in foote,
To blast the branches of that house,
  and vndermine the roote:
Their eldest sonne *Henry* Lord *Rosse*,
  possest with sicknesse strange,
Did lingring, lye tormented long,
  till death his life did change.

15 Their second sonne Lord *Francis* next,
  felt like continuing woe:

Both day and night in grieuous sort,
   yet none the cause did know:
And then the Lady *Katherin*,
   into such torments fell:
By these their deuilish practises,
   as grieues my heart to tell.

The second Part. To the same tune.

16   YEt did this noble minded Earle,
     so patiently it beare:
As if his childrens punishments,
   right natures troubles were:
Suspecting little, that such meanes,
   against them should be wrought,
Untill it pleas'd the Lord to haue
   to light these mischiefes brought.

17   For greatly here the hand of God,
   did worke in iustice cause:
When he for these their practises
   them all in question drawes.
And so before the Magistrates,
   when as the yongest came,
Who being guilty of the fact
   confest and tould the same.

18   How that her mother and her selfe,
   and sister gaue consent:
To giue the Countesse and her Lord,
   occasions to repent
That ere they turnd her out of dores,
   in such a vile disgrace:
For which, or them or theirs should be,
   brought into heauy case.

19   And how her sister found a time,
   Lord *Rosses* gloue to take:

Who gaue it to her mothers hand
  consuming spels to make.
The which she prickt all full of holes,
  and layd it deepe in ground:
Whereas it rotted, so should he,
  be quite away consum'd.

20 All which her elder sister did,
  acknowledge to be true:
And how that she in boyling blood,
  did oft the same imbrew,
And hereupon the yong Lord *Rosse*,
  such torments did abide:
That strangely he consum'd away,
  vntill the houre he died.

21 And likewise she confest how they,
  together all agreed:
Against the children of this Earle,
  to practise and proceed.
Not leauing them a child aliue,
  and neuer to haue more:
If witchcraft so could doe, because,
  they turnd them out of dore.

22 The mother as the daughters told,
  could hardly this deny:
For which they were attached all,
  by Justice speedily.
And vnto Lincolne Citty borne,
  therein to lye in Iayle:
Vntill the Iudging Sizes came,
  that death might be their bayle.

23 But there this hatefull mother witch,
  these speeches did recall:
And said that in Lord *Rosses* death,
  she had no hand at all.

Whereon she bread and butter tooke,
   God let this same (quoth she)
If I be guilty of his death,
   passe neuer thorough me.

24 So mumbling it within her mouth,
   she neuer spake more words:
But fell downe dead, a iudgment iust,
   and wonder of the Lords.
Her Daughters two their tryalls had,
   of which being guilty found,
They dyed in shame, by strangling twist,
   and layd by shame in ground.

25 Haue mercy Heauen, on sinners all,
   and grant that neuer like
Be in this Nation knowne or done,
   but Lord in vengeance strike:
Or else conuert their wicked liues
   which in bad wayes are spent:
The feares of God and loue of heauen,
   such courses will preuent.

Finis.

There is a booke printed of these Witches, wherein you shall know all their examinations and confessions at large: As also the wicked practise of three other most Notorious Witches in Leceister-*shire with all their examinations and confessions.*

Printed by *G. Eld* for *Iohn Barnes*, dwelling in the
long Walke neere Christ-Church.
1619.

Murther unmasked

Pepys, 1, 108, B.L., three woodcuts, four columns.

Barnevile (Johan Van Oldenbarneveldt, 1547–1619) was arrested by order of Prince Maurice of Nassau on August 18, 1618, arraigned for treason on February 20 following, sentenced to death, and executed at the Hague on May 13, 1619. The accusations brought against him were, it is now agreed, without foundation, while a packed jury made his trial a travesty of justice. "There was," said John Lothrop Motley (*The Life and Death of John of Barneveld*, 1879, 11, 315), "no bill of indictment, no arraignment, no counsel. There were no witnesses and no arguments. The court-room contained, as it were, only a prejudiced and partial jury to pronounce both on law and fact without a judge to direct them." Perhaps the chief blot on the fame of Prince Maurice is his base desertion of Barnevile, when a word could have saved him. *The Tragedy of Sir John Van Olden Barnavelt* (A. H. Bullen's *Old Plays*, vol. 11) was acted with considerable success in London in the autumn of 1619. The authors (Massinger and Fletcher?), according to Mr Bullen, "saw partially through the mists of popular error and prejudice; they refused to accept a caricature portrait, and proclaimed in unmistakeable accents the nobility of the fallen Advocate" (cf. also Sir A. W. Ward's *English Dramatic Literature*, 11, 716). The balladist, on the other hand, had a very prejudiced view, and distorted Barnevile's fall into a warning against Arminians and Popery. The printer W.I. was probably William Jones, Sr, who is known to have printed during the years 1601–1626. For the tune see Chappell's *Popular Music*, 1, 176.

Murther vnmasked,

Or

BARNEVILES base Conspiracie against his owne Country, discouered: who vnnaturally complotted to surrender into the Arch-dukes power, these foure Townes, *Vtreicht, Nimingham, Bergen-op-zome,* **and** *Brill*: **Together with his horrible intent to murther** *Graue Maurice,* **and others.**

To the tune of *Welladay*.

1 ALl you that Christians be
    vsefully, vsefully,
Consider now with me
    Gods bounteous mercie:
Though *Truth* hath bin denide
And Papists it defide,
Yet still it doth abide
    free from suppression.

2 How many Treasons vile
    haue bin layd, haue bin layd,
Gods pure Word to defile,
    in euery Country:

Yet still he keepes the same
From blemish, hurt, or blame,
And brings them all to shame
    that fight against it.

3 What strange cōplots haue bin
    gainst the truth, gainst ye truth,
Throughout the world is seene[1]
    t' haue beene attempted:
Yet Christ his church wil haue,
And his Professors saue,
In spite of Pope, or slaue
    that would confound it.

4 Approued this may be
    at this time, at this time,
By *Barnviles* trecherie
    gainst the Low-countries:
Who with vain hopes mis-led,
Deuis'd t' haue strucke all dead,
And to haue murthered
    men, wiues, and children.

5 He did consult with Hell
    impiously, impiously,
Their frontier townes to sell
    to *Austria's* Duke:
To murther great and small,
With th' English souldiers all,
That slept within the wall
    of euery Citie.

6 Yet here he did not stay,
    but conspir'd, but conspir'd
Graue Maurice for to slay,
    with other Princes.

---

[1] *Text* seeue.

Thus midst this bloodie broyle,
He would haue made a spoyle
Of his owne natiue soyle,
  without all pittie.

7 This Tyger fierce of mind,
    mercilesse, mercilesse,
  these townes wold haue resignd
    to Tyrants power:
  Who would haue banisht there
  The Gospel shining cleare,
  And in its stead vpreare
    trash and Traditions.

8 But this discouer'd was
    wondrously, wondrously:
  And nothing brought to passe
    what he intended:
  For God did from the skie,
  Cast downe his watchfull eye,
  His treasons to descrie,
    and crosse his purpose.

The Second Part.

9 NOw are his Treasons knowne
    to his shame, to his shame:
  And to all Statesmen showne,
    for their example:
  That God pursues his foes,
  With heauie ouerthrowes,
  Who doe their Hate disclose
    gainst Gospellizing.

10 What sauage Monster would
    thus haue slain, thus haue slain
  His friends; and Country sold
    for filthy lucre:

MURTHER UNMASKED

Outmatcht this Deed cannot,
Except with *Powder-plot*,
Which ne're will be forgot
    till the last Iudgement.

11 Of grace he had no touch
    in his heart, in his heart,
But still did fauour much
    th' Arminian Faction:
And did his God forsake,
Which did him ouertake,
And drencht him in the Lake
    of deepe destruction.

12 His Secretary then
    seeing well, seeing well
Their damned plots made plain
    to both their ruines:
Himselfe kil'd in the night,
With knife made sharpe & bright
So gaue the diuell his right
    by his despayring.

13 You Politians all,
    carefully, carefully,
Be warn'd[1] by *Barnviles* fall
    midst his fowle actions:
See you no mischiefes weaue,
That will your selues deceiue,
And soules of blisse bereaue
    past all redemption.

14 And let each English heart
    speedily, speedily,
From Poperie depart
    as from fell poyson.

[1] *Text* war'nd.

May he his birthday rue,
That striues for to subdue
The Gospell pure and true
    in this our Nation.

15 God guide our gracious King
    peacefully, peacefully:
And at the last him bring
    to ioyes eternall;
Where he amongst the best
Of Saints and Angels blest,
May liue in ioy and rest
    time without ending.

16 So blesse our vertuous Queen
    with this gift, with this gift:
That still her Fruit be seene
    mongst vs to flourish:
As long as Cedars bud,
And streames glide from the flood,
So long her royall Blood
    here sway the Scepter.

17 And powre on vs thy Grace
    plenteously, plenteously,
To mourne while we haue space
    for sinnes committed:
That when Death vs doth take
And we this world forsake,
We good account may make
    at our last ending.

Printed by W.I.

18

A prophecy of the judgment day

Pepys, 1, 36, B.L., three woodcuts, five columns. The margin of the first column is badly mutilated: missing letters have here been supplied in square brackets.

This ballad was printed about 1620, or a year or so earlier, presumably following a tract translated from the French. I have seen no such tract, but observe that in the diary of Richard Shanne, of Yorkshire (Additional MS. 38,599, fol. 58ᵛ), an entry is made of "A prophesie Found Vnder the ffoundation of A Church, didicated to the name of St Dinnis in Paris, in ffrance written in the Hebrew tongue, in Brasse, Inclosed in A tombe of Marble. Found An. 1617." Shanne then copied ten prophecies for the years 1621–1630, which correspond almost word for word with those given at the end of the ballad. There is a similar entry in the *Diary of Walter Yonge* for the year 1620 (ed. George Roberts, Camden Society, p. 38). The tune of *The Lady's Fall* is given in Chappell's *Popular Music*, 1, 196.

𝕬 𝔓𝔯𝔬𝔭𝔥𝔢𝔰𝔦𝔢 𝔬𝔣 𝔱𝔥𝔢 𝔍𝔲𝔡𝔤𝔪𝔢𝔫𝔱 𝔇𝔞𝔶.
𝕭𝔢𝔦𝔫𝔤 𝔩𝔞𝔱𝔢𝔩𝔶 𝔣𝔬𝔲𝔫𝔡 𝔦𝔫 𝔖𝔞𝔦𝔫𝔱 𝔇𝔢𝔫𝔦𝔰 𝔠𝔥𝔲𝔯𝔠𝔥 𝔦𝔫 𝔉𝔯𝔞𝔫𝔠𝔢, 𝔞𝔫𝔡 𝔴𝔯𝔞𝔭𝔭𝔢𝔡 𝔦𝔫 𝔏𝔢𝔞𝔡𝔢 𝔦𝔫 𝔱𝔥𝔢 𝔣𝔬𝔯𝔪𝔢 𝔬𝔣 𝔞𝔫 𝔥𝔢𝔞𝔯𝔱.

To the tune of *the Ladyes fall*.

1 [The w]onders of the Lord are great,
    [as] daylie may be seene,
[In F]ier, Water, Ayre, and Earth,
    [w]hich hath full often beene,
[But no exam]ple doe we take,
    [our wicked] courses runne,
[And in our] age more sinne commit,
    [than we] were new begun.

2 [Transgressions] daylie doe arise,
　　[as w]horedome, Theft, and Pride:
　[God's mini]sters we doe reiect,
　　[whose w]ordes should be our guide.
　[Nor is] there any yeare as yet,
　　[more wonder]full then now:
　[That whea]t, and Corne, & all thinges else,
　　[the heave]nly power did low.

3 [And for our] great vnthankefulnesse,
　　[from our] Gods powerfull hand:
　[There come] great store of Floods, and Raine,
　　[upon this] fruitefull Land;
　[And so I] thinke good people then,
　　[that He] will send a scourge:
　[Because that f]or our wickednesse,
　　[and s]innes, his wrath doth vrge.

4 [And mar]ke vpon the Latter day,
　　[which d]raweth to an end:
　[See how tha]t thou vpon this world,
　　[in smal]lest thoughtes depend.
　[We have] not always heere to liue,
　　[bethi]nke that thou must die:
　[Time] being come, you must away,
　　[in the twink]ling of an eye.

5 [But for] thy Gods owne promise made,
　　[thou could n]ot long endure:
　[For what] he sayd, is truth it selfe;
　　[there's] nothing else, so sure.
　For he hath P[romised th]at he will,
　　our time more [happy m]ake:
　And that heele Cut [down Princes],[1]
　　euen for his Elects [sake.]

6 As by a Prophesie in *France*,
　　the which was lately found:

　　　[1] *Text apparently* Cut...eeces.

A PROPHECY OF THE JUDGMENT DAY

In Parchment writ, and wrapt in Lead,
    most close vnto the ground.
Within a Churches wall, which then,
    was pulled downe to mend:
Which shew'd eare thirteene yeeres were past,
    the world should come to end.

The first Prophesie for the yeere, 1620.[1]

7 The wordes were these, which then were found:
    within this sacred place,
Great Warres shalbe in *Italy,*
    within this little space.
Which is no doubt Gods handy worke,
    to Plague them for their pride:
Which doth with foule Idolatry,
    his holy name deride.

The Second Prophesie for the yeere 1622.

8 There shall not be a *shepheard* left,
    to feed the silly *Flocke*:
Then let vs pray that in our hearts,
    he Graft a surer stocke;
And that we may not be bereft,
    of Pasters, vs to teach:
But that amongst vs he will send,
    good men his word to Preach.

The third Prophesie for the yeere 1623.

9 The wrath of God shall shew it selfe,
    throughout the world so wide:
Which he will powre vpon vs all,
    for our incessant Pride,
Then let vs pray with full consent,
    that he may hold his hand:
And that he will not wreake his wrath,
    vpon our sinfull Land.

[1] *Read* 1621?

A PROPHECY OF THE JUDGMENT DAY

The fourth Prophesie for the yeere 1624.

10 God shall be knowne but of a few,
     which is a grieuous thing:
   That wee so little should regard,
     our God, the heauenly King.
   Who sent his Sonne to saue our Soules,
     from Sathan, Death, and Hell:
   And that we should in heauenly blisse,
     with him for euer dwell.

The fifth Prophesie for the yeere 1625.

11 A great man shall arise, they say,
     which is a thing conceald:
   And vnto few but Godly men,
     the same shall be reueald.
   Then let vs pray which little know,
     that wee may ready bee:
   For him the which in glory sits,
     from all eternite.

The sixth Prophesie for the yeere 1626.

12 The fourt part of the Earth shall burne,
     the Sunne shall darkned bee,
   The Moone shall powre foorth streames of blood,
     which fearefully will see,
   Unto the Soules which ill haue done:
     but ioyfull to the rest:
   The bad twill terryfie to death,
     and greatly ioy the rest.

𝕿𝖍𝖊 𝕾𝖊𝖈𝖔𝖓𝖉 𝖕𝖆𝖗𝖙 𝖔𝖋 𝖙𝖍𝖊 𝕻𝖗𝖔𝖕𝖍𝖊𝖘𝖎𝖊. 𝕿𝖔 𝖙𝖍𝖊 𝖘𝖆𝖒𝖊 𝖙𝖚𝖓𝖊.

The seuenth Prophesie for the yeere 1628.

13 AN vniuersall Earthquake shall
     vpon this Globe remaine:
   The earth shall seeme to mooue and stir,
     so shall the Oceans maine:

113

Then if his breath can shake the same,
    which is the God of might.
How could he plague vs if he pleas'd
    but with his force to smite.

The eight Prophesie for the yeere 1629.

14 The *Infidels* true God shall know,
    and Trinity professe:
God graunt which wee that Christians are,
    may neuer doe the lesse:
If those which doe not feare the Lord,
    shall truest Christians turne.
Then wee which know the liuing God,
    in Hels hot flame shall burne.

The ninth Prophesie for the yeere 1630.

15 The Riuers shalbe dryed vp,
    one Shepheard shall remaine,
And but one Shepefold shall be left,
    Gods glory to maintaine.
Which is the latter day of all:
    where but one God shall raigne,
Then let vs labour day and night:
    his fauour to obtaine.[1]

16 Great God which sit'st in heauēly Throane
    graunt that we sinners may,
Haue place in thy eternall Court,
    where holy Saints doe pray.
Still holy, holy Lord of Lords
    and Spirit full of grace,
God graunt that in thy Kingdome wee,
    may haue a resting place.

Finis.

[1] Text has a comma.

A PROPHECY OF THE JUDGMENT DAY

Behold I come shortly : blessed is hee that keepeth the words of the Prophesie.

Reuelation. 22. 7.

These here vnder written, are the true words of the Prophesie of the last Iudgement, which were translated into English, out of the Hebrue copy, being found vnder Saint Denis *Church in the great City of* Paris *in* France, *and was wrapped in Lead in the forme of a Heart.* 1616. *Which copy hath been sent to diuers great Princes of Christendome from France.*

1620.[1] There shall be great warres through Italy.

1622. There shall not be a Shepheard to feed the Flocke.

1623. The wrath of God shall shew it selfe through the whole World.

1624. God shall be knowne but of a few.

1625. A Great Man shall arise.

1626. *Affrica* shall burne: the Sunne shall be darkned, &c. *Math.* 24. 29. And the Moone shall be bluddy. *Reue.* 6. 12.

1628. There shall be an vniuersall Earthquake.

1629. Infidels shall know the Trinity and vnitie of the Godhead.

1630. The Ryuers shall be dryed vp, and there shall be but one Shepheard, and one Sheepefolde.

Finis.

At London Printed for I.W.

[1] *Read* 1621?

19

The pedlar opening his pack

Pepys, 1, 238, B.L., two woodcuts, five columns.

A highly interesting picture of the cosmetics, gew-gaws, and trinkets that formed the mysteries of a seventeenth-century woman's toilet is given in this satirical song. The pack itself was a chest with drawers and compartments for the various articles here enumerated. Strangely enough, the pedlar does not mention ballads—something that every self-respecting member of his trade invariably carried. A similar ballad, written some twenty-five years later, is "The New Exchange" in *Merry Drollery*, 1661 (ed. J. W. Ebsworth, pp. 134–138).

The stanza-form is unusual but attractive. I have not met with the tune elsewhere. The printer was E[dward] A[llde], whose publications appeared during 1584–1628. The date may be assumed to be 1620, but was probably much earlier.

The Pedler opening of his Packe, To know of Maydes what tis they lacke.

To the tune of, *Last Christmas 'twas my chance*.[1]

1 WHo is it will repaire,
    or come and see my packet:
Where there's store of Ware,
    if any of you lacke it,
      view the Fayre.

2 Faire Maydens come and see,
    if heere be ought will please you:
And if we can agree,
    Ile giue you iust your due,
      or nere trust me.

[1] Comma in the text.

3 And if that you do please
    to see my Fardle open,
My burden for to ease,
    I hope that we shall Copen
    then straight waies.

4 From *Turky*, *France* and *Spaine*,
    doe come my cheifest Treasure,
Which doth cost much paine,
    I sell by waight and measure,
    for small gaine.

5 Farre-fetcht *Indian* ware,
    and *China* hard to enter:
Which to get is rare,
    costs many liues to venter,
    we nere care.

6 From *Venice* Citie comes
    great store of rare Complection,
From westerne Iles your Gummes
    to keep Teeth from infection,
    and from Rhewmes.

7 Heere is a water rare,
    will make a wench that's fiftie,
For to looke more fayre
    then one that wants of twenty,
    stil'd from the Ayre.

8 A Perriwig to weare,
    or Couer for bare places:
If you haue lost your heare,
    full many one it graces:
    tis not deare.

9 Heeres Poking stickes of steele,
    and Christall Looking Glasses:
Here globes that round will wheele
    to see each one that passes,
    Dildo Dill.

10 Pomado for your Lips,
    to make them soft and ruddy:
And sweet as Cipres chips,
    a lustre like a Ruby
      soone it gets.

11 Heres Bracelets for your arm
    of Corall, or of Amber:
A Powder that will Charme
    or bring one to your Chamber,
      tis no harme.

12 A water can restore
    a Maydenhead that's vanisht,
You'le say she is no whoore,
    although that it were banisht
      long before.

13 A paire of Bodye[s feat][1]
    to make you fine and slender:
A Buske as blacke as Ieat,
    to keepe your bellies vnder
      that are great.

14 And if you please to weare,
    a Bodkin of pure Siluer:
To thrust into your hayre,
    it comforteth the Liuer
      without feare.

15 Rebatoes, Tyres, and Rings,
    Sissers and a Thimble:
And many pretty thinges,
    to keepe your fingers nimble,
      weauing stringes.

[1] Torn.

𝕿𝖍[e 𝕾𝖊𝖈]𝖔𝖓𝖉[1] part.

16 Silkes of any hew,
    and Spanish needles plenty:
Thred both white and blew,
    like me not one 'mongst twenty,
      can fit you.

17 Balles of Camphyre made,
    to keepe your face from pimples:
An Unguent that's alayd,
    you neuer shall haue wrinckles,
      if a Mayde.

18 Spunges for your face,
    or Sope that came from *Turkey*:
Your fauour it will grace,
    if that you be not durty,
      in no place.

19 Rich imbroydered Gloues,
    to draw vpon your white hand:
Or to giue your Loues,
    a Ruffe or falling band,
      my pretty Doues.

20 Scarfes that came from *Cales*,
    or points and Laces lacke you:
Inckle made in Wales,
    I finely can beknacke you:
      tell no tales.

21 Bone lace who will buy,
    that came from *Flaunders* lately:
Pray doe not thinke I lye,
    but I will serue you straightly,
      by and by.

[1] Torn.

22 Pinnes both white and red,
    of all sortes and all sizes:
Plumbes and Ginger bread,
    my Wares of diuers prizes,
      Bookes to read.

23 *Venice* Glasses fine,
    were newly made in London:
To drinke your Beere or Wine,
    come now my Pack's vndone,
      speake betime.

24 Lawne and Cambricke pure,
    as good as e're was worne:
Like yron it will dure,
    vntill that it be torne,
      be you sure.

25 Heer's many other thinges,
    as Iewes trumps, pipes & Babies:
St. *Martins* Beades and Ringes,
    and other toyes for Ladyes,
      knots and stringes.

26 All you that want my Ware,
    approach vnto my Standing:
Where I will vse you faire,
    without deceit or cunning,
      to a hayre.

27 And as my Ware doth proue,
    so let me take your mony:
My pretty Turtle Doue,
    that sweeter is then hony,
      which is Loue.

Finis.

Printed at London by E.A.

20

The lamenting lady

Pepys, I, 44, B.L., two woodcuts (both of which are here reproduced), five columns.

F. J. Child (*English and Scottish Popular Ballads*, II, 68; cf. p. 511) thought that the probable source of this ballad was a sixteenth century ballad of Juan de Timoneda. I have not been able to see Timoneda's ballad, but in any case the source of "The Lamenting Lady" is undoubtedly one of the two early English accounts of the story—preferably Thomas Coryate's—given below.

Probably the first occurrence of the story in English is that in Edward Grimeston's *A Generall Historie of the Netherlands*, 1608 (pp. 51–52), a work translated from Jean François Le Petit's *Grande Chronique Ancienne et moderne, de Hollande, Zélande, West Frise, etc. jusques à la fin de l'an 1600* (2 vols., Dordrecht, 1601), where the "Lamenting Lady" story is printed in volume I, pp. 229–30. As this French history was published at Dordrecht, or Dort, where the marvel happened, Grimeston, Coryate, and the ballad-writer—none of whom had visited that city—may readily be pardoned for believing the astonishing tale of Countess Marguerite of Henneberg.

Grimeston's version follows, and I have indicated in foot-notes every important instance in which his Latin differs from that of Jean François Le Petit:

Floris the fourth of that name...was the seuenteenth Earle of Holland and Zeeland...and...had to wife *Mathilda*, daughter to *Henry* duke of Lothier and Brabant, by whom he had...*Marguerite* wife to *Herman* earle of Henneberg, who had that great number of children, whereof we shall speake by and by....

We haue formerly said, that this Cont *Floris* had among his other children, one daughter called *Mathilde* (some say *Marguerite*) married to Cont *Herman* of Henneberg; *William* King of the Romanes and Earle of Holland was her brother, *Otto* bishop of Vtrecht her vncle by the father, & *Henry* duke of Brabant her vncle by the mothers side, *Alix* Contesse of Henault her aunt, *Otto* earle of Geldres, and *Henry* bishop of Liege, her cousins. To describe the monstrous child-birth or deliuerie of this Lady, you must vnderstand, that on a time this Contesse of Henneberg did see a poore widow woman begging her bread for Gods sake, hauing in eyther arme a child, both which she had had at one birth: This poore woman crauing her almes, the Contesse reiected her with reprochfull words: whereupon this poore woman, hauing her heart full of discontent, for her bitter speeches, lifted vp her eyes to heauen, and said: O great and mightie

God, I beseech thee for a testimonie of mine innocencie, that it will please thee
to send vnto this Lady as many children as there be daies in the yeare. A while
after this Contesse was big with child by her husband; and for her lying in,
she went into Holland to see the Earle of Holland her nephew, lodging in the
Abbey of religious women of Losdunen: whereas she grew so exceeding great,
as the like was neuer seene. Her time being come, the friday before Palme-
sunday [*i.e.* on March 29], in the yeare 1276. she was deliuered of three hundred
sixtie and fiue children, halfe sonnes and halfe daughters, the odde one being
found a Hermaphrodite, all complete and well fashioned with their little members: the which were layed in two basins and baptized by *Guidon,* Suffragan to
the bishop of Vtrecht, who named the sonnes *Iohn* and the daughters *Elizabeth.*
As soone as they had been baptized, they died all, and their mother with them.
The two basins are yet to be seene in the said church of Losdunen, with their
Epitaph both in Latine and Dutch: the Latine was[1] as followeth:

Margareta[2] Comitis Hennebergae vxor, & Florentii Comitis Hollandiae &
Zeelandiae filia; cuius mater fuit Mathilda,[3] filia Henrici Ducis Brabantiae,
fratrem quoq; habuit[4] Allemaniae regem. Haec praefata domina Margareta,
Anno salutis 1276. ipso die Parasceues hora nona ante meridiem, peperit
infantes viuos promiscui sexus numero trecentos, sexaginta quinque: qui
postquam per venerabilem Dom. Guidonem, Suffragan[5] Episcopi Traiec-
tensis, praesentibus nonnullis proceribus & magnatibus, in peluibus duabus
ex aere, baptismum percepissent, & masculis Iohannes, foemellis vero Elizabeth
nomina imposita fuissent, simul omnes cum matre vno eodemq; die satis
concesserunt, in hoc Lodunensi templo[6] iacent. Quod quidem accidit ob
pauperculam quandam foeminam, quae ex uno partu gemellos in vlnis
gestabat pueros: quam rem admirans ipsa Comitissa dicebat, id per vnicum[7]
virum fieri non posse, ipsamq; contumeliose reiecit: vnde haec paupercula
animo turbata[8] & perculsa, prolium tantum numerum ac multitudinem ex
uno partu ei[9] imprecabatur, quod vel totius anni dies numerentur.[10] Quod
quidem praeter naturae cursum, obstupenda quadam ratione ita factum est,
sicut in hac tabula in perpetuam rei memoriam, ex vetustis tum manuscriptis,
quam typis excusis Chronicis, breuiter positum & narratum est. Deus ille ter
maximus hac de re suspiciendus, honorandus, & laudibus extollendus in
sempiterna saecula. Amen.

And vnderneath it were these two verses:

En tibi monstrosum & memorabile factum,
Quale nec a mundi conditione datum.

The account in *Coryat's Crudities,* 1611 (1776 reprint, III, 81–83),
which is probably the immediate source of the ballad, was brought to my
attention by my colleague, Professor A. L. Bouton. It runs as follows:

There is a Monument extant in a certaine Monastery called Laudun neere the
famous vniuersity of Leyden in Holland, where a certaine Countesse called
Margarite was buried, who was the wife of one *Hermannus* Earle of Henneberg,
the daughter of *Florentius* the fourth of that name, Earle of Holland and Zeland,
and the sister of *William* King of the Romanes. This Countesse hapned to be
deliuered of three hundred sixty fiue children at one burden, about three hundred

[1] est.	[2] Margareta Hermani.	[3] Mathildis.
[4] habuit Guillelmum.	[5] Suffraganeum.	[6] templo sepulti.
[7] unum.	[8] perturbata.	[9] ipsi.	[10] numerantur.

and fourteene yeares since, euen iust as many as there are daies in the yeare. All which, after they were baptized by one *Guido Suffragan* of Vtrecht, the males by the names of *Iohns*, and the females by the names of *Elizabeths*, died that very day that they came into the world: and were buried all together in one monument in the Church of the foresaid Monastery of Laudun, which is to this day shewed (as I haue heard many worthy trauellers report that were the eie witnesses of the matter) with a most memorable Latine inscription vpon it, together with two brasen basons wherin all those infants were baptized. This strange history will seeme incredible (I suppose) to al readers. But it is so absolutely and vndoubtedly true as nothing in the world more. The occasion of which miraculous and stupendious accident I will here set downe (seeing I haue proceeded thus farre in the narration of a thing I haue not seene) because it may confirme the stronger belief in the reader. It hapned that a poore woman came a begging to the foresaid Countesse *Margarite*, bearing a twinne of young babes in her armes. But the Countesse was so farre from hauing any commiseration vpon her, that she rather scornefully reiected her, affirming that it was not possible shee should haue those two children by one man. The poore soule being much vexed in spirit through these iniurious words of the Lady, pronounced such a bitter imprecation vpon her, that she wished that God would shew a miracle vpon the Lady, as well for a due reuenge vpon her that had so slandered her, as for the testifying of her vnspotted honesty and chastity; she wished, I say, that God would shew this miracle, that the Lady might bring forth as many children at one burden, as there are daies in the yeere; which indeed came to passe, according as I haue before mentioned. For the Ladie in the fortieth yeare of her age was deliuered of iust so many vpon a saturday, about nine of the clocke in the morning, in the yeare of our Lord 1276. The truth of this most portentous miracle is confirmed not so much by that inscription written in a certaine table vpon her tombe, as by sundry ancient Chronicles of infallible certainty, both manuscript and printed.

The story is also referred to in *A certaine Relation of the Hog-faced Gentlewoman* (cf. No. 79), 1640, sig. A 3ᵛ (E. W. Ashbee's *Occasional Fac-Simile Reprints*, vol. ii):

In the Bishopricke of *Colen* a woman, some thinke a Witches Curse, some otherwise, brought forth into the World at one birth one [*sic*] hundred three-score and five children: all which though they were of wondrous small stature, yet they were borne with life, and christned, and a monument remaynes for them to this day, her prayer or curse being, that shee might haue as many children at one birth, as there were dayes in the yeere.

A similar situation, so far as concerns an insult offered to a mother of twins, occurs in Marie de France's *Le Fraisne* (*Lais*, ed. R. Köhler, p. lxiv ff.). Professor Kittredge has given me these additional references: *Chevalier Assigne*, ed. Gibbs, verses 29–31, 41–42; *Helyas*, in W. J. Thoms's *Early English Prose Romances*, 2nd ed., iii, 33, 41; Harris's *Voyages*, 1764, ii, 1019; Elphinstone Dayrell, *Folk Stories from Southern Nigeria*, 1910, p. 133; *Journal of the Anthropological Institute*, xxvii, 480; Mary H. Kingsley's *Travels in West Africa*, 1897, p. 473; Baldwin Spencer and F. J. Gillen's *Native Tribes of Central Australia*, p. 52; *Report on the Work of the Horn Scientific Expedition*, ed. Baldwin Spencer, 1896, Pt. IV, p. 129. A curiously decayed form of the story, Professor

THE LAMENTING LADY

Kittredge adds, is given in Sarah Hewett's *Nummits and Crummits, Devon-shire Customs*, 1900, p. 19, and a better form in Bechstein's *Volkssagen und Legenden des Kaiserstaates Oesterreich*, 1841, No. 10, p. 121, and in Karl Reiser's *Sagen, Gebräuche und Sprichwörter des Allgäus*, I, 409–411.

Possibly there is a faint reference to the lamenting lady in *King Lear*, II, iv, 54, where the Fool says: "Thou shalt have as many dolours for thy daughters as thou canst tell in a year." Compare also the remark of Robert Waring, in verses "To the Memory of his deceased Friend, Mr William Cartwright," prefixed to the 1651 edition of Cartwright's *Comedies*:

> As the *Dutch Lady,* who at once did bear
> Numbers, not Births, to date each day i' th' year,
> Grew barren by Encrease; and after all,
> None could Her, Mother, or them Children, call.
> So whilst All write, None judge, we multiply
> So many Poems, and no Poetry.

Samuel Pepys himself was one of the Englishmen who had seen the basins and the inscription. In his *Diary* for May 19, 1660, Pepys notes that he went "by waggon to Lausdune, where the 365 children were born. We saw the hill where they say the house stood wherein the children were born. The basins wherein the male and female children were baptized do stand over a large table that hangs upon a wall, with the whole story of the thing in Dutch and Latin, beginning, 'Margarita Herman Comitissa,' &c. The thing was done about 200 years ago." See further *Notes and Queries*, 2nd S., VII, 260.

For the tune see Chappell's *Popular Music*, I, 196. The date of the ballad may be assumed to be 1620.

The Lamenting Lady,
Who for the wrongs done by her to[1] a poore woman, for hauing two children at one burthen, was by the hand of God most strangely punished, by sending her as many children at one birth, as there are daies in the yeare, in remembrance whereof, there is now a monument builded in the Citty of *Lowdon*, as many English men now liuing in *Lowdon*, can truely testifie the same and hath seene it.

To the tune of *the Ladies fall*.

[1] by her to: *text* to her by.

1 REgard my griefe kinde Ladies all,
   my heart now bleeding dyes,
And shewers of siluer pearled teares
   falls from my weeping eyes:
I once was louely, faire, and young,
   by nature sweet and kinde,
And had those ioyes that might content
   a gallant Ladies minde.

THE LAMENTING LADY

2 But barren grew my wished hopes,
　　　no children I could haue,
　　Which twixt my wedded Lord and me
　　　much cause of sorrowes gaue:
　　My tender body pure and faire,
　　　and of a princely frame
　　Could not abstaine these sugred ioyes
　　　that came by Cupids game.

3 Yet beggers borne of low degree
　　　such blessings did possesse,
　　Which when I saw my heart grew full
　　　of woes and heauinesse:
　　O why should people poore (quoth I)
　　　those happy ioyes obtaine
　　When I that am a Lady braue
　　　should barren thus remaine?

4 I feed on sweet delicious meates,
　　　and drinke of purest wine,
　　Yet are there homely bodies still
　　　as faire and cleere as mine,
　　and haue more sweetfac'd smiling babes
　　　then Ladies of degree,
　　And of as tender flesh and bloud
　　　as can be shewed by me.

5 In griefe of heart complaining thus,
　　　by chance a woman poore
　　With two sweet children in her armes
　　　came begging to my doore:
　　Poore pretty babes they smiled sweete,
　　　whereat I needs must know
　　If those two smiling children were
　　　the womans owne or no?

6 They are (sweet Madam) both (said she)
　　　and both borne at one birth,
　　The which are now my chiefest wealth
　　　and blessings on the earth:

THE LAMENTING LADY

Can Beggers haue what Ladies want
    in anger I repli'd,
And can thy wombe be fruitfull made
    when mine is still deni'd?

7 I goe attyr'd in garments rich
    bedeck'd with burnish'd gold,
And waited on with worldly pompe,
    and pleasures manifold,
Whilst thou in rags all rent and torne
    for thy reliefe dost craue,
And with two children blest at once,
    when I not one can haue.

8 Thou art some Strumpet[1] sure I know,
    and spend'st thy dayes in shame,
And stained sure thy marriage bed
    with spots of black defame:
Else vnto these two louely babes
    thou canst no mother be,
When I that liue in greatest grace
    no such content can see.

9 A hundreth such like taunting tearmes
    I gaue this woman poore
Whilst she for pitty and reliefe
    stood begging at the doore:
Reuiling her most spightfully
    with harlots hatefull name,
Dissembling with a shamelesse face
    to couer vp her shame.

10 Her heart hereat with inward griefes
    did feele such mortall paine,
And as it were before my face
    did seeme to breake in twaine:

[1] *Text* Strumpt.

127

Her pretty babes which at her breasts
   did sweetly sucking lye
To see their mothers bitter moane
   did sadly sob and crye.

11 Whereat, halfe kild with woe alas,
   I wish my wrongs (quoth she)
That these my babes may be reueng'd
   proud Lady, vpon thee:
And as I am both true and iust
   vnto my marriage bed
so let Gods wondrous works be shown[1]
   on thee when I am dead.

12 And for these children two of mine
   heauen send thee such a number
At once, as dayes be in the yeare,
   to make the world to wonder.
For I as true a wife haue beene,
   vnto my husbands loue:
As any Lady on the earth,
   vnto her Lord can proue.

13 Hereat relenting I began,
   to mourne for this misdeed:
And houre by houre in griefe thereof,
   my sorrowing hart doth bleed.[2]
At last a heauie hand of heauen,
   reuengd this womans woes:
And on my bodies pampred pride,
   a fearefull Iudgement shoes.

14 My cheekes that were so louely red,
   of natures choycest dye:
Grew blacke and vgly to behould,
   to euery weeping eye.

---

[1] *Text* show.   [2] No period in the text.

And in my wombe distempered griefes,
    so vext me day and night:
I sweld so big that I appeard,
    a strange and monstrous wight.

15 Remembring then the womans words
    she grieuing did impart,
A thousand strange misdoubting feares
    incompast round my heart.
And then me thought I sawe her come,
    in person vnto me,
With her two children in her armes,
    my sodaine shame to see.

The second part.

16 AT which affright my bigg sweld wombe
     deliuered forth in feare
As many children at one time
    as daies were in the yeare:
In bignesse all like newbred mice,
    yet each one shap'd aright,
And euery male from female knowne,
    by Gods great power and might.

17 My husband hereat grieued much,
    with inward cares and woe,
And knew not in what place he should
    these pretty ympes bestowe:
The strange report of this rare birth
    made people much admire,
And of the truth thereof to know
    the neighbours did desire.

18 Which caus'd my sorrowes still increase
    being made my Countryes scorne,
I wish'd I had in child-bed dyed
    before they had beene borne:
Then had this shame vnto my friends
    beene neuer seene nor knowne,
Nor I in Countries farre and neere
    a wonder thus be[1] showne.

19 But marke faire women of the world
    how Heauen did pitty me,
When I made sorrowe for my sinnes,
    and in extremity:
God tooke from hence my cause of shame
    my children, weake and small:
The which poore creatures in one graue
    were strangely buried all.

---

[1] *Read* been.

20 And on the graue where now they lye
    a monument still stands
To shew this wondrous hap of mine
    vnto all Christian lands,
That such as be of high degree
    may beare a meeker minde,
Least they despising of the poore
    the like misfortune finde.

21 The Lord we see his blessings sends
    to many women poore
As well as to the noble sort,
    that haue aboundant store:
Therefore let none desire to haue
    the ioyes of worldly things
Except it be his sacred will
    that is the King of Kings.

Finis.

Printed at London for *Henry Gosson*,
and are to be sold at his shop on
London Bridge.

2 1

A country new jig

Pepys, 1, 260, 278, B.L., four woodcuts, four columns.

Another splendid example of a dramatic jig, dating perhaps about 1620. There are four *dramatis personae*, a fair plot, and considerable opportunities for effective singing and dancing. This jig no doubt made a satisfactory conclusion to a play. Neither of the tunes is given in Chappell's *Popular Music*. The first is derived from "A Maiden's Lamentation for a Bedfellow. Or, I can, nor will no longer lye alone. As it hath often been sung at the Court. To the tune of *I will give thee kisses, one, two, or three*," and is used also in No. 13. A ballad of "The Northamptonshire Lover," printed early in the seventeenth century by Henry Gosson, is to the tune of *Falero lero lo* (Pepys, 1, 324).

In stanza 16 the curious notion that women who died maids were doomed to "lead apes in hell" is referred to. There are innumerable statements of this queer idea in the English dramatists from Peele and Shakespeare to Cibber (cf. *The Double Gallant*, ed. 1749, p. 63). That the idea has not entirely been lost seems to be shown in a remark made by the heroine of Mary Hastings Bradley's short story, "The Fairest Sex," in the *Metropolitan Magazine* for March, 1919 (p. 32): "I told him that rather 'n kiss him I'd lead apes through hell a thousand years." Professor Kittredge thinks that the phrase is still in common use. He refers me to No. 21 A in F. J. Child's *English and Scottish Popular Ballads*, where leading apes in hell for seven years is mentioned as a punishment or penance; to discussions in *Germania*, xxxiii, 245, and the *Modern Language Quarterly*, vii, 16; and to a comparatively recent use of the expression in Allan Ramsay's *Poems* (1800), ii, 259.

𝕬 𝕮𝖔𝖚𝖓𝖙𝖗𝖞 𝖓𝖊𝖜 𝕵𝖎𝖌𝖌𝖊 𝖇𝖊𝖙𝖜𝖊𝖊𝖓𝖊 *Simon* 𝖆𝖓𝖉 *Susan*, 𝖙𝖔 𝖇𝖊 𝖘𝖚𝖓𝖌 𝖎𝖓 𝖒𝖊𝖗𝖗[𝖞]¹ 𝖕𝖆𝖘𝖙𝖎𝖒𝖊 [𝖇𝖞]² 𝕭𝖆𝖈𝖍𝖊𝖑𝖔𝖗𝖘 𝖆𝖓𝖉 𝕸𝖆𝖞𝖉𝖊𝖓𝖘.

To the tune of *I can nor will no longer lie alone.* Or, *Falero lero lo.*

Simon.

1   O Mine owne sweet heart,
     and when wilt thou be true:
Or when will the time come,
    that I shall marry you,
That I may giue you kisses,
    one, two or three,
More sweeter then the hunny,
    that comes from the Bee.

Susan.

2 My Father is vnwilling
    that I should marry thee,
Yet I could wish in heart,
    that so the same might be:
For now me thinks thou seemest,
    more louely vnto me:
And fresher then the Blossomes,
    that bloomes on the tree.

Simon.

3 Thy mother is most willing,
    and will consent I know,
Then let vs to thy Father
    now both together goe:

¹ Cut off.   ² Blurred.

A COUNTRY NEW JIG

Where if he giue vs his good will,
    and to our match agree:
Twill be sweeter then the hunny
    that comes from the Bee.

Susan.

4 Come goe, for I am willing,
    good fortune be our guide:
From that which I haue promised,
    deare heart, Ile neuer slide:
If that he doe but smile,
    and I the same may see,
Tis better then the blossomes,
    that bloomes vpon the tree.

Simon.

5 But stay heere comes my[1] Mother,
    weele talke with her a word:
I doubt not but some comfort,
    to vs she may afford:
If comfort she will give vs,
    that we the same may see,
Twill be sweeter then the hunny,
    that comes from the Bee.

Susan.

6 O Mother we are going
    my Father for to pray,
That he will giue me his good will,
    for long I cannot stay.
A young man I haue chosen
    a fitting match for me,
More fayrer then the blossomes
    that bloomes on the tree.

---

[1] Perhaps the text should read *thy*, though (as later stanzas show) "mother" and "father" were "very common forms of address from a betrothed person to the father and mother of the other party to the engagement" (Professor Kittredge).

A COUNTRY NEW JIG

Mother.

7 Daughter thou art old enough
    to be a wedded wife,
You maydens are desirous
    to lead a marryed life.
Then my consent good daughter
    shall to thy wishes be,
For young thou art as blossomes
    that bloome vpon the tree.

Simon.

8 Then mother you are willing
    your daughter I shall haue:
And Susan thou art welcome
    Ile keepe thee fine and braue.
And haue those wished blessings
    bestowed vpon thee,
More sweeter then the honey
    that comes from the Bee.

Susan.

9 Yet Simon I am minded
    to lead a merry life,
And be as well maintained
    as any Citie wife:
And liue a gallant mistresse
    of maidens that shall be
More fayrer then the blossomes
    that bloome vpon the tree.

A COUNTRY NEW JIG

Simon.

10 THou shalt haue thy Caudles,
    before thou dost arise:
For churlishnesse breeds sicknesse
    and danger therein lies.
Young lasses must be cherisht
    with sweets that dainty be,
Farre sweeter then the honey
    that commeth from the Bee.

Mother.

11 Well said good Son and Daughter,
    this is the onely dyet
To please a dainty young wife,
    and keepe the house in quiet.
But stay, here comes your father,
    his words I hope will be
More sweeter then the blossomes
    that bloome vpon the tree.

Father.

12 Why how now daughter Susan
    doe you intend to marry?
Maydens in the old time
    did twenty winters tarry.
Now in the teenes no sooner
    but you a wife will be
And loose the sweetest blossome
    that bloomes vpon thy tree.

Susan.

13 It is for my preferment
    good father say not nay,
For I haue found a husband kinde
    and louing euery way:
That still vnto my fancy
    will euermore agree,
Which is more sweet then honey
    that comes from the Bee.

A COUNTRY NEW JIG

Mother.

14 Hinder not your daughter,
    good husband, lest you bring
Her loues consuming sicknesse,
    or else a worser thing.
Maydens youngly married
    louing wiues will be
And sweet as is the honey
    which comes from the Bee.

Simon.

15 Good father be not cruell,
    your daughter is mine owne:
Her mother hath consented
    and is to liking growne.
And if your selfe will giue then,
    her gentle hand to me,
Twill sweeter be then honey
    that comes from the Bee.

Father.

16 God giue thee ioy deare Daughter,
    there is no reason I
Should hinder thy proceeding,
    and thou a mayden die:
And after to lead Apes in hell,
    as maidens doomed be:
That fairer are then blossomes
    that bloome vpon the tree.

Simon.

17 Then let's vnto the Parson
    and Clerke to say Amen:

A COUNTRY NEW JIG

Susan.

With all my heart good *Simon*,
    we are concluded then,
My father and my mother both
    doe willingly agree
My *Simon's* sweet as honey
    that comes from the Bee.

All together sing.

18 You Maidens and Bachelors
    we hope will lose no time,
Which learne it by experience
    that youth is in the prime,
And dally in their hearts desire
    young married folkes to be
More sweeter then the blossomes
    that bloome vpon the tree.

Finis.

Imprinted at London for *H. Gosson*.

22

The post of Ware

Pepys, 1, 212, B.L., three woodcuts, four columns.

The Post, perhaps as a burlesque on the "Currants of News" that were just being introduced into England, begins with some references to affairs on the Continent, but soon degenerates into satirical comments about the general state of England and its trades and professions. The Post-Boy is directed to ride from London twenty-two miles to Ware (the first important town, in Hertfordshire, on the road north from London), spreading his news in every village through which he passes. From the references to Spinola (1569–1630) and the imminence of another war between Spain and the Netherlands, it is evident that the ballad was printed in or slightly before 1621, when the war actually was renewed. In the third stanza of Part Two Paul's steeple is mentioned. It had been destroyed by lightning on June 4, 1561, but was never reconstructed.

THE POST OF WARE

**The Post of Ware:
With a Packet full of strange Newes out of
diuers Countries.**

To a pleasant new Tune.

1 AWay, Away; make no delay,
   this Newes requireth hast;
Boy, mount thy Mare, post hence to *Ware*,
   thou canst not ride too fast;
And as thou rid'st through euery Towne,
   blow forth this liuely blast:
All Cittizens Wiues
   Are grown constant and sound,
And say, That Truth doth abound,
In euery Taylors
   Shop to bee found.

2 I'th Street of *Ware*, good Boy, declare,
    we shall haue money store,
The *Hollanders* heere did tast our Beere,
    while they could drinke no more;
Some lost their gold, which struck thē cold
    though they were hot before:
And vexing for anger,
    their money to leese,
They dranke old Sacke *Vpse-freeze*;
And lustily eate vp
    their red-coted Cheese.

3 Relate againe, this Newes from *Spaine*,
    that they are wondrous rich,
The Fleet of late, hath helpt their State,
    by bringing home so much;
The *States* and *Spaine*, will too 't againe;
    the Wars were nere none such,
And *Spinola* vowes,
    he no longer will stay,
But raise his men by breake of day:
Heele burne vp their Forts,
    and goe marching away.

4 Say, *France* with peace hath great increase
    from euery Country neere,
The Boores betimes renew their Vines,
    which lately spoyled were,
And some suppose, while Vinyards grows
    they make a shift with Beere:
And tell them the next time
    thou comst thither Post,
Thou shalt bring news frō *Englands* Coast
For that is the Newes,
    that concernes vs all most.

5 Away againe, Post hence amaine,
    and stranger Newes declare,
To euery Towne, both wise and Clowne,
    that hath abiding there,

For certaine tell, that all is well,
   and bid them banish feare;
Say, Courtiers are honest,
   they lead vertuous liues,
The one by the other louingly thriues,
And all haue gi'n ore
   to wrong Citizens Wiues.

The Second Part. To the same Tune.

6 THe Country large, maintain their charge
   and good Hospitality vse,
The Farmers bate of their hie rate,
   and do great Measures choose;
The Land-lords they, at Quarter day
   doe Fines or Bribes refuse;
The poore well are clothed,
   and victuals haue store,
The trades ar increasd which late did deplore,
And Constables scorne
   for to fauour a Whore.

7 A Soldier true, come ouer new,
   may quietly to his friends passe,
Without being staid, no wayes are laid,
   by any inquisitiue Asse,
And Carriers sing, they'l neuer bring
   London a broken Glasse;
The Knights and the Gentry,
   each keeps his house,
The neighbors welcome to Brawn & Souse,
And Beggers so proud,
   that they all hate a Louse.

8 All Citty Dames maintaine their fames,
   their pride they doe impayre,
The rich each day their money lay,
   Pauls Steeple vp to reare;

Each Prisoners Fee discharg'd shall be,
    to quit them from their care;
The Bride-wells are alter'd,
    and Hospitalls made,
And maymed Soldiers therein laid.
And euery Batchelor
    marries a Mayd.

9 By Merchants rich is giuen much,
    to Bankrupts newly decay'd,
The Merchants store, shall help the poore,
    that want, to set vp their Trade;
From *Lud-gate* stones none shal heare mones
    which haue so long beene made;
The Usurers, fiue
    in the hundred will take,
Promoters[1] all shall Soldiers make,
And Whores are turnd honest,
    for conscience sake.

10 More mightst thou say my fine-tongu'd Boy,
    of this our happy Newes,
If any grieue for to beleeue,
    I prethee bid them choose;
And those that will to *London* still
    these obiects come and peruse;
Where you shall find honestly
    all that I say,
Prouide, make hast, vse no delay:
For all this shall be
    betwixt this and Doomes-day.

Finis. *The Post.*

Printed at London for *I. Trundle.*

[1] *Text* Promooter.

23

The downfall of a corrupted conscience

Pepys, 1, 142, B.L., two woodcuts, four columns.

Sir Francis Michell—Justice of the Peace of Middlesex and commissioner for enforcing monopolies—is a pathetic figure. On October 20, 1618, he was appointed, along with Sir Giles Mompesson (the Sir Giles Overreach of Massinger's *New Way to Pay Old Debts*), on a commission charged with enforcing a monopoly of gold and silver thread. In this capacity for two years he exercised his powers corruptly and harshly. He was knighted in December, 1620. In the following February, however, he was committed for contempt to the Tower by the House of Commons. Examined by the Commons on March 6, 1621, he was tried, on April 26, at the bar of the House of Lords, where the chief accusation was that he had erected an office, kept a court, and exacted bonds, and that he had taken money in a suit to compound the same. On May 4 he was sentenced by the Lord Chief Justice to degradation from knighthood, fined £1000, debarred from holding office in the future, and ordered to be imprisoned during the King's pleasure. On June 30, 1621, Michell petitioned for release "from the rest of his censure, being old and sickly," and the petition was granted (*Calendar of State Papers, Domestic*, 1619–23, p. 269). A sentence similar to Michell's had been passed on Mompesson, who was exceptionally unpopular because of his patent on inns and alehouses; but he escaped to the Continent.

In his *Chronicle of England* Sir Richard Baker simply remarks that Michell was "made to ride with his Face to the Horse's Tail through the City of *London*." The ballad, which has remained unknown to Michell's biographers, is a far more valuable and picturesque account of the public degradation inflicted on him by the Earl Marshal's Commissioners at the King's Bench, Westminster Hall, on June 20, 1621. Equally unknown is the splendid "good-night" preserved in Bodley's Library (MS. Tanner 306, fols. 247–248ᵛ) under the title of "A lamentable newe Ballade expressing the Complaynte of Sʳ Fraunces Michell, Knighte, Dwellinge in Pickt hatche, lateley Justice of Peace. To a scuruey tune." It begins:

> You Justices & men of myghte,
> You Constables that walke by nyghte,
> And all you officers more lowe,
> But marke my sudden overthrowe.

DOWNFALL OF A CORRUPTED CONSCIENCE

The tune is not known to me. The printer's initials are those of George
Elde or George Edwards.

𝕲𝖍𝖊 𝖉𝖊𝖘𝖊𝖗𝖚𝖊𝖉 𝖉𝖔𝖜𝖓𝖋𝖆𝖑𝖑 𝖔𝖋 𝖆 𝖈𝖔𝖗𝖗𝖚𝖕𝖙𝖊𝖉 𝖈𝖔𝖓𝖘𝖈𝖎𝖊𝖓𝖈𝖊,
𝖉𝖊𝖌𝖗𝖆𝖉𝖊𝖉 𝖋𝖗𝖔𝖒 𝖆𝖑𝖑 𝕬𝖚𝖙𝖍𝖔𝖗𝖎𝖙𝖞 𝖆𝖓𝖉 𝖙𝖎𝖙𝖑𝖊𝖘 𝖔𝖋 𝕶𝖓𝖎𝖌𝖍𝖙𝖍𝖔𝖔𝖉,
𝖈𝖊𝖓𝖘𝖚𝖗𝖊𝖉 𝖎𝖓 𝖙𝖍𝖊 𝖍𝖎𝖌𝖍 𝕮𝖔𝖚𝖗𝖙 𝖔𝖋 𝕻𝖆𝖗𝖑𝖎𝖆𝖒𝖊𝖓𝖙, 𝖆𝖓𝖉 𝖊𝖝=
𝖊𝖈𝖚𝖙𝖊𝖉 𝖆𝖙 𝖙𝖍𝖊 𝕶𝖎𝖓𝖌𝖘 𝕭𝖊𝖓𝖈𝖍 𝖇𝖆𝖗𝖗𝖊 𝖚𝖕𝖔𝖓 𝖙𝖍𝖊 𝟚𝟘. 𝖉𝖆𝖞
𝖔𝖋 𝕵𝖚𝖓𝖊 𝖑𝖆𝖘𝖙, 𝟙𝟞𝟚𝟙. 𝖎𝖓 𝖙𝖍𝖊 𝖕𝖗𝖊𝖘𝖊𝖓𝖈𝖊 𝖔𝖋 𝖋𝖔𝖚𝖗𝖊 𝖌𝖗𝖊𝖆𝖙
𝕻𝖊𝖊𝖗𝖊𝖘 𝖔𝖋 𝖙𝖍𝖎𝖘 𝕶𝖎𝖓𝖌𝖉𝖔𝖒𝖊.

To the tune of, *The humming of the Drone.*

1   I T was my chance of late
    in Westminster to be,
Whereas in gallant state
    great numbers I did see,
      attending all
      in that great Hall,
Where Iustice is decreed,
      and people store
      came more and more,
Which did amazement breed.

2   At last, my longing eyes
    (expecting some strange thing)
Knight Marshals men espies.
    with Harrolds of our King,
      awaiting there
      as duties were,
To haue some action done,
      where presently
      I heard a cry,
[Mak]e[1] roome, for now they come.

3   It seem'd he was a Knight,
    and Iustice by degree,

[1] Torn. Only a few words of the stanza that followed this remain.

DOWNFALL OF A CORRUPTED CONSCIENCE

By wrongs in stead of right,
  great benefits gain'd he:
    by wrested Lawes
    much wealth he drawes
From many a poore mans state,
  for which it seem'd,
  he thus was deem'd
A bribed Magistrate.

4 Unto the Barre thus brought,
  foure Nobles of our Land,
By wisedome fittest thought,
  did in Commission stand,
    to take away
    his titles gay
Of Knighthood and renowne,
  and that high grace
  of Iustice place,
In open Court lay downe.

5 In that the King him gaue
  these honors by his loue,
So likewise must they haue
  an order of remoue,
    by noble States
    and Magistrates
Of great account and place:
  and thus was he
  from dignity,
Made seruile, meane, and base.

6 Before high Iustice seat,
  the Harrolds there him set,
And did at full repeat
  his knightly titles great,
    and him attir'd
    as place requir'd,

In robes of Knighthood braue,
  with spurs and sword,
  as did accord
What grace his Highnesse gaue.

7 All which was taken quite,
  by order and command,
From this degraded Knight,
  by a Marshals seruants hand,
   in open Court,
   before a sort
Of Barons, Lords and Knights:
   to his disgrace,
   euen in that place
Where Iustice pleadeth rights.

The second Part. To the same Tune.

8 HIs Sword of Knighthood, first
  was cut from off his side,
And ouer his head there burst,
  that should haue beene his pride,
   and Knighthoods grace,
   in courtly place

But he the same hath wrong'd,
    and now cast downe
    the faire renowne
To his knighthood that belong'd.[1]

9 His spurs of Knighthood then,
    was from his heeles there hewen,
And by the Marshals men
    in high disgraces throwne
    into the Hall,
    amongst them all
That stood with gazing eyes,
    to marke and see
    in what degree
Degraded Knighthood lies.

10 His sword, his spurres, his name,
    his titles, and his state,
His knighthood and his fame,
    which he possest so late
    thus all disgrac't
    and cleane defac't
For euer claiming more,
    and chang'd him quite
    from being Knight
And what he had before.

11 This Censure by command,
    vpon him then was layd,
That no where in this Land,
    of him be iustly said,
    or nam'd to be
    in his degree
A iust and honest man,
    but one whose vaine,
    for greedy gaine,
To shamelesse dealing ran.

[1] No period in text.

12 And so with vile reproach
    he was from thence sent backe,
And hurried in a Coach
    where did no wondring lacke,
    of cries and shouts
    with mocking flouts,
Untill he came where he
    should lye againe,
    and there remaine,
A prisoner close to be.[1]

13 No Knight nor Iustice now,
    nor of no other stile,
Our Land will him allow,
    but that which makes me smile,
    for what I heard
    I am afeard
To adde vnto his name,
    but let that rest
    within my brest,
And so be free from blame.

14 But thus much I will say,
    true iustice here was done,
To him that many a day
    did to Much euill run:
    much good thereby,
    assuredly
Now comes vnto our Land,[2]
    in driuing hence,
    this plague of pence,
That stood with open hand.

Finis.

Printed at London by G. E.

[1] Text has a comma.   [2] Text has a period.

24

A battle of birds

Pepys, 1, 70, B.L., three woodcuts, four columns.

A more complete account of this marvel in Ireland is given, with some variations in dates and minor details, in a nine-page pamphlet called "*The Wonderfvll Battell of Starelings: Fought at the Citie of Corke in Ireland, the* 12. *and* 14. *of October last past.* 1621. *As it hath been credibly enformed by diuers Noble-men, and others of the said Kingdome,* &*c.* London, Printed for N. B[ourne]. 1622" (British Museum, C. 32. e. 7). The preface, referring to this ballad and others now lost, complains "that so many poeticall fictions haue of late passed the print, that they [*i.e.* readers] haue some cause to suspect almost euery extraordinary report that is printed"; but says that the facts in the pamphlet are confirmed by "Letters, from Right Honorable persons in Ireland where the accident fell out, to Right Honourable persons at Court, and diuers in London at this present: as also by the testimony of Right Honourable and Worshipfull persons, & others of good reputation now in London, who were eye-witnesses." It also adds that "these strange newes out of Ireland had beene printed before this time, but that it hath beene stayed till the truth were fully certified and examined."

To summarize the body of the pamphlet: "About the seuenth of October last, *Anno* 1621. there gathered together by degrees, an vnusual multitude of birds called Stares, in some Countries knowne by the name of Starlings"; "they mustered together at this aboue-named Citie of *Corke* some foure or fiue daies, before they fought their battels, euery day more and more encreasing their armies with greater supplies, some came from the East, others from the West, and so accordingly they placed themselues"; "some twenty or thirty in a company, would passe from the one side to the other, as it should seem imployed in embassages." On October 12, Saturday, at nine a.m., the battle began. It continued "till a little before night, at which time they seemed to vanish." On Sunday they were seen fighting "betwixt *Grauesend* and *Wolwigge*," but on Monday they returned to Cork for a further battle. There is a contemporary copy (1621) of most of this pamphlet in Richard Shanne's diary (Additional MS. 38,599, fols. 53–54), and the battle of birds is commented on, also, in the *Diary of Walter Yonge* for September, 1621 (ed. George Roberts, p. 45).

A similar prodigy, and one of equally dire import, happened "Neere *Troppaw* in *Silesia,* in the Moneth of *February, Anno.* 1625. [where] a great multitude of little Crowes (*Corniculae*) appeared in the Ayre, which fought as it were in a set Battaile, and skirmished so eagerly, killing many amongst themselves, that the Boores gathered some sacks full of them dead, and transported them unto the City. The yeere after, *Anno.* 1626. fell out a hard and sharpe fight, betwixt the Imperialists, and the *Weinmarish* Forces in this place" (L. Brinckmair, *The Warnings of Germany*, 1638, p. 25). Compare also No. 26, which deals with a much later battle of birds in France, and No. 25, in which the burning of Cork in 1622 is taken to be the calamity predicted in the ballad.

For another contemporary reference to the battle of the birds see the *Court and Times of James I*, II, 302.

For the tune of *Shore's Wife* see Chappell's *Popular Music*, I, 215; for *Bonny Nell*, see the same work, II, 502.

A battell of Birds
Most strangly fought in Ireland, vpon the eight day of September last, 1621. where neere vnto the Citty of Corke, by the riuer Lee, weare gathered together such a multytude of Stares, or Starlings, as the like for number, was neuer seene in any age.

To the tune of *Shores wife*. Or to the tune of *Bonny Nell*.

1 MArke well, Gods wonderous workes, and see,
  what things therein declared be,
Such things as may with trembling feare,
  fright all the world, the same to heare:
   for like to these, which heere I tell,
   no man aliue remembreth well.

2 The eight day of September last,
  which made all Ireland much agast:
Were seene (neere Corke) such flights of Birds,
  whose numbers, cannot well by words,
   acounted be: for greater store,
   was neuer seene, nor knowne before.

3 The flights, so many legions seem'd,
  as thousand thousands they were deem'd,

A BATTLE OF BIRDS

All soaring vp, along the skye,
 as if the battle were on hie:
  in multytudes, without compare,
  which like black clowds, made dim the are.

4 First from the easterne skyes apeared,
 a flight of Stares, which greatly feared,
The people there, the same to see,
 as like could not remembred be:
  for they in warlike squadrons flew,
  as if they others would persue.

5 And as this flight, thus houering lay,
 prepared all in battle ray:
From out the west, another came,
 as great in number as the same,
  and there oppos'd in warlike might,
  themselues against the other flight.

6 Whereas these Stares, or starling Birds,
 for want of Helmetts, Glaues and Swords,
They vsed their Tallents, Bills, and Beakes,[1]
 and such a battle vndertakes:
  that trembling feare and terror brought,
  to all which saw this battle fought.

7 For first, the Easterne flight sat downe,
 with chattering noyes vpon the ground,
As if they challenged, all the rest,
 to meete and fight euen brest to brest,
  where presently was heard from farre,
  the same like chattering sound of warre.

8 And therevpon the westerne flight,
 downe by the easterne Birds did light,
Where after they a while had sat,
 together in their Birdlike chat,
  they all vpon a sudaine rose,
  and each the other did oppose.

[1] *Text* Bekaes.

152

A BATTLE OF BIRDS

The second part, to the same tune.

9 ANd filling thus the Azure skie
 with these their troupes vp mounted hie,
They seem'd more thick, then moats ith Sunne,
 a dreadfull battle there begun:
  and in their kind more strongly fought,
  then can immagen'd be by thought.

10 Thousands of thousands, on a heape,
 vpon the others backes did leape,
With all their forced strengths and might,
 to put their Bird-like foes to flight:
  and as it were in battle ray,
  long time they kept them, thus in play.

11 To fight this battle in the ayre,
 their bills and beakes their weapons were,
Which they performed in such a sort,
 as makes me doubtfull to report:
  that silly Birds should thus arise,
  and fight so fircely in the skyes.

12 But so it was and strange withall,[1]
 that Birds should thus at discord fall,
And neuer cease, till they had slaine,
 thousands, starke dead vpon the plaine:
  where people tooke them vp in feare,
  a thing most strange to see and heare.

13 With broken wings, some fell to ground,
 and some poore silly Birds were found,
With eyes pickt out, struck downe halfe dead,
 and some no braines left in their head;
  but battered forth, and kil'd outright,
  most strangly in this ayery fight.

[1] Text has a period.

A BATTLE OF BIRDS

14 Yet long with loud and chattering cryes,
     each company gainst other flyes:
  With bloody beakes, remorselesse still,
     their fethered foes to maine or kill,
       where whilst this battle did remaine
       their bodies fell like dropes of raine.

15 Thousands were to the Citty borne,
     with wounded limbes, and bodies torne:
  For all the fields were ouerspread,
     with mangled starlings that lay dead,[1]
       in bloud and feathers strang to se,
       which men tooke vp aboundantly.

16 It was a wonder to explaine,
     the number of them hurt and slaine,
  And being a wonder let it rest,
     the Lord aboue he knoweth best:
       what these poore creatures did intend,
       when thus to battle they did bend.

17 But such a battle nere was fought,
     by silly Birds which haue no thought:
  In doing ill, nor any mind,
     to worke contrary to their kind,
       but yet as nature gaue them life,
       so here they strangly fell at strife.

18 What now for trueth is publisht forth
     esteeme it as a newes of worth:
  And by the wonder of these dayes,
     learne to leaue off all wicked wayes,
       for sure it is that God it sent,
       that of our sinnes we should repent.

Finis.

Printed at London by W.I.

[1] Text has a period.

154

25

The lamentable burning of Cork

Pepys, 1, 68, B.L., three woodcuts, four columns.

By a strange coincidence a disastrous fire swept the city of Cork (see Caulfield's *Council Book of Cork*, p. 102) shortly after the battle of the birds there (cf. No. 24); and in this coincidence ballad-writers and Jacobean journalists naturally exulted. At the conclusion of the ballad the author, or more probably the printer, invites his readers to go to "the full Relation at large in the Booke newly Printed," an invitation that we shall accept, as the "book," of nine pages, is preserved in the British Museum (C. 32. 3. 6)[1]. It is entitled:

A Relation Of The Most lamentable Burning of the Cittie of Corke, in the west of Ireland, in the Province of Monster, by Thunder and Lightning. With other most dolefull and miserable accidents, which fell out the last of May 1622 after the prodigious battell of the birds called Stares, which fought strangely over and neare that Citie the 12. & 14. of May 1621. As it hath beene Reported to divers Right Honourable Persons. [Cut] Printed this 20. of Iune. 1622. London Printed by I.D. for Nicholas Bourne, and Thomas Archer, 1622.

In the preface, mention is made of the earlier book that Nathaniel Bourne had printed on the battle of the birds: "This report being so strange, was of some censured as an vntrue and idle invention; Of others, which vnderstood, and by enquirie were resolved of the truth, it was imagined to prognosticate some strange and dreadfull accident to follow...the *Omnipotent Maiestie* of heaven hath not onely reprooved their vanitie, who would not beleeue so strange a Relation, but hath further by a most dreadfull and lamentable demonstration of his power and Iustice, resolved what that battell of Birds might or did prognosticate."

The writer then proceeds to show that, like Sodom and Gomorrah, Cork was first warned and next destroyed for her sins: "The Citizens, and Inhabitants of *Corke*, haue beene taxed and noted for *Vsury*, (the chiefest Daughter of Covetousnesse) to exceed any Cittie in the Kings Dominions, except some Cities in *England*." Of the actual burning of the city, on Friday, May 31, 1622, between eleven and twelve a.m., the pamphleteer adds nothing to the balladist's account. He concludes by reminding his readers: "These inhabitants of the Cittie of *Corke*, were not the onely and greatest sinners, aboue all other Cities in *England* or *Ireland*": they were merely chosen as an example of God's punishment because they disregarded the warning given by the birds.

[1] It was licensed for publication on June 19, 1622.

More interesting than the pamphlet is the brief personal note in Richard Shanne's diary (Additional MS. 38,599, fol. 54ᵛ):

The 30 daie of may was the Cittie of Corke in Ireland Burned with fyre from heaven, over which Cittie the yeare befor, the great battell of Shepsternells was fought, as ye may reed in the yeare An. Do. 1621 [*i.e.* on fol. 53 of his own diary]. There was verie manie pore people of Ireland came into this Cuntrie A begginge, which was vtterlie vndune by reasone of the said fyre. I my owne selfe did talke with divers of those people that dwelled in the Cittie of Corke, and did enquire of them whether of A trueth there was such A battell of Shepstarnell as reporte went, and whether the Cittie was burned as is afforesaid. A[nd] they all agreed and tould me that there was whole Cart-lodes taken vp of those Shepstares that was slayne in the fight.

The tune is given in Chappell's *Popular Music*, i, 162.

The lamentable Burning of the Citty of *Corke* (in the Prouince of *Munster* in *Ireland*) by Lightning: which happened the Last of May, 1622. After the prodigious Battell of the *Stares*, which Fought most strangely ouer and neere that Citty, the 12. and 14. of May. 1621.

To the tune of *Fortune my foe.*

1   WHo please to heare such newes as are most true,
    Such newes to make a Christians hart to rue:
    Such Newes as may make stoutest hearts to shake,
    And Sinners iustly to tremble and to quake.

2   Reade this, and they shall haue iust cause to feare,
    Gods heauy hand on sinne reported heere:
    Twas lately heard that Birds all of a feather,
    Did strangely meete, and strangely fought together.

3   At *Corke*, in *Ireland*, where with might and maine,
    They fought together till store of them were slaine:
    Their Fight began and ended with such hate,
    Some strange euent it did Prognosticate.

4   What was presag'd fell out this last of *May*,
    Which was at *Corke* an heauy dismall day:
    This last of *May* the Morning was most faire,
    Towards xij. a clocke, Cloudes gathered in the Ayre.

5 Which Cloudes obscur'd, and darkened so the light,
  That Midday almost was as darke as Night:
  Whilest at such darknes Cittizens did wonder,
  Forthwith they heard a dreadfull clap of Thunder.

6 And with the Thunder, presently there came
  Such Lightning forth the Clouds did seeme to flame:
  But heere obserue, this Citty towards the East,
  Stands high, but falleth lowe towards the West.

7 As at the East the *Stares* began their Fight,
  And there fell downe the Birds first, kild outright:
  So at the East began the Fire to flame,
  Those at the West did soone beholde the same.

8 And towards the East, to see and helpe they ranne,
  Before halfe way, a wofull Cry began:
  Behinde them, seeing the West end was on Fire,
  They so recalld, began for to retire.

9 As from the East, towards the West they turne,
  They saw the middest of the Citty burne:
  So at an instant all was on a flame,
  There was no meanes to helpe to quench the same.

10 Although great store of Water was in place,
   Water could not helpe there in such a case:
   For why that Fire which from the Skyes doth fall,
   Is not with Water to be quencht at all.

11 Now were the Cittizens ouerwhelm'd with woe,
   For no man knew, which way to runne or goe:
   For in the Citty no man could abide,
   The Fire raged so on euery side.

12 Some were enclosed with Fire, they for their safety
   Fled to the Churches, which were in the Citty:
   Some to an Iland, and the Fields hard by,
   To saue their liues, with grieued hearts did flye.

13 Who was not then tormented in his minde,
To flye and leaue all that he had behinde?
When that the Husband, for to saue his life,
Might not make stay to bring away his Wife,

14 Or saue his Children: in like case the Mother,
Fled from her Children, Sister fled from Brother:
All were amazed in this wofull Day,
Not knowing where to flye nor where to stay:

15 Nor where to seeke or after Friends enquire,
They knew not who was sau'd, who burnt by Fire:
A dolefull thing it was men might not tarry,
Out of the flames, their dearest Friends to carry.

The Second part. To the same tune.

16 O That this wofull chance of *Corke* might rent,
The hearts of men and cause them to repent
Their wicked liues for to escape the Rod,
Which they haue cause to feare, will fall from God.

17 *Corke* to all Citties, may example bee,
To know they are not from Gods Iustice free:
For being Sinners they may feare the like,
As fell to *Corke*, God in his wrath will strike.

18 But they will say, God's mercifull, 'tis true,
But in this case, let them giue God his due:
Let them not so vnto his mercy trust,
But let them know that God is also Iust.

19 God's mercifull to Sinners which repent,
His Iustice is towards lingring sinners bent:
Who will take holde of mercy and of Grace,
Let them repent whilest they haue time and space.

20 Repentance onely pacifies Gods Ire,
Preserues from sodaine, and Eternall Fire:
This word Repentance, is a wicked thing,
To wicked Liuers, 'tis a Serpents sting.

21 Why should Repentance be so bitter, when
Tis the onely salue to Cure sinfull men?
And furthermore when as we are most sure,
That dye we must wee cannot long endure.

22 When we are sure, we from this world must goe,
But by what kinde of Death, we doe not know:
No more then *Corke* did when that God did powre
The Fire vpon them in a dreadfull houre.

23 Why should not we be well prouided then,
Against a certaine Death, but know not when:
Nor by what kinde of death, Death will vs take,
Then let Repentance our attonement make.

24 If men Repentance in this life doe stay,
Let them consider of the Iudgement day:
When God to Sinners, shall say in his Ire:
Goe hence yee Cursed to Eternall Fire.

25 But who in Life did faithfully Repent,
    When they shall come to appeare at that Iudgement
    The Iudge will say: *Goe Children of all Blisse,*
    Enter the Kingdome, for you prepared is.

26 The God of Heauen graunt, that all Sinners take,
    That course which may them blessed creatures make,
    That come yee Blessed, with a ioyfull eare,
    They from the Iudge at that maine day may heare.

Finis.

Printed at London by E.A.

You shall see the full Relation at large in the Booke
newly printed.

26

The Frenchmen's wonder

4to Rawlinson 566, fol. 78; Wood E. 25 (64), B.L., two woodcuts, four columns.

The ballad is summarized from a book called *A True Relation of The Prodigious Battle Of Birds, Fought in the lower Region of the Air, Between the Cities of Dole and Salines, The 26th of February last* 167⅝. *According to the Letters from Besancon, of the First of this Instant March,* 1676 (Wood D. 28 (22)). In the opinion of the authors of both tract and ballad "the like of this marvel hath never been." But to say nothing of the earlier prodigy at Cork (No. 24), more startling still must have been the sight seen in the air in Austria, 1621, as reported in Richard Shanne's diary (Additional MS. 38,599, fol. 53) from "the historie of Gallobelgicus":

In the moneth of August there was both seene and hearde in the higher Austria, A most straunge wonder, that is to saie: of two great Armies in the Ayre, fightinge one against an other, and thundringe of, and dischardginge greate Ordinance, with A hidious clamore.

Hone's *Every-Day Book* (1889, II, 570) reports that in August, 1736, near Preston two large flocks of birds met "with such rapidity, that one hundred and eighty of them fell to the ground," and that the carcasses were picked up and sold.

The enormously long title gives quite as much information as the text of the ballad itself. The reason for this was that the printers wished to use the title, torn from the remainder of the broadside, as advertising matter to be pasted on walls or posts. Salins and Dôle are towns on the eastern frontier of France, in the department of Jura.

The music for *In summer time* as given in Chappell's *Popular Music*, II, 392, 542, does not fit this ballad. That music is written for iambic septenary couplets, while the present ballad (like those, for example, in the *Roxburghe Ballads*, VI, 567, 789; VII, 702) is in iambic tetrameter quatrains. Few tunes are more frequently cited than the *Summer time* written for the latter measure. It is named as an alternative tune to *Callino* in J. P. Collier's *Book of Roxburghe Ballads*, p. 64; to *Flora farewell* and *Love's Tide* in the *Roxburghe Ballads*, VI, 567. Frequently it is given as equivalent to *My bleeding heart* or *Sir Andrew Barton* (*Roxburghe Ballads*, I, 9; III, 23), neither of which is known. I have seen, however, in the Manchester Free Reference Library a ballad of "The Great Turk's Terrible Challenge" to

the tune of *My bleeding heart* or *Let's to the wars again*. The latter is
equivalent (cf. No. 73) to *Maying Time* (for which see Chappell's *Popular
Music*, I, 377), and to *Maying Time* the present ballad can readily be sung.

𝕿𝖍𝖊 *Frenchmens* 𝖂𝖔𝖓𝖉𝖊𝖗;

𝕺𝖗,

𝕿𝖍𝖊 𝕭𝖆𝖙𝖙𝖑𝖊 𝖔𝖋 𝖙𝖍𝖊 𝕭𝖎𝖗𝖉𝖘

Relating that on the 26*th*. of *Feb*. last, about 9 in the
morning were seen between *Dole* and *Salins* in *France*, a
most incredible number of Birds, who by their multitude
darkened the Sky; after having for some time, as it were
skirmished together in great confusion, they seperated
into two bodies; and after most horrible cries, they en-
gaged against each other with such fury, that several
thousands were faln dead to the Earth; some smothered
with most of their feathers off, and others all bloody and
torn; These Birds were of a hundred several sorts, of
several sizes, and several colours. Those which were most
Numerous weighed four or five pounds a piece; their
claws were like those of *Indian* Hens, Nibs crooked like
Parrots, and their feathers of an Ash colour; about 500
Paces of Ground were covered with these dead carkasses
to a mans height. Besides several Thousands that were
found dispersed here and there: Insomuch that it being
feared that the Air might be infected by them, Pioneers
were sent from *Dole* to bury them.

𝖂𝖎𝖙𝖍 𝕬𝖑𝖑𝖔𝖜𝖆𝖓𝖈𝖊, 𝕽𝖔𝖌𝖊𝖗 𝕷'𝕰𝖘𝖙𝖗𝖆𝖓𝖌𝖊.

To the tune of, *In Summer time*.

1 COme give attention young and old,
   whilst in my story I proceed,
Strange wonders dayly we behold,
   yet pass them over without heed.

2 From places strange, by Sea and Land,
   and from all parts beneath the Sun;
Of wonders great we understand,
   which by the Lord on high are done.

3 Yet few doth lay it unto heart,
    nor to themselves the same apply,
Or from their sins strive to depart,
    though threatn'd judgements are so nigh.

4 But at the same they make a scoff,
    which are for warnings dayly sent,
To tell them they shall be cut off,
    except they of their sins repent.

5 'Tis known that pride, and drunkeness,
    and swearing, doth so much abound,
Men are so bent to wickedness,
    that soul and body they confound.

6 Which makes the Lord above to send
    such signs our spirits to abate;
That we our lives may all amend,
    by what hath happened of late.

7 Near unto *Dole* in firtile *France*,
    a wonder strange was lately seen,
Which doth fames Trumpet so advance,
    because the like hath never been.

8 Great multitudes of Birds appear'd,
    one morning being clear and fair,
The like whereof was never heard,
    for why they darkned all the ayr.

The second Part, to the same Tune.

9 THe people stood amaz'd to see,
    that wondrous sight which did appear,
Or what the sad event might be,
    why such strange Fowls was gathered there.

10 For sometimes they were seen to fight,
    and skirmish in confused wise,
To tug and pull, to claw and bite,
    sometimes to fall, and sometimes rise.

11 At length as it were by consent,
    into two parties they devide;
As if it were two Armies bent,
    to fight it out on either side.

12 And then with fearful hideous cries,
    each party did the other dare,
The like was never seen with eyes,
    how they proclaimed open war.

13 At last each other did engage,
    with fury great on either side,
Both parties being in a rage,
    like two brave armies in their pride.

14 Most fiercely they did fight it out,
    whilst thousands to the ground did fall;
They were so furious and so stout,
    they freely ventured life and all.

15 Their bodies mangled, rent, and torn,
    upon the earth most thick did lye,
So that the child that's yet unborn;
    may wonder at this prodigy.

16 At length their forces being spent,
    those that were left, away did flie,
But whence they came, or whither went,
    there's no one ever could descry.

17 These birds which did the battle fight,
    were of a hundred sundry sorts,
Of several colours and of shape,
    as doth appear by all reports.

18 The greatest of their bodies were,
    of four or five pounds weight each one;
As to the people did appear,
    which view'd them over as 'tis known.

19 Their claws like those of *Indian* hens,
    their crooked nibs, like Parrots just;
 Their feathers of an Ash colour,
    if we may the relation trust.

20 Five hundred paces, as 'tis said,
    of ground were covered with the dead,
 Unto the height of any man,
    besides some thousands scattered.

21 The people being sore afraid,
    their bodies should infect the air,
 Sent Pioneers to bury them,
    which is a thing most strange and rare.

22 Thus was this bloody combate past,
    within the sight of many a one;
 Who at the wonder stood agast,
    for to behold what there was shown.

23 What is the meaning of the same,
    there's none doth know but God above,
 Then let us fear his holy name,
    and live in concord, peace and love.

24 For cruel wars, and bloody strife,
    doth cause great ruine at the last:
 Then let us ad a holy life,
    and pardon crave[1] for what is past.

𝔉inis.

Printed for *F. Coles, T. Vere, J. Wright,* and *J. Clarke.*

[1] *Text* rave.

27

The back's complaint

Pepys, 1, 446, B.L., five woodcuts, four columns.
"The backes complaint for the bellyes wronge" was licensed to Cuthbert Wright on July 10, 1622, and, again, on July 18, 1623 (Arber's *Transcript*, IV, 74, 101). Edward Culter appears to be unknown save by this one production. Professor Kittredge suggests a comparison with "The Back and the Belly" in *Songs. By Thomas Hudson*, London, 1820, pp. 9–10 (Second Collection), which begins:

A story I'm going to tell ye,
Which if you'll attend to, you'll hear in a crack;
'Tis about a man's hungry belly
Conversing along with his back.

A pleasant new Song,
Of the backes complaint, for bellies wrong:
Or a farwell to good fellowship.

To the tune of *A, B, C.*

1 GOod fellowes all to you I send,
    These verses which in loue I pend:
   Desiring you will compasse keepe,
       and bid farwell *good fellowship*.

2 I once did beare a good fellowes name,
   And still am counted for the same:
   But now my vow is ingaged deepe,
       to bid farwell *good fellowship*.

3 I haue beene of that sett so long,
   Till backe complaines of bellies wrong:
   With great exclaimes in euery street,
       to make me leaue *good fellowship*.

166

THE BACK'S COMPLAINT

4 Me thinkes I oft doe heare it say,
    Mongst drunkards thou consum'd away:
    Thy monny memory and witt,
      all wasted by *good fellowship*.

5 Of me thou takest but little care,
    Though bellies full yet backe is bare:
    And frostie winter will thee nipe,
      vnles thou leaue *good fellowship*.

6 Thou thinkest good fellowes be thy friends
    And what thou hast on them thou spends:
    What thou by worke gainst all yᵉ weeke,
      comsumeth by *good fellowship*.

7 But when that all thy money is gone,
    And score nor credit thou hast none:
    These friends from thee away will slipe,
      and farewell all *good fellowship*.

8 When being gon, at thee they'l laugh,
    Tis bad to trust a broaken staffe:
    For feare thou fall in danger deepe,
      giue ouer in time *good fellowship*.

9 For dayly doth attend the same,
    Too sisters, call'd begery, and shame:
    Whose hands & hearts full fast are knit,
      and ioyned to *good fellowship*.

10 Besides deseases that doth flow,
    From drunkennes as many know:
    Who to their smart, haue felt the whipe
      that followeth *good fellowship*.

11 Surfetes, dropsies, and diuers paines,
    Ach of the head, breach of the braines:
    Like festred fistolles, foule and deepe,
      attendeth on *good fellowship*.

THE BACK'S COMPLAINT

12　Ten thousand misseries alacke,
　　Fall's both on bodie and on backe:
　　As ancient writters, large haue write,
　　　to warne vs from *good fellowship*.

The second part, wherein is declared,
The backes complaint, hath the bellie reformed:
To bid farwell good fellowship. To the same tune.

13　THis sad complaint when I did heare
　　　Vewing my back, I see it was beare:
　　And cheifest cause I knew of it,
　　　was keeping of *good fellowship*.

14　Being much moued at the same,
　　A solemne oath then did I frame:
　　This hainious wrong, for to aquite,
　　　to bid farwell *good fellowship*.

15　And therefore here I bid farwell,
　　To that which once I lou'd to well:
　　Henceforth I will in compasse keepe,
　　　therefore farwell *good fellowship*.

16　Farwell all such as take delight,
　　To drinke and gousell day and night:
　　Their sole sicke healths, & healthles whiff
　　　and causes the same *good fellowship*.

17　Farwell all such that dayly vse,
　　Themselues and others to abuse:
　　Intising all that they do meete,
　　　with them to keepe *good fellowship*.

18　Farwell all such that well are knowne,
　　To haue a charge to keepe at home:
　　As wife, and child, yet from them flitt
　　　and fly out to *good fellowship*.

19 Farwell good fellowes more and lesse,
No tongue is able to expresse,
The wofull wants that dayly hitte,
   on them that keepe *good fellowship.*

20 Some that were famous throw all parts,
For workmanship and skill in Arts:
Hath beggery cought vpon the hippe,
   for keeping of *good fellowship.*

21 Some that haue had possessions store,
Lands, goods, and cattell, few had more:
But lands, & goods, oxe, horse, and sheepe,
   were wasted by *good fellowship.*

22 Many examples are dayly seene,
Of such that haue good fellowes beene,
Bacchus braue souldiers, stout and stiffe,
   which now lament *good fellowship.*

23 And to conclud the sin is such,
The wise man sayes, none shall be ritch
Except he shun that bitter sweete,
   which drunkards call, *good fellowship.*

24 Then learne this vice for to refraine,
The onely cause of griefe and paine:
Least yee like me in sorrow sit,
   lamenting of *good fellowship.*

Finis.

Per me Edward Culter.

Printed at London by W.I.

28

A new-year's gift for the Pope

Pepys, 1, 62. Only half of the sheet, containing Part I of the ballad, is preserved. This half itself is badly mutilated. There is, accordingly, no way of determining the author's or the printer's name. The first part is in B.L. It has two columns and one very large woodcut, the "emblem" referred to in stanza 1. The date of the ballad is perhaps after May 6, 1624, when James I issued his last proclamation against Jesuits and seminary priests. For this proclamation and for two other ballads (one the work of Martin Parker) in which it is celebrated, see my *Old English Ballads* (Cambridge University Press, 1920), pp. 184–195. The music for *Thomas, you cannot* is given in Chappell's *Popular Music*, 1, 337, and the words are printed in *Bishop Percy's Folio Manuscript. Loose and Humorous Songs*, p. 116.

A New-yeeres-gift for the Pope.
Come see the difference plainly decided, betweene
Truth and Falshood.

Not all the Popes Trinkets, which heere are brought forth,
Can ballance the Bible for weight, and true worth:
Your Bells, Beads and Crosses, you see will not doo't,
Or pull downe your Scale, with the Diuell to boot.

To the Tune of, *Thomas, you cannot, &c.*

1 ALl you that desirous are to behold
   the difference twixt falshood and faith,
Marke well this Emblem, one piece of pure gold,
   a Cart-load of false Coyne outwayeth,
Then wisely consider and beare in your mind,
Though Sathans Instruments true faith to blind,
A thousand deuises dayly doe find:
   Yet all is in vaine, they cannot, they cannot,
   Yet all is in vaine they cannot.

2 The [diff]erence 'twixt Papist and Protestant here,
    you [h]aue in a moment debated,
The o[n]e loues the Gospell that shineth still cleare,
    the other is more subtile-pated,
He will not be ruld by the Scriptures large scope,
But trusts in Traditions deriu'd from the Pope,
By which to be sau'd he doth constantly hope:
    Fond fooles, y' are deceiued, you cannot, &c.

3 True Justice, 'gainst whom no falshood preuailes,
    the case for both Parties decideth
[An]d here she doth hold vp her vnpartiall Scales,
    no fictions nor lyes she abideth:
The Pope like a Martialist hardy and stout,
[C]omes marching in pompe with all his braue rout,
[To] win by his multitude he makes no doubt:
    but alas father Pope you cannot, &c.

4 Thus are these two opposites come to the place,
    where truth must be proued by tryall,
The Pope thinks with greatnesse to carry the grace,
    but Iustice hath eyes to descry all:
The Scales are made euen, the Bible's in one,
Which is the true meanes of Saluation alone,
They striuing to passe it, doe striue till they grone:
    Yet all is in vaine, they cannot, &c.

5 The Pope seeing he must be tride by the Bible,
    did seeke to orecome it by might,
He tride by all meanes that for him was possible;
    but all he could bring was too light:
Their Masses and Dirges, with such superstitions,
Decrees and Decretals, with other Traditions,
The golden Legend with late new additions:
    Yet all is in vaine, they cannot, &c.

6　Thus stil the pure Gospell gainst falshood preuailes,
　　　which when the proud Prelate did see,
　　A Cart-load of Trinkets he puts in the Scales,
　　　and thrust it as full as might be,
　　With great wooden Crosses and many great babies,
　　The Pictures and Saints of a bevy[1] of Ladies,
　　Who dayly are worshipped by these grand Rabbies:
　　　　Yet still father Pope you cannot, &c.
　　　　Yet still father Pope [*&c.*]

[1] *Text* bemy. *Perhaps the line should read* With Pictures of Saints and a bevy of Ladies.

29

The soldier's farewell

Pepys, IV, 42. There is a printed copy also in the collection of the Earl of Crawford (*Catalogue of English Ballads*, No. 793). B.L., one woodcut, two columns. The Pepys copy of this jig is printed on a broadside with another ballad called "A Pleasant Song Made by a Soldier," beginning "In summer time when Phoebus' rays" and included in the *Roxburghe Ballads*, VI, 284. Both ballads were registered at Stationers' Hall on December 14, 1624, as "Margarett, my sweetest" and "In summer time" (Arber's *Transcript*, IV, 131), though the latter was originally licensed on April 24, 1588 (*ibid.* II, 488). There is another copy of "The Soldier's Farewell," preserved under the significant title of "A Iigge," in the *Percy Folio Manuscript* (ed. Hales and Furnivall, II, 355). That copy was evidently made from memory: it has hardly a line in which verbal changes, all without significance, are not made, and is inferior in every way to the printed sheet.

Ballads on this theme—the cruel trials to which a young woman's love is put—are common: see the traditional ballad of "Child Waters," No. 63, in F. J. Child's *English and Scottish Popular Ballads* and the notes there. Perhaps the author of "The Soldier's Farewell" was influenced directly by the beautiful lyric of "The Nut-Brown Maid."

The Souldiers Farewel to his love.
Being a Dialogue betwixt *Thomas* and *Margaret*.

To a pleasant new Tune.

Thomas.

1 MArgaret my sweetest, Margaret I must go.[1]
Margaret.
Most dear to me, that never may be so:
T. Ah, Fortune wills it, I cannot it deny.[1]
M. then know my love your Margaret must dye.

[1] Text has a comma.

173

2 *T.* Not for the gold my Love that *Croesus* had,
Would I once see thy sweetest looks so sad.[1]
M. Nor for all that the which my eye did see,
Would I depart my sweetest Love from thee.

3 *T.* The King commands, & I must to the wars.[2]
M. Ther's others more enough may end the jars.[2]
T. But I for one commanded am to go,
And for my life I dare not once say no.

4 *M.* Ah marry me, and you shall stay at home,
Full thirty weeks you know that I have gone.[1]
T. There's time enough another for to take
He'l[3] love thee well, and not thy child forsake.

5 *M.* And have I doted on thy sweetest face?
and dost infringe that which thou suedst in chase.[2]
Thy faith I mean but I will wend with thee.[1]
T. It is too far for Peg to go with me.

6 *M.* I'le go with thee my Love both night and day.[2]
I'le bear thy sword, i'le run and lead the way.
T. But we must ride, how will you follow then,
Amongst a Troop of us thats Armed men?

7 *M.* Ile bear the Lance, ile guide thy stirrop too,
Ile rub the horse, and more then that ile do.[1]
T. But Margarets fingers they are all too fine,
To wait on me when she doth see me dine.

Margaret.

8 Ile see you dine, ile wait still at your back,
Ile give you wine, or any thing you lack.

Thomas.

But youl repine when you shall see me have
A dainty wench that is both fine and brave.

---

[1] Text has a comma.   [2] No period in the text.   [3] *Text* He l.

9 *M.* Ile love your wench, my sweetest, I do vow,
I'le watch time when she may pleasure you.
T. But you will grieve to see me sleep in bed,
And you must wait still in anothers stead.

10 *M.* I'le watch my love to see you sleep in rest,
And when you sleep then I shall think me blest.
T. The time will come you must delivered be,
If in the Camp it will discredit me.

11 *M.* Ile go from you before the time shall be,
When all is well my love againe ile see.
T. All will not serve for Margaret must not go,
Then do resolve my Love, what else to do.

12 *M.* If nought wil serve why then sweet love adieu.[1]
I needs must die, and yet in dying true.
T. Nay stay my love, for I love Margaret well,
And here I vow with Margaret to dwell.

13 *M.* Give me your hand, your Margaret livs again.[1]
T. Here is my hand, ile never breed thy pain.
M. I'le kiss my Love in token it is so.
T. We will be wed, come Margaret let us go.

𝔉inis.

London, Printed for F. Coles, T. Vere, and J. Wright.

[1] No period in the text.

30

A dream of a sinner

Pepys, 1, 39; 11, 7, B.L., one woodcut, two columns. There is also a copy in the Douce Collection (11, 200ᵛ), at the Bodleian, on the same sheet with Sir Edward Dyer's "My mind to me a kingdom is." "In slumberinge sleepe" was licensed for publication on December 14, 1624 (Arber's *Transcript*, IV, 131). A similar production is the ballad of "Even in the twinkling of an eye" (*Roxburghe Ballads*, VII, 783).

Rogero is given in Chappell's *Popular Music*, 1, 93, but has a different movement from that of this ballad. Nor does the Pepysian ballad of "John Spenser" (No. 45) or "The Poor Man Pays for All. To the Tune of *In slumbering sleep I lay*" (*Roxburghe Ballads*, 11, 334) agree with it in metre or stanza form. To a still different measure is a ballad to the tune of *Rogero* in the *Roxburghe Ballads*, 111, 87.

𝕬 comfortable new 𝕭allad of a 𝕯reame of a 𝕾inner, being very sore troubled with the assaults of 𝕾athan.

To the tune of *Rogero*.

1   IN slumbring sleepe I lay
    all night alone in bed,
  A vision very strange
    there came into my head.[1]

2   Me thought the day of doome
    vndoubtedly was come,
  And Christ himselfe was there
    to iudge both all and some.

3   My selfe was sent for there
    with sound of Trumpet shrill,
  Which said, All soules come heare
    your sentence good or ill.

[1] Text has a comma.

A DREAM OF A SINNER

4 I sate in minde amaz'd,
    at that same sudden voyce,
For in mine owne good life
    no whit I could reioyce.

5 With panting brest I paus'd
    at that same sudden sight,
Not trusting to my selfe,
    but to Christs mercies great.

6 I was no sooner meant,
    but Sathan came, me thought,
With him a role full large
    of all my life he brought.

7 And laid before the Lord
    how that I was his owne,
And would haue had me then,
    my sinnes so great were growne.

8 I quaking lay with feare,
    and wist not what to doe,
But in the blood of Christ
    I trusted still vnto.

9 Then said our Sauiour Christ,
    foule Sathan end thy strife,
Looke if the sinners name
    be in the booke of life.

10 If he be entred there,
    then must he needes be blest,
His sinnes be washt away,
    his soule with me shall rest.

11 Then Sathan tooke the booke,
    did leafe by leafe vnfold,
And there he found my name
    in letters limb'd with gold.

A DREAM OF A SINNER

12 Then Sathan sorrowed much
 at that same sudden sight.
And said vnto the Lord,
 thy Iudgements are not right.

13 And thus our Sauiour sweet
 said to him by and by,
Thou, Sathan, know'st full well
 that I for sinne did dye.

14 Redeeming all the world,
 once ouerthrowne by thee,
And so will saue all such
 as truly trust in mee.

15 My mortall foe was wroth,
 that he had lost his prey,
Extreamely vexed was,
 and vanisht quite away.

16 But I that thus was bill'd
 within that blessed booke,
Out of my slumbring sleepe
 so ioyfully awoke.

17 Still praying to the Lord,
 that alwayes sinners may
From Sathan be set free,
 at the last dreadfull day.

18 That after earthly toyles,
 we may heauen ioyes attaine,
Here learne to liue to dye,
 that we may liue againe.

19 Our noble royall King,
 God grant him long to raigne,
To liue in ioy and peace,
 the Gospell to maintaine.

Finis.

London Printed for *E. Wright*.

178

3 1

Collins' conceit

Pepys, 1, 455, B.L., no woodcuts, three columns.

"Coullins Conceits" was registered for publication on December 14, 1624 (Arber's *Transcript*, IV, 132). One Collins was evidently the author of the ballad: he enumerates a great number of "ifs," the observance of which should, and would, result in pious, godly living. Perhaps he was also the author of "Collins and the Devil," a ballad registered by Edward Blackmore on December 14, 1632 (*ibid.* p. 289), and, though now lost, known to Ditty, the ballad-singer in the *London Chanticleers*, 1659 (Dodsley-Hazlitt's *Old Plays*, XII, 329), who cried it among his wares. *Wigmore's Galliard* is given in Chappell's *Popular Music*, 1, 242.

𝔄 most excellent 𝔇itty, called *Collins* ℭonceit.

To the tune of *Wigmores Gallard*.

1 COnceits of sundry sorts there are,
    but this Conceit of mine,
Doth wish all men to haue a care,
    to liue by wisedomes line.
In my conceit if men would looke,
    where sacred vertues dwell,[1]
And liue according to Gods Booke,
    then all things should be well.

2 If wisedome were once made our guide,
    she would direct vs right,
Where now we daily slip aside,
    for want of wisdomes light.
If we had faith, we need not feare
    the Deuill nor powers of Hell:
If godly faith our Anchor[2] were,
    then all things should be well.

[1] Text has a period.   [2] *Text* Auchor.

179

3 If we could learne to loue the Lord,
    with an vnfayned loue,
And willingly obey his Word,
    as duty doth vs moue:
If we would leaue our wickednesse,
    wherein we doe excell,
And giue our mindes to godlines,
    then all things should be well.

4 If people did not goe to Church,
    onely for fashion sake:
If one would not another lurch,
    nor yet bad courses take:
If all those that seeme so pure,
    would not by false weights sell,
But iustly deale, we might be sure
    that all things should be well.

5 If men would not, to purchase gain,
    falsly themselues forsweare,
Nor take the name of God in vaine,
    but liue in dread and feare:
If all hypocrisie were left,
    which daily doth excell:
If we were not of zeale bereft,
    then all things should be well.

6 If conscience were not ouerstrain'd,
    for to oppresse the weake:
If subtill mates were not maintain'd,
    if none would promise breake:
If spitefull men did not delight,
    in wrangling suites to dwell:
If one kept not anothers wife,
    then all things should be well.

7 If no man would false witnesse bear
    for lucre or for loue:
If no contentious people were
    disquiet for to moue:

If none would hurt the innocent,
    nor yet for money sell
Anothers life, twere time well spent,
    then all things should be well.

8 If bloody murthering would cease,
    which doth for vengeance cry:
If euery man would seeke for peace,
    and liue contentedly:
If drunkennesse and gluttony,
    that doth so much excell:
If none would practise cruelty,
    then all things should be well.

9 If Parents would instruction vse,
    and youth in time correct:
Would youth good counsell not refuse,[1]
    but thereto haue respect:
If seruants were obedient
    to those with whome they dwell,[2]
If they were quicke and diligent,
    then all things should be well.

10 If fornication were not vs'd,
    nor foule adultery:
In euery place were bribes refus'd,
    and partiality:
If no man would his neighbour wrong
    which far or neere him dwell,
Nor stain their credits with his toūg,
    then all things should be well.

11 If scolding queanes were punished,
    did witches hang or burne:
If bawds and whores not suffered,
    some had a blessed turne:

---

[1] *Text* note rfuse.   [2] No comma in the text.

If we did not delight to sit
in sins darke shadow Cell:
If godly wisedome gouernd wit,
then all things should be well.

12 If crafty heads wold once grow scant,
which scrape and claw for gaine,
The poore and needy soules that want
would not so much complaine.
If trust might lye safe in his bed,
if truth might buy and sell,
If double dealing once were dead,
then all things should be well.

13 If cunning Cutpurses and Theeues,
were cleane out of the way,
Then some false knaues that true men grieue
should not remaine this day.
If swearing were once out of vre,
that none of oathes could tell:
If lyes were left, we might be sure,
that all things would be well.

14 If carry-tales, that breed debate,
were hid from Man and Wife:
Then surely each man with his mate,
might lead a quiet life:
If neighbors would like friends agree
and loue among vs dwell:
If pride might once expelled be,
then all things should be well.

15 If Landlords would leaue racking rent,
if vsurie would cease:
If we had not great male-content,
this Land might liue in peace.
If Justice would not swerue at all,
if malice would not swell:
Might high aspiring climbers fall,
then all things should be well.

16 If rash and hasty people would
    to patience giue place:
  If wrath were left, a number would
    not be so void of grace:
  If hatred were abandoned,
    were enuie driuen to Hell:
  If Idlenesse were punished,
    then all things should be well.

17 If deedes of charity were vs'd,[1]
    if poore men were not proud,
  If Officers were not abus'd,
    if dice were not allow'd:
  If Lawyers would not suits prolong,
    but to their Clients tell
  How cases stand, if right or wrong,
    then all things should be well.

18 If flattering pick-thanks were expeld
    out of the Common-wealth:
  If men a moderate dyet held,
    they might liue long in health:
  If hel-bred couetousnesse and pride
    did not amongst vs dwell:
  If rich men were not mercilesse,
    then all things should be well.

19 If poore mens states were pittied,
    which doe in prison lye:
  If sick folke were much comforted,
    in their necessitie:
  If Trades-men did not vse deceit,
    if fraud did not excell:
  Did wicked men practise no sleights,
    then all things should be well.

[1] Text has a period.

20 If these false traitors were found out,
    which would this Realme betray,
Then should all *England* round about,
    stand at a better stay.
That wicked vices may decay,
    and vertue beare the bell,
To God let vs most humbly pray,
    and so we shall doe well.

Finis.

Printed at London for H. Gosson.

32

A passing bell tolling

Wood 276 B (103), B.L., two woodcuts, four columns. The sheet is badly mutilated, five stanzas being, in whole or in part, torn off. Mutilated words and lines are filled in as far as possible between square brackets.

The ballad, doleful as it is, is worth reprinting, for it is a copy, apparently unique, of the ballads called "A passinge bell to call us to minde &c," registered by John Allde on October 30, 1582, and "Harke man what I thi God," registered by Francis Coles and others on December 14, 1624 (Arber's *Transcript*, II, 416; IV, 131). Neither of these entries has hitherto been identified. Wood's copy is probably from the 1624 edition. On the tune see Chappell's *Popular Music*, I, 229; II, 775.

𝔄 passing 𝔅ell towling to call us to mind,
𝔒ur time ebill spending, a plague now we find:
𝔚hich plague if it cease not is for our sin,
𝔗herefore to repent now let us begin.

To the tune of *Triumph and Ioy.*

1 HArk man what I thy God shal speak,
      My Laws thou daily seem'st to break
   What though the flesh of man be weake,
      yet I thy God will love thee:
   Give eare I say to *Ieremie*,
   And learne with him to live and die,
   The Scriptures they doe testifie,
      that I God doe love thee.

2 First I thee fram'd of earth and clay,
   And made all things thee to obey,
   The Sun, the Moone, the Night and day,
      because that I doe love thee:

185

A PASSING BELL TOLLING

I gave thee strength to terrifie
The beasts and foules that multiply,
Yet this will not thee satisfie,
   but thou wilt seeme to move me.

3 I made the[1] King of Sea and Land,
I made each subject to thy hand,
The Heaven, the Ayre, the Earth & Sand,
   because that I did love thee:
I made thee like to Christ my Son,
In hope thy love for to have won,
I charg'd thee Satans wyles to shun,
   yet thou dost daily move me.

4 I gave thee wit, with wisedome rife,
To rule aright while thou hast life,
I gave thee *Evah* to thy wife,
   because that I did love thee:
I placed thee in Paradice[2],
Yet fleshly pride did thee entice,
Thou would not follow my advice,
   but thou didst daily move me.

5 Yet mercy did I take on thee,
My Son I sent to set thee free,[3]
   because that I did love [thee.]
I lent thee earth wherein to joy,
The fruits of all things to imploy,
I fostred thee from all annoy,
   yet daily thou dost move me.

6 Remember man why Christ was borne,
He scourged was and laught to scorne,
To save thee man that was forlorne,
   because that I did love thee:
He taught you how to fast and pray,
That Satan might be driven away,
I meane you belly-gods I say,
   for you doe daily move me.

[1] *I.e.* thee.   [2] *Text* Pardaice.   [3] The printer omitted a line here.

7 Christ fasted forty daies we know,
All fleshly lusts to overthrow,
Though you be weak, your good will show
   so shall I say you love me:
But if you doe not fast and pray,
The wiles of Satan will lead you away,
To desolation for ever and aye,
   where you no more shall move me.

8 There shall you languish still and cry,
Because the truth you doe defie,
For ever living and never die,
   because you doe not love me:
Take heed therefore of *Bacchus* cheare,
Let *Dives* fall put thee in feare,
Else shall you die when I appeare,
   where you no more shall move me.[1]

The second part, To the same tune.

9 REmember if thou Heaven wilt win,
How Sodom I did sinke for sinne
All saving a few that were therein,
   because they still did move me:
I drown'd the world also before,
I promised then to doe no more,
If that your sins you will deplore,
   and turne anew to love me.

10 But if you daily me provoke,
And draw a worse plague to your yoke,
Your sins deserve a greater stroke,
   because you daily move me.
For if that Sodome ever was,
A greater Sodome now doth passe,
All Christian hearts may cry alas,
   if that thou [still doth move me.][2]

[1] Only a few words of the stanza that followed this now remain.
[2] Two entire stanzas are here torn away.

A PASSING BELL TOLLING

11 Thinke on the fall of *Ninivie*
And how the Israelites went awry.
For usurie Jesus did defie
    the Jewes, because they move me:
For in *Iudah* none was righteous found
But now in usury you abound,
My plagues shall beat you to the ground,[1]
    because you doe not love me:

12 Therefore give eare, and marke me well,
The Scriptures they doe plainely tell,
That greedy Carles will burne in hell,
    because they still doe move me:
For banqueting and belly cheare,
Doth make thee man to live in feare,
The poore they pinch, as doth appeare,
    and yet you say you love me.

13 The Scriptures read and understand,
That Christ[2] did sell no lease of Land,
But greedy Satan breakes the band:
    that brotherlie love should move ye:
Thinke well what will become of you,
When you despise my Gospell true.
You passe the Ninivite, Turke and Jew;
    and yet you say you love me.

14 Read over *Ieremy* Once againe,
Then shall you see these vices plaine,
Your Heathenish customes are but vaine
    in which you daily move me.
You cog, you sweare, you foist forth lies,
Against the which my Preachers cries,
Amend, repent, lift up your eyes
    and turne anew to love me.

15 So shall I blot out all thy sin,
If to repent you doe b[egin]...[3]

[1] Text has a period.   [2] *Text* Chist.
[3] Two stanzas and the colophon are here torn away.

33

A statute for swearers

Pepys, I, 214, B.L., two woodcuts, four columns.

The date of this interesting ballad is 1624. By an Act of 3 James I profane or jesting use of the name of the Deity in stage-plays had been prohibited under penalty of a fine of £10. The Act of 21 James I, ch. 20, referred to in the ballad, enacted "by the authority of this present Parliament, That no person or persons shall from henceforth profanely Swear or Curse" under penalty of a fine of 12*d*. (For striking illustrations of the high value set on a shilling by Jacobeans see Nos. 13, 60, 66, 73.) Fines incurred under this Act were to be used for the relief of the poor. The Act provided, further, that if the fine were not paid, the offender was, if over twelve years of age, to be set in the stocks for three hours; if under twelve, to be whipped by the Constable, his Master, or his parents. It was to continue "until the end of the first session of the next Parliament, and no longer." In Ben Jonson's *Masque of Owls* (1624), the Sixth Owl is described as a bird

> Who since the Act against Swearing
> (The tale's worth your hearing)
> In this short time's growth,
> Hath at twelve-pence an oath,
> For that, I take it, is the rate,
> Sworn himself out of his estate.

In 1645 Oliver Cromwell wrote with pride of his regiment of Ironsides: "Not a man swears but he pays his twelve pence." The ballad refers also to the Act for the Repressing of Drunkenness of 21 James I, ch. 8, according to the provisions of which any person proved to have tippled "in any Inne Ale house or Victualling house" was to be fined five shillings.

The tune (used also in No. 70) comes from the refrain of a ballad (beginning "Brave Mars begins to rouse"), the words and music of which are preserved only in John Forbes's *Cantus, Songs and Fancies* (1662, Song XXXVIII). In James Shirley's *Love Tricks*, 1625, II, i, Bubulcus replies to the statement that ballads are "whipping-post, tinkerly stuff": "For all that, I have read good stuff sometimes, especially in your fighting ballads: *When cannons are roaring and bullets are flying, &c.*" This quotation has not hitherto been explained.

A Statute for Swearers and Drunkards,

Or

**Forsake now your follies, your booke cannot saue you,
For if you sweare and be drunke, the Stockes will haue
you.**

To the tune of *When Canons are roaring.*

I Y Ou that in wicked wayes
long time haue ranged;
Now must be with the times;
turned and changed.
The Realmes carefull keepers
such Lawes haue ordained,
By which from your vices base,
you must be weaned.
Let high and low, rich and poore,
striue for to mend all;

A STATUTE FOR SWEARERS

And forbeare for to sweare,
　　curse, drinke, and spend all:
Forsake now your follies,
　　your booke[1] cannot saue you:
For if you sweare and be drunke,
　　the Stockes will haue you.

2　You that doe swim in silkes,
　　　in gold and brauery;
Thinke not, your gawdy clothes
　　can hide your knauery:
You that consume your states,
　　by debosht courses;
Riding the Turnbole Iades,
　　like hackney horses:
Banish your new base trickes,
　　your drinking and drabbing,
Your cursing, your swearing,
　　your roring and stabbing:
Forsake now your follies,
　　your booke cannot saue you:
For if you sweare and be drunke,
　　the Stockes will haue you.

3　You that thinke, he's no man
　　　of reputation,
That cannot sweare and be drunke,
　　and do't in fashion;
You that doe thinke your selues
　　ne're better graced;
Then when 'mongst drunkards you
　　are set and placed:
You that do brag, and say,
　　your braines are stronger,

---

[1] An allusion to "benefit of clergy."

A STATUTE FOR SWEARERS

Then shallow pates, who at pots
cannot hold longer.
Forsake now your follies
your booke cannot saue you:
For if you sweare and be drunke,
the stockes will haue you.

4 You that cry, Kergo, boyes,
hang vp all sorrowe;
Drinke stiffe, our Landlord shall
stay till to morrow:
Then reeling out of dores
into the kennell;
Yet sweare, you sweeter smell
then does the Fennell:
You that lie bathing
from morning till twilight,
In Tauerne and Tipling house,
to cleare the eye-sight.
Forsake now your follies,
your booke cannot saue you:
For if you sweare and be drunke,
the Stockes will haue you.

5 You that will whoot at him,
as at some wonder,
That will not rap out othes
lowd as the Thunder;
You that familiarly
vse in your talking,
Prophanely for to sweare,
sitting or walking:
And you that deeme them not
men of good fashion;
That has not learnt the rules
of Prophanation.
Forsake now your follies,
your booke cannot saue you,
For if you sweare and be drunke,
the Stockes will haue you.

A STATUTE FOR SWEARERS

The second Part. To the same tune.

*Be warned by me you Swearers and Drunkards for
I first broke the Statute.*

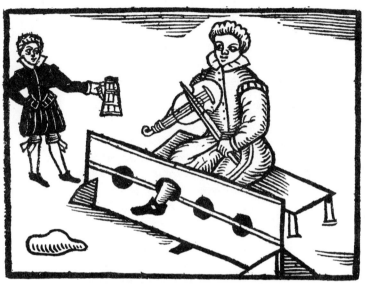

6 YOu that sweale out your life
   in beastly drinking;
Vntill your bodies
   and breaths be stinking:
You that sit sucking still
   at the strong barrell,
Till into tatters rent
   turnes your apparell:
You that by guzling
   transforme your best features,
Changing your selues from men,
   to swinish creatures:
*Forsake now your follies,
   your booke cannot saue you:
For if you sweare and be drunke,
   the stockes will haue you.*

A STATUTE FOR SWEARERS

7 You that doe scorne abroad
    for to be scanting,
You that to your wife at home,
    bread may be wanting.
And your poore children eke
    likely to perish:
Whilst you with Taplash strong
    your corps doe cherish:
Crying still, let them starue,
    tush, 'tis no matter.
With drinke ile stuffe my guts,
    let them drinke water.
Forsake now your follies,
    your booke cannot saue you:
For if you sweare and be drunke,
    the Stockes will haue you.

8 You that at midnight can
    outsweare the watchmen;
And braue a Constable,
    that stands to catch men.
You that with giddie braines
    by the wall holdeth,
And ith' darke euery post
    in his armes foldeth.
And you that in the durt,
    thrust deepe your noses;
There sleeping sweetly as
    in beds of Roses:
Forsake now your follies,
    your booke cannot saue you:
For if you sweare and be drunke,
    the Stockes will haue you.

9 You that in dregs of drinke
    so drowne your reason;
That you are loth to leaue
    in timely season:

A STATUTE FOR SWEARERS

But drinke still following,
  neglect your vocation;
Till you haue nor meanes left,
  nor habitation,
You that will spend as much,
  iust at one sitting;
As would a weeke yours keepe
  with victuals fitting,
Forsake now your follie,
  your booke cannot saue you:
For if you sweare and be drunke,
  the Stockes will haue you.

10 You that desire to dwell
  in heauen hereafter,
Must not of this deuice
  make iest or laughter:
But must shake off these crimes,
  with much discasting,
If you hope to enioy
  life euerlasting.
To honest men let this be
  sound admonition,
To bewaile their past sinnes
  with sad contrition.
Forsake now your follies,
  your booke cannot saue you:
For if you sweare and be drunke,
  the Stockes will haue you.

Printed at London[1] for *J.T.* and are to be sold at his shop
  in Smithfield.

[1] *Text* Londondon.

34

A merry new catch of all trades

Pepys, 1, 164, B.L., two woodcuts, four columns. The fourth line is to be repeated at the end of each stanza as a refrain. Since the ballad was printed by John Trundle it may date about 1624. The tune is given in Chappell's *Popular Music*, 11, 425.

𝔄 merry nebb catch of all 𝔗rades.

To the tune of *The cleane Contrary way.*

1 ALL Trades are not alike in show,
    All Arts doe not agree:
  All Occupations gaines are small,[1]
  As heere they all shall see,
  As heere they all shall see.

2 The Courtier woes, his seruant does,
  Farre more then he can answer,
  The Baker weighes with false essayes,
  The Cuckold's turn'd a Monster. The Cuck. &c.

3 The Taylor sowes, the Smith he blowes,
  The Tinker beates his pan:
  The Pewterer ranke, cries tinke a tanke tanke,
  The Apothecary ranta tan tan. The Apoth: &c.

4 The Bricklayer high doth rise to flye,
  The Plummer oft doth melt,
  The Carpenter doth loue his rule,
  And the Hatmakar loues his felt. And the, &c.

[1] Text has a period.

5 The Weauer thumps, his olde wife mumps,
 The Barber goes snip snap,
 The Butcher prickes, the Tapster nickes,
 The Farmer stops ap ap. The Farmer, &c.

6 The Curryer toyles, and deales in oyles,
 The Cobler liues by his peece:
 The Chamberlaine cheates with musty meates,
 And doth the Countrey fleece. And doth, &c.

7 The Carter whips, the Begger skips,
 The Beadle liues by blowes,
 Yet whores wil be whores at honest mens doores
 Disphight a'th Beadles nose. Dispight a'th, &c.

8 The Broome-man cryes, mayd seruants buyes,
 And swaps with him for wares,
 The Countrey asse doth to the Cosse,
 Sell Orchards full of Peares. Sell, &c.

9 Some Schoole-masters teach beyond their reach,
 The Mason deales with his square,
 The Fletcher doth nock, and workes by the clock,
 The Beareward liues by his Beare. The, &c.

10 The Grosers pates 'bout thinges of weight,
 Is often troubled sore,
 The Taylors yard is seldome marde,
 Tho it measure many a score.
 Tho it measure many a score.

The second part. To the same Tune.

11 THe Iron-monger hardly deales,
 All Fruterers loose by th'rot:
 The Hagler buyes and liues by lyes,
 The Drunkard plyes the pot,
 The Drunkard plyes the pot.

12 The Collier sweares heele loose his eares,
    But he will falsly deale:
    And such are glad as mand the Pad,
    For trifles for to steale. For trifles, &c.

13 The Budget maker oftentimes,
    Doe deale in brasen nayles:
    And Tradesmen store, turne Porters poore,[1]
    When other trading failes. When other, &c.

14 The Water-man will carry *Nan*,
    For two-pence crosse the Riuer:
    Yet this heele say, if she cannot pay,
    Her passage free heele giue her. Her passage, &c.

15 The Glouer pokes, the Gallant smoakes,
    Yet liues in Tradesmen debts,
    The Drawer thriues by honest wiues,
    The Cheater liues by bets. The Cheater, &c.

16 The Cooke doth broyle, the Fencer foyle,
    The footman he doth sweat:
    And Apple-Iohn doth vsher Nan,
    And she giues him a heate. And she, &c.

17 The Ostler rubs, the Cutler scrubs,
    The Semsters deale in Ruffes:
    The smoakie man with his small cole pan,
    Maintained is by puffes. Maintained is, &c.

18 The Chandelors deeds great pennance needs,
    And Faggots they doe beare:
    The Vintner drawes, yet makes no frayes,
    The Begger is voyde of care. The Begger, &.

19 The Morris dance doth brauely prance,
    And about the Countrey goes:
    And May-poles hie shall mount to th' skie,
    Despight of the Hobby horsenose. Despight, &c.

[1] Cf. Parker's ballad on Porters (No. 64).

20   Dissentions feede, the Parators neede,
And Scoulds him money giue:
And if there were no swaggering Whore,
The Pander could not liue. The Pander, &c.

21   Thus all arise by contraries,
Heauen send them crosses ten:
Unlesse they all both great and small,
Doe liue and dye honest men,[1]
Doe liue and dye honest men.

Finis.

Printed at London for *I. Trundle.*

[1] Text has a period.

35

News out of East India

Pepys, 1, 94, B.L., one woodcut (which is reproduced here), four columns.

English colonists founded a small settlement at Cambello in the island of Amboyna, Dutch East Indies, about 1615. It was destroyed by the Dutch in the massacre of February, 1623. Many pamphlets, both in Dutch and English, were written on the massacre; for example, *Waerachtich Verhael Vande Tidinghen ghecomen wt de Oost-Indien, met the Iacht ghenaemt de Haze, in Iunio 1624. in Texel aenghelandt...Ghedruckt int Iaer 1624*, and *A Trve Relation of the Vnivst, Crvell, And Barbarovs Proceedings against the English at Amboyna In the East-Indies, by the Neatherlandish Governor and Covncell there*, 1624 (British Museum, 106. a. 58 and 802. k. 1). From these pamphlets the ballad was summarized, and from them it borrowed its lugubrious woodcut.

A play dealing with the massacre was "ready to be acted" in 1625, but was suppressed by the Privy Council (*Court and Times of James I*, 11, 500; C. H. Firth, Royal Historical Society *Transactions*, Third Series, v, 49). Jacobean playwrights frequently allude to the Amboyna affair; for example, in Fletcher's *Fair Maid of the Inn*, iv, ii, this passage occurs:

> *Forobosco.* Thence to Amboyna i' th' East Indies,
> for pepper to bake it.
> *Clown.* To Amboyna? so I might be pepper'd.

In 1630 (according to H. Lestrange's *Reign of King Charles I*, 1656, p. 117) two English captains who were serving in Germany waylaid with a troop of horse, near Frankfort, "Eighteen *Hollanders* (whereof three had been actours in the *English* Tragedy at *Amboyna*)," hanged seventeen of them, including "*Johnson* the chief of the *Amboinists*," and sent "the odde man home" to tell the story; in 1654 Cromwell extorted £300,000 and a small island from Holland to compensate the descendants of the victims of the massacre; and in 1673 Dryden produced his tragedy of *Amboyna, or the Cruelties of the Dutch to the English Merchants*. See further F. S. Boas, "The Amboyna Outrage," *Times Literary Supplement*, December 14, 1917, p. 614.

On the tune see No. 49.

Nebbes out of East India:
Of the cruell and bloody bsage of our English Merchants
and others at *Amboyna*, by the Netherlandish Gouernour
and Councell there.

To the tune of *Braggendary*.

NEWS OUT OF EAST INDIA

1 FRom *India* Land such newes I haue,
    of death and deadly dole,
As may inforce a deepe remorse,
    to each good Christian soule,[1]
To thinke what English blood was shed,
Upon a small occasion bred.
    Oh heauen looke downe,
    vpon poore innocent soules.

2 Betweene the English and the Dutch,
    hath beene a long debate:
And mischiefes many hath beene wrought,
    against our Merchants state,
Where Merchant-men haue lost their liues,
Their goods, their children, and their wiues:
    Oh heauen looke downe,
    vpon poore innocent soules.

3 A towne there stands *Amboyna* call'd,[1]
    a Castle in the same:
Made rich by these Low-Country States,
    and Merchants of great name:
Who on a time a plot deuiz'd,
To haue our Englishmen surpriz'd.
    Oh heauen looke downe, &c.

4 They gaue out words our Englishmen,
    by secret treason wrought,
The towne and Castle to blow vp,
    and so in question brought,
Our English Merchants dwelling there,
With all that held our Country deare.
    Oh heauen looke downe, &c.

5 Their Gouernor a Councell cal'd,
    and yet no reason why,
That twenty of our Englishmen
    should there their causes try:

[1] Text has a period.

And answer for a thing not done,
Nor any way there thought vpon.
Oh heauen looke downe, &c.

6 To cruell tortures day by day,
      our English thus were brought:
Where strange tormenting instruments
      vpon their bodies wrought:
To make them all confesse and say,
They sought *Amboyna* to betray.
      Oh heauen looke downe, &.

7 The first they laid vpon a Racke,
      with armes and legs abroad,
And spred him, till he did confesse
      and most vntruly show'd,
How that our Englishmen conspir'd,
To haue the town and castle fier'd.
      Oh heauen looke downe,
      vpon poore innocent soules.

𝕿𝖍𝖊 𝖘𝖊𝖈𝖔𝖓𝖉 𝖕𝖆𝖗𝖙, 𝕿𝖔 𝖙𝖍𝖊 𝖘𝖆𝖒𝖊 𝖙𝖚𝖓𝖊.

8 THe second of these wofull men,
      they bound vnto a stake:
And throtle him about the necke,
      till he could hardly speake.
Which cruell torments to auoyd,
Said that the towne should be destroyd.
      Oh heauen looke downe, &c.

9 The third they bound in Iron chaines,
      which griped him so sore,
That all his body round about,
      did gush out bloody gore:
From which to find some ease he sayd,
Amboyna should haue beene betrayd.
      Oh heauen looke downe, &c.

10 They whipt the fourth man at a post,
    vniustly without fault:
And washt his bloody body ore,
    with vineger and salt.
And to the fifth like punishment,
Though to no ill he gaue consent.
    Oh heauen looke downe, &c.

11 With water they stuft vp the sixth,
    vntill his body swel'd:
The seuenth likewise with twisted coard,
    most barbarously compeld,
To say our English friends were those,
That were the townesmens greatest foes.
    Oh heauen looke downe, [*&c.*][1]

12 The eighth[2] with burning pincers pul'd,
    made challenge of the rest:
Though most vntrue, to ease himselfe,
    and so false things confest.
So did the nynth by their pretence,
Bring in most wrongfull euidence.
    Oh heauen looke downe, &c.

13 The tenth they hung vp by the armes
    two foot aboue the ground:
And so with scorching candles burn'd
    his back and body round:
With all the other parts about,
Till drops of fat the lights put out.
    Oh heauen looke downe, &c.

14 The rest of these distressed soules,
    were vsed in like sort:
At which the cruell Gouernor,
    made his tormenting sport.
Till nyneteene of our Englishmen,
Felt more then common tortures then.
    Oh heauen looke downe,
    vpon poore innocent soules.

[1] Text omits.   [2] *Text* eight.

15 Then Captaine *Towerson* came in place,
    to answer with the rest:
To whom was told the treason was
    by those before confest.
Though all as false as God was true,
Yet they affirme, the same he knew.
    Oh heauen looke downe, &c.

16 For which his goods were seized on,
    which all our English had:
And so vnto the Iudgement seat,
    as traitors they were led.
And there vniustly iudg'd to dye,
Which was performed immediately.
    Oh heauen, looke downe, &c.

17 Ten of our men they hang'd forthwith,
    the other ten went free:
Which was a wrongfull Iudgement giuen,
    and full of griefe to see,[1]
That after all those torments past,
They thus should suffer death at last.
    Oh heauen looke downe, &c.

18 But on the execution day,
    as God did so dispose,
A sudden darkenesse and a gust
    of violent winds arose,[1]
Which cast two of their ships away,
As they at road in harbour lay.
    Thus heauen lookes downe, &c.

19 Yea here to make Gods vengeance more,
    the chiefest of that plot,[1]
In this tormenting of our friends,
    as then escaped not,
But felt Gods heauy Iron hand,
And could no way the same withstand,
    Thus Heauen lookes downe &c.

[1] Text has a period.

20 For comming to the graues whereas
   the murthered bodies lay:
He fell starke mad, and would not thence,
   with life depart away.
But dyed most strangely in that place,
Euen as a wretch bereft of grace:
   Thus heauen lookes downe, &c.

21 Thus haue you heard what bloody deeds,
   were late in *India* done:
To make vs all in *England* heere,
   with sorrow to thinke vpon,
What sad misfortune should be hap,
To take our friends in such a trap.
   Yet heauen lookes downe,
   Vpon poore innocent soules.

𝕿𝖍𝖊 𝖓𝖆𝖒𝖊𝖘 𝖔𝖋 𝖙𝖍𝖔𝖘𝖊 executed.	𝕿𝖍𝖊 𝖓𝖆𝖒𝖊𝖘 𝖔𝖋 𝖙𝖍𝖔𝖘𝖊 pardoned.
1 *Captaine Gabriel Towerson.*	1 *Iohn Beomont.*
2 *Samuel Colson Factor.*	2 *Edward Collins.*
3 *Emanuel Tomson Assistant.*	3 *William Webber.*
4 *Timothy Iohnson Assistant.*	4 *Ephraim Ramsey.*
5 *Iohn Wetherall Factor.*	5 *George Sharocke.*
6 *Iohn Clarke Assistant.*	6 *Iohn Sadler.*
7 *William Griggs Factor.*	7 *Iohn Powell.*
8 *Abel Price Chyrurgian.*	8 *Thomas Ladbrooke.*
9 *Robert Browne Taylor.*	9 *A Portingall.*
10 *Iohn Fardo steward of the English house.*	*You may read more of this bloody Tragedy in a booke printed by authority.*[1] 1624.
As also nyne natiue Indians suffered together with them.	

Printed at London for *F. Coules*,
dwelling at the vpper end of the Old-Baily.

[1] Text *authory.*

36

A pleasant new ballad

Pepys, 1, 376, B.L., five woodcuts, four columns. There is a coarse *refacimento* of the ballad in *Westminster Drollery*, Part I, 1671 (ed. J. W. Ebsworth, pp. 44–47), called "The kind Husband, but imperious Wife. The first part of the Tune his, and the latter part her's." It is almost identical with the version called "The Patient Man, and the Scolding Wife" in *Grammatical Drollery*, 1682, pp. 109–110, by W.H. (*i.e.* Captain William Hicks).

Coarse as the language is, there is a boisterous mirth about this jig that must have given it great appeal in the theatre. With good actors and singers in the rôles of Husband and Wife and with emphasis on stage business—which is suggested but not expressed—even to-day the jig would be more comic than are many vaudeville performances. Shrewish wives were often chastened by being forced to light the wrong ends of candles and by "pinning the basket." Those who are interested in the latter procedure may enjoy reading an early Elizabethan ballad by T. Rider, "A merie newe Ballad intituled, the Pinnyng of the Basket" (*A Collection of Seventy-Nine Black-Letter Ballads and Broadsides*, London, 1867, p. 105), one stanza of which runs:

> Her housebande, sore insenste, did sweare
> By stockes and stones,
> She should, or els he would prepare
> To baste her bones,—
> Tantara, tara, tantara;—
> Quoth he, Ile tame your tongue,
> And make you pinne the basket to,
> Doubt not, ere it be long.

The tune of *How shall we, good husband, live* comes from the first line of a ballad (for which no tune is indicated) registered under that title on December 14, 1624 (Arber's *Transcript*, IV, 131; *Roxburghe Ballads*, I, 122). The jig, then, dates about 1625.

A PLEASANT NEW BALLAD

A pleasant new Ballad, both merry and witty,
That sheweth the humours, of the wiues in the City.

To the tune of, *How shall a good Husband.*

Husband.

1 WIfe, prethee come hither & sit thee down by me,
 For I am best pleased when ẙ art most nie me.

Wife.

2 I scorne to sit by such a blockheaded Clowne,
 No thou shalt not touch the worst hem of my Gowne,
 For I could haue had men both proper and good,
 That would haue maintaind me euen as I wood.

Husband.

3 Wife pray you forgiue me if I haue offended,
 Let me know my fault Loue, and all shall be mended.

Wife.

4 Away you base Rascall, get out of my sight,
 Thou shalt not come neere me by day nor by night,
 For dost thou not see it, euen to my disgrace,
 My neighbours exceed me in dressings and Lace.

Husband.

5 If that be the matter wife, let it not moue thee,
 Thou shalt haue as good as they; come kisse & loue
  me.

Wife.

6 I will haue a silke Gowne, a Maske and a Fanne,
 I will neuer walke abroad without my man,
 And he shall be handsome to, with a good face,
 Not such a Clowne as You, me to disgrace.

208

A PLEASANT NEW BALLAD

Husband.

7 Wife I will attend thee if that may suffice,
And lay all things ready against you doe rise,
And then if you please to walke and take the ayre,
Wife I will waite on thee, be it foule or faire.[1]

Wife.

8 Nay, thou art not worthy to carry my Fan,
I will be supplied by a propperer man:
And wee'l haue our Coach and horse to ride at pleasure
And thou shalt run by on foot, and wait our leisure.

Husband.

9 Wife thou shall haue horses and Coach, and a man
To driue for thy pleasure through Cheapside &
Strand,
And I will goe with thee, and always attend thee,
My care shall be such Loue, as none shall offend thee.

Wife.

10 Ile not be attended by any such Foole.
No, thou art not worthy, to empty my close stoole,
For thou hast no complement, Courtship, nor wit,
And therefore not worthy to kisse where I sit.

The second part: To the same tune.

Husband.

11 COme Dame I will tell you, for I cannot hold
No longer, but tell thee that thou art turn'd
Scold,
For I haue borne long with your blockhead and foole,
Not worthy you say, for to empty your stoole.

Wife.

12 Why so I say still, if you mend not your manners,
It were better you liued among *Brewers* or *Tanners*.

[1] Text has a comma.

209

A PLEASANT NEW BALLAD

Husband.

13 Come Huswife Ile teach you to vse your tongue better
Or else I will tye it vp with such a fetter;
Shalt cause you to wish you neuer had vsed it,
With such ill-be-fitting tearmes and so abusing it.

Wife.

14 Why what haue I said now you take in such dudgeon,
Which makes you to grumble so like a Curmudgeon.

Husband.

15 Dame Ile make you know how that I am your head,
And you shall be ready at board, or in bed,
To giue me content, or else be sure of·this,
Both gowne and lace, horse & Coach all you shall
misse.

Wife.

16 Alas Sir, you wrong me, to vse me so ill,
In not giuing way to my humour and will:
For tis for your credit man, all this I craue,
And you are esteemed for my going braue.

Husband.

17 I like no such credit Dame, let them that will,
Retaine it and hold it, twill giue them their fill,
But as for your selfe Wife, Ile cause you to know,
What duty and seruice to me you doe owe.

Wife.

18 I pray you be quiet, if I haue offended,
Forgiue me my fault Loue, and all shall be mended:
And here I doe promise and giue my consent,
To doe whatsoeuer may giue you content.

A PLEASANT NEW BALLAD

Husband.

19 Well, that I will try ere you part from my sight,
Fetch vp all the Candles, and see you doe light
Euery one of them, euen at the wrong ends,
And then pinne the basket, and so we are friends.

Wife.

20 All this am I willing, and more I will doe,
To shew my respect, thus I stoope to your shooe.

Husband.

21 Why that's a good Wench, now come kisse & be
friends
Put out all the Candles Ile make thee amends.

𝕱inis.

Printed at London for *H.G.*

37

Two Welsh lovers

Pepys, I, 270, B.L., four woodcuts, four columns. The last stanza and the colophon are badly mutilated: the gaps have been filled in by guess. There can, however, be no doubt that the torn signature was that of Martin Parker, though the ballad has not before been given in any list of his works. The date is after December 14, 1624, when the ballad of "The Blazing Torch" (*Roxburghe Ballads*, I, 418), for which the tune is named, first appears in the Stationers' Register (Arber's *Transcript*, IV, 131).

Due gwin, so Professor F. N. Robinson, of Harvard, kindly informs me, is the Welsh exclamation *Duw gwyn*, equivalent to "Good Lord" or "Good God." The ballad may be quoted in Fletcher's *Monsieur Thomas*, IV, iv, where Lancelot says: "Oh, *Deu guin!* Can you deny you beat a constable Last night?"[1] There is in the Pepys Collection (I, 451) a ballad written in Welsh—"Byd Y bigail [*i.e.* "Byd y bugail" = "The Shepherd's World"?]...to a daintie new tune...Terfyn R.H. Printed by A.M. for H. G[osson]."

𝕿𝖍𝖊 𝖙𝖜𝖔 𝖂𝖊𝖑𝖘𝖍 𝕷𝖔𝖚𝖊𝖗𝖘,

𝕺𝖗

𝕿𝖍𝖊 𝕭𝖗𝖎𝖙𝖎𝖘𝖍 𝕹𝖞𝖒𝖕𝖍 𝖙𝖍𝖆𝖙 𝖑𝖔𝖓𝖌 𝖜𝖆𝖘 𝖎𝖓 𝖍𝖊𝖗 𝖑𝖎𝖋𝖊,
𝕬 𝖈𝖍𝖆𝖓𝖌𝖎𝖓𝖌 𝕸𝖆𝖎𝖉, 𝖇𝖚𝖙 𝖆 𝖗𝖊𝖈𝖆𝖓𝖙𝖎𝖓𝖌 𝖂𝖎𝖋𝖊.
𝕷𝖊𝖙 𝖊𝖚𝖊𝖗𝖞 𝖒𝖆𝖓 𝖙𝖍𝖆𝖙 𝖜𝖔𝖚𝖑𝖉 𝖜𝖎𝖓 𝖆 𝕸𝖆𝖎𝖉𝖘 𝖋𝖆𝖚𝖔𝖚𝖗,
𝕬𝖙 𝖍𝖔𝖒𝖊 𝖐𝖊𝖊𝖕𝖊 𝖜𝖎𝖙𝖍 𝖍𝖊𝖗, 𝖎𝖋 𝖍𝖊 𝖒𝖊𝖆𝖓𝖊 𝖙𝖔 𝖍𝖆𝖚𝖊 𝖍𝖊𝖗.

To the tune of *the Blazing Torch.*

1   AS late I walkt the Meades along,
      where *Seuerns* streames did glide;
   I heard a mournfull Shepherds tong,
      and him at last espide.

[1] The date of *Monsieur Thomas* is uncertain. It was first printed in 1639. The appearance of *Due gwin* here may indicate merely that that phrase was in Elizabethan slang use.

He wrung his hands and wept apace,
   to mourne he did not lin:
Riuers of teares ran downe his face,
   and still he cride Due gwin.

2 I drew me neere vnto the Swaine,
   and prayd him tell the cause,
Why he so sadly did complaine,
   he silent made a pause.
At length he raisd himselfe to speake,
   yet e're he could begin;
He sigh'd as if his heart would breake,
   and cryde alas Due gwin.

3 Quoth he, Among yon Brittish hills,
   where *Zephirus* doth breathe:
Where flowers sweet the Meadows fills,
   and valleys vnderneathe,
And neere vnto that fountaine head,
   where *Dee* comes flowing in:
Ah me, that fatall Nymph was bred,
   for whom I cryde Due gwin.

4 I loued her once, but now I rue,
   that I was such an Asse:
For she did proue the most vntrue,
   that euer woman was.
Faire was her face, great was her fame,
   had she still constant bin:
But, Oh, her heart was not the same:
   which makes me cry Due gwin.

5 Once had I power, till her command
   forbad that power to rise,
Further then touching of her hand,
   or looking on her eyes.
I feard to contradict her will,
   as though it were a sinne:
Yet she rewards my good with ill,
   which makes me cry Due gwin.

6 I thought I had her free consent,
    but it prou'd quite contrarie:
  For while I on a iourney went,
    another she did marrie.
  Cause I was absent for a space,
    and thought no hurt therein:
  Another did possesse my place,
    which made me cry Due gwin.

7 When I returned home againe,
    I thought with her to wed:
  But there I found my labour vaine,
    for she before was sped.
  Which when I saw, I sigh'd and sobd,
    and made a pitious din:
  Wishing him hang'd that had me robd,
    and made me cry Due gwin.

8 It seemes by this, 'tis hard to finde
    a woman true in heart:
  Beleeue them not, though they seeme kind,
    they can deceiue by art.
  We men may woe and vse the meanes,
    at vs they laugh and grin:
  Thus we are crost by faithlesse queanes,
    which makes vs cry Due gwin.

The second Part. To the same tune. With the Nymphs Recantation.

9 NOw when the Nymph did see yᵉ swain
    was safe returned at last:
  Most petuously she did complaine,
    to thinke of what was past.
  The sting of conscience did her pricke,
    calling to minde her sinne:
  Immediatly she fell sore sicke,
    and cryde alas Due gwin.

10 No comfort could she take at all,
      to cure her inward smart:
  She thought it bootlesse to recall
      the folly of her heart.
  It might haue greeu'd a man to see,
      the case that she was in:
  My fond mistrust of him, quoth she,
      thus makes me cry Due gwin.

11 Oh had I neuer seene mans face,
      since my deere shepheard went:
  Then had I neuer knowne disgrace,
      but liu'd still continent.
  Or if within some sacred cell,
      I had included bin:
  I had remained constant still,
      but now I cry Due gwin.

12 Thus hauing wept for her offence,
      she sent vnto her swaine:
  Desiring that without offence,
      she might his sight obtaine.
  At her request he went apace,
      her husband not within:
  As soone as e're she saw his face,
      she wept and cryde Due gwin.

13 What speeches past betweene these twaine
      were needlesse here to tell:
  The Nymph imbrac'd and kist her Swain,
      and all was wondrous well.
  He needs no elegance of phrase,
      her fauour now to win,
  Her griefe was turn'd to fond loue plaies,
      she cryde no more Due gwin.

14 Deare loue, quoth she, what's done & past,
      I cannot now recant:
  Yet what I haue, while life doth last,
      my shepheard shall not want.

What though my husbands forehead ake,
 I weigh it not a pin:
Yet if by chance he should vs take,
 we both must cry Due gwin.

15 Thus were the louers perfect friends,
 the Nymph, as best became her,
Did make her shepheard such amend,[1]
 he knew not how to blame her.
Yet let all young men keepe [at home]
 if they their loues w[ould win,]
If they be lost while [they are gone,]
 then they may cry [Due gwin.]

𝕱𝕴𝕹[𝕴𝕾]

By Martin [Parker].

London Printed for *Ioh[n Wright* and are]
to be sold at his shop [near the Hospi]tall
gate in S[mithfield.]

[1] *Read* amends.

216

38

News good and new

Pepys, 1, 210, B.L., four woodcuts, four columns.

The date of the ballad is not later than 1625. This is a jig without a dramatic plot. There are only two characters, but the lines afford ample opportunity for humorous action, and in the mouths of clever actors and dancers can easily have furnished a comic and enjoyable entertainment. I can find no trace of the tune.

𝕹𝖊𝖜𝖊𝖘 𝖌𝖔𝖔𝖉 𝖆𝖓𝖉 𝖓𝖊𝖜𝖜 𝕿𝖔𝖔 𝖌𝖔𝖔𝖉 𝖙𝖔 𝖇𝖊 𝖙𝖗𝖚𝖊.

To the tune of *Twenty pound a yeere*.

1 *Iohn* NOw welcome neighbour *Rowland*,
　　　　　　From London welcome home,
　　What newes is there I pray you?
　　　　From thence I heare you come.
　　Row. The best that ere you heard,
　　　　Youle say't when I you shew.
　　Iohn. I hardly can beleeue it,
　　　　Tis too good to be true.

2 *Row.* The Lawyer in his pleading
　　　　to gaine giues no respect,
　　Though Clients haue no mony,
　　　　he doth not them neglect:
　　But truly pleades their cause,
　　　　of these there be not few.
　　Iohn. I neuer will beleeue it,
　　　　Tis too good to be true.

NEWS GOOD AND NEW

3   In[1] Lords there's no ambition,
    in Ladies theres no pride,
The Clergie loues no monie,
    no woman's wanton-eyde,
Each one that wicked liu'd,
    doth striue to liue anew.
Iohn. I neuer will beleeue it,
    Tis too good to be true.

4   *Row.* I there did know an Usurer,
    ith hundred tooke threescore:
But he is now repented,
    and gaue all to the poore,
And daily fasts and prayes,
    and hates that damned Crew.[2]
Iohn. I neuer will beleeue it,
    Tis too good to be true.

5   *Row.* Your Tradesmen hate short measures
    false lights, and falser waights:
Nor will they in their bargaines,
    vse oathes as cunning baites,
To fetch the simple ore,
    theres no such cunning Iew.
Iohn. I neuer will beleeue it,
    Tis too good to be true.

6   *Row.* No Vintner there doth mingle,
    his wine with water pure:
And then doth sweare tis neatest:
    in London's no such Brewer.
Of that they all are cleare,
    they can, but will not brew.
Iohn. I neuer will beleeue it.
    Tis too good to be true.

---

[1] Supply *Row.*   [2] Text has a comma.

7 *Row.* No Ostler there will rob you,
    of either oates or hay:
No Tapster nickes the pot there,
    but fils it as he may:
No hoast will there be drunke,
    no hostesse proues vntrue.
Iohn. I neuer will beleeue it,
    Tis too good to be true.

8 *Row.* Your Brokers there are honest
    and are not ranckt with knaues,
They lend their coine for conscience,
    which makes them ore their graues
To haue their good deeds writ,
    whose number is but few.
Iohn. I neuer will beleeue it,
    Tis too good to be true.

The Second Part.

9 *Row.* A Sergeant late turn'd honest,
    and not abus'd his place:
A Baily became pitifull,
    and wail'd his prisoners case:
And both to goodnesse fram'd
    their former course anew.
Iohn. I neuer will beleeue this,
    Tis too good to be true.

10 *Row.* The Landlords there are pitiful
    and racke not poore mens rents,
The tenant there is dutifull,
    and payes what he indents.
The rich the poore doe loue:
    of these there are but few.
Iohn. I neuer will beleeue this,
    Tis too good to be true.

11 *Row.* Iailors are tender hearted,
  that doe their prisons keepe:
To thinke on poore mens miseries,
  their yron hearts doe weepe:
The poore men they relieue,
  and giue the rich their due.
Iohn. I neuer will beleeue this,
  tis too good to be true.

12 *Ro.* You there shall see no drunkards,
  in walking through the street:
The stockes stand euer emptie,
  all's sober that you meet.
He's hated that's but seene,
  amidst a drunken crew.
Iohn. I neuer will beleeue this,
  Tis too good to be true.

13 *Row.* Picthatch, and garden Allies,
  Turnebull, and Mutton lane,
Of truth are now turn'd honest,
  and hate vnlawfull gaine.
Bridewell did them conuert,
  and clad their backes in blew.[1]
Iohn. I neuer will beleeue this,
  tis too good to be true.

14 *Row.* Fleetstreet has[2] nere a cheater,
  White-fryers ne're a whore:
Tiburne is now deliuered,
  and beareth theeues no more.
And Smithfield now is rid,
  of those horse-cheating crew.
Iohn. I neuer will beleeue this,
  tis too good to be true.

[1] Cf. No. 6, above.   [2] *Text* ha's.

15 *Row*. Ludgate has[1] nere a bankrupt
    that can, but will not pay:
The Counter nere a Prodigall,
    that turnes the night to day,
By vile disordered life,
    which age doth after rue.
Iohn. I neuer will beleeue this,
    tis too good to be true.

16 This newes doth much amaze me,
    the which you haue me told,
And truely to beleeue it,
    I dare not be too bold.
I would that true it were,
    as it to me is new.
But I will not beleeue it,
    tis too good to be true.

Printed for I. Trundle.

[1] *Text* ha's.

39

The cries of the dead

Pepys, I, 116, B.L., three woodcuts, four columns.

Richard Price, weaver, was a genuine monster if our ballad can be trusted —such a monster that only Dickens, perhaps, could have painted him in true colours. The ballad is decidedly unpleasant but has some sociological value. If it had a large contemporary circulation, Price may well have found a partizan jury and a hostile audience when he appeared for trial. Unhappily official documents, like those printed in Jeaffreson's *Middlesex County Records*, prove that barbarous treatment of apprentices was only too common. For example (*op. cit.*, III, 239), on October 8, 1655, Mathew Nicholas was discharged from his apprenticeship to an Uxbridge toolmaker, William Lovejoy, because it was proved that Lovejoy had grossly mistreated the boy, "tyinge and fetteringe him to the shoppe, and that the said master his wife and mother did most cruelly and inhumanely beate his said apprentice, and also whip'd him until he was very blooddy and his flesh rawe over a great part of his body, and then salted him, and held him naked to the fyre, beinge soe salted to add to his paine."

"Ned Smith," a ballad, was entered at Stationers' Hall for transfer on December 14, 1624 (Arber's *Transcript*, IV, 131; *Roxburghe Ballads*, II, 465). It is to be sung to the oft-mentioned tune of *Dainty, come thou to me* (cf. Chappell's *Popular Music*, II, 517). The date of the present ballad is perhaps about 1625.

The cryes of the Dead.

Or the late Murther in South=warke, committed by one Richard Price Weauer, who most vnhumaynly tormented to death a boy of thirteene yeares old, with two others before, which he brought to vntimely ends, for which he lyeth now imprissoned in the White= Lyon[1], till the time of his triall.

To the tune of *Ned Smith*.

1 MEe thinkes I heare a grone,
   of death and deadly dole,
Assending from the graue
   of a poore silly soule:
Of a poore silly soule,
   vntimely made away,
Come then and sing with me,
   sobbs of sad welladay.

[1] The common prison of Surrey.

THE CRIES OF THE DEAD

2 One *Price*, in South-warke dwelt
    a Weauer by his trayde,
But a more graceles man
    I thinke was neuer made:
All his life wicked was,
    and his minde bent to blood,
Nothing but cruelty
    did his heart any good.

3 Many poore Prentisses
    to himselfe did he bind,
Sweete gentle children all
    of a most willing mind:
Seruing him carefully
    in this his weauing Art,
Whome he requited still,
    with a most cruel heart.

4 Lawfull corrections, he
    from his mind cast aside,
Beating them cruelly
    for no cause, tel they dyed:
Spurning and kicking them,
    as if dogs they had beene,
Careles in cruelty,
    was this wretch euer seene.

5 Neuer went they without
    brused and broken eyes,
Head and face blacke and blew,
    such was their miseries:
What so came next his hand,
    tongs or forke from the fier
Would he still lay on them,
    in his madd moody ire.

6 Parents come bend your eares,
    listen what followed on,

Masters come shed your teares,
   mothers come make your moane,
Seruants with sad laments,
   rue the calamity,
Those gentle children had;
   liuing in missery.

7 The first a pretty boy,
   had with a suddaine spurne,
One of his eares strooke off,
   woefully rent and torne:
Where vnder surgeons hands,
   he liued long in woe,
By this same grieuous wound,
   this vilaine gaue him so.

8 Most heauy was his hand,
   and his heart full of strif,
Ungodly all the dayes
   of this his passed life,
Who so perswading him
   to patient Charity,
Was still abussed much,
   by this wretch wilfully.

9 Witness this harmles child,
   that he misused sore,
Scourging him day by day,
   not knowing cause wherefore,
Unlawfull gouernment
   brings him vnto his end,
From such like cruelty
   all seruants God defend.

The second part. To the same tune.

10 THis his deeds was not known
   which he kept secretly
Nor to light, many a day
   came this vile villany

Till that his heart did thirst,
    more humain blood to shed,
VVhich in the same full sone
    crewell conditions bred.

11 No sparke of gentlenes,
    but flames of cruelty,
Burned within his brest
    mischiefes blacke treasury,
So that to further ills,
    and to more bloody deeds
VVanting grace, wilfully
    to the same he proceeds.

12 A poore mans child he had
    whome he beat backe and syde
Continuing it day and hower
    till this poore prentis dyed,
For which he was arraigned
    and by Law had beene cast,
But mercy quitted him
    for those offences past.

13 Yet those faire warnings here
    wrought in him little good,
But rather drew him on
    For to shed further blood:
And being blinded thus
    with a persewing ill,
Another poore harmles child
    he did by beating kill.

14 Harmelesse indeed was he,
    and a poore neighbours sonne
Whom he did beat and bruze
    ere since this frost begun:
Onely because that hee
    could not worke in the cold
Nor performe such a taske
    as he by custome should.

15 Wherefore this cruell wretch,
        whipt him from top to toe,
    With a coard full of knotts,
        of leather yet to show,
    Wherby his tender limbes,
        from his foote to the head,
    Are with wounds blacke & blew,
        couered ore all and spred.

16 Oh cursed cruelties,
        this did not him suffice,
    But kept him lokt vp closse,
        from sight of neighbors eyes,
    And from his parents deare,
        when they came him to see,
    Little misdouting this,
        their sonnes extremetye.

17 Thus weary woefull dayes,
        did this poore child abide,
    Where he lay languishing,
        till the hower that he dyed,
    Where his poore mangled corpes,
        By neighbors there was found,
    bruzed and beaten sore,
        with many a deadly wound.

18 His braines ny broaken forth,
        and his neck burst in twaine,
    On his Limbs ouer all,
        spotts of blood did remaine.
    And the rim of his wombe,
        spurned in peeces is,
    Neuer such Marterdome,
        of a poore child like this.[1]

[1] Text has a comma.

THE CRIES OF THE DEAD

19 (Oh *Price,*) deare is the price
    for this blood thou must pay,
Life for life, bloud for bloud,
    on thy domes dying day,
Pray thou for mercy there,
    to saue thy sinfull soule,
For me thinks I doe heare,
    thy pasing Bell doth toule.

Finis.

Printed at London for T.L.

40

A proverb old, yet ne'er forgot

Pepys, I, 386, B.L., three woodcuts, four columns. This is an admirably printed and illustrated sheet, of which Francis Grove could justly have been proud.

A number of other ballads by Martin Parker are written on proverbs—"Faint heart never won fair lady," "The proof of the pudding is all in the eating," and the like. "Strike while the iron is hot" is a proverb that occurs in Chaucer's *Melibeus* (line 70) and his *Troilus and Criseyde* (II, 1275), in John Heywood's *Proverbs* (*Works*, 1562, ed. J. S. Farmer, pp. 8, 221), in 3 *Henry VI*, v, i, 49, in Webster's *Northward Ho*, II, ii, and in many other places. Here Parker advises young men to marry widows, though in "The Wiving Age" (No. 41) he scoffs at this practice.

The tune is given in Chappell's *Popular Music*, I, 143.

𝕬 𝖕𝖗𝖔𝖚𝖊𝖗𝖇𝖊 𝖔𝖑𝖉, 𝖞𝖊𝖙 𝖓𝖊𝖗𝖊 𝖋𝖔𝖗𝖌𝖔𝖙,
𝕿𝖎𝖘 𝖌𝖔𝖔𝖉 𝖙𝖔 𝖘𝖙𝖗𝖎𝖐𝖊 𝖜𝖍𝖎𝖑𝖊 𝖙𝖍𝖊 𝕴𝖗𝖔𝖓𝖘 𝖍𝖔𝖙𝖙.

𝕺𝖗,

𝕮𝖔𝖚𝖓𝖘𝖊𝖑𝖑 𝖙𝖔 𝖆𝖑𝖑 𝖄𝖔𝖚𝖓𝖌 𝖒𝖊𝖓 𝖙𝖍𝖆𝖙 𝖆𝖗𝖊 𝖕𝖔𝖔𝖗𝖊,
𝕿𝖔 𝕸𝖆𝖗𝖗𝖞 𝖜𝖎𝖙𝖍 𝖂𝖎𝖉𝖔𝖜𝖊𝖘 𝖓𝖔𝖜 𝖜𝖍𝖎𝖑𝖊 𝖙𝖍𝖊𝖗𝖊 𝖎𝖘 𝖘𝖙𝖔𝖗𝖊.

To the Tune of, *Dulcina*.

1 ALl you Young-men who would Marry,
   and enioy your hearts content,
In your mindes this Counsell carry,
   then you shall no whitt repent:
     now is the time
     that Men may clime
Unto promotion by good lot,
     this Prouerbe old
     hath oft bene told,
Tis good to strike while the Iron's hott.

229

2 Wealthy Widowes now are plenty,
    where you come in any place,
For one Man thers Women twenty,
    this time lasts but for a space:
        She[1] will be wrought,
        though it be for nought,
But wealth which their first Husband got,
    let Young-men poore
    make hast therefore,
Tis good to strike while the Irons hott.[2]

3 Now is the Wooing time or neuer,
    Widowes now will loue Young-men,
Death them from their Mates did seuer,
    now they long to match agen,
        they will not stand
        for House or Land,
Although thou be'st not worth a groat,
    set foorth thy selfe,
    thou shalt haue Pelfe,
If thou wilt strike while the Irons hott.

4 Doe not dote on Maydens features,
    Widowes are the only ware,
It is many Young-mens natures
    to loue Maydens young and fayre,
        tis *Cupids* wile
        thus to beguile
Young Louers, therefore trust him not,
    get one with Gold,
    though nere so old,
Tis good to strike while the Irons hott.

5 Lads and Lasses often marry,
    ritch in nothing but in Loue,

---

[1] *Read* They.   [2] Text has a comma.

Want of meanes will make them vary,
  as we often times doe prooue,
    how ere they fare,
    they must take care
To kepe their Children when they are got:
    of this take hede,
    and learne with speed
To strike the Iron while tis hott.

6 Let not such a time oreslip thee,
    rayse thy fortunes while thou mayst,
Maydens can but coll and clip thee,
  so will Widowes when they tast
    a Young mans loue,
    most kind theyle prooue,
The youngest best that can be got,
    sith this is so,
    then be not slow,
But strike the Iron while tis hott.

The second Part, to the same Tune.

7 ALl waies take this for a maxime,
    that old Widowes loue young men,
Oh then doe not spare for asking,
  though she's old, shele toot agen:
    she scornes to take
    for Ritches sake.
Thy Money she regardeth not,
    with loue her winne,
    together ioyne,
And strike the Iron while tis hott.

8 Some perhaps may make obiection
    that Old-women ielous are,
Let not that change thy affection,
    though they be doe thou not care
    if thou be true,
    and give her due,

Shele nere mistrust thee feare it not,
 shele loue thee deere,
 then doe not feare,
But strike the Iron while tis hott.

9 Maydens loues are coy and fickle,
 they too much their equalls looke,
If of wealth thou hast but little,
 fye away you[1] are mistooke,
  replyeth she,
  come not to me:
Then art thou daunted soone God wot,
  then woe an old,
  feare not, be bold,
And strike the Iron while tis hott.

10 And besides thers many Lasses,
 dares not marry when they list,
Cause her Portion ere she passes
 must come from her Fathers fist:
  but still you see
  a Widowes free,
For friend or foe she careth not,
  then who would misse
  such time as this,
Tis good to strike while the Irons hott.

11 Many Matches haue bene broken,
 though both Parties were content,
When the Maides good-will is gotten,
 then her Friends will not consent:
  would it not vexe
  a Man, to fixe
His mind on whats an others lot?
  then he thats poore
  to mend his store,
Must strike the Iron while tis hott.

[1] *Text* your.

12 If a poore Young-man be matched
  with a Widdow stord with gold,
And thereby be much inritched,
  though hes young and she is old,
   twill be no shame
   vnto his Name,
If he haue what his Friends haue not,
  but every Friend
  will him commend
For striking the Iron while twas hott.

13 Young-men all who heare[1] this Ditty,
  in your memories kepe it well,
Chiefely you in *London* City,
  where so many Widowes dwell,
   the Season now
   doth well alow
Your practise, therefore loose it not,
  fall toot apace,
  while you haue space,
And strike the Iron while tis hott.

Finis.

Martin Parker.

Printed at London for Francis Groue, and
are to be sold at his Shop on Snow-Hill.

[1] *Text* hreae.

41

The wiving age

Pepys, 1, 384, B.L., four woodcuts, four columns.

The ballad dates at least as early as 1625, as appears from the fact that the ballad next following (No. 42), which is an answer to it, came from the press of John Trundle. Perhaps another limit to the date is to be inferred from the fact that "The siluer Age, or, The VVorld turned backward. To a pleasant new Court tune" (Pepys, 1, 154), which is apparently the first of the popular "Age" ballads, was licensed on November 16, 1621 (Arber's *Transcript*, IV, 61). On that same day "the brasen age" (now lost) was registered by Henry Gosson, and it may have been followed by an "Iron Age," since a ballad of that title is mentioned in Fletcher's *Coxcomb*, II, ii. Possibly the popularity of Thomas Heywood's dramas on the various ages had something to do with suggesting these ballads, though the subject-matter of the dramas and the ballads is widely different.

Parker delighted in writing satirical ballads of this nature. Here he ridicules the marriage of young men with widows, while in "A Proverb Old" (No. 40) he strongly urges the wisdom of such a procedure. By following this method consistently, Parker hoped to placate and amuse every class of his hearers: those whom he attacked in one ballad could be sure that in another he would soon defend them or satirize their rivals.

The tune comes from a ballad in the Pepys Collection, 1, 152, called "The Golden Age; or, An Age of plaine-dealing. To a pleasant new Court tune: Or, *Whoope, doe me no harme, good man*." To the latter tune, which is given in Chappell's *Popular Music*, 1, 208, *The Golden Age* is, of course, equivalent.

THE WIVING AGE

The wiuing age.

Or

A great Complaint of the Maidens of London,
Who now for lacke of good Husbands are vndone,
For now many Widowes though neuer so old,
Are caught vp by young men for lucre of gold.

To the tune of *the Golden age.*

1 THe Maidens of *London* are now in despaire,
   How they shall get husbands, it is all their care,
Though maidens be neuer so vertuous and faire,
Yet old wealthy widowes, are yong mens chiefe ware.
    Oh this is a wiuing age.
    Oh this is a wiuing age.

2 A yong man need neuer take thought how to wiue,
For widowes and maidens for husbands doe striue,
Heres scant men enough for them all left aliue,
They flocke to the Church, like Bees to the Hiue.
    Oh this is a wiuing age,
    Oh this is a wiuing age.

3 Twixt widowes and maids there is a great strife,
And either of them would faine be a wife,
They all doe cry out on this fond single life,
And long to dance after a Taber and Fife.
    Oh this is a wiuing age.
    Oh this is a wiuing age.

4 The maidens I doubt will be put to the worst,
And widowes though old, will be maried all first,
To drinke the bride Posset good Lord how they thirst,
Though they haue foule faces the're beautifull purst.
    Oh this is a wiuing age.
    Oh this is a wiuing age.

5 Most Widowes are impudent, they cannot blush,
  For speech of the people they care not a rush:
  They are very free and their money is flush,
  They will haue a young-man their aprons to brush.[1]
         Oh this is a wiuing age.
         Oh this is a wiuing age.[2]

6 Yong maidens are bashfull, but widowes are bold,
  They tempt poore yong men with their siluer and gold,
  For loue now a daies for money is sold,
  If she be worth treasure no matter how old.
         Oh this is a wiuing age.
         Oh this is a wiuing age.

7 For one maid now maried theres widowes a score,
  Their husbands scant dead a whole fortnight[3] before,
  They cannot liue single they'le mary therefore,
  With any yong man though hees neuer so poore.
         Oh this is a wiuing age.
         Oh this is a wiuing age.

8 Oh is not this a pitifull case,
  That many a delicate beautifull lasse,
  Should thus by old widowes be put to disgrace,
  For euery yong lad has his widow in chase.
         Oh this is a wiuing age.
         Oh this is a wiuing age.

The second part, to the same tune.

9 LEt Maidens be patient, and neuer take thought,
    But stay vntill all the old widowes be caught,
  For now like to horses for coyne they are bought.
  They say that in *Smithfield* they'r cry'd twelue a groat.
         Oh this is a wiuing age.
         Oh this is a wiuing age.

[1] No period in the text.   [2] Text has a comma.
[3] *Text* fornight.

10 Yet some of these widowes that marry so fast,
   I doubt will haue cause to repent of their haste:
   If they marry yong men their shoulders to bast,
   Oh then they will whine when the remedy is past,
       And curse such a wiuing age.
       And curse, &c.

11 Likewise many yongmen perhaps may repent,
   When all the old Angels are wasted and spent,
   Theyle wish the tongue out, that gaue first consent,
   Theyle say then I muse what a deuill I meant
       To match in that wiuing age.
       To match in that wiuing age.

12 A young man that marries a widow for wealth,
   Does euen much dammage vnto his soules health,
   For he will be toying and playing by stealth,
   Shee's iealous though neuer so iustly he dealth.
       Take heed of this wiuing age.
       Take heed, &c.

13 When young Lads and Lasses as them doth behoue,
   Doe lawfully marry together in loue,
   God poures downe his blessings on them from aboue,
   But youth and old dotage contrary doe proue,
       As tis in this wiuing age.
       As tis, &c.

14 It may be accounted a wonder to see
   An old crasse croane with a young man agree:
   Tis onely for wealth that they married be,
   Then take them who list, a young maid is for me.
       Oh this is a wiuing age,
       Oh this is a wiuing age.

15 Then let no yong maidens be displeased in minde,
   Though widowes are maried, and they left behinde:
   Those yong men who are thus contrary to kinde,
   You were better lose, then euer to finde,
       Leaue them to this wiuing age.
       Leaue them, &c.

16 Yet must I confesse many widowes there be
    Who from all libidinous thoughts are so free,
    They wed not for lust, but for loue as we see,
    Finde me such a one, and Ile quickly agree,
            To match in this wiuing age.
            To match in this wiuing age.

17 Of all sorts and sexes theres some good some bad,
    Theres choyce of both widowes and maids to be had;
    He that happens well hath cause to be glad,
    And therefore let euery honest young Lad
            Make choyce in this wiuing age,
            Make choyce, &c.

18 My song vnto Virgins is chiefly directed,
    Who now in this age are little respected,
    Though widowes be chosen and maids be reiected,
    They will be esteemed, though now they'r neglected,
            Yet not in this wiuing age,
            Yet not in this wiuing age.

Finis.   *M.P.*

Printed for Francis Coules at the vpper end of the
old Baily neere Newgate.

42

The cunning age

Pepys, I, 412, B.L., four woodcuts, four columns.

As John Trundle printed this ballad, it cannot have appeared later than 1626. Perhaps, as is pointed out in the introduction to the ballad immediately preceding, it as well as No. 41 was printed a year or two earlier. It was registered at Stationers' Hall by John Wright and his five partners on June 1, 1629, under the title of "The Conning cosening age" (Arber's *Transcript*, IV, 213).

The song was written as a direct answer to Martin Parker's "Wiving Age" (No. 41). The author, John Cart, represents an irate widow as bitterly denying the truth of Parker's attack on her sisterhood, as scoffing at the thought of remarrying, and as anxious to get her clutches on Parker. J. C., probably Cart, was the author of "A Lesson for all True Christians" (*Roxburghe Ballads*, VII, 814); a later ballad entitled "A Warning for Swearers" (*ibid.* VIII, 76), though signed J. C., can hardly have been his work.

The tune is equivalent to *Whoop, do me no harm, good man* (cf. No. 41).

The cunning Age.

Or

A re-married Woman repenting her Marriage, Rehearsing her Husbands dishonest carriage.

Being a pleasant Dialogue between a re-married Woman, a Widdow, and a young Wife.

To the Tune of *The Wiuing Age*.

Widdow.

1 GOod morrow, kind Gossip, why whither so fast?
     I pray stay a while, I know ther's no haste,
   And let's chat a while of some things that are past;
   I heare say y' are married since I saw you last;
        O this is a hasty Age,
        O this is a hasty Age.

239

Mar. Woman.

2 'Tis true, I am marry'd, which hath beene my bane,
But if that I were now a Widdow againe,
I so would continue; but griefe is in vaine,
I must be contented to sing this sad straine,
> *Oh fie on this coozening Age,*
> *Oh fie on this &c.*

Wid.

3 Oh, doe you so quickly your bargaine repent,
And yet you thought long e're about it you went?
If marriage bring trouble, in time Ile preuent
All future vnquietnesse, and be content
> *To shun such a coozening Age,*
> *To shun &c.*

Mar. Wo.

4 Oh, woe is me, Gossip, that e're I was borne,
I marry'd a Boy, that now holds me in scorne,
He comes among Whoores both euening and morne,
While I sit at home, like a creature forlorne.
> *Oh, this is a coozening Age,*
> *Oh, &c.*

Wid.

5 Oh, who would imagine that such a young Lad,
That scarce was worth twelue pence with al that he had,
Should wed a rich woman, and vse her so bad?
I trust I shall neuer be so doting mad,
> *To match in this coozening Age, &c.*

Mar. Wo.

6 The griefe that I suffer can hardly be told,
Among Whores and Knaues he consumeth my gold,
And if I reprooue him, he tels me I scold,
I dare not dispose of mine owne as I would.
> *Oh fie on this doting Age,*
> *Oh fie on this doting Age.*

Wid.

7 Well, by your example I warning will take,
With no Skip-iacke boy a match I will make;
Two Sutors I haue, but I both will forsake,
For some that are fond, as they brew let them bake;
  I'le take heed of this cunning Age,
  I'le take heed of this cunning Age.

Mar. Wo.

8 Well, doe so, good Gossip; and[1] so Fare you well,
My goodly new husband will curse me to hell:
Old *Iohn*, (God be with him) my neighbours can tell,
Did neuer in 's life giue me mouthfull of ill.
  Oh fie on this doting Age,
  Oh fie on this doting Age.

Wid.

9 There is an old Prouerbe, that oft hath bin try'd,
Set a Beggar on horse-back, to th' Gallowes heel ride;
So, wed a young Boy, hee's so puft vp with pride,
They'l marry rich Widdowes, to scoffe and deride.
  Oh this is a coozening Age,
  O this is a coozening Age.

𝔉inis.

      John Cart.

𝕿𝖍𝖊 𝕾𝖊𝖈𝖔𝖓𝖉 𝕻𝖆𝖗𝖙. 𝕿𝖔 𝖙𝖍𝖊 𝖘𝖆𝖒𝖊 𝕿𝖚𝖓𝖊.

Married Woman.

10 BUt stay, who comes yonder? 'tis well y[t] I tarry'd:
My kinswoman *Katherin*, she lately was mary'd,
Shee had better gone to the Church to be bury'd,
With her now, I doubt, things are otherwise carryd,
  She curseth this coozening Age,
  She curseth this coozening Age.

Young Wife.

11 What Cousin and neighbour, are you met together?
'Tis well that I hapned so luckily hither,

    [1] *Text* aod.

I long haue desired to talke with you either;
Come, stand not i'th street, let's go trauel somwhither.[1]
  Oh fie on this coozening Age,
  Oh fie on this &c.
Both to the young Wife.

12 Well, how dost thou like of thy Husband, good *Kate?*
We heare of a certaine th' art marry'd of late
With a wealthy old widdower, to better thy state,
Who loues thee as deare as the Turtle his mate:
  That's rare in this coozening Age,
  That's rare &c.

Yong Wife.

13 Oh woe is me, Cousin, that euer 'twas done,
A beggarly slaue my affection hath wonne;
He brag'd of his riches, whereof he had none,
But fiue little Children, foure Girles, and a Sonne,
  Oh fie on this coozening[2] Age,
  Oh fie on this &c.

14 VVhen he came a wooing, he borrow'd a Cloake,
And Rings to his fingers, my loue to prouoke;
The diuell a word of his Children he spoke,
But now we are marry'd, I find that hee's broke,
  Oh fie on this coozening Age,
  Oh fie on this &c.

15 Besides, hee's so ielous, that if I but looke
On any Yong-man, hee'l be sworne on a booke,
That I make him Cuckold by hooke or by crooke;
This doting suspition no woman can brooke.
  Oh fie on this doting Age, &c.

Mar. Wom.

16 It seemes then, good *Kate,* we are both alike sped.
Ill fortune had we, with such Husbands to wed:
For if all be true that heere thou hast sed,
I would either we, or our Husbands were dead.
  Oh fie on this coozening Age,
  Oh fie on this coozening Age.

[1] No period in the text. [2] Text *coozennig.*

THE CUNNING AGE

Wid.

17 Your speeches will make me still willing to tarry,
Sith VViddowes and Batchelors both doe miscarry;
Yet 'tis said in *London*, that when we doe bury
Our Husbands, next moneth we are ready to marry:
  Oh this is a lying Age,
  Oh this is &c.

18 Nay more, to abash vs, the Poets o'th times,
Doe blazon vs forth in their Ballads and Rimes,
VVith bitter inuectiue satyricall lines,
As though we had done some notorious crimes.
  Oh this is a scandalous Age,
  Oh this is &c.

19 I would I the Poet could get in my clutches,
He were better write ballads against ye Arch-dutches:
There is one mad ballad that sorely vs touches,
The hetroclite Singer, that goes vpon Crutches,
  Doth roare out the Wiuing Age,
  Doth roare out &c.

20 But 'tis no great matter, let Knaues say their worst,
And swell with foule enuy vntill they doe burst.
I keepe you so long, I shall make you be curst,
I could find in heart to stay still, if you durst:
  Oh now comes the parting Age,
  Oh now comes the parting Age.

Finis.

Printed at London for *Iohn Trundle.*

43

The cheating age

Pepys, 1, 158, B.L., four woodcuts, four columns.

"The Cheating Age," one of a series of "Age" ballads, was printed before 1626. Cf. the introductions to Nos. 41 and 42. Lincolnshire Leonard tells rather a stupid story, though not half bad are his descriptions of typical London sharpers. Presumably the Poet whom he mentions as being among his dubious companions was a ballad-writer. William Cooke is not, so far as I can find, represented by other extant ballads. The "pleasant new tune" to which the ballad is to be sung is equivalent to *Whoop, do me no harm, good man* (cf. No. 41).

The Cheating Age:
Or *LEONARD* of *Lincolnes* iourney to *LONDON* to buy Wit.

To a pleasant new tune.

1 FRom olde famous *Lincolne* that's seated so hye,
    Well mounted and furnisht, with gold did I flye,
  To *Londons* fam'd Citie some wit for to buy,
  Which cost me so deare, makes me sigh, sob, and cry.
      For this is the cheating Age,
      For this is the cheating Age.

2 Before I had entered Bishops wide gate,
  The Mouth made an offer as if it would prate:
  But one scrapt acquaintance vnto my hard fate,
  And made me consume there most part of my state.
      For this is the cheating Age, &c.

3 For after a neate comly French salutation,
  His tongue he did order in such a feat fashion,

244

As I for to heare him amazed did stand,
But he in the Tauerne me pull'd by the hand.
For this is the cheating Age, &c.

4 When each one had tasted a cup two or three,
What knowledge of Country and kindred had wee,
How bountifull *Bacchus* with vs did agree,
That ne're till this houre did each other see.
For this is the cheating Age, &c.

5 He askt my affaires? I made him reply:
And tolde him my comming was wit for to buy:
(Quoth he) I'le befriend you with that presently,
He vnlatcht a window that Westward did flye.
For this is the cheating age, &c.

6 Then straight a strange whistle he to the street sends,
Audaciously blowne from his Theeues fingers ends,
The Drawer runs vp, sayes, there's some of your friends
Hath call'd for some wine, and your comming attends.
For this is the cheating Age, &c.

7 He cheard me, and tolde me, for them he had sent:
Should teach me wit *gratis* ere homeward I went:
But I ne're misdoubting, the Knauery he meant,
Haue swallow'd a baite which hath made me repent.
For this is the cheating Age, &c.

8 Up straight comes a Roarer with long shaggy lockes,
New broke out frō Newgate, the Cage, or some Stocks
Or else from the Spittle, halfe cur'd of the Pox,
But I'le carefull be, least he pepper my box.
For this is the cheating Age, &c.

9 This totterd grim Rascall amaz'd me to heare,
The terrible oathes which for nothing he sware,
With that stampt his foote, and straightway did appeare
Such horrible faces that made me to feare.
For this is the cheating age, &c.

10 Up marches two creatures in torne totterd cases,
   With long rustie Rapiers, swolne eyes, & patcht faces
   As if that black *Pluto* from *Limbo* had sent,
   These horrid grim visions to make vs repent.
   For this is the cheating age, &c.

The second part. To the same tune.

11 MY former Companion straight rise from the boord,
   And courteous kinde greeting to them did afford:
   Saying, pray sir bid welcome my friends of the sword,
   That gaine credit by deeds sir, and not by their word:
   For this is the cheating age, &c.

12 First hauing saluted, we sate downe againe,
   And call'd for Tobacco, burnt Claret amaine:
   The Drawer officious to giue vs our bane,
   With cups plyde vs hard to put's out of our paine.
   For this is the cheating age, &c.

13 These chimney-nos'd Rascals did make such a smother,
   I ne're saw the like since I came from my mother:
   Such cloude of blew vapour frō their nosthrils did come,
   Had like for to choakt me and fired the roome.
   For this is the cheating age, &c.

14 Then vp comes a Poet with a Rooke at his taile,
   That feedes all the Winter of Toasts drown'd in Ale,
   And in the Summer so setteth to sale,
   Inuentions of others before, his time stale.
   For this is the cheating age, &c.

15 Then straightway one calls to the barre-Boy for Dice,
   Which wrapt in a paper, was brought in a trice,
   Requesting to put off a little odde time,
   They would play for no more then a pottle of Wine.
   For this is the cheating age, &c.

16　I gaue my consent, and with them did play,
　　From wine for dry money, till next breake of day,
　　Where vext at my losses, I set at one cast,
　　Full forty good pounds to be rid of my last.
　　　　For this is the cheating age, &c.

17　My money being set, the cast straight was throwne,
　　And he like the diuell cride, All is mine owne:
　　So euery penny he from me did get,
　　And bad me to *Lincolne* goe backe by my wit.
　　　　For this is the cheating age, &c.

18　They hauing my money, did all steale away,
　　And left me with nothing, fiue pound for to pay:
　　But my cloake lin'd with veluet, & my rapier guilt gay,
　　Did make cleane the score, and all charges defray,
　　　　For this is the cheating age, &c.

19　A Pox of all Cheaters, and grim roaring Boyes:
　　All rooking base Pandars and nitty Decoyes:
　　And all that make practise to thriue by such fits,
　　The three cornerd night-cap once cocker their wits.
　　　　For this is the cheating age, &c.

20　Now *Leonard* of *Lincolne* with griefe bids adiew:
　　My iourney to *London* long time I shall rue:
　　I ne're in my life met with villaines so vilde,
　　To send a man home like the Prodigall Childe.
　　　　For this is the cheating age,
　　　　For this is the cheating age.

ℱinis.　　　　*By William Cooke.*

Printed at London by *E.A.* for Iohn Wright.

44

The life and death of Mr George Sandys

Pepys, 1, 128, B.L., two woodcuts, four columns.

This is a fine example of a "hanging ballad," though a bit more hostile in tone than is customary. The hostility of the ballad-writer is certainly excusable, for Mr George Sandys, his father Sir George, and his mother Lady Susanna were notorious rotters, inveterate criminals. Abundant information about the three—for much of which I am indebted to Professor Kittredge—is available.

On August 10, 1616, Sir George Sandys was indicted in the Middlesex Sessions on four counts: (1) for assaulting and robbing Anthony Culverwell of a cloak and a watch worth forty shillings each; (2) for assaulting and robbing John Foxe of personal property to the value of fifteen shillings; (3) for assaulting and robbing John Marston of "a blacke roned gelding worth ten pounds" and valuable personal property; (4) for assaulting and robbing Robert Wright of "a grey gelding worth seven pounds, a chestnutt bay gelding worth eight pounds, three saddles worth forty shillings," and so on. Sir George pleaded "not guilty," and the trial resulted in his acquittal (Jeaffreson's *Middlesex County Records*, II, 125). On August 21 M. de Tourval wrote to Francis Windebank (*Calendar of State Papers, Domestic*, 1611–18, p. 391) that Sir George Sandys and others were hanged for highway robberies at Kensington "of twelve or thirteen persons in an evening." It is hardly credible that there were two highway robbers of the same name and title; and as our Sir George was acquitted by the courts sometime in August after the tenth, it seems reasonable to suppose that Tourval had this trial in mind and was misinformed about the verdict.

On June 1, 1617 (Jeaffreson, *op. cit.* II, 131), "Sir George Sandes knt., his wife Susannah Lady Sandes, and George Sandes gentleman, all three of Endfield," were indicted for being absent for a whole month from church!—evidence that, whatever their other faults, they were not sanctimonious lip-servers of religion. But in spite of these peremptory warnings, Sir George did not mend his ways; and, according to a letter written by Sir Gerard Herbert to Sir Dudley Carleton (*Calendar of State Papers, Domestic*, 1611–18, p. 527), he was hanged about March 10, 1618, "at Wapping for taking purses on the highway, having been formerly pardoned for like offences; his lady and son [are] in prison as accomplices."

LIFE AND DEATH OF MR GEORGE SANDYS

The son and mother were, as the ballad says, thoroughly depraved. John Chamberlain wrote to Carleton on January 23, 1619 (*Calendar of State Papers, Domestic*, 1619–23, p. 8), that "Lady Sandys, whose husband was hanged for robbery, has herself turned thief." Similar charges were soon made against George. On September 22, 1619 (Jeaffreson, *op. cit.* II, 149), he was indicted on the charge of stealing "a gray gelding worth five pounds of the goods and chattels of Sir Peter Temple knt.", but pleaded "not guilty" and was acquitted. The following passage gives an account of the crime which in stanza 8 Sandys is said to have committed:

25 July, 2 Charles I.—True Bill that, at the parish of St. Pancras co. Midd. on the said day, George Sandes late of St. Giles's-in-the-Fields co. Midd. gentleman assaulted Jane Wrighte,...and murdered her by putting one leather brayded rayne round her neck, and forthwith strangling and suffocating her with the said rayne, so that she then and there died instantly; and that afterwards on the same day, knowing him to have committed the said murder, Suzan Lady Sandes, James Jones yoman and Edward Gent gentleman [or rather *yeoman*], all three late of St. Giles's-in-the-Field, received, harboured and comforted the said George Sandes at the same last-named parish.

Jeaffreson (*op. cit.* III, 11) remarks that over the names of the accused "appear the words 'po se' = he (or she) put himself (or herself) 'Not Guilty' on a jury of the country. No other minute [appears] on the face of the indictment." From the comments made by the ballad-writer it seems that Sandys with his companions was acquitted of this charge though afterwards he made an inadvertent confession of its truth to another woman whom he assaulted—to the Honor Rudston of the following indictment:

28 August, 2 Charles I.—True Bill that, at St. Giles's-in-the-Fields co. Midd. on the said day, George Sandes gentleman, James Jones yoman, and Edward Gent yoman, all late of the said parish, assaulted Honor Rudston,... and that the said George Sandes gentleman then and there 'rapuit et carnaliter cognovit' the said Honor Rudston, against her will and without her consent.

On this indictment all three men were found guilty and were sentenced to be hanged (Jeaffreson, *op. cit.* III, 11). After their execution the ballad was written.

From these records it appears that the author of the ballad, though rightly hostile to Sandys, has too much sympathy for James Jones and Edward Gent and that they were not the passive tools and dupes he describes. The valedictory poem—said to be of Jones's own composition —with which the ballad ends, hardly suggests that English poetry suffered a loss by the untimely end of Jones. In any case his claim to the authorship of this poem is very doubtful indeed. "Neck verses" like these were the stock in trade of the professional balladists, who with no compunction thrust them on any criminal that was available.

The tune is given in Chappell's *Popular Music*, I, 198.

𝕿𝖍𝖊 𝖑𝖎𝖋𝖊 𝖆𝖓𝖉 𝖉𝖊𝖆𝖙𝖍 𝖔𝖋 𝕸. *Geo: Sands,* 𝖜𝖍𝖔 𝖆𝖋𝖙𝖊𝖗 𝖒𝖆𝖓𝖞 𝖊𝖓𝖔𝖗𝖒𝖔𝖚𝖘 𝖈𝖗𝖎𝖒𝖊𝖘 𝖇𝖞 𝖍𝖎𝖒 𝖈𝖔𝖒𝖒𝖎𝖙𝖙𝖊𝖉, 𝖜𝖎𝖙𝖍 *Iones* 𝖆𝖓𝖉 *Gent* 𝖍𝖎𝖘 𝖈𝖔𝖓𝖋𝖊𝖉𝖊𝖗𝖆𝖙𝖊𝖘, 𝖜𝖆𝖘 𝖊𝖝𝖊𝖈𝖚𝖙𝖊𝖉 𝖆𝖙 𝕿𝖞𝖇𝖚𝖗𝖓𝖊 𝖔𝖓 𝖂𝖊𝖉𝖓𝖊𝖘𝖉𝖆𝖞 𝖙𝖍𝖊 6 𝖔𝖋 𝕾𝖊𝖕𝖙𝖊𝖒𝖇𝖊𝖗, 1626.

To the tune of *Flying Fame.*

1 COme hither yongmen and giue eare,
  and good example take,
By this which is related here
  for admonitions sake,
Wherein is showne the life and death,
  of *Sands* that noted theefe.
The reason why he lost his breath,
  is here declar'd in briefe.

2 That all young men from him may learne
    to liue in better awe,
  Foule vice from vertue to discerne,
    according to the law:
  A wicked life this caitiffe led,
    reiecting vertues lore,
  The grace of God from him was fled,
    all good he did abhorre.

3 Since first he came to any strength,
    he practis'd nought but stealing,
  Which brought a shamefull death at length
    for his vngracious dealing,
  He alwayes hath himselfe maintain'd
    by base sinister courses,
  And oftentimes hath beene araign'd
    by Law, for stealing horses.

4 Yet still it was his lucke to scape;
    which hardned him in euill,
  From theft to murder, and to rape,
    suborned by the Deuill,
  His wicked heart so bent to sin,
    in villany tooke pride,
  There liued scarce the like of him,
    in all the Land beside.

5 His name so infamous was growne
    to all both far and neere,
  And he tooke pride to haue it knowne,
    as by him did appeare.
  For when he was araign'd of late,
    at the Tribunall seat,
  He seemed to exhilerate,
    at his offences great.

6 And boasted that he oftentimes
    had scap't the fatall cord,
  For stealing horses, and such crimes,
    as high wayes doe afford,

And with a brauing impudence,
    he did the Bench outface,
Not shewing any reuerence,
    to any in that place.

7 The facts he was indited for,
    were three enormous[1] sinnes,
Which God and nature doth abhor,
    the least damnation winnes,
Without the speciall grace of God,
    for which he neuer sought,
Nor neuer seemed to be sad,
    for that which he had wrought.

8 The Maid that on Saint *Iames* his day,
    was found neere Holborne dead,
Tis thought this wretch did make away,
    if all be true that's sed.
From her he tooke away twelue pound,
    and then to make all sure,
He strangled her, as she was found,
    his safety to procure.

The second part. To the same tune.

9 BUt no such crimes can be conceal'd,
    old time will find them out,
And haue them to the world reueal'd,
    and publisht all about,
As this strange murder came to light,
    by *Sands* his owne confession,
When as he sought with all his might,
    to act a foule transgression,

10 Vpon the body of a Maid,
    whom he perforce did rauish,
If she oppos'd his will he said,
    with speeches somewhat lauish:

[1] *Text* enornous.

That if she did deny to yeeld
  to him, hee'd serue her so,
As he did one in Holborne field
  not very long agoe.

11 To this foule sin of rauishment
  he likewise did seduce
Another youngman, whose consent
  gaue ayd to this abuse.
For which by law he hath his doome,
  to suffer shamefully,
Take heed young men how you do come
  into leud company.

12 For if young *Iones* had neuer seene
  this wicked *Sands* his face,
He surely now had liuing beene,
  but wanting Gods good grace,
He was allured by his meanes
  to liue by lawlesse stealth,
Thus to maintaine strong drink & queanes
  he robd the commonwealth.

13 Some other men of good regard,
  he did to robbery draw,
All these with him in death haue shar'd,
  according to the Law.
But he the chiefe occasion was
  of these same youngmens ends,
Whose deaths haue brought to wofull passe
  their parents and their friends.

14 Among the rest one father *Iones*,
  an honest ancient man,
With lachrimable teares bemones
  the losse of his owne son.
But *Sands* hath run so vild a race,
  that few bewaile his death,
How many flockt with ioy to th' place
  where he did lose his breath.

15 His father named Sir *George Sands*,
    when by his carelesse dealing,
He had quite wasted goods and lands,
    did liue long time by stealing:
And with his wicked Lady wife,
    did rob the highway side,
For which at length he lost his life,
    and by base hanging dyde.

16 Thus both the father and the sonne
    did end their liues alike,
The Lady yet hath scapt that death,
    and sorrow doth her strike.
God grant her life may now be such,
    that men of her may say,
Her life was leud, yet now shee's prou'd
    a conuert at last day.

17 Loe here you see a fearfull end,
    of Sir *George Sands* his sonne,
Let euery one a warning take,
    and better courses runne:
Which to effect let vs all pray
    to him that gaue vs breath,
That of his mercy he'll vs keepe
    from such vntimely death.

The following lines Iones *writ with his owne hand, a
little before his death.*

18 *TO me death is no death, but life for euer.
    My ioy in heauen is, which endeth neuer.
Lord thou hast promist to the penitent,
That thou wilt saue him if he doe repent:
And now most gratious Lord, I craue of thee,[1]
Mercy for him that hath contemned thee,*

[1] Text has a period.

LIFE AND DEATH OF MR GEORGE SANDYS

I am a sinner (Lord) thou knowst I am,
And full of ill, aboue an other man,
Yet am I free from th'[1] *fault for which I dye,*
But haue transgrest the Lawes most hainously.
Oh saue my soule, O Lord of thee I craue,
Let that mount vp, though body rot in graue.

𝔉inis.

Printed at London for F. Couls, and are to be sold
at his shop at the vpper end of the Old Baily
neere Newgate.

[1] Text *'th.*

45

John Spenser, a Cheshire gallant

Pepys, 1, 114, three woodcuts, four columns. The first part is in B.L., the second in roman and italic type.

Some Cheshire antiquary may know the facts of John Spenser's lewd life and melancholy death, but I have found nothing to add to the account given in the ballad. Thomas Dickerson, too, is a name unfamiliar in balladry: had he come earlier, his initials at the end of ballads would have caused confusion with those of Thomas Deloney. Dickerson, of course, also wrote the second part, though he foists the authorship upon John Spenser himself. This is a splendid ballad of its particular kind. Spenser's repentance is thoroughly edifying: it is a bit curious, perhaps, that a man so widely loved as he is said to have been should have kept this love during a whole life of dissipation and have lost it for "one offence but small," even though that small offence was murder. It is also a pity that he delayed so long in subscribing to the sentiments of "A Constant Wife and a Kind Wife, a Loving Wife and a Fine Wife, Which Gives Content unto Man's Life," a ballad (Pepys, 1, 390; IV, 82; Lord Crawford, *Catalogue of English Ballads*, No. 1456; etc.) to which in several verses he seems to be referring. For Spenser the author evidently had much sympathy, and the mention of the two milk-white butterflies and the two milk-white doves that alighted on the body of the dangling corpse seems to indicate that Spenser actually was innocent. At least it is an unmistakable sign that Spenser's repentance had been so sincere as to win complete forgiveness. As John Trundle printed the ballad, its date may be assumed to be 1626. The tune may be equivalent to *Rogero* (*Popular Music*, 1, 94).

JOHN SPENSER, A CHESHIRE GALLANT

𝕴𝖔𝖍𝖓 𝕾𝖕𝖊𝖓𝖘𝖊𝖗 a 𝕮𝖍𝖊𝖘𝖘𝖍𝖎𝖗𝖊 𝕲𝖆𝖑𝖑𝖆𝖓𝖙, 𝖍𝖎𝖘 𝖑𝖎𝖋𝖊 𝖆𝖓𝖉 𝖗𝖊𝖕𝖊𝖓𝖙𝖆𝖓𝖈𝖊, 𝖜𝖍𝖔 𝖋𝖔𝖗 𝖐𝖎𝖑𝖑𝖎𝖓𝖌 𝖔𝖋 𝖔𝖓𝖊 𝕽𝖆𝖓𝖉𝖆𝖑𝖑 𝕲𝖆𝖒: 𝖜𝖆𝖘 𝖑𝖆𝖙𝖊𝖑𝖞 𝖊𝖝𝖊𝖈𝖚𝖙𝖊𝖉 at *Burford* a 𝖒𝖎𝖑𝖊 𝖋𝖗𝖔𝖒 *Nantwich*.

To the tune of *in Slumbring Sleepe*.

1   K Ind hearted men, a while geue eare
     and plainely Ile vnfold
The saddest tale that euer yet,
   by mortall man was told.
One *Spenser* braue, of *Cheshire* chiefe,
   for men of braue regarde:
Yet hee vnto his Countries griefe,
   did good with ill reward.

2 At *Acton*, neere *Nantwich* was borne
   this man, so famde of all;
Whose skill at each braue exercise,
   was not accounted small:
For beating of the war-like Drumme,
   no man could him surpasse:
For dauncing, leaping, and such like,
   in *Cheshire* neuer was.

3 For shooting none durst him oppose,
   hee would ayme so faire and right;
Yet long he shot in crooked Bowes,
   and could not hit the white:
For striuing still more things to learne,
   the more he grew beloued;
No Shomaker but *Spenser* braue,
   by women was so prooued.

4 Those qualities did draw his minde,
   from reason quite and cleane,
And vildly hee'd forsake his wife,
   for the loue of euery Queane:
By Women he maintayned was
   in parill fine and braue,

JOHN SPENSER, A CHESHIRE GALLANT

Iohn Spenser could no good thing want,
  for he could but aske, and haue.

5 In Silkes and Sattins would he goe,
    none might with him compare;
  No fashion might deuised be,
    but his should be as faire;
  When as (God knowes) his wife at home
    should pine with hungry griefe,
  And none would pitty her hard case,
    or lend her some reliefe.

6 Whilst hee abroad did flaunt it out
    amongst his lustfull Queanes,
  Poore soule of force she sits at home,
    without either helpe or meanes.
  Thus long he liued basely vild,
    contemd of all thats good,
  Till at the last by hard mischance,
    he did shead Giltlesse Blood.

7 One *Randall Gam* being drunke,
    with *Spenser* out did fall:
  And he being apt to Quarilling,
    would not be rul'd at all.
  But about the Pledging of a Glasse,
    to which he would not yeeld,
  He vowed he either would be pledg'd
    or answered fayre in field.

8 This answer *Randall Gam* did deny,
    which *Spencer* plainly found,
  And being rag'd he strucke on[1] blow,
    feld *Randal gam* to the ground.
  Seuen weekes vpon this he lay,
    ere life from him did part:
  And at the last to earth and clay,
    his Body did conuert.

[1] *I.e.* one.

9 Then *Spenser* was in prison cast
    his friends full farre did ly,
For frindship in them proued cold,
    and none would come him nie.
That man being kild, beloued was well
    of all men farre and neare,
And some did follow Law so farre,
    did cost poore *Spenser* deare.

10 For though he kild him by mischance,
    yet Law him so disdaines,[1]
That for his vnrespected blow,
    he there was hangd in Chaines.
He that was kild, had many friends,
    the other few or none,
Therefore the Law, on that side went,
    and the other was orethrone.

11 He being dead, two Milkewhite Doues,
    did houer ouer his head,
And would not leaue that hartlesse place,
    after he three howers was dead.
Two milke white Butterflies did light,
    vpon his Breches there:
And stood Confronting peoples sight,
    to their amase and feare.

12 Though he was vildly bent in life,
    and hangd the Law to quit:
Yet he was stolne away by his wife,
    and Buryed in the night.
His true repentance is exprest,
    within the second part:
With all his Gilt he hath confest,
    when troubled was his heart.

Finis. *by Thomas Dickerson.*

[1] Text has a period.

JOHN SPENSER, A CHESHIRE GALLANT

John Spenser his Repentance in Prison, Written with his owne hands as he lay in Chester Castle. To the same tune.

13 *K*Ind Youngmen all to mee giue eare,
    obserue these lessons well;
For vndeserued my death I tooke,
    and sad is the tale I tell.
I prisond pent, I lie full fast,
    sure Heauen hath decreed:
That though I thriued, yet at last,
    bad fortunes should proceed.

14 *I that for practise passed all,*
    in exercises strong,
Haue heere for one offence but small,
    been pent in Prison long.
Kind Countrymen faire warning take,
    beeing bad, amend your liues,
For sure Heauen will them forsake,
    that doe forsake their wiues.

15 *I haue a wife, a louing wife,*
    a constant, and a kind;
Yet proud of gifts, I turnd my life,
    and falce she did me find:
Heauen shewed his part in making me,
    proper in limbes and face,
Yet of it I no true vse made,
    but reapt thereby disgrace.

16 *For being proud in dancings art,*
    most womens loues I gaynd:
By them a long time was my life
    in gallant sort maintaynd:
No Mayden young, about the towne,
    but ioyfull was to see
The face of Spenser, *and would spend,*
    all for to daunce with mee.

17 *I spent my time in Ryoting,*
    and proudly led my life,
I had my choyce of damsels fayre,
    what card I for my wife,
If once she came to intreat me home,
    I'd kick her out of doors,
Indeed I would be ruld by none,
    but by intising whores.

18 *At length being pledging of a Glasse,*
    my hopes I did confound:
And in my rag[1] I feld my friend,
    with one blow to the ground.
For this offence, he being dead,
    and I in Prison cast:
Most voyd of hopes this rashing hand
    hath Spensers name disgrast.

19 *None but my wife will visit me,*
    for those I lou'd before,
Being in this sad extremytie,
    will visit me no more.
No helpe I find from these false friends,
    no food to inrich my life:
Now doe I find the difference true,
    twixt them and a constant wife.

20 *But she poore soule, by my bad meanes,*
    is quit bereft of all:
She playes the part of a Constant wife,
    although her helpes be small.
Young men, youngmen, take heed by me
    shun Dangers, Brawles, and Strife:
For though he fell against my will,
    I for it loose my life.

21 *O liue like men and not like me,*
    of no good giftes be proud:

[1] *I.e.* rage.

JOHN SPENSER, A CHESHIRE GALLANT

For if with you God angry be,
from his vengeance nought can shroud.
Make vse of what you haue practis'd well,
and not in vitious meanes,
If in rare gifts you do excell,
yet trust not Vitious Queanes.

22 *For lust doth fully fill their Vaynes,*
and apt they be to intise:
O therefore shunne their company,
like good men still be wise.
Example truely take of me,
all Vitious courses shunne:
For onely by bad company,
poore Spenser is vndone.

Finis. *by Iohn Spenser.*

Imprinted at London for I. Trundle.

46

Nobody's counsel to choose a wife

Pepys, 1, 382, B.L., two woodcuts, six columns.

The printer, A.M., was probably Augustine Matthewes, whose publications appeared during 1619–1638. The exact date of this ballad cannot be determined, but may be assumed to be about 1626. It is only another instance of the enjoyment ballad-writers derived from comparing the respective merits of widows and maidens as wives. Here the comparison is all to the advantage of widows, and the author found it convenient to hide his identity under the *nom de guerre* of Nobody. In spite of their merits, however, widows were, according to ballad-writers, often unlucky in choosing husbands: an interesting ballad in which this ill luck is pointed out occurs in the Pepys Collection (1, 284)—"A merry new Song of A rich Widdowes wooing, That married a young man to her owne vndooing." For comments on the tune see the introduction to No. 49.

𝕹𝖔𝖇𝖔𝖉𝖞 𝖍𝖎𝖘 𝕮𝖔𝖚𝖓𝖘𝖆𝖎𝖑𝖊 𝖙𝖔 𝖈𝖍𝖚𝖘𝖊 𝖆 𝖂𝖎𝖋𝖊 :
𝕺𝖗, 𝕿𝖍𝖊 𝖉𝖎𝖋𝖋𝖊𝖗𝖊𝖓𝖈𝖊 𝖇𝖊𝖙𝖜𝖊𝖊𝖓𝖊 𝖂𝖎𝖉𝖉𝖔𝖜𝖊𝖘 𝖆𝖓𝖉 𝕸𝖆𝖞𝖉𝖊𝖘.

To the Tune of *the wanton Wife of Westminster.*

1   LEt Young men giue eare
   vnto that I reherse,
And thinke good the subiect
  though set downe in verse:
Nobody vnto you,
  will kindly relate:
The difference twixt Maydens
  and Widdowes estate,
When ere they be had,
  they both will proue bad:

Yet he that a Widdow takes,
    most may be glad:
For Maydens are wanton
    and often times coy:
But Widdowes be wilfull
    and neuer say nay.

2 That man that doth woe a mayd,
    must be compeld:
To liue like an honest life
    ere she will yeeld:
He sometimes must coll her
    and often times kisse her,
Yet may another gaine,
    he may chance misse her:
He liues like a slaue,
    must doe what she'le[1] haue:
He must not deny
    whatsoere she doth craue.
For Maydens, &c.

3 But take me a Widdow,
    who if you doe woe her:
Will yeeld with the soonest,
    when ere you come to her:
She will be as willing,
    to yeeld to a man:
As he that doth woe her,
    make what speede he can:
Shee'le[2] giue him content,
    for what he hath spent:
If he that doth woe her,
    to true loue be bent.
For Maydens, &c.

4 He that a Mayd marries
    is caught in the lurch,
He must neuer let her
    goe often to Church:

[1] *Text* shel'e.   [2] *Text* Sheel'e.

Least thinking by that meanes,
    some goodnesse to teach her:
She larne some new fashion,
    and minde not the Preacher:
Then when she comes home,
    shee'le[1] pine, and sheele mone:
With sweete heart let me
    haue that fashion or none.
For maydens, &c.

5 He that's matcht with a widdow,
    by that is a winner:
Shee'le[1] stay and heare Seruice,
    and then prouide dinner:
Shee is twise in a Saboath,
    at Church like a Woman:
And not to learne fashions,
    as some doe most common:
Shee loues to goe plaine,
    let who will disdaine:
Shee needs must goe so,
    that hath had Husbands twain:
For Maydens, &c.

6 And if a young Bell[e][2]
    doe chance for to swell:
That man that begot it,
    were as good liue in Hell:
For she will be calling
    for one thing or other,
It may be shee's ioyfull
    shee shall be a Mother:
Then the man must disburse,
    to hire a Nurse,
With twenty things more,
    which is marryed mens curse.
For Maydens, &c.

[1] *Text* Sheel'e.   [2] Torn.

7 He that deales with a Widdow,
  hath these at command:
He takes a commodity
  broke to his hand,
He neede not stand carking,
  for linnen nor Cradle:
If he bestow getting,
  to keepe it shees able:
She seldome will pray,
  her Husband to pay:
If he bestow night worke,
  then sheele bestow day.
For Maydens are wanton
  and often times coy:
But Widdowes be wilfull,
  and neuer say nay.

𝕿𝖍𝖊 𝖘𝖊𝖈𝖔𝖓𝖉 𝖕𝖆𝖗𝖙,[1] 𝖙𝖔 𝖙𝖍𝖊 𝖘𝖆𝖒𝖊 𝖙𝖚𝖓𝖊.

8 A Younge Wife must haue gossips,
    were nere had before
She scornes to haue any
  are iudgd to be poore:
Great Banquets sheele make them,
  no cost shall be spard:
Her poore husbands purse
  shee doth neuer regard,
With pray be not sad,
  tis the first that I had:
My Husband and I,
  haue cause to be glad.
For Maydens are wanton,
  and often times coy:
But widdowes be wilfull,
  and neuer say nay.

9 A widdow to saue all
  these charges will shift.

---

[1] Text has a period.

For she can haue Gossips
    at any dead lift:
Sheele bid them as welcome,
    to one ioynt of rost:
As your new married Cupple,
    shall with all their cost:
Sheele say man be wise,
    spend what may suffice:
For Houserent and all things,
    beginneth to rise.
  For Maydens, &c.

10 A young Wife is crabbed,
    and takes a delight:
If her mayd doe but crosse her,
    to speake and then smight:
Shee neuer is well
    but a breeding debate,
Shee'le make her young husband,
    his prentises hate:
No seruants will stay,
    man and mayde will away:
By this meanes she worketh,
    her Husbands decay:
  For Maydens, &c.

11 A Widdow will neuer
    be froward to such,
Sheele vse them as kindly,
    and then theyle doe much:
Theyle call her kind Mistris,
    and alwayes worke faster:
Because they liue quiet
    with her, and their master:
She still beares the mind,
    to vse seruants kinde:
That she and her husband
    much profit may finde.
  For Maydens, &c.

12 A young wife must allwayes,
 in house be halfe Master:
Or else her tongue gallops,
 no Mill-clacke goes faster:
If he doe denie her,
 a needlesse request:
Sheed haue it by some meanes,
 or make him a beast:
With rascall and slaue,
 giue me what I craue:
Or else by this light,
 thou no quiet shalt haue:
For Maydens, &c.

13 A Widdow will always,
 looke well to her home:
Let him doe his businesse
 or let it alone,
Sheele buy what is needfull
 to serue her owne vse:
In words she will neuer
 her Husband abuse,
Abroad she is kinde,
 in bed he shall finde:
A woman that striue will,
 to pleasure his mind:
For Maydens, &c.

14 A young Wife will wauer[1]
 as oft as the winde,
An old wife is fixed
 naught changeth her mind:
A young wife once crost,
 continually doth frowne:
But crosse once an old wife,
 her mind will reforme:
A young wife will brawle,
 if she rule not all:

  [1] *Text* vauer.

A widdow will rule
what to her doth befall:
For Maydens, &c.

15 Much more I could speake,
but to tell you the troth:
To prayse and to disprayse
too much, I am loath:
I would not be partiall,
on one side nor other:
Did they to their deserue,
I would speake well of tother:
My iudgements not blind,
I speake as I find:
None will take exceptions,
for speaking my mind.
For Maydens, &c.

16 I speake not of all Maydes,
that are to be had:
Tis pitty mongst thousands,
if all should be bad:
Nay some widdowes likewise,
may worse be then they:
Both sortes are too wicked,
no man will gaine say:
With this I doe end,
hoping none I offend:
If I wed, with a widdow
my dayes I will spend.
For Maydens are wanton,
and oftentimes coy:
But Widdowes be wilfull,
and neuer say nay.

𝕱inis.

Printed at London by *A.M.*

47

Every man's condition

Pepys, I, 220, B.L., four woodcuts, four columns.

Ll[ewellyn] Morg[an] is a name new to English balladry: I have found no further trace of his name or his ballads, unless he was the L.M. whose initials are signed to "An excellent Ditty, both merry and witty, Expressing the love of the Youthes of the City.... To a pleasant new tune, or the two lovely Lovers," printed by John Grismond (Pepys, I, 242). Similar in theme to "Every Man's Condition" is "A Merry Catch of All Trades" (No. 34). Compare also Dekker and Webster's *Northward Ho*, Act I: "the Northerne man loues white-meates, the Southery man Sallades, the Essex man a Calfe, the Kentishman a Wag-taile, the Lancashire man an Egg-pie, the Welshman Leekes and Cheese, and your Londoners rawe Mutton." Such characterizations enjoyed an extraordinary vogue among seventeenth-century Englishmen.

The ballad dates after March 5, 1627 (Arber's *Transcript*, IV, 173), the day on which Francis Grove registered ballads called "2 slippes for a Teston" (whence the tune) and "3 slips for a Teston." The latter is extant: it is called "A Quip for a scornfull Lasse. Or, Three slips for a Tester. To the tune of *Two slips for a Tester*" (Pepys, I, 234).

"Three slips for a testern" (*i.e.* three counterfeit twopenny coins for a sixpence) was a more or less proverbial expression with the same meaning as the Elizabethan slang phrase "to give him the slip," that is, to elude, to get away. Thus the *Faithful Post* for September 7–14, 1655, in telling of a criminal who escaped from the gallows as the noose was being adjusted around his neck, but was recaptured, says: "He wanted agility of body to give them three slips for a Tester." Cf. also the ballad of "The Forlorn Lover; Declaring How a Lass Gave Her Love Three Slips for a Tester" (*Roxburghe Ballads*, VI, 233).

EVERY MAN'S CONDITION

Euery Mans condition.
Or euery Man has his seuerall opinion,
VVhich they doe affect as the *Welchman* his Onion.

To the Tune of *two Slips*.

1   ALL men are inclinde,
         To follow their minde
       although their courses be bad.
    Some men will laugh,
    And some men will quaffe,
       and some againe looke very sad.
    Other sorts there be,
    That loue flattery,
       but they are base in my opinion,
    Your swaggerers will rore,
    And your knaues run on score,
       but your *Welchman* he still loues an Onyon.

2   Your Citizens fine,
    Loue a cup of neat wine,
       their wiues[1] doe loue good Canary,
    Your Lawyer he,
    Well loues a large fee,
       your Courtyier he loues to be merry:
    Your Gallants and Knights,
    For their sports and delights,
       will spend out their time amongst women:
    The sparkes of our age,
    In their drinke they will rage,
       but your *Welchman* he still loues an Onyon.

3   The Merchants[2] likewise,
    Though they seeme precise,
       yet they couet more wealth, and more pleasure:

---

[1] *Text* wiuus.   [2] *Text* Merchauts.

EVERY MAN'S CONDITION

By crossing the Sea,
Inriched are they,
   thus still multipled is their treasure.
So they may get gaine,
They care not for paine,
   but they are not of my opinion:
Though small be my wealth,
I pray still for health,
   but the *Welchman* he still loues an Onyon.

4 The Taylor[1] loues bread
With a bottom of thred:
   his sheares, his needle and thimble:
The sawyer his Saw,
And the Miser loues Law,
   the Carpenter he loues his wimble:
The Cooper his ads,
The children their Dads,
   but this still is my chiefe opinion,
To be merry and wise,
And trust mine owne eyes,
   but the *Welchman* he still loues an Onyon.

5 The Thrasher his flaile,[2]
The Spanyel his taile,
   the Carman his whip and his whistle:
The Butcher his dogge,
the Swineherd his hogge,
   the Bore delights for to brissle:
the Rorer his wench,
The Lecher the French,
   pray let them both packe with a winion:
For I loue my health,
As the Farmer loues wealth,
   or the *Welchman* a peece of an Onyon.

---

[1] *Text* Taylors.   [2] No comma in the text.

The second part. To the same tune.

6 YOur pure-seeming man
    Will deceiue if he can,
      Your Papist deales all in crosses,
The Theefe liues by stealth
On other mens wealth,[1]
      the Traueller endures great losses.
But time giues free scope
For the theefe to haue a rope,
      tis fit for him in my opinion,
If you will shunne shame
Then loue your owne fame,
      as a Welchman his Leeke or his Onion.

7 The Mercer loues Gloues,
The Dutchwomen stoues,
      the Groser's a man of some reason:
The Farmer loues corne,
And the huntsman his horne,
      the Unthrift doth spend out of season:
The Weauer his Loome,
The Miller his thumbe,
      thus all are of seuerall opinion,
Giue me good old Sherry,[1]
I loue to be merry,
      as well as the Welchman his Onion.

8 The Usurer Gold,
Idle Knaues endure cold,
      because that they wil not labour,
The Fiddler the[2] fiddle,
The Iester his riddle,[1]
      the Piper his pipe and his tabour,

---

[1] No comma in the text.   [2] *Text* he.

EVERY MAN'S CONDITION

The Cobler his last,
The Bowler his cast,
   thus men are of seuerall opinion,
The fish loues the poole,
And my Lady her foole,
   but the Welchman, &c.

9 The Smith loues his Hammer,
And the Captaine his Drummer,
   the Souldier[1] loues a good blade,
The Pedler his packe,
And the Collyer his Sacke,
   and the Horse-courser he loues a Iade.
The Brazier his kettle,
The Bell-founder mettle,[2]
   addicted to seuerall opinions,
The Broome-man loues Broome,
And the Pope he loues Rome,
   but the Welchman, &c.

10 The Dutchman loues Beere,
And the Beareward his Beare,
   the Porter his Frock and his Basket,
My Mamesey nose Host
Loues a pot and a toste,
   and the Landresse she loues a neat Flasket,
The hangman the Gallowes,
and all cheating fellowes,
   deserueth in my opinion
To end in that place,
That liues by disgrace,
   but the *Welchman* he still loues an Onion.

11 Let no body grudge,
Nor ill of me iudge
   because I haue pend this same ditty.

---

[1] *Text* Soulder.   [2] No comma in the text.

EVERY MAN'S CONDITION

But let euery man,
These verses well scan,
   and if he please say they are pretty.
But yet howsoeuer
I doe not endeauour
   to please your base ones or coy minions:
But to end my tale,
I loue good strong Ale
   as well as the *Welchman* loues Onions.

Ll. Morg.

Printed for Fr. Coules.[1]

[1] Text has a comma.

48

The tragedy of Doctor Lamb

Pepys, 1, 134, B.L., two woodcuts, four columns.

According to the pamphlet quoted below (and it is rightly followed by the *Dictionary of National Biography*), Dr Lamb was mobbed on June 13, 1628, and died on June 14. In the ballad Martin Parker mistakenly gives the dates as June 14 and June 15[1]. Lamb, a minion of the Duke of Buckingham, was execrated not only because of his own "lewd life" but, also, because of the popular belief that he used magical powers to enable his patron to seduce chaste women. Buckingham exerted himself to secure vengeance on Lamb's assailants. At his instigation, Charles I threatened to withdraw the charter of London and fined the city £6000. The Duke himself was assassinated a few weeks later (on August 23), and the fine was reduced to 1500 marks. The ballad is an historical document of real value, particularly interesting as showing the reaction towards Lamb of a man in the streets. Parker tried hard to be fair, but his feelings overcame him.

For other ballads referring to Dr Lamb see Fairholt's *Songs and Poems Relating to George Villiers, Duke of Buckingham*, Percy Society, 1850, pp. xiv, 58–63, 65. Contemporary references to his murder abound. Bulstrode Whitelocke notes in his *Memorials* (1732, p. 10) that "Dr Lambe was set upon in the Streets by the Rabble, and called Witch, Devil and the Duke's Conjurer, and beaten that he died; the Council wrote to the Lord Mayor to find out, and punish the chief Actors therein, but none were found." Richard Smyth, in his *Obituary* (Camden Society, ed. H. Ellis, p. 3), remarks: "March 12[, 1628]. Dr Lamb killed in the Old Jurie by a rude multitud, for which the City was fined." John Rous jots down in his diary (ed. Camden Society, pp. 17, 31): "We received newes that doctor Lambe (called the duke's wisard) was knocked on the heade on the 12th of June or thereabout, at 6 at night: he and his minion came from a play, and being houted and wondered at by prentises and water-

---

[1] Both pamphlet and ballad say that Dr Lamb was assaulted on Friday. According to Table C in H. Nicolas's *Chronology of History* (2nd ed., p. 51) June 13, 1628, fell on Friday. For further notes on Lamb see an article by Professor Kittredge in *Studies in the History of Religions. Presented to C. H. Toy*, 1912, pp. 50–51.

men, was at length battered with stones and otherwise, and so slaine. The devill is dead." In October he noted that "a booke is come forth of Doctor Lambe." A copy of this book is preserved in the British Museum (C. 30. d. 18). It is called *A Briefe Description of the Notorious Life of Iohn Lambe, otherwise called Doctor Lambe. Together with his Ignominious Death. [Cut.] Printed in Amsterdam*, 1628. The following passage (pp. 20–21) may be quoted:

Vpon Friday being the 13. of Iune, in the yeare of our Lord 1628. hee went to see a Play at the *Fortune*, where the boyes of the towne, and other vnruly people hauing obserued him present, after the Play was ended, flocked about him, and (after the manner of the common people, who follow a Hubbubb, when it is once a foote) began in a confused manner to assault him, and offer violence. He in affright made toward the Citie as fast as he could out of the fields, and hired a company of Sailors, who were there present to be his guard. But so great was the furie of the people, who pelted him with stones, and other things which came next to hand, that the Sailors (although they did their endeauour for him) had much adoe to bring him in safetie as farre as *Moore-gate*. The rage of the people about that place increased so much, that the Sailors for their owne safetie, were forced to leaue the protection of him; and then the multitude pursued him through *Coleman street* to the old *Iurie*, no house being able, nor daring to giue him protection, though hee had attempted many. Foure Constables were there raised to appease the tumult; who all too late for his safety brought him to the Counter in the Poultrey, where he was bestowed vppon the commaund of the Lord Maior. For before hee was brought thither, the people had had him downe, and with stones and cudgels, and other weapons had so beaten him, that his skull was broken, one of his eyes hung out of his head, and all partes of his body bruised and wounded so much, that no part was left to receiue a wound. Whereupon (although Surgeons in vaine were sent for) hee neuer spoke a word, but lay languishing vntill Eight a clocke the next morning, and then dyed. This lamentable end of life had Doctor *Iohn Lambe*, who before prophecied (although hee were confident hee should escape Hanging,) that at last he should die a violent death. On Sunday following, hee was buried in the new Church-yard neere Bishops-gate.

In a long account of Lamb's death Dr Joseph Mead (*The Court and Times of Charles I*, 1, 367 f.) informed a friend that "a ballad being printed of him [Lamb], both printer, and seller, and singer, are laid in Newgate." Beyond much doubt Mead was referring to the ballad by Parker here reprinted.

The tune of *Gallants, come away* is used also for Richard Climsal's ballad of "The Essex Man Cozened" (Pepys, 1, 290). It does not, so far as I can find, occur among the Roxburghe Collection, and the music is apparently unknown.

The Tragedy of Doctor *Lambe*,

The great suposed Coniurer, who was wounded to death by Saylers and other Lads, on Fryday the 14. of June, 1628. And dyed in the Poultry Counter, neere Cheap-side, on the Saturday morning following.

To the tune of *Gallants come away.*

1   NEighbours sease to mone,
    And leaue your lamentation:
For Doctor *Lambe* is gone,
The Deuill of our Nation,
    as 'tis knowne.

2 A long time hath he liued,
By cursed coniuration:
And by inchantments thriued,
While men of worthy fashion,
    haue coniued.

278

3 The pranks that he hath played,
    (By the help o'th Deuill)
    Are wondrous: but his trade
    And all his actions euill,[1]
        at one time fade.

4 The name of Doctor *Lambe*,
    Hath farre and neere beene bruted,
    The Deuill and his dame
    So cuning were not reputed,
        sure I am.

5 But now he's gone the way
    That's fit for such a liuer;
    To Hell I dare not say,
    Some iudge so, howsoeuer:
        as well they may.

6 For such a wicked wretch
    In *England* hath liu'd seldome,
    Nor neuer such a Wich,
    For his skill from Hell came,[1]
        that made him rich.

7 I neede name none on's feates,
    That are well knowne olready:
    But this my ditty treates,
    Of Doctor *Lambe's* Tragedy,
        my muse intreates,

8 Your patience for a space,
    Whil'st I make his narration,
    That liued voyde of grace,
    And did in desperation
        end his race.

[1] Text has a period.

9 The fourteenth day of Iune
Which was vpon a Friday,
In the afternoone,
We may count it a high day,
    for what was done.

10 This man vpon that day,
As it is knowne for certaine,
Went to see a play
At the house cald *Fortune:*
    and going away,

11 A crew of Sea-men bold,
That went to see the action,
Followed the Doctor old,
And rose vnto a faction,
    as 'tis tolde.

12 Ouer the fields went he,
And after him they follow'd,
His Deuill could not free
Him, for they whoop'd and holowd,
    till they see.

The second part. To the same tune.

13 HIm enter in a house,
   The Horshoe neere to More-gate,
Where he did carouse,
But they to him still bore hate,
    the story shewes.

14 Assone as he had supt,
Which was with halfe a pig there,[1]
This multitude abrupt,
Said were a Deuill as big there,
    they'd interrupt.

[1] Text has a period.

15 His coming by his death,
   Some Prentises did ayde them,
   To take the Doctors breath,
   No fairemeans could perswad them,
     each one hath

16 A resolution bent,
   To kill the English Deuill,
   About which, at they went,
   Though I confesse that euill
     was their intent.

17 With cudgels and with stones,
   The followd him with fury,
   To bruse and breake his bones:
   And iust in the old *Iury*,
     all at once

18 They beate him to the ground,
   And meaning to dispatch him,
   They gaue him many a wound,
   The Deuill could not watch him,
     to keepe him sound.

19 They broke one of his armes,
   And yet they would not leaue him,
   But did him further harmes,
   And still they bad him saue him-
     selfe by's charmes.

20 His scull in piteous wise,
   Was battered and brused,
   They put out both his eyes,
   So cursely then they vsed
     him, who spyes

21 No rescue from his Spirits,
   That vsed to attend.
   So ill had beene his merits,
   That few men to defend,
     shew'd their mights.

22 Now breefely to conclude,
to'th Counter he was carried
By the multitude,
Where all that night he tari'd,
with blood imbrude.

23 And then he did depart,
In lamentable manner,
Yet few are grieu'd at heart,
To heare of his dishonour,
and his smart.

24 Thus Doctor *Lambe* is dead,
That long hath wrongd our Nation.
His times accomplished,
And all his coniuration,
with him is fled.

25 As his life was lude,
Damnable and vitious:
So he did conclude
His life, and none propitious,
pitty shew'd.

Finis.

M.P.

Printed at London for H.G.

49

The unnatural wife

Pepys, I, 122, roman and italic type, two woodcuts, five columns. The use of "white letter" in so early a ballad is most unusual.

This ballad, printed by Margaret Trundle,—widow of the celebrated John Trundle,—supplements Coles's ballad of "A Warning for All Desperate Women" (No. 50), as each deals with the same crime. According to an entry in Jeaffreson's *Middlesex County Records* (III, 107), which Professor Kittredge has brought to my attention, Alice Davies was tried for the murder of her husband, Henry Davies, at the Middlesex Sessions of July 9, 1628, and found guilty. Mrs Davies made a plea of pregnancy, but this was disallowed because a jury of matrons found her "Not Pregnant." She was then sentenced to be burned.

The tune of *Bragandary*[1], though used for many ballads (cf. Nos. 3, 35, 52, 76, 77), appears to be unknown. "The Fair Widow of Watling Street," in two long parts, was registered on August 17, 1597 (Arber's *Transcript*, III, 88; *Roxburghe Ballads*, VIII, 8; *Shirburn Ballads*, p. 1). Its first part is to be sung to *Bragandary*, the second to *The Wanton Wife* (perhaps *The Wanton Wife of Westminster*, a tune named from a lost ballad of that title registered in two parts on July 3, 1597). Ebsworth argued that *The Wanton Wife of Westminster* and *Bragandary* were identical tunes: his argument (*Roxburghe Ballads*, VIII, 14) is fallacious, and, in any case, the *Wanton Wife* is still an undiscovered tune. There is, also, among the *Roxburghe Ballads* (VIII, 14; Wood E. 25 (17)) "A Description of Wanton Women. To the Tune of *Bragandary*, or, *Southampton*." But *Southampton*, too, is unknown. It is very likely, however, that somewhere the music will be found under the names already mentioned or under those of *O Folly*, *Desperate Folly*, *O Roundheads*, *Desperate Roundheads*, and the like.

[1] A ballad "to the Tune of *Braggendarty*" was entered in the Stationers' Register on March 29, 1604 (Arber's *Transcript*, III, 257).

THE UNNATURAL WIFE

𝕿𝖍𝖊 𝖚𝖓𝖓𝖆𝖙𝖚𝖗𝖆𝖑𝖑 𝖂𝖎𝖋𝖊:

𝕺𝖗,

𝕿𝖍𝖊 𝖑𝖆𝖒𝖊𝖓𝖙𝖆𝖇𝖑𝖊 𝕸𝖚𝖗𝖙𝖍𝖊𝖗, 𝖔𝖋 𝖔𝖓𝖊 𝖌𝖔𝖔𝖉𝖒𝖆𝖓 *Dauis*, 𝕷𝖔𝖈𝖐𝖊-𝕾𝖒𝖎𝖙𝖍 𝖎𝖓 𝕿𝖚𝖙𝖑𝖊-𝖘𝖙𝖗𝖊𝖊𝖙𝖊[1], 𝖜𝖍𝖔 𝖜𝖆𝖘 𝖘𝖙𝖆𝖇𝖇𝖊𝖉 𝖙𝖔 𝖉𝖊𝖆𝖙𝖍 𝖇𝖞 𝖍𝖎𝖘 𝖂𝖎𝖋𝖊, 𝖔𝖓 𝖙𝖍𝖊 29. 𝖔𝖋 *Iune*, 1628. 𝕵𝖔𝖗 𝖜𝖍𝖎𝖈𝖍 𝖋𝖆𝖈𝖙, 𝕾𝖍𝖊 𝖜𝖆𝖘 𝕬𝖗𝖆𝖎𝖌𝖓𝖊𝖉, 𝕮𝖔𝖓𝖉𝖊𝖒𝖓𝖊𝖉, 𝖆𝖓𝖉 𝕬𝖉𝖎𝖚𝖉𝖌𝖊𝖉, 𝖙𝖔 𝖇𝖊 𝕭𝖚𝖗𝖓𝖙 𝖙𝖔 𝕯𝖊𝖆𝖙𝖍 𝖎𝖓 *Smithfield*, 𝖙𝖍𝖊 12. 𝖔𝖋 *Iuly* 1628.

To the tune of *Bragandary*.

1   IF woefull obiects may excite,
       the minde to ruth and pittie,
    Then here is one will thee affright
       in Westminsters faire Citie:
    A strange inhumane Murther there,
    To God, and Man as doth appeare:
          oh murther,
          most inhumane,
    To spill my Husbands blood.

2   But God that rules the host of Heauen,
       did giue me ore to sinne,
    And to vild wrath my minde was giuen,
       which long I liued in;
    But now too late I doe repent,
    And for the same my heart doth rent[2]:
          oh murther,
          most inhumane,
    To spill my Husbands blood.

3   Let all curst Wiues by me take heed,
       how they doe, doe the like,
    Cause not thy Husband for to bleed,
       nor lift thy hand to strike:

[1] *I.e.* Tothill Street.   [2] The *n* is upside down in the text.

THE UNNATURAL WIFE

Lest like to me, you burne in fire,
Because of cruell rage and ire:
    oh murther,
    most inhumane,
To spill my Husbands blood.

4 A Locke-Smith late in Westminster,
   my Husband was by trade,
And well he liued by his Art,
   though oft I him vbbraide;
And oftentimes would chide and braule,
And many ill names would him call:
    oh murther,
    most inhumane,
To spill my Husbands blood.

The second part. To the same Tune.

5 I And my Husband foorth had bin,
  at Supper at that time,
When as I did commit that sin,
   which was a bloody crime;
And comming home he then did craue,
A Shilling of me for to haue:
    oh murther,
    most inhumane,
To spill my Husbands blood.

6 I vow'd he should no Money get,
   and I my vow did keepe,
Which then did cause him for to fret,
   but now it makes me weepe;
And then in striuing for the same,
I drew my knife vnto my shame:
    oh murther,
    most inhumane,
To spill my Husbands blood.

THE UNNATURAL WIFE

7 Most desperately I stab'd him then,
    with this my fatall knife,
Which is a warning to Women,
    to take their Husbands life:
Then out of doores I streight did runne,
And sayd that I was quite vndon,
      oh murther,
      most inhumane,
To spill my Husbands blood.

8 My Husband I did say was slaine,
    amongst my Neighbours there,
And to my house they straite way came,
    being possest with feare;
And then they found him on the floore,
Starke dead all weltring in his goore,
      oh murther,
      most inhumane,
To spill my Husbands blood.

9 Life faine I would haue fetcht againe,
    but now it was too late,
I did repent I him had slaine,
    in this my heauie state;
The Constable did beare me then
Vnto a Iustice with his men:
      oh murther, &c.

10 Then Iustice me to Newgate sent,
    vntill the Sessions came,
For this same foule and bloody fact,
    to answere for the same:
When at the Barre I did appeare,
The Iury found me guiltie there:
      oh murther[1], &c.

[1] *Text* muther.

THE UNNATURAL WIFE

11 The Iudge gaue sentence thus on me,
    that backe I should returne
To Newgate, and then at a Stake,
    my bones and flesh should burne
To ashes, in the winde to flie,
Vpon the Earth, and in the Skie.
    oh murther, &c.

12 Vpon the twelfth of Iuely now,
    I on a Hurdle plac't,
Vnto my Execution drawne,
    by weeping eyes I past;
And there in Smith-field at a Stake,
My latest breath I there did take:
    oh murther, &c.

13 And being chayned to the Stake,
    both Reedes and Faggots then
Close to my Body there was set,
    with Pitch, Tarre, and Rozen,
Then to the heauenly Lord I prayd,
That he would be my strength and ayde.
    oh murther,
    most inhumane,
To spill my husbands blood.

14 Let me a warning be to Wiues,
    that are of hasty kinde,
Lord grant that all may mend their liues,
    and beare my death in minde,
And let me be the last I pray,
That ere may dye by such like way.
    Oh Father
    for thy Sonnes sake,
Forgiue my sinnes for aye.

Finis.

Printed at London for *M.T.* Widdow.

287

5○

A warning for all desperate women

Pepys, I, 120, B.L., two woodcuts, four columns.

Richard Harper secured a license for this ballad on December 11, 1633 (Arber's *Transcript*, IV, 310), as "A warning for all desperate weomen," but this was a reissue of the present sheet, which Francis Coles published in 1628. It is a remarkable example of a good-night written (as the ballad-monger would have us believe) after the guilty woman had actually been burned. Verisimilitude was the least of the ballad-writer's troubles. To be sure, he began with the idea of writing a mere conventional farewell such as all criminals made (or were expected to make) before their execution. Accordingly, with the lighting of the faggots in the second stanza from the end, he changes to the third person, but, forgetting realism, in the final stanza takes up the first person again and makes the dead woman utter a doleful warning. A record of Mrs Davies's trial and condemnation is cited in the introduction to No. 49.

For the tune see Chappell's *Popular Music*, I, 196.

𝕬 warning for all desperate 𝔚omen.
𝕭y the example of *Alice Dauis* who for killing of her husband was burned in 𝔖mithfield the 12 of 𝔍uly 1628. to the terror of all the beholders.

To the tune of *the Ladies fall.*

1   VNto the world to make my moane,
        I know it is a folly,
    Because that I have spent my time,
        which haue beene free and iolly,
    But to the Lord which rules aboue,
        I doe for mercy crie,
    To grant me pardon for the crime,
        for which on earth I dye.

288

2 Hells fiery flames prepared are,
    for those that liue in sinne,
And now on earth I tast of some,
    but as a pricke or pin,
To those which shall hereafter be,
    without Gods mercy great,
Who once more calls vs to account,
    on his Tribunall Seate.

3 Then hasty hairebraind wiues take heed,
    of me a warning take,
Least like to me in coole of blood,
    you burn't be at a stake;
The woman which heere last did dye,
    and was consum'd with fire,
Puts me in minde, but all to late,
    for death I doe require.

4 But to the story now I come,
    which to you Ile relate,
Because that I haue liu'd like some,
    in good repute and state,
In Westminster we liued there,
    well knowne by many friends,
Which little thought that each of vs,
    should haue come to such ends.

5 A Smith my husband was by trade,
    as many well doe know,
And diuers merry dayes we had,
    not feeling cause of woe,
Abroad together we had bin,
    and home at length we came,
But then I did that fatall deede,
    which brings me to this shame.

6 He askt what monies I had left,
    and some he needes would haue,
But I a penny would not giue,
    though he did seeme to craue,

But words betwixt vs then did passe,
    as words to harsh I gaue,
And as the Diuell would as then,
    I did both sweare and raue.

The second Part, To the same tune.

7 ANd then I tooke a little knife,
      and stab'd him in the heart.
Whose Soule from Body instantly,
    my bloody hand did part,
But cursed hand, and fatall knife
    and wicked was that houre,
When as my God did giue me ore
    vnto his hellish power.

8 The deede no sooner I had don,
      But out of doores I ran,
And to the neighbours I did cry,
    I kil'd had my goodman,
Who straight-way flockt vnto my house,
    to see that bloody sight,

Which when they did behold with griefe,
    it did them much affright.

9 Then hands vpon me there was lay'd,
    And I to Prison sent,
Where as I lay perplext in woe,
    and did that deede repent,
When Sizes came I was arraign'd,
    by Iury iust and true,
I was found guilty of the fact,
    for which I haue my due.

10 The Iury hauing cast me then,
    to iudgment then I came,
Which was a terrour to my heart,
    and to my friends a shame,
To thinke vpon my husbands death,
    and of my wretched life,
Betwixt my Spirit and my flesh,
    did cause a cruell strife.

11 But then the Iudge me sentence gaue
    to goe from whence I came,
From thence, vnto a stake be bound
    to burne in fiers flame,
Untill my flesh and bones consum'd,
    to ashes in that place,
Which was a heauie sentence then,
    to on[1] so uoyd of grace.

12 And on the twelfth of Iuly now,
    I on a sledge was laid,
To Smithfield with a guard of men
    I streight way was conueyd,
Where I was tyed to a stake,
    with Reedes was round beset,
And Fagots[2], Pitch, and other things
    which they for me did get.

---

[1] *I.e.* one.   [2] *Text* Fagtos.

13 Now great *Iehouah* I thee pray,
  my bloudy sinnes forgiue,
For on this earth most wretched I
  vnworthy am to liue.
Christ Iesus vnto thee I pray,
  and vnto thee I cry,
Thou with thy blood wilt wash my sinnes
  away, which heere must dye.

14 Good wiues and bad, example take,
  at this my cursed fall,
And Maidens that shall husbands haue,
  I warning am to all:
Your Husbands are your Lords & heads,
  you ought them to obey,
Grant loue betwixt each man and wife,
  vnto the Lord I pray.

15 God and the world forgiue my sinnes,
  which are so vile and foule,
Sweete Iesus now I come to thee,
  O Lord receiue my Soule.
Then to the Reedes they fire did put,
  which flamd vp to the skye,
And then she shriek'd most pittifully,
  before that she did dye.

16 The Lord preserue our King & Queene,
  and all good Subiects blesse,
And Grant the Gospell true and free,
  amongst vs may encrease.
Betwixt each husband and each wife,
  send loue[1] and amitie,
And grant that I may be the last,
  that such a death did dye.

[F]inis.

Printed for F. Coules.

[1] *Text* lond.

5 I

Rochelle her yielding

Pepys, 1, 96, B.L., four woodcuts, four columns.

The failure of the expedition (June–October, 1627) which Charles I
sent to the Island of Rhé under command of the Duke of Buckingham, and
the fall of La Rochelle on October 28, 1628, aroused great interest in
Protestant England, which Martin Parker's ballad faithfully reflects.
Parker has no hostility towards King Louis XIII (the "Dolphin" of No. 4):
he was too firm a believer in the sanctity of Royalty and Nobility to have
much sympathy with rebels, even though they were Protestants and their
King a Roman Catholic. In the Great Rebellion Parker, with his loyal
ballads and pamphlets, gave to the Royal Cause aid that was by no means
despicable. For the tune see Chappell's *Popular Music*, 1, 179; 11, 773.

𝕽𝖔𝖈𝖍𝖊𝖑𝖑 𝖍𝖊𝖗 𝖞𝖊𝖊𝖑𝖉𝖎𝖓𝖌 𝖙𝖔 𝖙𝖍𝖊 𝖔𝖇𝖊𝖉𝖎𝖊𝖓𝖈𝖊 𝖔𝖋 𝖙𝖍𝖊 𝕱𝖗𝖊𝖓𝖈𝖍 𝕶𝖎𝖓𝖌, 𝖔𝖓 𝖙𝖍𝖊 28. 𝖔𝖋 𝕺𝖈𝖙𝖔𝖇𝖊𝖗 1628. 𝖆𝖋𝖙𝖊𝖗 𝖆 𝖑𝖔𝖓𝖌 𝖘𝖎𝖊𝖌𝖊 𝖇𝖞 𝕷𝖆𝖓𝖉 𝖆𝖓𝖉 𝕾𝖊𝖆, 𝖎𝖓 𝖌𝖗𝖊𝖆𝖙 𝖕𝖊𝖓𝖚𝖗𝖞 𝖆𝖓𝖉 𝖜𝖆𝖓𝖙.

To the tune of *In the dayes of old*.

1 YOu that true Christians be
  assist me with your sorrow,
 While the misery
  of *Rochell* I relate:
 And in loue let me
  your attention borrow,
 Ile in breuity
  shew you their estate.
 Being besieged long
 With an Army strong,
  by land and sea inuirond close:
 France and Spaine combinde,
 To haue them all pinde,
  yet brauely they did them oppose,

ROCHELLE HER YIELDING

And with constant valour,
They indur'd such dolour,
   that a heart obdure may melt,
To heare this relation,
And haue commiseration,
   on the wants that long they felt.

2 While this warlike Towne
   stood in her chiefe glory,
Still when Fate did frowne
   on the Protestants,
Thither haue they flowne,
   while their foes were sory,
But that old renowne
   now braue *Rochell* wants.
For through want of meat,
Famine was so great,
   that the liuing ate the dead:
It grieues me to report,
How that in wofull sort
   many Christians perished,
Through the want of victuall,
Whereof they had so little,
   that as I before did touch,
Those who dy'd by hunger,
Were eate by the stronger,
   their necessity was such.

3 Horses, Dogs, and Cats,
   were esteemed dainty,
Frogs, and Mice, and Rats,
   were meat for the best.
Some did eate old Hats,
   to maintaine them faintly,
Shooes and Gloues were cates
   that seru'd among the rest:
Such is hungers power,

ROCHELLE HER YIELDING

Twill make one deuoure
   that which we will scarce beleeue:
Ere a man will starue,
Hee'le his life preserue
   with that which our smell would grieue,
Thus this wofull City,
Whose distresse I pitie,
   suffered most extreame famine,
The like I scant haue read of,
To the feare and dread of
   all that shall their case examine.

4 About twelue thousand soules
   perished by hunger,
While many needlesse bowles
   in England were ill spent.
Neither fish nor fowles
   had they to keepe them longer,
Many cryes and houles
   to the ayre were sent.
Nor any kinde of meat
Could they haue to eate,
   when their store was fully spent.
The Spaniard and the French
Put them to such a pinch,
   hauing round begirt their Towne,
That they needs must yeeld
What they could not weild,
   hunger brings stout stomaks down.[1]
So it hath constrained
Them with heart vnfained
   to surrender vp their Towne.

[1] No punctuation in the text.

The second part. To the same tune.

5 THe eight and twentieth day
    of the last October,
Seeing there was no way
    but to yeeld the Towne,
They without delay
    aduis'd by Counsell sober,
Yeelded to obey
    the King who weares that crown
And therewithall they straight
Opened the gate,
    and put the Town, their liues and goods
Into his Highnesse hands,
To doe as he commands,
    who did not seek to spil their bloods.[1]
Beyond our expectation
He had commiseration,
    on those miserable soules,
And mildly he dispenses
With their bold offences,
    and their cases much condoles.

6 When they had open set
    the Gates vpon aduenture
And that the French did get
    possession of the same,
They freely without let
    into the streets did enter,
The Townesmen yeelded it,
    and did all right disclaime,
Protesting that they would
Be euer as they should
    obsequious to his Maiesty,
And like subiects true,

[1] No period in the text.

Liue in obedience due,
　　and he with their humility
So graciously was pleased,
That he then released
　　them of what they had offended,
He giues them leaue to vse
The faith which they doe chuse,
　　thus all contention shall be ended.

7　It was a piteous thing
　　　that befell them after,
For when some did bring
　　victualls as was needing,
Sent thither by the King,
　　it caus'd a wofull slaughter:
Many, surfetting,
　　dy'd with too much feeding,
So weake their stomacks were
That they could not beare
　　meat as other people can:
Thus as some dy'd through need,
So want of taking heed
　　broght death to many a hungry man.
God grant that we here dwelling
May haue a fellow feeling
　　of those Christians misery,
Who haue indur'd such sorrow,
And let vs from them borrow,
　　a patterne of true constancy.

8　God blesse our Royall King,
　　　who is true faiths defender,
That he to passe may bring
　　euery good designe:
Blesse also in each thing
　　his Queene, and in time send her
Power in grace to spring
　　like a fruitfull Vine:

ROCHELLE HER YIELDING

The Nobles of this Land
Protect with thy right hand,
   that they may fructifie in good:
And let those Christians true
The right way still pursue,
   oh let them stand as they haue stood,
Let not thy flocke disturbed,
Be by Tyrants curbed,
   but like the Arke let it still swim,
Among those raging billowes,
Though with cares they fill vs,
   let's not be dismaid for them.

Finis.

M.P.

Printed at London for I. Wright.

5²

A warning for wives

Pepys, 1, 118, B.L., four woodcuts, four columns.

This ballad has not previously been included in any list of Martin Parker's works. It is an adequate news-story in verse—though hardly, as Parker professes, "in tragicke stile." There is a remarkable similarity between the murders committed by Mrs Francis, of this ballad, and Mrs Davies, of Nos. 49 and 50. The following account of the crime, as Professor Kittredge reminds me, is given in Jeaffreson's *Middlesex County Records* (III, 26):

8 April, 5 Charles I. True Bill that, at Cowcrosse co. Midd. on the said day, Katherine Francis, late the wife of Robert Francis *alias* Katherine Francis late of the said parish spinster, assaulted the said Robert then her husband, and then and there murdered him by stabbing him with a pair of scissors in the neck, so that he then and there died instantly.

Marriage seems to have entailed many dangers to husbands of this period. John Rous, in his *Diary* for December 13, 1632 (ed. Camden Society, p. 76), notes that "A woman was burned in Smithfield December 13, who in a falling-out with her husband, stabbed him in the necke with a knife; so that, following her doune a payer of stayers, and crying out to stay her, he died at the bottome of them immediatly." Richard Smyth's *Obituary* (ed. H. Ellis, Camden Society, p. 8) records that on December 12, 1634, "A taylor's wife, for killing her husband, [was] burnt in Smithfield." Many other crimes of this nature are enumerated in a book called *The Adultresses Funerall Day: In flaming, scorching, and consuming fire: OR The burning downe to ashes of Alice Clarke late of Vxbridge in the County of Middlesex, in West-smithfield, on Wensday the 20. of May, 1635. for the unnaturall poisoning of Fortune Clarke her Husband...By her daily visiter H. G[oodcole]. in life and death* (British Museum, 6495. c. 38).

Burning was the usual mode of inflicting the death penalty on women who were convicted of petty treason. For other offences, such as theft (to the proper amount), murder, and witchcraft, English women were freely hanged (cf. No. 76). Lucy Cole, for example, who poisoned her master, Anthony Trott, was in November, 1605, acquitted on the charge of [petty] treason, which would have involved burning, but convicted of murder and sentenced to be hanged (Jeaffreson, *op. cit.* II, 9). See Nos. 14, 49 and 50, where the crimes mentioned were petty treason. Strangulation may sometimes have preceded the actual burning, but was not (if ballads

299

and pamphlets can be trusted) the rule. All the steps involved in burning a woman to death are minutely described in a pamphlet printed by Henry Gosson in 1608 on *The Araignement & burning of Margaret Ferne-seede, for the Murther of her late Husband Anthony Ferne-seede, found deade in Peckham Field neere Lambeth, hauing once before attempted to poyson him with broth, being executed in S. Georges-field the last of Februarie.* 1608 (British Museum, C. 21. b. 5). Mrs Ferneseed, who vehemently denied her guilt and against whom the evidence now appears very dubious, was burned on Monday, February 28, at two p.m. "She was stripped of her ordinary wearing apparell, and vppon her owne smocke put a kirtle of Canuasse pitched cleane through, ouer which she did weare a white sheet, and so was by the keeper deliuered to the Shreue, one [*i.e.* on] each hand a woman leading her, and the Preacher going before her. Being come to the place of execution, both before and after her fastning to the Stake, with godly exhortations hee admonished her that now in that minute she would confesse that fact for which she was now ready to suffer, which she denying, the reeds were planted aboute, vnto which fier being giuen she was presently dead."

The taking refrain of the ballad, characteristic of the tune of *Bragandary* (cf. No. 49), had been used earlier, and is referred to in John Webster's play, *The Devil's Law Case*, 1623, iv, ii:

> O women, as the ballad lives to tell you,
> What will you shortly come to!

Parker's refrain is also given as the tune of ballads in *Wit Restored*, 1656, pp. 157 ff., *Musarum Deliciae*, 1656, pp. 88 ff., *The Rump*, 1661, pp. 82 ff., and the *Roxburghe Ballads*, III, 117; VII, 826. It is the tune also of "The Careless Curate and the Bloody Butcher" (beginning "Black Murther and Adultery"), 1662, in the Wood Collection (Wood 401 (187)).

A warning for wiues,
By the example of one *Katherine Francis*, alias *Stoke*, who for killing her husband, *Robert Francis* with a paire of Sizers, on the 8. of Aprill at night, was burned on *Clarkenwell-greene*, on Tuesday, the 21 of the same moneth, 1629.

To the tune of *Bragandary*.

1 ALas what wretched bloody times
   doe we vile sinners liue in!
What horrid and what cruell crimes
are done in spight of heauen!

A WARNING FOR WIVES

What barberous murders now are done,
   none fowler since the world begun!
     Oh women,
     Murderous women,
     whereon are your minds?

2 The Story which I now recite,
   expounds your meanings euill.[1]
Those women y^t in blood delight,
   Are ruled by the Deuill,
Else how can th' wife her husband kill,
Or th' Mother her owne childs blood spill,
     Oh women,
     Murderous women, &c.

3 At *Cow-crosse,* neere to *Smithfield-barres,*
   adiacent to the City,
A man ands wife at houshold iarres
   long liu'd, the more's the pitty,
Like Cat and Dog they still agree'd;
Each small offence did anger breed:
     Oh Women, &c.

4 She oftentimes would beat him sore,
   and many a wound she gaue him,
Yet hee'd not liue from her therefore,
   to stay ill fate would haue him,
Till she with one inhumane wound,
Threw him (her husband) dead toth' ground,
     Oh women, &c.

5 Upon the 8 of Aprill last,
   betweene this man and wife,
Some certaine words of difference past;
   and all their cause of strife,
Was but about a trifle small,
   yet that procur'd his fatall fall,
     Oh women, &c.

[1] No period in the text.

6 This was about the houre of tenne,
  or rather more that night,
When this was done, whereof my Pen
  in tragicke stile doth write;
The maner of's death most strange appeares
Being struck ith' neck with a pair of sheeres,
  Oh women, &c.

7 As many of the neighbours say,
  that thereabout doe dwell,
This couple had most part oth' day
  beene drinking, so they tell,
And comming home at night so late,
She did renew her former hate.
  Oh women, &c.

𝕿𝖍𝖊 𝖘𝖊𝖈𝖔𝖓𝖉 𝖕𝖆𝖗𝖙 𝕿𝖔 𝖙𝖍𝖊 𝖘𝖆𝖒𝖊 𝖙𝖚𝖓𝖊.

8 ANother woman that was there,
  she out oth' doores did send,
And bad her fetch a Pot of Beere,
  oh then drew nere his end,
For ere the woman came againe,
This wife had her owne husband slaine:
  Oh women,
  Murderous women,
  whereon are your minds?

9 She long had thirsted for his blood,
  (euen by her owne confession)
And now her promise she made good,
  so heauen gaue permission
To Satan, who then lent her power
And strength to do't that bloody houre.
  Oh women, &c.

10 It seemes that he his head did leane
  toth' Chimney, which she spide,
And straight she tooke, (O bloody queane)
  her Sisers from her side,

And hit him therewith such a stroake
Ith necke, that (some thinke) he nere spoke.
   Oh women, &c.

11 She hauing done that monstrous part,
   (woe worth her for her labour)
No power had from thence to start,
   but went vnto a neighbour,
And told him, that she verily thought,
that she her husbands death had wrought.
   Oh women, &c.

12 The man amaz'd to heare the same,
   caught hold of her, and said,
Ile know the truth, and how this came,
   if such a part be plaid,
No sooner had he said the same,
But neighbours did her fact proclaime.
   Oh women &c.

13 Then to New Prison was she sent,
   because it was so late,
And vpon the next day she went
   (through *Smithfield*)[1] to *Newgate*,
Where she did lye vntill the Session,
To answer for her foule transgression.
   Oh women, &c.

14 Where she condemned was by Law,
   in *Clarkenwell* to be burned,
Unto which place they did her draw,
   where she to ashes turned,
A death, though cruell, yet too milde
For one that hath a heart so vilde.
   Oh women, &c.

---

[1] *Text* (through *Swithfield*).

A WARNING FOR WIVES

15 Let all good wiues a warning take,
    in Country and in City,
And thinke how they shall at a stake
    be burned without pitty.
If they can haue such barbarous hearts,
What man or woman will take their parts,
     Oh women,
     Murderous women,
    whereon are your minds?

Finis.

M.P.

Printed at London for *F.G.* on Snow-hill.

53

The western knight

Pepys, I, 312, B.L., four woodcuts, four columns.

This ballad was licensed as "Western Knight" on June 1, 1629 (Arber's *Transcript*, IV, 213). It is a romance with possibly a traditional ballad as a source and with a few traditional features. Of somewhat similar nature are "The False Lover Won Back" and "Child Waters" in F. J. Child's *English and Scottish Popular Ballads* (Nos. 63 and 218). Even closer is the resemblance to the early part of Child's No. 4, "Lady Isabel and the Elf-Knight," which in one stall copy (dating about 1749) is, as Professor Child noted (*op. cit.* I, 23), called "The Western Tragedy." Professor Kittredge remarks that the Harvard College Library has an American edition of "The Western Tragedy" that was printed late in the eighteenth, or early in the nineteenth, century.

𝕿𝖍𝖊 𝖂𝖊𝖘𝖙𝖊𝖗𝖓𝖊 𝕶𝖓𝖎𝖌𝖍𝖙, 𝖆𝖓𝖉 𝖙𝖍𝖊 𝖞𝖔𝖚𝖓𝖌 𝕸𝖆𝖎𝖉 𝖔𝖋 *Bristoll*, 𝕿𝖍𝖊𝖎𝖗 𝖑𝖔𝖚𝖊𝖘 𝖆𝖓𝖉 𝖋𝖔𝖗𝖙𝖚𝖓𝖊𝖘 𝖗𝖊𝖑𝖆𝖙𝖊𝖉.

To a pretty amorous tune.

1 IT was a yong knight borne in the West,
　　that led a single life,
And for to marry he thought it best
　　because he lackt a wife.

2 And on a day he him bethought,
　　as he sate all alone,
How he might be to acquaintance brought,
　　with some yong pretty one.

3 What luck, alas, (quoth he) haue I
　　to liue thus by my selfe?
Could I find one of faire beauty,
　　I would not sticke for pelfe.

305

4 Oh, had I one though nere so poore,
    I would her not reiect:
  I haue enough, and aske no more,
    so she will me affect.

5 With that his man he then did call
    that nere vnto him staid,
  To whom he soone vnfolded all,
    and vnto him he said,

6 Come saddle me my milke white Steed,
    that I may a wooing ride,
  To get some bonny Lasse with speed,
    whom I may make my Bride.

7 On horsebacke mounted this gallant young Knight,
    and to try his fate he went,
  To seeke some Damsell faire and bright,
    that might his mind content.

8 And as he through *Bristoll* Towne did ride,
    in a fine window of Glasse,
  A gallant Creature he espide,
    in the Casement where she was.

9 His heart then taught his tongue to speake
    as soone as he her saw,
  He vnto her his mind did breake,
    compel'd by *Cupids* Law.

10 Faire Maid, quoth he, long may you liue,
    and your body Christ saue and see,
  Fiue hundred Crownes I will you giue,
    to set your loue on me.

11 Though I am faire, qd. she, in some sort,
    yet am I tender of age,
  And want the courtesie of the Court,
    to be a yong Knights Page.

12 A Page, thou gallant Dame, quoth he[1],
     I meane thee not to make;
  But if thou loue me, as I loue thee,
     for my Bride I will thee take.

13 If honestly you meane, quoth she,
     that I may trust your word,
  Yours to command I still will be,
     at bed and eke at boord.

The second part. To the same tune.

14 THen he led her by the lilly white hand,
     vp and downe a Garden greene,
  What they did, I cannot vnderstand,
     nor what passed them betweene.

15 When he to her had told his mind,
     and done what he thought best,
  His former promises so kind,
     he turned to a Iest.

16 Yet he gaue to her a Ring of gold,
     to keep as her owne life:
  And said, that in short time he would,
     come and make her his wife.

17 Then mounted he vpon his Steed,
     and rode from the Damsell bright,
  Saying he would fetch her with speed,
     but he forgot it quite.

18 When fifteene weeks were come and gone,
     the Knight came riding by,
  To whom the Lasse with grieuous moane,
     did thus lament and cry.

19 Sir Knight, remember your vow quoth she
     that you to me did say,
  With child, alas, you haue gotten me,
     and you can it not denay.

[1] *Text* she.

20 So mayst thou be, quoth he, faire Flowre,
    and the child be none of mine,
  Unlesse thou canst tell me the houre,
    and name to me the time.

21 Full fifteene weeks it is, quoth she,
    that you lay my body by;
  A gay gold Ring you gaue to me,
    how can you this deny?

22 If I (quoth he) my gold Ring gaue,
    to thee, as to my friend,
  Thou must not thinke I meane to haue
    thee till my life doth end.

23 Nor do I meane to take for my wife,
    a Lasse that is so meane,
  That shal discredit me all my life,
    and all my kindred cleane.

24 Quoth she, false Knight, why didst thou then
    procure my ouerthrow,
  Oh, now I see that faithlesse men,
    will sweare, yet meane not so.

25 Now may I liue from ioyes exilde,
    like a bird kept in a Cage,
  For I am fifteen weeks gone with child,
    and but fourteen yeeres of age.

26 Farewel, farewel, thou faithlesse Knight,
    sith thou wilt me forsake,
  Oh heauens grant all Maidens bright,
    by me may warning take.

27 When as the Knight did heare what she
    poore harmelesse wretch did say,
  It mou'd his heart, and quickly he
    made her a Lady gay.

Finis.

Printed at London for *F. Coules*.

54

The father hath beguiled the son

Pepys, 1, 362, B.L., two woodcuts, four columns.

"The father beguild his sonne" was registered for publication by Francis Coles and his ballad-partners on June 20, 1629. A lost ballad called "The sonne beguils the Father" was registered by Francis Grove on July 3, 1630, and was probably a reply, by Martin Parker himself, to the present work. (Cf. Arber's *Transcript*, IV, 216, 238.) A tune of *The Mother Beguiled the Daughter* (cf. *Roxburghe Ballads*, VII, 161) is often used: the ballad from which it was derived is not known, but I suspect that it, too, was the work of Parker. He was very fond of writing of a subject from various angles, especially when he could in turn satirize men and then women. The tune of *Drive the cold winter away* is given in Chappell's *Popular Music*, I, 194.

What basis—whether fact or imagination—Parker had for this doleful tragedy, with its pointed warning to deceitful fathers, is not determined. But the story reads like fiction. The third line, "a spokesman hath woo'd for himself," is an anticipation of a well-known passage in Longfellow's *Courtship of Miles Standish*.

𝔗𝔥𝔢 𝔣𝔞𝔱𝔥𝔢𝔯 𝔥𝔞𝔱𝔥 𝔟𝔢𝔤𝔲𝔦𝔩'𝔡 𝔱𝔥𝔢 𝔰𝔬𝔫𝔫𝔢.
𝔒𝔯, 𝔞 𝔴𝔬𝔫𝔡𝔢𝔯𝔣𝔲𝔩𝔩 𝔗𝔯𝔞𝔤𝔢𝔡𝔶, 𝔴𝔥𝔦𝔠𝔥 𝔩𝔞𝔱𝔢𝔩𝔶 𝔟𝔢𝔣𝔢𝔩𝔩 𝔍𝔫
𝔚𝔦𝔩𝔱𝔰𝔥𝔦𝔯𝔢, 𝔞𝔰 𝔪𝔞𝔫𝔶 𝔪𝔢𝔫 𝔨𝔫𝔬𝔴𝔴 𝔣𝔲𝔩𝔩 𝔴𝔢𝔩𝔩.

To the tune of *Drive the cold Winter away.*

1 I Often haue knowne,
    And experience hath showne,
      that a spokesman hath woo'd for himselfe
  And that one rich neighbour
  Will vnderhand labour
      to ouerthrow another with pelfe:
  But I neuer knew,[1]
  Nor I thinke any of you,
      since wooing and wedding begun,

      [1] Text has a period.

309

That ith way of marriage,
Or such kinde of carriage
the father beguil'd his owne sonne.

2 Yet of such a thing
I purpose to sing:
   and tis of a certaine truth,
A widower old
Well stored with gold:
   had one onely sonne a fine youth,
In *Wiltshire* of late
Neere to Bodwin the great:
   this strange and true story was done,
Then list and giue eare
And you truly shall heare:
   how the father beguil'd his owne sonne.

3 A pretty young maid,
In the place aforesaid:
   in a Gentlemans house did dwell
And this youthfull lad
So much view of her had,
   that with her in loue he soone fell:
By day and by night
He wisht for her sight,
   and she at the last was wonne,
To plight him her troth,
Yet she broke her oath,
   for the father beguil'd his owne sonne.

4 For once on a day
The young man did say:
   vnto his wise and aged dad,
That twas his intent
(Worse things to preuent)
   with marriage to make him glad:
Me thinkes first quoth he,
Your wife I might see,
   why will you hastily run:

On such brittle ware?
Yet for all his care,
   (*old fox*) *he beguil'd his owne sonne.*

5 The sonne told his father,
  How that he had rather:
    to haue in the same his consent,
  So to haue a view
  Of his Louer true,
    the sonne with his father went:
  And when they came there
  The Lasse did appeare,
    so faire and so louely a one,
  That the old doting churle,
  Fell in loue with the girle
    and sought to beguile his owne sonne.

6 With such pleasant words
  As to loue accords,
    they all did depart for that season,
  The honest young Lad,
  Was ioyfull and glad:
    his sweet-hart had shew'd him good reasō,
  The loue-sicke old man,
  Did looke pale and wan,
    and could to no pleasure be wonne,
  By night and by day,
  Still musing hee lay,
    how he might beguile his owne sonne.

7 Yet none did mistrust,
  A thing so vniust:
    for he was neere threescore yeeres old:
  Which yeeres one would thinke,
  Should make a man shrinke,
    when his vitall spirits are cold:
  But now to be briefe,
  That was all his griefe,
    from loue all this mischiefe begun:

And nothing could serue,
His life to preserue,
  but that vvhich must kill his owne sonne.

8 So once on a day,
When his sonne to make hay:
  was gone a good mile from the house,
Away the old man,
Is gone to see *Nan*,
  as briske as a body louse:
And with a bold face,
He told her his case,
  and into what care he was runne,
Unlesse that she,
Would kindly agree,
  to take him in stead of his sonne.

The second part, To the same tune.

9 SHe mused in mind,
  Such greeting to find,
  and thus vnto him shee said,
Can such an old knaue,
With one foot in the graue:
  set loue on a young tender maid,
That hardly sixteene
Cold winters had seene,
  sure such thing cannot be done:
Nay more then all this
You know what past is,
  tvvixt me and your onely sonne.

10 Sweet *Nan* quoth hee,
Ne're dally with me,
  I loue thee as well as may be,
And though I am old
I haue siluer and gold
  to keepe thee as braue as a Lady,

All my whole estate
Upon thee shall wait,
   and whatsoere thou wouldst haue done,
With gold in thy hand
Thou shalt it command,
   if thou wilt take me instead of my sonne.

11 If me thou doe shun,
In hope of my sonne
   then take him and ift be thy minde,
But into the bargaine
Looke not for one farthing,
   then be not with folly let blind,
For it lies in my power,
At this instant houre
   (if thou say no it shall be done)
To giue all I haue,
Away from the knaue,
   then take me and leaue off my sonne.

12 When she heard these words,
To him shee accords
   vpon the same condition,
That of all his pelfe,
He should his owne selfe,
   her set in full possession,
To which he agreed,
And gaue her a deed,
   by which the poore Lad was vndone,
Unnaturally
To please his fancy,
   he did dis-inherit his sonne.

13 These things being [said,][1]
And they both contriued,
   by witnesse [conspires][1] so the Lad,
The old man home went

[1] These words are blurred so that only a few letters can be read. *Con-spires* is very doubtful.

With hearty content,
  reioycing at his courses bad,
And thus the next day,
He carryed away
  the Lasse which with wealth he had won.[1]
He maried was,
Twelue miles from the place,
  thus the father beguil'd his own sonne.

14 The young-man with griefe,
Heard of this mischiefe
  and blaming this monstrous part,
Before both their faces,
Unto their disgraces,
  he stab'd himselfe to the heart:
The vnnaturall dad,
Ran presently mad:
  repenting of what he had done,
He runs vp and downe,
From towne vnto towne,
  and hourely calles on his sonne.

15 The faithlesse young wife,
Weary of her life,
  (to thinke what folly befell)
Ran straight in all hast,
And headlong shee cast
  herselfe in a deepe draw-well.
And there shee was found,
Next morning quite drown'd
  these things for certaine were done,
Some sixe weekes agoe,
As many men know,
  that knew both father and sonne.

16 Let euery good[2] father
A warning here gather,
  by this old mans punishment:

---

[1] No period in the text.   [2] *Text* god.

And let euery young Lasse,
(As in a glasse,)
　looke on this disastrous euent;
For both were to blame,
And both suffer'd shame,
　the old man yet liuing doth run
In mad franticke wise
And alwayes he cryes,
　for casting away his owne sonne.

𝔉inis.

M.P.

Printed at London for Francis Coules.

55

A fool's bolt is soon shot

Pepys, 1, 178, B.L., six woodcuts, four columns.
Both the proverbial title of this ballad and the fine large woodcut of Part I were borrowed from Samuel Rowlands's satiric pamphlet, *A Fooles Bolt is soone shott*, which was printed by George Loftus in 1614 (*Complete Works of Samuel Rowlands*, Hunterian Club, 1880, vol. II). The ballad may have been printed by John Grismond immediately after Rowlands's book, but it was first entered in the Stationers' Register on June 20, 1629 (Arber's *Transcript*, IV, 216), by Francis Coles. Approaching the same subject from another angle is the much older ballad (1569) of "The xxv. orders of Fooles" reprinted in *A Collection of Seventy-Nine Black-Letter Ballads*, 1867, p. 88.

The author, T.F., translated in 1616 a sensational news-pamphlet called *Miraculous Newes, From the Cittie of Holdt, in the Lord-ship of Munster* (*in Germany*) *the twentieth of September last past. 1616. Where There Were Plainly beheld three dead bodyes rise out of their Graues, admonishing the people of Iudgements to come* (British Museum, 1103. d. 53. For a ballad on the subject see the *Shirburn Ballads*, pp. 76–80). He can hardly have been the T.F., a Kentishman, who in 1585 published *Newes From the North. Otherwise called the Conference between Simon Certain and Pierce Plowman* (C. 40. d. 12).

The tune is given in Chappell's *Popular Music*, 1, 378.

A FOOL'S BOLT IS SOON SHOT

𝕬 𝕱ooles 𝕭olt is soone shot.
𝕲ood 𝕱riends beware, 𝕴'me like to hit yee,
𝖂hat ere you be heer's that will fit yee;
𝖂hich way soeuer that you goe,
𝕬t you 𝕴 ayme my 𝕭olt and 𝕭owe.

To the Tune of, *Oh no no no not yet.*

1 STand wide my Masters, and take heed,
    for feare the Foole doth hit yee,
If that you thinke you shall be shot,
    I'de[1] wish you hence to get yee;
My Bowe you see stands ready bent,
    to giue each one their lot,
Then haue amongst you with my Bolts,
    for now I make a shot.

2 He that doth take delight in Lawe,
    and euer to be brangling,
Would be[2] like to the Bells were hang'd,
    that loues still to be iangling;

      [1] *Text* Id'e.   [2] *Text* he.

A FOOL'S BOLT IS SOON SHOT

His Lawyers purse he fills with Coine,
　himselfe hath nothing got,
And proues a begger at the last,
　at him I make a shot.

3 Who all the weeke doth worke full hard,
　　and moyle both night and day,
Will in a trice spend all his coine,
　and foole his meanes away,
In drinking and in rioting,
　at pipe and at the pot,
Whose braines are like an adled egge,
　at him I make a shot.

4 The Prodigall that is left rich,
　　that wastes his state away,
In wantones and surfeting,
　in gaming and in play,
And spends his meanes on Whores and Queanes,
　doth make himselfe a sot,
May in a Spittle chance to dye,
　at him I make a shot.

5 He that is apt to come in bands
　　for euery common friend,
May shake a begger by the hands[1],
　and pay the debt i'th[2] end,
By selling Goods and Lands away,
　or in a Prison rot,
Where none will pitty his poore case,
　at him I make a shot.

6 The Man that wedds for greedy wealth,
　　he goes a fishing faire,
But often times he gets a Frog,
　or very little share;
And he that is both young and free,
　and marries an old Trot,
When he might liue at libertie,
　at him I make a shot.

　　[1] *Text* hand.　　　　　　[2] *Text* it'h.

A FOOL'S BOLT IS SOON SHOT

The Second Part. To the same Tune.

7 THe Miser that gets wealth great store,
  and wretchedly doth liue,
In 's life is like to starue himselfe,
  at 's death he all doth giue
Unto some Prodigall, or Foole,
  that spends all he hath got,
With griping vsury and paine,
  at him I make a shot.

8 He that doth early rise each morne,
  and worketh hard all day,
When he comes home can not come in,
  his Wife is gone to play;
And lets her to drinke and spend all
  the moneys which he got,
Shall weare my Coxcombe and my Bell,
  and at him heers a shot.

9 An Old-man for to dote in age
  vpon a Wench thats young,
Who hath a nimble wit and eye,
  with them a pleasing tongue,
Acteons plume I greatly feare
  will fall vnto his lot,
That stoutely in his crest he'le beare,
  at him I make a shot.

10 A Widow that is richly left,
  that will be Ladifide,
And to some Gull or Roaring-boy
  she must be made a Bride,
His Cloathes at Broakers he hath hir'd
  himselfe not worth a groat,
That basts her hide and spends her meanes
  at her I make a shot.

A FOOL'S BOLT IS SOON SHOT

11 A Mayden that is faire, and rich,
    and young, yet is so proud,
That fauour vnto honest men
    by no meanes can be low'd;
And thus she spends her chiefest prime,
    refusing her good lot,
In youth doth scorne in age is scornd,
    at her I make a shot.

12 But she that wanton is and fond,
    that fast and loose will play,
When that her reconings are cast vp,
    must for it soundly pay,
And may the Father chance to seeke
    of that which she hath got,
Besides her standing in a sheete,
    at her I make a shot.

13 Who spends his time in youth away,
    to be a Seruing-man,
Doth[1] seldome grow for to be rich,
    doe he the best he can;
And then when age doth come, God knows
    this Man hath nothing got,
But is turnd out amongst the dogges,
    at him I make a shot.

14 He that doth sell his Lands away,
    an Office for to buy,
May keepe a quarter for a time,
    but will a begger dye;
For he hath sold his Lambes good man,
    and younger Sheepe hath got,
Although he thinke himselfe so wise,
    at him I make a shot.

15 He that will goe vnto the Sea,
    and may liue well on shore,
Although he venture life and goods,
    may hap to come home poore,

[1] *Text* Dotd.

Or by the Foe be made a Slaue,
  with all that he hath got,
Whose Limbes in peeces are all torne,
  at him I make a shot.

16 Those that their Parents doe reiect,
    and makes of them a scorne,
  Who wishes then with griefe and woe
    they neuer had been borne;
  For portion they may Twelue-pence haue
    beside a heauy lot,
  For disobedience ordaind,
    at them I make a shot.

17 The Parents which their Child brings vp
    to haue their owne free will,
  The wise and antient *Salomon*
    doth say they them will spill:
  And when correction comes too late,
    they wish they'd nere been got:
  But for their folly which is past,
    at them I make a shot.

18 They that continue still in sinne,
    and thinke they nere shall dye,
  Deferring off repentance[1] still,
    and liues in iollitie,
  Death quickly comes and ceases them,
    and then it is their lot
  In hells hot flame for to remaine,
    at them I make a shot.

19 And so farewell my Masters all,
    God send 's a merry meeting;
  Pray be not angry with the Foole
    that thus to you sends greeting:

[1] Text has the *p* upside down.

A FOOL'S BOLT IS SOON SHOT

And if that any haue escap'd,
    and saies I did not hit them,
It is because my Bolts are spent,
    but Ile haue more to fit them.

𝔉inis.

T.F.

Printed at London for I.G.

56

Fourpence halfpenny farthing

Pepys, I, 274, B.L., three woodcuts, four columns.

The ballad was licensed to Francis Grove on June 22, 1629 (Arber's *Transcript*, IV, 216), though it was printed by Cuthbert Wright. An extract of one stanza from the Pepysian copy is printed in the *Roxburghe Ballads*, VIII, 720.

This ditty shows Martin Parker in a naughty mood, but seems desirable in print merely because it *is* his work. No other ballad-writer was half so clever in dealing inoffensively, so far as concerns language, with an offensive situation. In his class he was a master of innuendo. This "Jest" maintained its popularity for years: answers and imitations, dating from the years 1685–1689, will be found in the Pepys Collection, III, 41, 238; IV, 249, 257, and in the *Roxburghe Ballads*, VIII, 710. The tune is given in Chappell's *Popular Music*, I, 366.

𝕱ourepence 𝖍alfepenney 𝕱arthing:

𝕺r,

𝕬 𝖂𝖂oman 𝖜ill 𝖍aue t𝖍e 𝕺dde𝖘.

To the tune of *Bessy Bell*, or *a Health to Betty*.

1 ONe Morning bright, (for my delight)
    Into the Fields I walked,
  There did I see
  A Lad, and hee
    with a faire Maiden talked.
It seem'd to me, they could not agree,
About some pretty bargaine,
    He offer'd a groat,
    But still her note
   was foure pence halfe penney farthing.

2 Whats that thought I, that he would buy
  at such a little value,
And as much I mus'd
Wherefore he vs'd
  that summe of which I tell you,
The price was small, but that's not all.
The rest is worth regarding,
   for nothing she,
   would doe, till he,
  gaue foure pence halfe penney farthing.

3 Quoth he faire Maid, let me perswade,
  you to vnfold a reason,
Why you request,
Boue all the rest
  that price now at this season,
Quoth she, good Sir, I doe preferre,
My humour, before the bargaine:
   by all the gods,
   Ile haue the ods,
  iust foure pence halfe penny farthing.

4 I made an oath, which I am loth
  to violate, I tell you.
Though 't be more worth,
If 'twere set forth
  the Iewell which I tell you,
The number three, best liketh me,
Therefore I aske according,
   three pieces of you,
   as 'tis my due,
  thats foure pence halfe penney farthing.

5 When this yong Lad, receiued had,
  to his demand, an answer:
He laught outright,
As well he might,
  for he, nor his great Granser,

The like nere heard, it well appear'd,
She knew how to make her bargin.
    he drew his purse,
    and did disburse,
iust foure pence halfe penney farthing.

6 When he had paid, the pretty Maid,
    and gaue what she desired,
To haue the same,
For which he came,
    he eagerly required,
But ere they could, doe what they would,
I (who had vnaware bin,
    and heard and seene,
    what past betweene,
for foure pence halfe penney farthing)[1]

The second part, To the same tune.

7 VNto them stept, by which I kept
    the yongster from his pleasure,
The best on't[2] was,
The witty Lasse,
    before had got his Treasure,

---

[1] Text *farthing. (Sic.)*   [2] *Text* ont'.

She swore to me, that neuer she,
Would haue perform'd the bargin,
    her meaning was,
    to make him an Asse,
    for foure pence halfe penney farthing.

8 And truely I, thinke verily,
    in that she did dissemble:
Poore Fellow hee,
At sight of mee,
    began to quake and tremble.
His sword I found, upon the ground,
With which I did reward him,
    with a knocke or twaine,
    twas all his gaine,
    for foure pence halfe penny farthing.

9 When I had beate him with 's own weapon,
    and might haue run him thorow,
To th'[1] Alehouse we,
Did goe all three,
    to drinke away all sorrow.
The honest Lasse, most willing was,
To call her whole reward in.
    and freely spent,
    with merriment,
    her foure pence halfe penny farthing.

10 And he likewise, was not precise,
    but, (as it seemed) willing,
To call for drinke,
As much I thinke
    as came vnto a shilling.
I would haue paid but he denaid,
And thus I got by th'[1] bargin,
    good sport and drinke,
    which makes me thinke
    of foure pence halfe penny farthing.

[1] *Text* 'th.

11 But ere they went, I, to preuent
    their meeting againe together,
Sent her away,
And made him stay,
    I'me sure he met not with her.
If she be nought, as 't may be thought,
Ioue send her a Whores rewarding,
      but good or bad,
      she guld the Lad
    of foure pence halfe penny farthing.

12 The tother[1] day, vpon the way,
    it was my chance to meet her.
She blushed red,
And nothing sed,
    but I began to greet her.
How now sweet Lasse, can you thus passe
By me without regarding.
      though you haue forgot,
      yet I haue not,[2]
    the foure pence halfe penny farthing.

13 Kind Sir (quoth she) I well doe see,
    you haue not it forgotten,
Quoth I, I protest,
This may be a Iest,
    when we are dead and rotten.
She went[3] her way, and since that day,
I thought it might be a rare thing:
      to cause this Iest,
      thus t' be exprest
    of foure pence halfe penny farthing.

𝔉inis.

M.P.

Printed at London for *C.W.*

---

[1] *Text* to'ther.   [2] Text has a period.   [3] *Text* whent.

57

A banquet for sovereign husbands

Pepys, I, 402, B.L., three woodcuts, four columns. The first column is badly mutilated, so that the third and fourth stanzas have been filled in by guess.

The date of the ballad is after June 22, 1629, for at that time was licensed the ballad of "The Woman to the Plough and the Man to the Hen-Roost," after which the tune is named (Arber's *Transcript*, IV, 216; *Roxburghe Ballads*, VII, 185). "The Woman to the Plough" was to be sung to *I have for all good wives a song*, a tune named from the first line of Parker's "Merry Dialogue betwixt a Married Man and His Wife. To an Excellent Tune" (*Roxburghe Ballads*, II, 159).

The idea of cuckoldry that underlies the "eating of the ram" is broadly implied: there is innuendo rather than actual coarseness of expression. The last stanza is cleverly designed to increase the sale of the ballad.

𝕬 𝖂𝖆𝖓𝖖𝖚𝖊𝖙 𝖋𝖔𝖗 𝕾𝖔𝖚𝖊𝖗𝖆𝖎𝖌𝖓𝖊 𝕳𝖚𝖘𝖇𝖆𝖓𝖉𝖘.

𝕺𝖗,

𝕿𝖍𝖊 𝕽𝖔𝖘𝖙𝖎𝖓𝖌 𝖔𝖋 𝖙𝖍𝖊 *Ramme* 𝖜𝖍𝖔𝖑𝖊 𝖆𝖙 𝕾𝖆𝖎𝖓𝖙 *Giles* 𝖎𝖓 𝖙𝖍𝖊 𝖋𝖎𝖊𝖑𝖉𝖘 𝖔𝖓 𝖂𝖊𝖉𝖓𝖊𝖘𝖉𝖆𝖞 𝖙𝖍𝖊 𝖙𝖜𝖊𝖓𝖙𝖞 𝖋𝖔𝖚𝖗𝖊 𝖔𝖋 𝕵𝖚𝖓𝖊, 1629. 𝖇𝖊𝖎𝖓𝖌 𝕸𝖎𝖉𝖘𝖔𝖒𝖒𝖊𝖗 𝖉𝖆𝖞, 𝕳𝖊𝖆𝖉, 𝕳𝖔𝖗𝖓𝖊𝖘, 𝖆𝖓𝖉 𝖆𝖑𝖑.

To the tune of *The Woman to the Plow, and the Man to the Hen-Roost.*

1 ON Midsommer day I chanc't to goe
   Unto a place which many know:
   And there was done a merry Iest,
   Which in my song shall be exprest.
   Let no man thinke this is a flamme,
   I sing the rosting of a *Ramme*.

2 Saint *Giles'es* in the fields, that towne,
   Which no place can for mirth put downe:

328

Especially about the City,
They haue such sport and pastime pretty:
But this excels all, sure I am,
  I meane the rosting of the *Ramme*.

3 [The *Ram*]*me* was for this purpose fed,
  [Was cooked] whole both feet and head:
  [Head an]d hornes and all to boot,
  [And now her]e all that would come too't.
  [Come *John*,] come *George*, come *William*,[1]
    [So preciou]s is the rosted *Ramme*.

4 [And many a man there] thither came,
  [Swearing he would] his wife rule and tame:
  [And that he s]hould eate vp the spit,
  [His wife also] should taste a bit.
  [But all be]held most sure I am
    [That nothing was ea]ten of the *Ramme*.

5 He lay so long o'th Spit Ile tell yee,
  Till most o'th puddings dropt out of's belly,
  And scarce a man durst draw his knife,
  For feare he should displease his wife:
  Many excus'd it with a flam,
    and few or none durst touch the *Ram*.

6 At last came in a good fellow o'th Towne,
  And swore it should cost him a Crowne,
  But he would haue a slash at th' Tuppe,
  This was before his wife was vp:
  Had she bin there, halfe sure I am,
    he had not tasted of the *Ram*.

7 Many were halfe resolued to enter,
  Yet on the *Ram* they durst not venter,
  For feare their wiues ere they had dinde
  Would fetch them home with words vnkind:
  Franke would fain, & so would *Sam*,
    yet neither of them durst taste the *Ram*.

---

[1] No comma in the text.

8   This being perceiued by mine Host,
Who fear'd this proiect would be crost,
Hee had it cut off bit by bit,
And sold for money from off the spit:
On these conditions many came
     to buy for money some o'th *Ram*.

𝕿𝖍𝖊 𝖘𝖊𝖈𝖔𝖓𝖉 𝖕𝖆𝖗𝖙 𝕿𝖔 𝖙𝖍𝖊 𝖘𝖆𝖒𝖊 𝖙𝖚𝖓𝖊.

9   NOw if this *Ramme* had beene a Bull,
And all his belly with pudding full,
If none but ruling women might
Haue come, it had bin swallowd quite
In the forenoone, for sure I am
     they best deseru'd to eate the *Ram*.

10   But now to make my story short,
This *Ram* all day did cause good sport,
As Moris-dancing, and such toyes,
That draw together Girles and Boyes.
And many a groat and tester came
     to th'[1] Host, for tasting of the *Ram*.

11   The Master Cooke that Iouiall blade,
All day good mirth and pastime made:
Though first a Tapster, next a Groome,
He for that day supplyde the roome
Of th' Cooke, and he with many a flam
     got money for the rosted *Ram*.

12   One man among the rest was there,
Who meant to tast of this good cheare,
But he was glad his share to hide,
For's wife came in and began to chide,
She sware he should dine with the deuil & 's Dam
     before he should eate a bit o'th *Ram*.

13   This poore mans credit being crackt,
Alack for woe the market slackt,
For all the women did consent,
To make her tongue their president:

       [1] *Text* 'th.

And many a one to hinder came
their husbands from the taste o th *Ram*.

14 One sort of wiues were not so bold,
In such a meeting place to scold:
Yet 'cause their husbands shall not eate,
On purpose they dispraise the meate.
But I eate some, and sure I am,
no Venson's sweeter then was that *Ram*.

15 Though ruling husbands few did taste,
The *Ramme* was eaten vp at last:
They shau'd him barely to the bones,
Nay some did cut his very stones:
Who did the same not sure I am:
who euer he was he well lou'd *Ram*.

16 Some eate the rumpe, and some the feet,
Not asking whether the meate was sweet,
The head and hornes I cannot tell,
Unto whose share by right they fel,
But he that hath a wanton wife,
might keepe them still to whet his knife.

17 Thus vnto you I haue exprest,
The manner of this mery feast:
He that is horned like a beast,
Perhaps is angry at this Iest,
But each good fellow sure I am,
will buy this Ballad of the *Ram*.

18 If here be any scolding wiues,
I wish them if they loue their liues,
In any case not buy this song,
Which doth to gentle wiues belong:
Thus from the Author told I am,
who made this ditty of the *Ram*.

Finis.

M.P.

Printed for Francis Coules.

331

58

A he-devil

Pepys 1, 398, B.L., one woodcut, four columns.

"The Hee divell" was registered for publication by Francis Grove on March 12, 1630 (Arber's *Transcript*, IV, 230). Several ballads are sung to a tune named from it (cf. *Roxburghe Ballads*, II, 509).

Martin Parker here espouses the cause of ill-treated married women, but not, one fears, with any real sympathy. The tune of *The She-Devil* is not known ("The she Divell of Westminster" was registered by Francis Coles on June 24, 1630), but at once suggests that Parker had first written a ballad of that title for the delectation of harassed husbands before turning to the woes of married women. This habit of his has already been mentioned: undoubtedly one reason for his enormous popularity with the common people was his impartiality, his custom of writing ditties on both sides of every question. Thus his satire against women, "Keep a Good Tongue in Your Head," was immediately followed by a ballad against brutal husbands called "Hold Your Hands, Honest Men. To the Tune of *Keep a Good Tongue in Your Head*" (*Roxburghe Ballads*, III, 237, 243).

A Hee-Diuell: or,
If this Womans Husband vse her well,
Ile say some kindnesse may be found in Hell.

To the tune of, *The Shee-diuell*.

1 WHen I a Maiden was,
     I long'd to be married,
But now (alas) such is my case,
    I wish I had longer tarried,
Matching ouer hastily
    hath wrought me mickle euill.
She that weds such a knaue as I,
    were as good to marry the Deuill.

332

2 I thought each day as long as a yeere,
  vntill that I was mated,
My Mayden-head I could not beare,
  so sore that life I hated:
I long'd to haue a man,
  with pleasure to content me,
But now that I haue gotten one,
  it sorely doth repent me.

3 For he is such a dogged wretch,
  and doth so basely vse me,
Many a sorrowfull sigh I fetch,
  when he doth beat and bruise me.
I married him for loue
  that was not worth a farthing,
And yet he doth ingratefull proue,
  iudge, is not this a hard thing?

4 Two hundred pounds in ready coyne,
  my father did bequeath me,
Which I (as freely as 'twas[1] mine)
  did giue to him that hath me.
Against my friends consent,
  I chose him for my pleasure,
But now my hasty match repent,
  I doe (as they say) by leasure.

The second part To the same tune.

5 HE doth consume & waste my means
  in lewd dishonest fashion,
Among a crew of Knaues and Queanes
  which turnes to my vexation:
And if I speake to him,
  in kindnesse, to reclaime him,
Heele with his girdle lace my skin,
  though all the neighbours blame him.

[1] *Text* t'was.

6 Euery day I labour sore
    and earne my food with sweating,
Yet all the thankes I haue therefore,
    is nought vnlesse 't be a beating.
What I haue earn'd all day,
    (alas) I speakt with sorrow,
The knaue at night takes all away,
    to spend vpon the morrow.

7 And glad am I to please him so,
    If I might but liue quiet:
While he doth to the Ale-house goe,
    I worke to get his dyet.
Though my labour earnes the meat,
    I nor my little daughter,
Till he hath done, dare nothing eate,
    but dine (like seruants) after.

8 When he comes home drunke at night,
    if supper be not drest,
Most diuellishly heele raile and fight,
    though humbly I request
Him to be patient,
    but there is no such matter,
And if the meat doe not him content,
    heele breake my head with the platter.

9 I like a seruile bond-slaue,
    doe wipe his boots and shooes,
And yet the domineering knaue,
    so basely doth me vse,[1]
That if one spot on them he find,
    about my head heele beat them,
And if with words I shew my mind,
    I were as good to eat them.

[1] Text has a period.

10 Though such a portion I did bring,
    as before is said,
Yet I doe euery droyling thing,
    heele let me keepe no Maide.
I wash and scowre,
    yet (if you will beleeue me)
I seldome liue a quiet houre.
    iudge whether this doth grieue me.

11 If any neighbour me inuite,
    to gossipping, or feasting,
I dare not goe (is not this a spight)
    for feare of his molesting.
I forth to supper went one night,
    but that may be my warning,
Heele not indure me out on's sight,
    he is so afraid of horning.

12 How can it chuse but griefe me still,
    to see some of my neighbours,
That money haue to spend at will
    out of their husbands labours,
And I that to my portion brought
    two hundred pounds in money,
Dare neuer doe, as women ought,
    nor hardly spend a penny.

13 If any time he money lacke
    and I cannot supply him,
Heel pawn my garments from my back,
    and I dare not deny him,
Tother day he tooke my smocke,
    and pawn'd it for a shilling,
I came, and found him at the Cocke,
    iust when the drinke was filling.

14 All you Maidens faire,
    that haue a mind to wed,

A HE-DEVIL

Take heed and be aware,
   lest you like me be sped.
And you good wiues,
   that heare my wofull Ditty,
If you ere bought Ballad in your liues,
   buy this, for very pitty.

Finis.

M.P.

Printed for F. *Groue*, on Snow-hill.

59

John Jarret

Pepys, 1, 170, B.L., four woodcuts, four columns.

There is no colophon, but the ballad was no doubt printed by Francis Grove, to whom it was licensed as "John Jarrett" on December 20, 1630 (Arber's *Transcript*, IV, 246).

New Year's gifts in verse were great favourites, and here the complacent Mrs Jarret is represented as sending to her thoroughly dissolute husband a "gift" in rhyme, urging him to repent. The gift was printed in good time for the beginning of the new style year (January 1), for although England retained the old style of dating until 1752, there were many seventeenth-century printers who consistently dated their publications *stilo novo*. A most forbearing and stolid wife was Mrs Jarret: apparently her objections to gentle John's bad courses are based sheerly on the economic misfortunes that will result, not at all on moral grounds. She feels little or no sense of personal injury because of his gross infidelity and libertinism. One hopes that her husband saw the error of his ways.

For the tune see the introduction to No. 41.

I tell you, John Jarret, you'l breake :

Or,

John Jarrets wiues counsell to her husband, to haue care to his estate in this hard time, lest he turne Bankerout.

To the tune of *the wiuing Age.*

1 PRay gentle *Iohn Iarret*, give eare to my words,
It is my true kindnesse this counsell affords,
And euery good husband to his wife accords:
If your time you wast away at Alehouse boords,
I tell you, Iohn Iarret, you'l breake,
I tell you, Iohn Iarret, you'l breake.

2 You see how the world to vices inclines,
Which if you doe follow, my soule thus diuines,
That you'l want the mony which you waste in wines:
Men being drunkards, are worse than base swines.
    I tell you Iohn Iarret, &c.

3 They say, at the *Talbot* you runne on the score,
Beside, at S. *Katherines* you keepe a braue whore,[1]
Where you on a night spent an Angell and more:
If you vse such dealings, twill make you full poore.
    I tell you, &c.

4 I heare y' haue a wench, they call her *Blacke Kate*,
Whose dwelling, they say, is neere to *Billingsgate*,
Besides, how you gaue her a new gowne of late:
If you vpon harlots doe thus waste your state,[1]
    I tell you, &c.

5 Besides, at S. *Toolies*, another mans wife,
They say that (*Iohn Iarret*) you loue as your life.
Twixt her and her husband you daily breed strife,
Consuming your meanes, if you lead still this life,
    I tell you, &c.

6 I heare say at *Wapping* that you keepe another,
And when you goe there, you say tis to your brother
But you maintaine her, with the old bawd her mother.[2]
Such scuruy dealings I by no meanes can smother:
    I tell you, &c.

7 You rise in the morning before breake of day,
And vnto the Alehouse you straight take your way, .
Where you in base manner at shuffle-boord play,
Untill you haue wasted your money away.
    I tell you, &c.

---

[1] Text has a period.   [2] No period in the text.

8 You haue a Bastard at *Brainford* to nurse,
That weekly dost cost you two shillings thats worse:
These things, sweet *Iohn Iarret,* will empty your purse.[1]
Besides, if you still perseuer this course,
  I tel you, &c.

9 You into ill company daily doe rome,
Whilst I and your children sit sighing at home,
With brown bread and small drink I sit like a mome
And sometimes at midnight you drunke in do come.[1]
  I tell you, &c.

10 This is a hard world, and euery thing's deare,
Sweet gentle *Iohn Iarret,* my counsell pray heare
Before all be wasted, I pray haue a care.
For if you doe hold this course one other yeere,[2]
  I tell you,[2] *Iohn Iarret, you'l breake,*
  I tell you, Iohn Iarret, you'l breake.

The second part. To the same tune.

11 YOu see how the Farmers doe hoord vp their graine,
No eare will they lend to the poore mens complaine,
Although we should starue, these Curmugins will gaine.[1]
They neuer thinke on vs, nor pitty our paine,
  I feare me, Iohn Iarret, you'l breake,
  I feare me, Iohn Iarret, you'l breake.

12 This is no world to borrow nor lend
Nor (if you consider it) vainely to spend:
Receiue this my counsell (good *Iohn*) as a friend,
For if you pursue this vaine course to the end,
  I tell you, &c.

---

[1] No period in the text.   [2] Text has a period.

13 When you in your shop should be plying your worke,
   In some scuruy blinde Alehouse you all day doe lurke,
   More like than a Christian to some Iew or Turke:
   If thus you neglect your liuing and worke,
        I tell you, &c.

14 Be rul'd by my counsell, good husband, I pray,
   For 'twill[1] be your owne I'm sure another day:
   Yet, if you please liue full well you may,
   But if you persist in your drinking and play,
        I tell you, &c.

15 You know, you haue wasted away a good Farme,
   And now we want firing for to keepe vs warme,
   Besides a good house for to shelter a storme:
   I giue not this counsell vnto you for harme:
        I tell you, &c.

16 Giue ouer in time your scuruy base whores,
   For feare they should fill you with scars & with sores
   And laboure besides to pay your old scores:
   If whores still you follow, with company that rores,
        I tell you, &c.

17 You see that the ould yeare is almost quite spent,[2]
   The new one is comming, good *Iohn* then repent
   Your wicked old follies, and with one consent,
   Your downe-sinking state with care to preuent.
        I tell you, &c.

18 Some that haue enough, at Gods blessings repine,
   But whilest I liue, that fault shall not be mine,
   Then to thy power, sweet *Iohn*, with me ioyne,
   And pray that God daily will guard thee and thine,
        I tell you, &c.[3]

---

[1] *Text* t'will.   [2] No comma in the text.   [3] Text &c,.

19 Be rul'd by your wife, that doth loue you full deare,
And all ill society see you forbeare,
And of these children I pray haue a care,
Begin a new course, I pray, with the yeare,
  Or else, sweet, &c.

20 There commeth no goodnes by following of queene[s][1]
But ryotous drinking, and wasting of meanes.
Who trusts to such harlots, on wickednes leanes,
And may with the Prodigall feed vpon beanes.
  I tell you, Iohn Iarret, you'l breake,
  I tell you, Iohn Iarret, you'l breake.

𝔉inis.

[1] Margin clipped.

60

A wonder in Kent

Pepys, 1, 72, B.L., two woodcuts, four columns.

This jocular ballad celebrates the "stomach's exploits" of Nicholas Wood, of Kent. It was suggested by and closely paraphrases (cf. the last stanza) a twenty-page pamphlet written by John Taylor, the Water Poet, and published by Henry Gosson in 1630 under the title of *The Great Eater, Of Kent, Or Part Of The Admi-rable Teeth And Stomacks Exploits of Nicholas Wood, of Harrisom in the County of Kent. His Excessive Manner Of Eating Withovt manners, in strange and true manner described* (British Museum, C. 31. c. 9; reprinted in Charles Hindley's *Old Book Collector's Miscellany*, vol. III). The pamphlet begins with an address by Taylor "To The Most Famous, Infamous, High and Mighty Feeder, Nicholas Wood," who is described on page 18 as follows:

he is swarty, blackish haire, Hawk-nosed (like a Parrot, or a Roman) hee is wattle-Iawde, and his eyes are sunke inward, as if hee looked into the inside of his intrayles, to note what custom'd or vncustom'd goods he tooke in, whilst his belly (like a Maine-sayle in a calme) hangs ruffled and wrinkled (in folds and wreathes) flat to the mast of his empty carkasse, till the storme of aboundance fills it, and violently driues it into the full sea of satisfaction.

A person of similar achievements, J. Marriot, of Gray's Inn, was written up in numerous tracts and ballads in 1652 (see Thomason Tracts, E. 667(8), E. 668(20)). Both men are referred to in *The Loves of Hero and Leander*, 1653, p. 51:

> Their teeth so sharp, their stomacks keen
> That *Marriots* you would them ween,
> Or *Wood* or *Kents* own Bastards.

Professor Kittredge suggests that Woolner of Windsor, the famous eater, be mentioned, and states that references to him are made in Arber's *English Garner*, 1897, VI, 276; Gabriel Harvey's *Works*, ed. A. B. Grosart, II, 231; *Nugae Antiquae*, ed. Park, II, 96; Archie Armstrong's *Jests*, ed. 1889, p. 112; and *Poor Robin's Almanac*, 1697, under "August." Perhaps the person who nowadays comes nearest to Wood's record is "America's tallest immigrant" "who is twenty-four years old, stands eight feet six inches and is said to eat twenty-four eggs for breakfast" (New York *Times*, September 26, 1920). The greatest possible contrast to Wood is the remarkable Miss Eve Fliegen, who lived for sixteen years on the smell of a rose: see the ballad on her in the *Shirburn Ballads*, p. 55, and cf. my notes in the *Journal of American Folk-Lore*, XXX (1917), 372.

342

A WONDER IN KENT

The tune of *The maunding soldier* is derived from Martin Parker's ballad, "The Maunding Soldier; Or, The Fruits of War Is Beggary. To the Tune of *Permit me, Friends*" (*Roxburghe Ballads*, III, III). Richard Climsal has left many other ballads (*e.g.*, *ibid.* I, 207, 499, 509; II, 7, 281).

𝔄 wonder in *Kent*:
𝔒f the admirable stomacke of one *Nicholas Wood*, dwelling at *Harrisom*[1] in the County of *Kent*.

The like of him was neuer heard, As in this Ditty is declar'd.

To the tune of, *The maunding Souldier.*

I   ALL you that valiant fellowes be,
      I pray giue eare a while to me,
      I tell you of a Champion bold,

---

[1] *I.e.* Harrietsham.

343

A WONDER IN KENT

That fights not for the fame of gold,
  but for good belly cheare,
  as well it doth appeare,
the like wherof you nere did heare.
  none may with him compare,
  as I will here declare,
the like liues not I dare to sweare.

2 In *Kent* this fellow now doth liue,
At *Harrisom* as report doth giue,
His Name is called *Nicholas Wood*,
As I for truth haue vnderstood,
  well knowne by men of fame,
  his worth and name,
  that well can iustifie the same,
    some Gentlemen and Knights,
    to satisfie delights,
  haue sent for *Wood* to see his sleights.

3 He is not like these puling ones,
That sits an houre picking bones,
A Sheepe or Calfe thats worth a Marke,
On them heele brauely fall to worke,
  or if a Hogge it be,
  all's one quoth he,
  in one houres space you none shall see,
    his stomacke is so strong,
    nothing will doe him wrong,
  the Deuill is sure his guts among.

4 What talke I of a Sheepe or Calfe,
Alas these exploits are not halfe,
A Hogs a thing that much will eate,
Fish, Flesh, Fowles, Frogges, or such like meat,
  yet *Wood* is of such power,
  that he within an houre
  a good fat Hogge he did deuoure,
    his like was neuer none
    as plainely may be shone,
  not one like him was euer known.

5 After that he had eate this Hogge,
I doe not meane to lye nor cogge,
Three pecks of Damsons he did eat,
For to digest his Swinish meat,
    Another time beside,
    he being tride:
seuen dozen of Rabbets he destroy'd,
    likewise he tooke in hand,
    to eat a Fleath of Brawne
as soone as from the Bore twas drawne.[1]

6 At Sir *William Sidleyes* house he eat,
As men of credit doe repeat,
As much as thorowly would suffice,
Full thirty men, Oh gurmundize,
    but then vnto the fire,
    he did retire,
and for some grease he did desire,
    thinking his belly he
    would breake immediately
vnlesse he had speedy remedy.[1]

7 A quarter of a good fat Lambe,
And threescore Egges he ouercame,
And eighteene yards of blacke pudding,
And a raw Ducke all but Bill and Wing,
    and after he had din'd,
    as I doe find,
he longed for Cherries y^t brauely shined;[2]
    thē threescore pound they brought,
    which he consumed to nought,
a thing vnpossible me thought.[1]

8 His mighty paunch doth harbour all,
Sheepe, Hoggs or Calues, tis like a stall,
A Parke it is likewise for Deare,

---

[1] Text has a comma.   [2] No punctuation in the text.

And Conneyes gray, or siluer haire;[1]
   a storehouse tis besides
   whereas he hides
all kind of fruits that him betides,[1]
   Cheese, Buttermilke and Whey,
   he bringeth in that way,
thus he brings all quite to decay.

The second part. To the same tune.

9 THe *Norfolke* Dumpling he ore came,
    The Deuonshire white-pot he made tame,[1]
The bag-pudding of *Glocester*,[1]
The blackepudding of Wostershire,
   the Shrop-shire pan-pudding,
   and such gutting,
and Somersetshire white-pudding,
   or any other Shire,
   their puddings heele not feare,[1]
none may w^t *Nicholas Wood* compare:

10 The Clothiers that in *Kent* doe dwell,
In *Sussex* of this man did tel,
To some o'th chiefest yeomen there,
Who greatly mused when they did heare,
   and ofred presently
   that they would lay,
a hundred pound of good money,
   that he could not deuoure,
   a whole calfe in an houer,
they thought it was not in his power.

11 The wager thus betwixt them laid,
The *Sussex* men grew sore afraid,
And of their match they did repent,
Desiring that they might recant;
   the kentish men did say,
   that they should pay,

[1] No punctuation in the text.

ten pounds or stand the match and day,
   then so they did agree,
   and spent it merrily,
but *Wood* mist of their company.

12 A Gentleman by chance did come,
Where friends of his was in the roome
And they were all at diner set.
But he with them eate not a bit,
   when the reckoning was paid,
   the tapster said
   that twelue pence more must be defraid,
   by him that last came in,
   which had not at diner ben
whereat the Gentleman in spleene,[1]

13 Did pay the same and said no more,
But after plagued them therefore,
An other time he did come there,
And brought *Wood* with him to a faire:[2]
   then to the Inne he went,
   whereas he spent,
   a shilling once by ill consent,[2]
   and telling *Wood* his mind,
   being thus inclin'd,
to call much meat & leaue *Wood* behind.[2]

14 Come hostes quickly let be brought
As much good meat as may be thought
To satisfie a dozen men,
The hostes quickly sent it in.[2]
   come sit downe *Wood* quoth he,
   and Ile goe see,
   for some more of our company,
   but ere hee came agen,
   the tapster he came in
thinking the deuill there had ben.

[1] Text has a period.   [2] No punctuation in the text.

15 The tapster did his Mistris call,
And said the man had eat vp all,
Then into th' roome she came with speed,
And found the same was true indeed,
 then she began to sweare
 and pull and teare
with *Wood* for money for his fare
 and he said he was willing,
 to pay her downe a shilling:[1]
he fitted her for former dealing.

16 Two Citizens from *London* went.
To see this *Wood* was their intent,
And being come to *Harrisom*,
They sent for him into the roome,
 for all the victuals they
 did call and pay,
that was within the house that day,
 and wished goodman *Wood*,
 to fall vnto his food.[1]
I marry quoth he that is good.

17 These Citizens found him to be,
So strange the like they ne'r did see,
Desiring him that he would goe,
To *London*, he resolued so,
 then at the last he said,
 he was afraid
the same to th'[2] King should be beraid;
 and so he hang'd might be,
 therefore this thought had he,
tis best staying in *Kent* for me[3].

---

[1] No punctuation in the text.   [2] *Text* to'th.
[3] According to the pamphlet, John Taylor himself made this offer to Wood.

18 His porrige boule is full two pecks,
      He is not of the weakest sexe,
      Good Ale graines some times he doth eate,
      For want of other sort of meat,
            I doe not tell no lye,
            those that will further try,
         a booke of him likewise may buy,
            where much more is declared,
            as I haue read and heard
      none like to him may be compared.

Finis.

R.C.

Printed at London for H.G.

61

The judgment of Solomon

Pepys, I, 30, B.L., one woodcut, four columns.

In the main, the ballad is a paraphrase of 1 Kings, iii, 16–28, with passages here and there from other books dealing with Solomon's life; as, 2 Chronicles, ix, 7, for the words of the Queen of Sheba in stanza four. Henry Gosson printed during the years 1603–1640. For the tune see Chappell's *Popular Music*, I, 196.

𝕿𝖍𝖊 𝕴𝖚𝖉𝖌𝖊𝖒𝖊𝖓𝖙 𝖔𝖋 𝕾𝖆𝖑𝖔𝖒𝖔𝖓:
𝕴𝖓 𝖉𝖎𝖘𝖈𝖊𝖗𝖓𝖎𝖓𝖌 𝖙𝖍𝖊 𝖙𝖗𝖚𝖊 𝕸𝖔𝖙𝖍𝖊𝖗 𝖋𝖗𝖔𝖒 𝖙𝖍𝖊 𝖋𝖆𝖑𝖘𝖊, 𝖇𝖞 𝖍𝖊𝖗
𝖈𝖔𝖒𝖕𝖆𝖘𝖘𝖎𝖔𝖓, 𝖌𝖎𝖚𝖎𝖓𝖌 𝖘𝖊𝖓𝖙𝖊𝖓𝖈𝖊 𝖙𝖔 𝖉𝖎𝖚𝖎𝖉𝖊 𝖙𝖍𝖊 𝕮𝖍𝖎𝖑𝖉𝖊.

To the tune of *the Ladies fall.*

1 WHen *Dauid* ouer Israel, had
  ruled full forty yeares,
And on his Throne securely sate,
  as plainely it appeares:

THE JUDGMENT OF SOLOMON

Stricken in yeares, and full of dayes,
    and nature almost spent,
To set his sonne vpon that Throne,
    his minde was fully bent.

2 For fearing lest that he should dye,
    without the choyse of one:
That might as he had done before
    sit still on Israels Throne:
And to preuent the discord that
    amongst his sonnes might rise,
He pickes out one, and makes him King,
    before Death closd his eyes.

3 Whose name was *Salomon*, a man,
    of rare, and excellent parts:
Yea, such a man he was, that if
    any by their deserts
Might claime a Crowne, then *Salomon*,
    of whom the earth did ring,
Deserud it, and none fitter could
    olde *Dauid* chuse for King.

4 Such was his wisedome, that the Queene
    of *Sheba* from the South
Came, for to heare those words that did
    proceede out of his mouth:
Which when sh'ad heard, pronounc'd them blest,
    and happy for to be:
That his Attendants were, and did
    wayte on his Maiestie.

5 His wisedome made him shine more bright
    then did the Roabes he wore,
And made him in the peoples sight
    to be respected more,
Then all the costly Iemms that hee,
    or ornaments had on:
Or then the Throne that thus adorn'd,
    he vsd to sit vpon.

THE JUDGMENT OF SOLOMON

6 Whose wisedome was principally
    vnto the world made knowne:
In a iust sentence that he gaue
    to th'[1] Harlots which did come
To him for Iustice, 'bout a childe,
    that both layd claime vnto,
Whose cause to heare he did assent,
    and did determine to.

𝕿𝖍𝖊 𝖘𝖊𝖈𝖔𝖓𝖉 𝖕𝖆𝖗𝖙. 𝕿𝖔 𝖙𝖍𝖊 𝖘𝖆𝖒𝖊 𝖙𝖚𝖓𝖊.

7 THe Harlots standing then before
    the presence of the King:
With faltring speech and trembling tongue,
    one straite declares the thing:
Saying, my Lord we women had
    lately two children small,
Which of all earthly ioyes we did
    esteeme them most of all.

8 We had them much about one time,
    and both were of one sex,
And one house doth containe vs both,
    tis this that doth perplex
My troubled soule th'one Harlot said,
    seeing her Childe is dead,
She labours all she can to haue
    mine, in her Infants stead.

9 For in the night she ouer-layd
    her childe, and it did dye:
But waking straitway, she perceiu'd,
    and this sad sight did spie:
She straightway rose, and forthwith came
    at midnight to my bed:
And tooke from me my liuing childe,
    and left with me hers dead.

[1] *Text* to' th.

10 But in the morning when I wak'd,
    not knowing what was done:
By this vilde woman which doth seeke,
    to bereaue me of my sonne:
And taking gently in mine armes,
    as then I thought, my childe:
I straight perceiu'd it was not mine,
    and that I was beguil'd.

11 Nay, said the other Harlot then,
    the childe that liues is mine:
And that same Infant that is dead,
    assuredly was thine:
That's false reply'd the other straight,
    for that that liues (said she)
Is none of thine, I did it beare,
    and it belongs to me.

12 Thus whatsoe'r the one did say,
    the other did deny:
And what the other did affirme,
    did th' other presently,
Cry[1] out vpon as false and vaine,
    nor would they ere they said,
Nor possibly could quietnesse
    betwixt them both be made.

13 Therefore they did implore the helpe,
    and wisedome of the King,
Whose eye could onely pierce into
    so difficult a thing:
That he would graciously be pleas'd,
    as he had heard it so:
He would giue sentence to their cause,
    which they would stand vnto.

[1] *Text* Cry'd.

14 *Salomon* causd the liuing childe
    in the midst to be plac'd,
Of both those Harlots that did seeke
    each other to disgrace:
And one of his seruants he charg'd
    to fetch a sword straightway;
Which to him presently was brought
    without the least delay.

15 Which sword he to his seruant gaue,
    putting it in his hand,
Enioyning him to execute
    whate're he did command.
Diuide the childe (saith he) and giue
    to each of them a part:
Which words did pierce the true Mother
    vnto the very heart.

16 Who humbly did beseech the King,
    rather then it should dye,
To giue it to the other all,
    that with her did stand by:
Nay answered the false Mother then,
    the King hath it decided:
Neither thine, nor mine, the childe shall be,
    but let it be diuided.

17 King *Salomon* weigh'd both their words,
    and looking on them both,
Did say, that she the Mother is
    that most compassion shew'th:
Giue her the childe that did lament,
    for such an Infant pretty,
And when it should haue mangled beene,
    was moued vnto pitty.

18 The Mother gladly did receiue
    her tender Babe againe:

THE JUDGMENT OF SOLOMON

Which the false Mother cruelly
   desired might be slaine:
And when the people heard the words,
   and sentence of the King:
Cry'd all with voyce most lowd, God blesse
   Salomon in euery thing.

𝔉inis.[1]

At London Printed for *Henry Gosson.*

[1] No period in the text.

62

'Tis not otherwise

Pepys, 1, 394, B.L., four woodcuts, four columns.

Perhaps the point of view of the average married man is well stated here, though possibly too much stress is laid on the mere physical comforts that attend marriage. After the many ballads in which that sacrament is abused, the present defence of marriage is a bit refreshing. From the opening lines it is evident that this song is a reply to some doleful ditty in which a young married man laments his loss of liberty and his never-ending woes. The printer was no doubt G[eorge] B[lackwall], whose publications appeared during 1626–1636. The date of 1630, accordingly, may be assumed for this ballad. For the tune see Chappell's *Popular Music*, 1, 380.

Tis not otherwise:
Or:
The praise of a married life.

To the tune of, *I'le neuer loue thee more.*

1 A Young man lately did complaine
    because that he was wed:
And counsel'd others to abstaine
    from *Hymeneal* bed:
Had years but giuen him man-like thoughts,
    hee'd[1] not bin so vnwise,
For wiues increase mans happines,
    then *'Tis*[2] *not otherwise.*

2 What ioy is there vpon the earth
    but Mariage makes it more,
It is to man a second birth,
    and openeth the doore
To happines, and such delight
    that none but they comprize:

[1] *Text* he'ed.   [2] Text throughout *t'is.*

'TIS NOT OTHERWISE

They pleasures haue both day and night,
    then *'tis not otherwise.*

3 When I was single I did stray
        in heart, in words, and life,
    But I haue found a better way
        I thanke my louing wife:
    I now liue free from all suspect,
        and many wicked lyes,
    The good I wisht, hath tooke effect,
        then *'tis not otherwise.*

4 Much company I vs'd to keepe,
        before I had a wife.
    The memory doth make me weepe,
        for 'twas[1] a wicked life:
    Such comfort now at home I finde,
        from Mariage to arise,
    I wish all men were in my minde,
        then *'tis not otherwise.*

5 Unthrifty games I now haue left
        as Tables, Cards and Dice,
    That oft hath me of wealth bereft,
        I curse no Ace, nor Sice:
    I do not now the Cards bid burne,
        that made my anger rise,
    A wife hath caused me to turne,
        then *'tis not otherwise.*[2]

6 So ciuill I am growne of late
        since that I made my choice,
    I hate each swearing swaggering mate,
        which makes me to reioyce:
    The company I now do keepe,
        are honest men and wise,
    That not with drinke, but sence do sleepe,
        then *'tis not otherwise.*

[1] *Text* t'was.   [2] No period in the text.

7 No Constable nor watch feare I,
  that cryeth *Who goes there?*
 I doe not reele, but soberly
  can passe them void of care:
 I vse no caudels in the morne,
  I drinke not out mine eyes,
 My wife hath made me these to scorne,
  then *'tis not otherwise.*

8 This diet makes me to forget
  the head-ach that some haue,
 Which makes them for all things vnfit,
  (to drinke I am no slaue.)
 Those men their vertue hath out-worne,
  that drinke doth so disguise,
 My wife hath made me this to scorne,
  then *'tis not otherwise.*

The second part. To the same tune.

9 AGainst I from my labour come,
  my wife prouides me meat:
 When I was single none at home,
  found I, or what to eate.
 At sight of me she layes the cloath,
  and then for meat she hies,
 Which makes me to forget all sloath,
  then *'tis not otherwise.*

10 If I seeme discontent with ought,
  she kindly prayes me tell,
 If that it may be beg'd or bought,
  (or where it is to sell:)
 That would me please, & merry make
  the teares stand in her eyes
 Till I my discontent forsake:
  then *'tis not otherwise.*

11   It is a comfort for to see,
        good women meeke and mild,
    That to her come in charity,
        when that she is with child:
    They comfort her if she do sound,
        one for strong water hies,
    And so their husbands healths drinke round,
        then 'tis not otherwise.

12   When that she doth in child-bed lye,[1]
        the neighbours in their loue,
    Will with her sit, and pleasantly
        to mirth they doe her moue:
    By christning of my little lad
        I did in credit rise:
    All this by my good wife I had,
        then 'tis not otherwise.

13   For gossiping they send in meat,
        would well serue forty men,
    As good as any man can eate,
        for mutton, pig, or hen;
    They eate not halfe but leaue it me,
        there profit doth arise:
    This cometh by a wife you see,
        then 'tis not otherwise.

14   One giues a peece, and one a spoone
        vnto my pretty childe,
    And wish that ere to morrow noone,
        their cradles to be fil'd
    With such a pretty child as this:
        ioy there to me doth rise,
    Had I no wife all this I misse,
        then 'tis not otherwise.

15   The babe doth grow, and quickly speaks,
        this doth increase my ioy,

---

[1] Text has a period.

'TIS NOT OTHERWISE

To heare it tattle, laugh, and squeake,
    I smile and hug the boy:
I with it play with great delight,
    and hush it when it cryes,
And euer wish it in my sight,
    then *'tis not otherwise*.

16 All Batchelors I wish you wed,
    if merry you would liue,
A single man is oft misled,
    and seldome doth he thriue:
I liu'd before, but better now,
    my ioy and wealth arise,
To liue well I haue showne you how,
    then *'tis not otherwise*.

Printed at London by G.B.

63

A goodfellow's complaint

Pepys, 1, 438, B.L., four woodcuts, four columns.
This "pussyfoot" complaint should be compared with Edward Culter's
(No. 27). It is worthy of notice that "honest Jack," the goodfellow, re-
forms not because of moral or religious scruples, but simply because he
has no money with which to buy strong beer—"a good cause why," as he
truly remarks. Similar in idea and expression is "Wade's Reformation"
(*Bagford Ballads*, 1, 6) with the refrain, "And 'tis old Ale has undone me."
The date is perhaps about 1630. The tune appears to be unknown.

𝕬 goodfellowes complaint against strong beere,
𝕺r
𝕿ake heed goodfellowes for heere you may see
𝕳ow it is strong beere that hath vndone me.

To the Tune of *a day will come shall pay for all.*

1 ALL you good fellowes who loue strong beere,
   In time be warned the same to flee
For I can make it plaine appeare
How tis strong beare that has vndon me.

2 I vsd all company to keepe,
Which was my downfall now I see
For pouertie on mee doth creepe,
And tis strong beerre[1] that has vndon mee.

3 I once enioyed both house and land,
But now 'tis[2] otherwise you see,
My moneys spent my cloathes are pawnd:
And tis strong beere that has vndone mee.

---

[1] *Sic.*   [2] *Text* t'is.

361

4 Now I haue wasted my estate,
  Which was enough to maintaine three,
  Ime faine to liue at an vnder rate,
  For this strong beere that has vndone me.

5 O how it greeues my hart to thinke,
  That they who had my money free,
  Now I am poore from me they shrinke,
  O this strong beere has vndone me.

6 When I had coine enough to spend,
  Among good fellowes who but me,
  Then each one stroue to be my friend:
  Until strong beere had vndon me.

7 Now all is gone and nothing left,
  It is not as it was wont to be,
  Of all my friends I am bereft,
  O thus strong beere has vndon me.[1]

8 For now my company they[2] shunne,
  And where I come away they flee,
  Which makes me sing this heauy tune:
  O tis strong beere that has vndon me.[3]

9 They say tis money makes a man,
  Experience prooues it true I see,
  For my assotiates from mee rane,
  When thus strong beere had vndone me.[1]

10 For when I had clothes to my backe,
   And coine to call for liquor free,
   I neuer did companions lacke,
   Untill strong beere had vndon me.

11 But now I haue consumed all,
   And am as poore as poore may be,
   Here's many laugh to see my fall,
   Now this strong beere has vndone me.

[1] Comma in the text. [2] *Text* thy.
[3] *Text* mo.

12 The world is growne to such a passe,
That if your meanes consumed be,
You shall be counted but an asse
And thus strong beere hath vndon me:

The second part. To the same Tune.[1]

13 WHen[2] I had coine no tapster durst,
Refuse to trust me shillings three,
But now thele see my money first,
Because strong beere has vndone mee.

14 Unto a Tapster once I came,
You'r welcome Sir, draw neere quoth he,
But now the slaue wo'not know my name,
Because strong beere has vndone mee.

15 My little hostes at the crowne,
Would often sit vpon my knee,
But now sheele cry away thou clowne,
Because strong beere has vndone me.

16 Besides ther's Tapsters three or foure,
Where I haue spent my money free,
Are like to thrust me out of doore,
And say there is no roome for me.

17 But if I could get vp my meanes,
As that I doubt will neuer be,
I sure would fit those Knaues and Queenes,
But now strong beere has vndone me.

18 O is not this a hellish spight,
That I should thus reiected be,
Who lately liu'd in such delight,
Before strong beere had vndone me.

19 When I doe call to minde the dayes,
Which I againe shall neuer see,
In which[3] torments me many wayes,
Alas strong[4] beere has vndone me.

---

[1] No period in the text.   [2] *Text* Wheu.
[3] *Read* It then?   [4] *Text* stroug.

20 Full many a shilling haue I spent,
And cride hang sorrow let it fly,
In drinke and smoke away it went,
And thus strong beere hath vndone me.

21 Then who but I among the rout,
Of Iouiall Blades should welcome be,
But now my pouerty they flout,
Because strong beere has vndone me.

22 Then would good fellowes to me say,
Heere honest *Iacke* ile drinke to thee,
Because they knew I still would pay,
Untill strong beere had vndone me.

23 Now they who hung vpon my purse,
If I through want should starued be,
Will not a groate for me disburse,
Because strong beere has vndone me.

24 And if I passe by the ale-house doore,
My host will say, looke there goes he,
I knew him rich but now hee's poore,
And thus strong beere has vndone me.

25 All you good fellowes that heare my case,
Take heede least it[1] your owne case be,
I might haue liu'd void of disgrace,
Had not strong beere thus vndone me.

26 Shake of ill company in time,
Which wrongeth many a man you see,
Now I through them am like to pine,
And tis strong beere that has vndone me.

27 Farewell strong beere my mortall foe,
Ile drinke no more therefore of thee,
A good cause why my purse is lowe,
For thou strong beere hast vndone mee.

Finis.

Printed for F. Groue.

[1] *Text* in.

64

The honest, plain-dealing porter

Pepys, I, 194, B.L., three woodcuts, four columns.

A didactic ballad of a type characteristic of Martin Parker. There is a sturdy independence, a pride in honest labour, in almost everything he wrote. That pride may also explain his deep veneration for the nobility and the throne. The present ballad in praise of porters should be compared with Thomas Brewer's much earlier production (No. 2). "The Proverb says, *Need makes the old wife trot*," remarks John Taylor, in his *Certaine Travailes of an Uncertain Journey* (1653). Many instances of this proverb far older than 1653 are given in Hazlitt's *Proverbs*, 1st ed., p. 288, and still older are the extraordinarily numerous uses of the proverb to which Professor Kittredge has referred me; as, "Besoing fet veille troter," of the thirteenth century (Haupt's *Zeitschrift*, XI, 115). The date of the ballad is about 1630. The tune is not known to me.

𝕿𝖍𝖊 𝖍𝖔𝖓𝖊𝖘𝖙 𝖕𝖑𝖆𝖎𝖓𝖊 𝖉𝖊𝖆𝖑𝖎𝖓𝖌 𝕻𝖔𝖗𝖙𝖊𝖗:
𝖁𝖁𝖍𝖔 𝖔𝖓𝖈𝖊 𝖜𝖆𝖘 𝖆 𝖗𝖎𝖈𝖍 𝖒𝖆𝖓, 𝖇𝖚𝖙 𝖓𝖔𝖜 𝖙𝖎𝖘 𝖍𝖎𝖘 𝖑𝖔𝖙,
𝕿𝖔 𝖕𝖗𝖔𝖚𝖊 𝖙𝖍𝖆𝖙 𝖓𝖊𝖊𝖉 𝖜𝖎𝖑𝖑 𝖒𝖆𝖐𝖊 𝖙𝖍𝖊 𝖔𝖑𝖉 𝖜𝖎𝖋𝖊 𝖙𝖗𝖔𝖙.

To the tune of *the Maids A.B.C.*

1   YOu who haue beene rich heretofore,
  and by ill fates are now grown poore,
In that estate doe not despaire,
  but patiently your crosses beare:
Though you haue quite consum'd your wealth,
  if God haue lent you limbs and health,
To labour daily murmur not,
  For need will make the old wife trot.

2   I haue had wealth as others haue,
  so much, I needed not to craue,
Among good fellowes some I spent,
  the rest to cosening knaues I lent:

Now all is gone, and nought is left,
    and I am faine to make hard shift,
Yet am contented with my lot,
    Thus need will make the old wife trot.

3 Now all my meanes is gone and spent,
    to fare hard I must be content,
To get my bread my browes must sweat,
    till I haue earnd I must not eate.
My charge I must take care to keepe,
    which makes me wake when others sleepe,
I trudge abroad be it cold or hot,
    Thus need will make the old wife trot.

4 At first to worke I was asham'd,
    but pouerty hath me so tam'd,
That now I thinke it no disgrace,
    to get my liuing in any place,
Tis more commendable to worke,
    then idlely at home to lurke,
Wishing for bread, and haue it not,
    Thus need will make the old wife trot.

5 Some idle knaues about this towne
    doe basely loyter vp and downe,
And ere they'le set their hands to worke,
    from place to place they'le liue by th shirke,
They'le sit i'th Alehouse all the day,
    and drinke and eate, yet nothing pay.
I scorne to drinke of anothers pot,
    though need doe make the old wife trot.

6 Such men as these I hold in scorne,
    Ile rather rise at foure i'th morne,
And labour hard til nine at night,
    ere I in shirking take delight:
What honestly I get I spend,
    and well accept what God doth send:
No man shall say he paid my shot,
    though need doth make the old wife trot.

7 My calling's honest, good and iust,
    well worthy to be put in trust,
I am a Porter my habit showes,
    my trade I doe not care who knowes,
I am a man that's borne to beare,
    I cary burthens farre and neere,
By which an honest meanes is got,
    thus need doth make the old wife trot.

8 When some who knew me rich before,
    doe shun to meet me now I'me poore,
I dare to looke them in the face,
    because my calling is not base.
For of all men we Porters be
    good vnderstanding men you see,
Then though I labour blame me not,
    for need will make the old wife trot.

The second part. The same Tune.

9 SUch pleasure in my worke I find,
    that I liue more content in mind,
To earne my liuing with my hands,
    then when I liued vpon my lands.
For many cares are incident
    to wealthy men, when sweet content
Doth fall vnto the meane mans lot,
    though need doth make the old wife trot.

10 When I doe meet with any friend,
    I seldome want a penny to spend,
Which brings me to a good report,
    because I liue in honest sort,
Ide rather earne my liuing deare,
    then steale or beg for bread or beere,
For charity is cold God wot,
    when need doth make the old wife trot.

11 We Porters are good fellowes still,
  and spend our money with good will,
When three or foure on's meet together,
  we needs must drinke come wind come wether,
In friendly sort our pence we ioyne,
  or more, if we be stor'd with coine,
We neuer wrangle at paying the shot,
  though need doth make the old wife trot.

12 When I all day haue labour'd hard,
  content at night is my reward.
When I come home, to quit my paines,
  my wife me kindly entertaines.
We sup with such as God hath sent,
  though nere so small we are content,
Come weale, come woe, we grumble not,
  For need will make the old wife trot.

13 Thus haue I showne you my estate,
  and how I first was crost by fate,
And how that crosse did proue a blis,
  because my mind contented is,
My meanes I did consume in wast,
  but there's no helpe for what is past,
I little dream'd of this my lot,
  but need will make the old wife trot.

14 By this I free my selfe of blame,
  my kindred I will neuer shame,
Well may they heare that I am poore,
  yet not to beg from doore to doore.
Let him who hath no house nor land,
  some honest calling take in hand,
Whereby a liuing may be got,
  For need will make the old wife trot.

15 If thou hast learning, strength, or wit,
  to vse it lawfully tis fit,

THE HONEST, PLAIN-DEALING PORTER

To sharke and shift from place to place,
  doth thee and all thy kin disgrace.
Tis base to beg, tis worse to steale,
  then if thou honestly doe deale,
Be not ashamed of thy lot,
  For need will make the old wife trot.

𝔉inis.

M.P.

Printed at London for F. Coules, dwelling at
the vpper end of the Old Baily.

65

A looking-glass for corn-hoarders

Pepys, I, 148, B.L., two woodcuts, four columns.

I have found no trace of John Russell, of St Peter's Chalfont, in histories of Buckinghamshire. It is worthy of note, however, that in 1631, when a dearth was threatening, Charles Fitz-Geffrie wrote *The Curse of Corne-hoarders: With The Blessing of seasonable Selling. In three Sermons, on Pro[verbs]. 11. 26. Begun at the general Sessions for the County of Cornwall, held at Bodmyn, and continued at Fowy* (British Museum, 4455. b. 13). Evidently he had not heard of Russell's calamity, for he mentions only the well-known traditional punishments inflicted upon Archbishop Walter Gray and Bishop Hatto. Ballad-writers never tired of writing fearful warnings against "ingrossers" of corn, many of whom in person sank into the ground. A very remarkable example of such a punishment occurs in "A true balett of Dening, a poore man, and a loffe of bred, which he paid for," printed as No. XLVII in H. Boeddeker's edition of the ballads from MS. Cotton Vespasian A. XXV (*Jahrbuch für romanische und englische Sprache und Literatur*, N.F., vols. II and III). Russell should have deemed himself lucky, for he escaped, and the yawning earth swallowed only one of his teams. But the punishments varied. Thus Goodman Inglebred, of Boughton, Norfolk, as one of Anthony à Wood's ballads ("A Warning-peice for Ingroosers of Corne," *ca.* 1643) tells us, suffered from a tornado, which the Devil sent suddenly and which "tore the Barne in pieces, and scattered all the Corne," doing such damage to his property as "the like was never heard of before." Many other engrossers hanged themselves "on the expectation of plenty," as the Porter in *Macbeth* remarks.

A LOOKING-GLASS FOR CORN-HOARDERS

**A Looking glasse for Corne-hoorders,
By the example of** *Iohn Russell* **a Farmer dwelling
at St Peters Chassant in Buckingham shire, whose
Horses sunke into the ground the 4 of March 1631.**

To the tune of *Welladay*.

1 OF wonders strange that was
      euer heard, euer heard,
  The like ne'r came to passe
    of this that followes.
  Let no man this truth doubt,
    but rather search it out:
  For tis spred farre about
    in euery place.

2 This woefull chance befell
    welladay, welladay,
  Which I with griefe doe tell,
    Lord, haue thou pitty.
  Since mens hearts are so hard,
    that poore from bread are bard,
  And diuers almost staru'd
    in this our Land.

3 In Buckingham Shire this
    Accident, Accident,
  Fell out at a place nam'd
    Saint *Peters Chassant.*
  This thing though strāge, 'tis[1] true,
    I doe assure all you
  That doe wrong, wrack and scrue,
    the needy poore.

4 The poore being abus'd
    by the rich, by the rich,
  And by them cruelly vs'd
    in euery Towne:

      [1] *Text* t'is.

371

But God that heares their moane,
    for their sakes hath this showne,
That's already noysd and blowne
    ouer the Land.

5 A Farmer there did dwell,
    rich he was, rich he was,
Who had much Corne to sell,
    and store of graine:
Iohn Russell was he nam'd,
    whose base fact hath him sham'd,
Because it is proclaim'd
    to his disgrace.

6 A poore man wanting graine,[1]
    came to him, came to him,
Requesting to obtaine
    some of his store,
The Farmer yeeldes thereto,
    seeming willing to doe
This for the poore man, so
    he might be payd.

7 The Farmer toke his price
    of his Corne, of his Corne,
The poore man was not nice
    but yeelded to it:
He bid him repaire home,
    and bring with him that summe
That they concluded on,
    and he should haue 't.

8 The poore man came and brought
    to the house, to the house,
Of the Farmer, and sought
    him, to fulfill
His former promise made,
    When he these words had said,
His mony downe he paid
    vnto the Farmer.

[1] Text has a period.

A LOOKING-GLASS FOR CORN-HOARDERS

𝕿𝖍𝖊 𝖘𝖊𝖈𝖔𝖓𝖉 𝖕𝖆𝖗𝖙. 𝕿𝖔 𝖙𝖍𝖊 𝖘𝖆𝖒𝖊 𝖙𝖚𝖓𝖊.

9   THe poore mā left his Sack
      with his quoine, with his quoine,
Thinking to returne back
    to him againe,
And for to fetch from thence
    that Corne, which he long since
Had giuen recompence
    vnto the full.

10 But afterwards he came
    to demand, to demand,
That Corne, yea that very same
    that he had bought,
The Farmers humour was such
    that he did grumble much.
Nor would he at all keepe touch
    with this poore man.

11 But told him, Corne did rise
    euery day, euery day,
And therefore a higher price
    must he giue him:

Otherwise he should not haue
   one Corne, though's life't might saue,
At which his speeches braue
   the poore man grieu'd.[1]

12 The poore man he went farre
   to his friend, to his friend,
To get some mony more,
   to buy that Corne.
Which when he had procur'd,
   though he was much iniur'd
He quietly indured,
   and gaue it him:

13 Who found him labouring
   in the field, in the field,
And hard a harrowing
   with his seruants,
But God will sure requite
   all those, that doe delight
To affront and affright
   those that are poore.

14 The ground strait opened wide,
   into which, into which
Did two of his horses slide:
   tis strange to heare.
They did sinke downe so lowe,
   thar[2] no man yet can know
Whither they fell, they did so
   strangely vanish:

15 The rest o' th' Teame did sinke
   presently, presently,
But twas good helpe, I thinke,
   that them releas'd.

[1] Comma in the text.
[2] *I.e.* there. *Possibly a misprint for* that.

They were rays'd vp againe,
   suffring but little paine.
This is a blot and staine
   to all our Mizers.

16 Let them take heed how they
   doe oppresse, doe oppresse
The poore that God obey,
   and are beloued.
God will not let these long
   alone, that doe his wrong,
Though ne'r so rich and strong
   that are oppressors.

Finis.

Printed at London for H. Gosson.

66

News from the Tower Hill

Pepys, I, 266, B.L., four woodcuts, four columns.

E[dward] B[lackmore] registered "Peg and Kate" on November 4, 1631 (Arber's *Transcript*, IV, 263). Parker was evidently fond of this "jest," to which he refers in his "Good Throw" (No. 67). But it is not edifying or, for that matter, moral, though Parker undoubtedly intended it to be a warning to young roarers to shun evil women. He commends his hero as a model, but most readers would be inclined to feel some indignation at the scurvy trick that insufferable young person plays on the two London prostitutes. As a picture of the times and for the light it throws on M.P. himself, the ballad is not without some interest. What appears to be a reference to it occurs in the two lines,—

> And have I met thee, sweet Kate?
> I will teach thee to walk so late,—

sung by Cuddy Banks in Ford, Dekker, and Rowley's *Witch of Edmonton* (printed 1658), III, i, although this play is usually regarded as having been acted *circa* 1621.

The music for *The North-Country Lass* which Chappell printed, with a specific reference to "News from the Tower Hill," in *Popular Music*, II, 457, is adapted neither to the measure nor to the stanza-form. In the same measure as the "News" and to the tune of *The North-Country Lass* is a ballad of "The Turtle Dove" in the *Roxburghe Ballads*, II, 592.

𝔑𝔢𝔴𝔢𝔰 from the 𝔗𝔬𝔴𝔢𝔯-𝔥𝔦𝔩𝔩:
𝔒𝔯,
𝔄 gentle warning to *Peg* and *Kate*,
𝔗𝔬 walke no more abroad so late.

To the tune of *the North countrey Lasse.*

1   A Pretty iest Ile tell,
     which was perform'd of late,
  Let Lasses all in generall,
     be warned by *Peg* and *Kate*.

2 These Lasses both doe dwell,
    neere Algate at this day,
A vse they had ith night to gad,
    abroad as I heard say.

3 To meete with some young men
    on them to shew affection,
Which vse they still on Tower-hill
    did keepe by due direction.

4 But now giue heede a while,
    and marke how they were serued,
Would all were so that thus doe goe,[1]
    then men might be preserued[2]

5 From these deluding bayts,
    which by the way doe catch them.[1]
Let all young men be carefull then,
    and marke how one did match them.

6 As they walkt forth one night,
    as twas their custome still,
A youngman kind did chance to finde
    them vpon Tower-hill.

7 And finding them so free,
    and easie to goe downe,
He got them both they were not loth
    with him to *Greenewich* Towne.

8 A payre of Oares he tooke,
    and thither went in hast,
While all that night they had delight,
    but marke what after past.

9 He brought them vp next day,
    and at the Posterne gate,
Into the Ship they all did skip,
    at night when it was late.

[1] No punctuation in the text.   [2] Text has a period.

10 Where they to supper had
    all dainties they could wish,
Young Rabbets fry'd they bade prouide
    and rost Beefe in a dish.

11 And Lambe they had beside,
    with Wine and Sugar store,
And musicke sweet which made the street
    to muse how they did roare.

12 At last the reckoning came
    to two and twentie shilling,
The Lad was wise and did deuise
    to make them pay for billing.

The second part, To the same tune.

13 SO out of doores he stept,
    and made a fine excuse,
The Lasses still their Wine did fill
    as twas their former vse.

14 But when they long[1] had stayd,
    and the Lad came no more,
The Vintner came of them to clayme
    money to cleere the score.

15 They sayd they had no money,
    to pay for what was drawne,
Their Aprons they vntill next day
    and Ruffes would leaue in pawne.

16 The Vintner would haue none,
    but swore he would be payd
Ere they did passe, or else alas
    in prison they must be stayd.

17 All night they tarryed there,
    ith morning *Peg* did send
To her Mother deare, who came to her
    as did become a friend.

[1] *n* upside down in text.

18 Her Husband came with her,
 and he did passe his word,
At a certaine day the shot to pay
 which they that night had scor'd.

19 And so they were dismist,
 well serued I protest:
If all base whores might pay such scores
 then men might passe in rest.

20 The youngman I commend,
 and wish that others would
Him imitate, then *Peg* and *Kate*
 would be no more so bold.

21 It is a great abuse,
 in *London* at this day,
Now in the street many nightly meet
 such wenches on the way.

22 Which causeth many a Man,
 that would goe home in quiet,
Upon such queans to spend his meanes,
 in filthinesse and ryot.

Finis.

M.P.

London Printed for E.B.

67

A good throw for three maidenheads

Pepys, 1, 314, B.L., one woodcut (which is reproduced in the *Roxburghe Ballads*, VIII, 641), four columns.

Granted the situation, Parker's ballad proceeds without offence. From the fourth line it is evident that this song was written to outjest the similar ballad of "Peg and Kate," or "News from the Tower Hill" (No. 66). Accordingly, the date of "A Good Throw" can be established as after November 4, 1631, at which time "Peg and Kate" was licensed. The ballad of "Over and Under," after which the tune was named (the music is given in Chappell's *Popular Music*, 1, 190), had been licensed on June 13, 1631 (*ibid.* p. 254). The dicing terms used by Parker are explained in the Glossary.

A good throw for three Maiden-heads.

Some say that mayden-heads are of high price,
But here are three maids that haue lost theirs at dice.

To the Tune, Of *Ouer and Vnder*.

1 THree maides did make a meeting,
    With one young man of late,
Where they had such a greeting,
As passes *Peg* and *Kate*.
They talke of many matters,
Not fitting to be told:
Also they dranke strong waters,
To heat their stomacks cold.
    and when they had,
    drunke with the Lad,
Vntill they were merry all:
    betweene them three,
    they did agree,
Into discourse to fall.

2 Concerning husbands getting,
  The question did arise,
  And each of them their sitting,
  Some reason did deuise.
  One was a milkemaid bonny,
  The other Ile not name,
  And shee did get much mony,
  By selling of the same,
        her name is *Ione*,
        as is well knowne,
  I hope tis no offence:
        to tell what they,
        did on that day,
  Before they went from thence.

3 They all did loue this young man
  And each for him did striue,
  It seemes he was a strong man,
  That could his worke contriue.
  Now which of them should haue him,
  They neither of them knew,
  But each of them did craue him,
  As her owne proper due.
        now meeting,
        and greeting,
  As maids and young men vse,
        with them he dranke,
        his money was franke,
  Indeed hee could not chuse.

4 And either of them telling,
  Her mind in full to him,
  Meane while the rest were filling,
  Their cupps vp to yee brim.
  Because in either of them,
  It seemes he had a share,

Unlesse he meant to scoffe them,
He now must choose his ware.
   and therefore they,
   without delay,
Being on the merry pinne:
   with good aduice,
   did throw the dice,
Who should the young man win.

5 The young man was contented,
And so the dice were brought.
The maids that this inuented,
Their lessons were well taught:
For the youngman all lusted,
And by this fine deuice,
They seuerally all trusted,
To win him by the dice.
   but harke now,
   and marke now,
The manner of their play:
   in their behalfe,
   I know youle laugh,
Before you goe away.

The second part, To the same tune.

6 IF any of the lasses,
  Doe ouerthrow the rest,
On her the verdict passes,
None should with her contest,
But she should haue her louer,
Cleane from the other twaine,
If euen not aboue her,
Then they must throw againe.
   but if hee,
   all them three,
Did win by throwing most:
   their mayden-heads all,
   to him must fall,
Without any paine or cost.

7 To this they all replied,
They ioyntly were agreed,
What words had testifyed,
Should be perform'd indeed.
The first maid threw, tray cater ace,
Which is in all but eight,
She hop'd from all the maids in place,
To win the lad by right,
 The second I thinke,
  threw tray dewce cinque,
There's ten (quoth she) for me.[1]
  the first was quell'd,
  for this excel'd,
Full sorely vext was she.

8 The third with courage lusty,
Did take the dice in hand,
Now dice if you be trusty,
Quoth she, this cast shall stand,
For I resolue for better for worse
As fortune shall dispose,
That either now ile win the horse
Or else the Saddle lose.
  she tooke them,
  and she shooke them,
And threw without feare or wit,
  tray cater sice,
  gramercy dice,
Quoth she, for that is it.

9 She thought herselfe most certain
The young man now to haue,
But false deluding fortune,
No such great fauour gaue.
The young man tooke the dice vp,[2]
Quoth he now haue at all,

---

[1] No period in the text.　　　[2] No comma in the text.

A GOOD THROW FOR THREE MAIDENHEADS

He threw sincke cater sice vp,
Which made her courage fall,
  who threw the last,
  for 'twas[1] surpast,
How now my girles, quoth hee,
  You must resigne,
  for they are mine,
Your maiden-heads to me.

10 For I haue fairely wonne them,
As you your selues can tell,
The lots were cast vpon them,
Which you all liked well.
The maydens all confessed,
That what he said was true,
And that they were distressed,
Should he exact his due.
  we hope sir,
  some scope sir,
You vnto vs will giue.
  if that we pay,
  whats lost by play,
Twere pitty we should liue.

11 Quoth he, Ile haue them all three,
For they by right are mine,
Or else in troth, they shall bee,
All painted on my signe.
The signe of the one maiden-head,
Hath oftentimes bin seene,
But ile haue three caus 't shall be sed
The like hath neuer beene.
  now whether this lad,
  his winnings had,
I cannot nor will not say:
  but likely tis,
  he would not mis,
What was won by faire play.

[1] *Text* t'was.

384

12 They thought they had bin priuat
Where none had hard their doing
But one did so contriue it,
That he heard all this woeing.
Thought he I haue heard many hold,
Their maiden-heads at high price,
But now hereafter it may be told,
How three were wonne at dice.
   this man ere long,
   did cause this song,
To be made on the same,
   that maidens faire,
   might haue a care,
And play at no such game.

𝔉inis.

                  M.P.

London, Printed for *I. Grissmond*.

68

A wonder beyond expectation

Pepys, I, 74, B.L., three woodcuts, five columns.

The "Wonder," which was registered for publication on January 2, 1632 (Arber's *Transcript*, IV, 268), is summarized from a thirty-five page pamphlet that was "Printed by R.Y. for Iohn Partridge" in 1631 under the title of *Gods Power and Providence: Shewed, In The Miracv-lous Pre-servation and Deliverance of eight Englishmen, left by mischance in Green-land Anno* 1630. *nine moneths and twelve dayes....Faithfully reported by Edward Pellham, one of the eight men aforesaid. As also with a Map of Green-Land* (British Museum, C. 59. g. 17). The pamphlet was also sum-marized in 1631 by John Rous in his *Diary* (ed. Camden Society, pp. 63–65), and is reprinted in Churchill's *Voyages*, volume II.

In his preface Pellham says: "If the first in inhabiting of a Countrey by a Princes Subiects (which is the King of *Spaines* best title to his *Indyes*) doth take possession of it for their *Soveraigne:* Then is *Green-land* by a second right taken *livery* and *Seisin* of, for his *Majesties* use; his Subiects being the first that ever did (and I beleeve the last that ever will) inhabite there." He declares that his experience was in every particular more re-markable than that of "the *Dutch-mens* hard Winter in *nova Zembla*" in 1596. Coming to his story, Pellham tells how he and his companions left London on May 1, 1630, in the ship *The Salutation of London* in the service of the Worshipful Company of Muscovie Merchants. Arriving at Greenland on June 11, the eight men were sent ashore to kill venison. They killed fourteen deer, but during their absence the winds and ice-drifts drove the *Salutation* away. As another English boat was known to be operating at Green Harbour, the eight men, loaded down with venison, set out for that place but arrived after the ship had sailed. Making the best of the matter, they settled down to a life that is described almost in Robinson Crusoe style. On May 25, 1631, two ships from Hull came to their port, and were followed three days later by the London fleet. At the end of the hunting season, on August 20, the rescued men and the fleet sailed for London.

The tune is named from a ballad called "The wonderful example of God shewed upon Jasper Coningham, a Gentleman born in Scotland, who was of oppinion that there was neither God, nor Divell, Heaven nor Hell. To the Tune of *O neighbour Robert*" (*Roxburghe Ballads*, III, 104). In MS. Rawlinson Poet. 185, fol. 21, is preserved "A Pleasant new

A WONDER BEYOND EXPECTATION

Sounge called The Carmen's Whistle. To the Tune of *O Neighbor Roberte*"
(cf. *ibid*. VII, xiv). Accordingly, it is evident that *O neighbour Robert* and
The Carmen's Whistle were identical. The music for the latter tune is
given in Chappell's *Popular Music*, I, 137.

**A wonder beyond mans expectation,
In the preseruation of eight men in** *Greenland* **from
one season to another, the like neuer knowne or heard
of before, which eight men are come all safely from
thence in this last Fleet, 1631. whose names are these,**
William Fakely **Gunner,** *Edward Pellham,* **Gunners
Mate,** *Iohn Wise, Robert Goodfellow* **Seamen,**
Thomas Ayers **Whalecutter,** *Henry Rett* **Cooper,**
Iohn Dawes, Richard Kellet **Landmen.**

To the tune of *Iasper Coningham*.

1 TO England comes strange tidings,
    from Greenland of eight men,
  Who there had their abidings,
    till season came agen:
  Beyond mans expectation,
    (as you shall vnderstand)
  Was their strange preseruation,
    within that barren land.

2 Where nothing for mans sustenance,
    most part o'th yeare doth grow,
  No Sun at all on them did glance,
    the hils are hid with Snow:
  White Beares and Foxes monstrous,
    and other sauage beasts,
  Within that Barren wildernesse,
    vpon each other feasts.

387

3 So that in mans coniecture,
    no man could there liue long,
But God the great Protector,
    of all both old and young,
Did shew his wondrous power,
    in helping these men there,
Whom beasts did not deuoure,
    nor hunger pinch too neare.

4 These men abroad there wandred,
    to hunt for Venson there,
Meane while the royall standard
    from heauen did appeare,
I meane the Starre so constant,
    which when they doe perceiue,
They must perforce that instant
    hoyst Sayles and take their leaue.

5 The Captaine he commanding
    his men to goe abord,
Alas there was no standing,
    the time would not afford,
So that these men being absent,
    were left behinde on shore
Because no time they had lent
    to linger any more.

6 But when these men returned,
    and found the ship was gone,
Alasse their hearts then burned,
    with woe they were[1] forlorne:
In pitious wise lamenting,
    their hard and heauy fate,
At last they all consenting,
    (to grieue it was too late.)

[1] *Text* we.

388

7 Then one man best experienc'd
    in pollicy and cunning,
The rest to try their wits incenc'd,
    quoth he, here is no running:
And seeing we are left here
    in this vnfertile place,
Lets doe our best with hearty cheare,
    the rest leaue to Gods grace.

8 Then with this resolution
    they firmely all agreed,
To search out the conclusion,
    and try how they could speed:
A Caue they dig'd i'th ground then,
    to shrowd them from the cold,
Wherein they liued sound men,
    most wondrous to behold.

9 Their Venson they dry baked,
    which serued them for bread,
For drinke their thirst they slaked
    with Snow water, in stead
Of English Beere and French Wine:
    to warme them they did burne
Three hundred Tunne of Casks,
    which stood there for their turne.

10 The flesh of Beares they boyled,
    in stead of powdered Beefe,
Their liues had all been spoyled,
    but for this course reliefe,
In oyle which they had left there,
    with shirts and other clothes,[1]
They made lamps to burn most cleer,
    beleeue it on their oathes.

[1] Text has a period.

11 And when their food was neare spent
   and fearing they should want
Vittaile for the remaining time,
   they did begin to scant
Themselues and feed but once a day,
   thus spare they did their meate,
And fasting dayes they did obserue,
   on which they naught did eate.

12 In this their extremity,
   when they did famine feare,
They spide to Sea horses
   that vnto them were neare,
And kild them as they a sleepe
   on th' Ice were set to rest,
Which fishes much comfort gaue
   these men so sore opprest.

The second part To the same tune.

13 VVHen much danger by these men
   they had past o're, much harme
They did receiue for want for clothes,
   wherewith to keepe them warme,
For by time, and their toyling
   their clothes were worne bare,
And torne, that they could not
   keepe out the piercing ayre.

14 But misery that makes men
   industrious, was so kinde,
To furnish them with a tricke
   to keepe them from the winde:
Their needle of Whales bone,
   vntwisted Ropes their thred,
They sow'd their clothes, & handsomly
   their bodies couered.

390

15 Foure of them watched duly,
 whilst th' other foure did sleepe,
Thus constantly and truly
 their houres they did keepe,
Els 't had beene impossible,
 they should themselues sustaine.
Thus they were neuer idle,
 but still were taking paine.

16 The Sabbath day they obserued,
 and spent it piously,
Yet not as they desired,
 nor yet so zealously
As they would haue been willing
 that holy day to keepe,
Because they had not any booke
 to keepe their eyes from sleepe.

17 Thus in that strange fashion,
 they liued in that place,
Till the ships of our English Nation,
 keeping their wonted space,
Did come againe and view them,
 clad with the skinnes of Beares,
The Captaine hardly knew them,
 his heart was full of feares.

18 But when he truly found them,
 so vnexpectedly,
To be all perfect sound men,
 he praised God on high:
Who had so well preserued
 these men of courage bold,
Whom he thought to be starued
 with hunger and with cold.

19 Now hauing past these dangers,
 they are come safe from thence,[1]

   [1] *Text* thnce.

A WONDER BEYOND EXPECTATION

And all both friends and strangers,
    not sparing for expence,
Are ioyfull for to see them,
    lauding in their behalfe,
That God which did free them,
    and brought them home so safe.

20 So long they there had tarried,
    vntill two of their wiues
Were in their absence married,
    not hoping of their liues.
This was the Lords owne doing,
    to him be giuen praise
For this strange wonder shewing,
    admired in our dayes.

Printed for *H. Gosson.*

69

It is bad jesting with a halter

Pepys, I, 440, B.L., four woodcuts, four columns. The sheet was wrinkled in the press, with the result that stanzas 1 and 2 were blurred in printing. Blurs and typographical errors are here silently corrected.

The ballad was registered on January 2, 1632 (Arber's *Transcript*, IV, 268). The refrain is musical, but not much can be said for Mr Guy's "merry jest," which, indeed, though it enforces an obvious moral, is rather stupid. The "jest," however, Professor Kittredge notes, is hoary with age, and he has been kind enough to give me these references to stories that illustrate the danger of playing at hanging: E. Meier, *Deutsche Sagen aus Schwaben*, I, 43; Kühnau, *Schlesische Sagen*, I, 559, 572, 592; Eisel, *Sagenbuch des Voigtlandes*, pp. 289–290; *Lincolnshire Notes and Queries*, I, 166; Grimm in Haupt's *Zeitschrift*, VII, 477. The oldest instance of all, he says, is the story of King Vikarr and Starkaðr in the Gautrekssaga.

Guy was a prolific ballad-writer: there are many of his signed pieces in the *Roxburghe Ballads* (*e.g.* II, 105, 164; III, 47). It can hardly be doubted that Robert Guy is referred to in the first and third of the following entries in John Parton's *Some Account of the Hospital and Parish of St Giles in the Fields, Middlesex*, 1822, p. 303:

> 1642.—P^d and given to *Guy*, a poore fellow   1^s
> ———. Geven to the *Ballet-singing Cobler*   1^s
> 1657.—P^d the collectors for a shroude for
>   *oulde Guy*, the poet   2/6

Possibly the second entry also refers to him. It is melancholy to think of a popular ballad-writer's being buried at the expense, complete or partial, of the parish!

The tune is named from the refrain of "A Choice of Inventions. To the tune of *Rock the Cradle, Sweet John*" (*Roxburghe Ballads*, I, 105). But *Rock the Cradle, Sweet John* and the tune given by Chappell (*Popular Music*, I, 189) as the equivalent of *Rock the Cradle, John* (see the ballad in *Roxburghe Ballads*, VII, 162) are evidently different tunes.

It is bad Jesting with a Halter.

A Merry Jest to you I'le make appeare,
That happened lately vnto London neere,
VVhereas good-fellowes were together drinking:
One of them in a jeering manner thinking
To scape shot=free, this fellow was in hope,
His shot to pay, by jeasting with a Rope:
VVhich jeasting might haue proued to his paine,
But hee'le be aduis'd how he jeasts so againe.

To the tune of *There was a Ewe had three Lambes.*

1 THree Iouiall sparkes together,
    merry they did make,
The coldnesse of the weather,
    made them their liquor take:
Their coyne they freely spent it,
    and quaft it merily,
And all as one consented
    merry for to bee:
One he for Tobacco cal'd,
    another cal'd for beere,
Another cal'd what haue you not
    some faggots bring vs heere:
They were three lusty souldiers,
    had seru'd in France and Spaine,
Germany and Italy,
    and were come home againe,
One in Warres had lost an eye,
    another shot quite through the thigh,
the third in Turkish slauery,
    endured had much paine.

2 These were no Maunding souldiers,
    maunding vp and downe,
With knap-sakes on their shoulders
    that trudge from Towne to Towne,

394

And by their Roking cunning
   poore *Ale-wiues* oft deceiue:
For meate and drinke, and lodging,
   and doe their charges saue:
These were no such they would keepe tutch,
   & pay their shot though ne'r so much,
To gaine the loue of poore and rich,
   their fauour still to haue.
They were three lusty Souldiers, &c.

3 Also three iouiall Saylers,
   vnto these Soldiers came,
And brought with them two Taylors,
   but none of them Ile name:
And brought with them a fellow,
   a Butcher and a Baker,
But all this time to make them euen
   did want the neat shooe-maker:
Quoth one of them I haue a friend,
   and he dwells here fast by,
A shooe-maker lets for him send
   he is good company,
They were three lusty Souldiers, &c.

4 He will sing and be merry,
   drinke and pay his share,
We wish then said his neighbors all
   that now we had him here:
They for him sent, incontinent,
   he came and gaue them good content,
And was so full of merriment,
   he pleas'd them all were there.
They were three lusty Souldiers, &c.

5 For nothing there was wanting
   that might giue them content,
They merry were, and made good cheere
   and liberally they spent,

Still calling on the Tapster,
　　of Beere, to bring the best:
Then silent be, and list to me,
　　for now beginnes the Iest,
This fellow he, most Iouially,
　　did for Tobacco call:
And sayes my noble Iouiall blades
　　a health vnto you all.
They were three lusty Souldiers,
　　had seru'd in France, and Spaine,
　　Germany and Italy,
　　and were come home, &c.

The Second Part To the same tune.

6　THus beeing blith together,
　　　vnto their hearts desire
Sayes he here is cold weather,
　　lets haue a better fire,
And bring vs more Tobacco,
　　and of your Beere the best,
For whilst I stay, my part Ile pay,
　　and be a Iouiall guest.
Hang money it is but an Asse,
　　for meanes I cannot lacke,
Then fill the other dozen in,
　　let sorrow and care goe packe.
They were three lusty Souldiers
　　and seru'd in France and Spaine,
　　Germany, and Italy,
　　and were come home againe, &c.

7　So calling for the Tapster,
　　　to know what was to pay,
Sayes he I haue no money,
　　but if you please to stay,
And drinke the tother dozen
　　whil'st[1] the Faggots burne,

[1] *Text* whls't.

I scorne you for to cozen
    but presently returne:
And money bring: then may I sing,
    a Flye, a figge for care,
Ile hast away, and make no stay,
    but come and pay my share.
They were three lusty Souldiers, &c.

8 So presently returning,
    they all were in good hope,
That he some money then had brought
    till pulling out a Rope,
Which he had in his breeches,
    on termes he did not stand,
But askt if any one were there
    would buy a Carelesse-Band:
A neate one a feate one,
    that was both strong and new,
And nere was worne, I dare be sworne,
    beleeue me it is true.
They were three lusty Souldiers, &c.

9 The company then smiling
    for to be Ieered so,
One of them to him calling,
    the price of it to know:
Is this a Carelesse-Band sayes he,
    I must commend thy wit:
Then presently, I meane to try
    how it thy necke will fit:
The Rope then, he tooke then,
    of trueth as I heard say,
And with a twitch his necke did stretch
    vntill he gasping lay.
They were three lusty Souldiers, &c.

10 But when he did recouer,
    and to his sences came,

IT IS BAD JESTING WITH A HALTER

Saith he I must acknowledge
   that I was much too blame,
In such a foolish manner
   my betters so to Ieere:
That here I should haue breath'd my last
   it put me in a feare:
Your gentle fauours crauing,
   and briefely to be plaine,
It shall to me a warning bee,
   for Iesting so againe,
They were three lusty Souldiers, &c.

11 Thus all the City ouer,
   by rumour it was spread,
E're he could well recouer
   that surely he was dead:
And that for trueth of certaine,
   he like a wretched Elfe,
Had by some dire misfortune
   vntimely hang'd himselfe:
This song therefore it written was,
   to cleare all doubts of it,
That all may know, it is not so,
   he is not dead as yet:
But hopes to liue, content to giue,
   and so continue by care to thriue,
Ne'r in that perill for to come
   of such a hanging fit.
They were three lusty Souldiers, &c.

Finis.

By *Robert Guy.*

London Printed for F.C.

398

70

News from Holland's Leaguer

Pepys, 1, 98, B.L., two woodcuts, five columns.

Holland's Leaguer was a notorious brothel kept by a Mrs Holland[1] on the Bankside, Southwark. It is described in a quarto pamphlet called *Hollands Leagver: OR, An Historical Discourse Of The Life and Actions of Dona Brit-tanica Hollandia the Arch-Mistris of the wicked women of Evtopia*, 1632 (Bodleian, Malone 227). Of this establishment J. W. Ebsworth (*Bagford Ballads*, 1, 507*) remarks:

> In general, the houses of ill-fame, attacked by the apprentices on Shrove-Tuesdays, were scarcely different from ordinary dwellings, and perhaps private spite often dictated the selection more than just cause of offence. But Holland's Leaguer was exceptional, and claimed to be an island out of the ordinary jurisdiction. The portcullis, drawbridge, moat, and wicket for espial, as well as an armed bully or Pandar to quell disagreeable intruders, if by chance they got admittance without responsible introduction, all point to an organized system. There were also the garden-walks, for sauntering and "doing a spell of embroidery, or fine work," *i.e.* flirtation; the summer-house that was proverbially famous or infamous for intrigues, and the river conveniently near for disposal of awkward visitors who might have met with misadventure.

Ebsworth (*ibid.* p. 508*) has reproduced from the 1632 pamphlet the famous woodcut of the brothel.

The pamphlet was licensed for publication on January 20, 1632; six days later Shackerley Marmion's comedy of *Holland's Leaguer* was licensed. Laurence Price's ballad followed on May 24 (Arber's *Transcript*, IV, 278), and deals with the same subject: it is simply a poetical paraphrase of the tract of January 20, although Ebsworth states positively (*Roxburghe Ballads*, VIII, 564) that it "is historical, on the Dutch alliance, and has nothing to do with the moated grange bearing the same name, on the Bankside in London."

For the tune see the introduction to No. 33.

---

[1] She was twice summoned before the Court of High Commission in 1631 (on January 26 and February 9), but failed to appear. She is called "Elizabeth Holland a woman of ill reporte," and mention is made of a husband. See S. R. Gardiner's *Reports of Cases in the Courts of Star Chamber and High Commission* (Camden Society), pp. 263, 268.

NEWS FROM HOLLAND'S LEAGUER

𝕹𝖊𝖜𝖊𝖘 from *Hollands* 𝕷𝖊𝖆𝖌𝖊𝖗 :
OR,

Hollands 𝕷𝖊𝖆𝖌𝖊𝖗 𝖎𝖘 𝖑𝖆𝖙𝖊𝖑𝖞 𝖚𝖕 𝖇𝖗𝖔𝖐𝖊𝖓,
𝕿𝖍𝖎𝖘 𝖋𝖔𝖗 𝖆 𝖈𝖊𝖗𝖙𝖆𝖎𝖓𝖊 𝖎𝖘 𝖘𝖕𝖔𝖐𝖊𝖓.

To the tune of, *Canons are roaring.*

1 YOu that desire newes,
   list to my story;
Some it will make to muse,
   some will be sorry,
Some will reioyce thereat,
   others will wonder,
To see the barke and tree
   parted asunder.
This of a certaine
   for truth it is spoken,
That Hollands Leager,
   up lately is broken.

2 Such Ensignes were displaid
   to amaze *Holland,*
The like hath seldome been,
   I thinke in no land.
From many parts there hath
   gallants resorted;
Because the fame thereof
   they heard reported:
Yet some their labour lost,
   for it is spoken,
That Hollands, &c.

3 The flaunting *Spaniard,*
   and boone Cauillera,
The bragging *Dutchman*
   thought cost him deare a:
Wallouns and *Switzer,*
   both *Iewes, Turke* and *Neager,*[1]
Scots, Danes and *French,*
   haue been at *Hollands* Leager.
Yet all would[2] not auaile,
   for it is spoken,
That Hollands, &c.

4 Though many sought to
   inuade the strong Iland,
And stratagems deuised
   by sea and by land,
Rumors were spred abroad,
   fames Trumpet sounding,
Their Sconce so firmely stood,
   they fear'd no wounding:
But yet for all their pompe,
   thus it is spoken,
That Hollands, &c.

---

[1] No comma in the text.
[2] *Text* wonld.

5 The great god *Iupiter*
    did well affect her:
And *Mars* the god of warre,
    did so protect her,
His martiall discipline
    made her so valiant,
She durst in battell ioyne
    with any Gallant:
Yet though she valour had,
    thus it is spoken,
That Hollands, &c.

6 Belloniaes blustring shot,
    they neuer feared,
But brauely face to face,
    the Champions dared:
She seldome tooke the foyle
    by friend or stranger,
Unlesse a backe recoyle
    put her in danger,
But yet for all their pomp,
    thus it is spoken,
That Hollands, &c.

7 Blow for blow, shot for shot
    still they returned,
But sliding Cowards
    she euer disdained:
If any younker
    the Island doe venter,
Without admittance
    no partie could enter.
But tho they were so stout
    thus it is spoken,
That Hollands Leager
    is lately up broken.

8 The draw-bridge being
    up taken they durst to,

Stand to push of pike
   and giue a thrust too:
Those that gaue onset
   sometimes got th' worst ont,
And at their parting
   most dearly haue curst ont.
But howeuer it is spoken
   that Hollands Leager
Vp lately is broken.

𝕿𝖍𝖊 𝖘𝖊𝖈𝖔𝖓𝖉 𝖕𝖆𝖗𝖙. 𝕿𝖔 𝖙𝖍𝖊 𝖘𝖆𝖒𝖊 𝕿𝖚𝖓𝖊.

9 BUlworkes and batteries
   and other fences
Daily manteined
   the Iland expences:
Store of musition,
   and all things at pleasure,
Fit for this company
   gold and rich treasure
They had at her command
   yet it is, &c.

10 Now since the Leager broke
   and they are excluded
The chiefe Commander
   by fate is subdued,
Those that did them assault
   thought it small purchase,
The *Lion* scornes to prey
   on a dead carkas.
This we heare certainly
   by many spoken,
That Hollands, &c.

11 All those that vsed to
   frequent this border
Are backe retired for
   there's a new order:

That none shall thither come
   to worke a violence,
Great and small, high and low,
   all must keepe silence,
For it is by many spoken,
   that Hollands, &c.

12 Yet youngsters[1] arme your selues,
      here comes new tidings
   Allthough the Campe be broke,
      for their abidings,
   They haue a refuge found,
      that can defend them,
   Drummes, pikes and musketers
      doth there attend them
   Then brauely march along,
      gallants in clusters,
   Arrive at Bewdly,
      where they keep their musters.

13 There front garded is
      with such strong forces
   Only they left behind
      some certaine Horses,
   Yet for a trifle
      they will not be daunted,
   When once their Colors
      o'th' wall is aduanced.
   Feare to march away,
      gallants in clusters,
   To Bewdly heigh, where
      they keep their musters.

14 Now if my newes in
      this song may content you,
   Buy it and try it
      and neuer repent you,

---

[1] *Text* younster.

NEWS FROM HOLLAND'S LEAGUER

For your recreation
    in loue I haue pend it:
Trusting no creature I
    haue here offended,
With telling of the newes
    which I heard spoken,
That Hollands Leager
    is lately up broken.

Finis.

L.P.

London, printed for I.W.

The honest age

Pepys, 1, 156, B.L., four woodcuts, four columns.

Henry Gosson and his partners registered "The Honest Age" on May 24, 1632 (Arber's *Transcript*, IV, 278). It is of very little interest apart from the fact that its author, Laurence Price, mentions—apparently with approval—*Robin Conscience,* a long ballad-poem among the most pretentious and popular of Parker's works. The ballad, then, is one of many proofs (cf. the introduction to No. 78) that Price and Parker, though great rivals, were on friendly terms. *Robin Conscience* was first registered for publication on April 20, 1630 (*ibid.* p. 233); a late edition of it (1683) is reprinted in the *Harleian Miscellany,* 1808, 1, 48–54.

For the tune cf. No. 41.

The Honest Age,

OR

There is honesty in all Trades; As by this Ditty shall appeare, Therefore attend and giue good eare.

To the tune of *the Golden age.*

1 YOu Poets that write of the ages that's past,
   I pray stay your hand and write not too fast,
   Ile write of an age that for euer shall last,
   Plaine dealing in Country and City is plac't.
   O this is an honest age,
   This is a plaine dealing age.

2 Some people at these strange tidings will muse,
   And some will be ioyfull to heare such rare newes,
   Then list to my Ditty for it briefly shewes,
   No man Ile offend, then let no man refuse,
   To heare of this honest age,
   This is a plaine dealing age.

THE HONEST AGE

3 And first to goe forward as now I intend,
I heare that the Broker his money will lend
To any poore Neighbour his estate to amend,
How well is that man that hath got such a friend.
     O this is an honest age,
     This is a plaine dealing age.

4 The Chandler that keepes coles and fewel to sell,
Doth top heape his measure and soundly it fill,
For Sope, Starch, and Candle he wayeth so well,
That of his plaine dealing his neighbors can tell.
     O this is an honest age,
     This is a plaine dealing age.

5 That Taylor doth scorne to deceiue any friend,
But vnto plaine dealing his mind he doth bend,
If once he were false he hath sworne to amend,
No more cloth, nor silke, lace, to hell he will send.
     O this is an honest age,
     This is a plaine dealing age.

6 The Cookes in Pye-corner deceit will not vse,
In rosting meat three times their trade to abuse,
They'l rather both custome and money refuse,
Than vse a man falsely if that they can chuse.
     O this is an honest age,
     This is a plaine dealing age.

7 The Tapster is willing to giue men content.
To sell them full measure his humour is bent
If a man score a dozen he will not repent,
Nor take of you hate for the beere which is spent
     O this is an honest age,
     This is a plaine dealing age.

8 I heare this of Bakers in sizing of bread,
Tho some think that conscience frō Bakers is fled
Since one through the Pillery put forth his head,
No more of their company will be misled.
     O this is an honest age,
     This is a plaine dealing age.

THE HONEST AGE

9 ALso the Butcher so iouiall and bold,
   Is turn'd a plaine dealer as you may behold,
   They'l put forth no tainted meat for to be sold
   To wrong any Neighbour for siluer nor gold,
        O this is an honest age,
        This is a plaine dealing age.

10 The Miller that vsed too deepe to take tole,
    Is now in great feare to endanger his soule,
    Of late *Robin Conscience* tooke him by the pole,
    And charg'd him to flye those offences so foule.
         O this is an honest age,
         This is a plaine dealing age.

11 The Brewer that made his beere very small,
    Hath changed his hand since Malt had a fall,
    And by this meanes gained the loue of them all,
    The rich and the poore, the great and the small.
         O this is an honest age,
         This is a plaine dealing age.

12 And the neat Shooemaker who merrily sings,
    Whose predecessors were heires vnto Kings,
    To such good perfection all matters he brings,
    That throughout all Europe his credit rings,
         O this is an honest age,
         This is a plaine dealing age.

13 The Weauer, the Glouer, the Mason also,
    The Painter that makes such a gorgious show,
    The Pewterer, the Plūmer with other trades mo
    Will vse no false dealing where euer they goe.
         O this is an honest age,
         This is a plaine dealing age.

14 The Cooper, the Blacksmith the ancient translater
  The Copper-nos'd tinker w^t his wife y^t kind creture
  And y^t swaggering Sowgelder & Iack y^t greater eater
  Hath sworne to his wife that he neuer will beat her
       O this is a quiet age,
       This is a plane dealing age.

15 The Spendthrift that vsed in Tauerns to rore,
  With wine and Tobacco and sometimes a whore[1],
  Say's now hee'l liue honest and doe so no more.
  If he haue spare money hee'l giue it to the poore,
       O this is an honest age,
       This is a plaine dealing age.

16 All this honest company which I haue nam'd,
  I trust will like of it I shall not be blam'd,
  For this rare new Ditty in loue I haue fram'd,
  I know no plaine dealing man will be asham'd,
       To heare of this honest age,
       This is a plaine dealing age.

17 Thus here you see honesty flyes vp and downe,
  through Citty, through Country through Village &
     Town
  Amongst other vertues it merits renown,
  By this for example that it may be knowne,
       That this is the honest age,
       The best and honestest age.

𝔉inis.[2]

L. P.

London, Printed for H.G.

[1] *Text apparently* whoroe.
[2] No period in the text.

72

Knavery in all trades

Pepys, 1, 166, B.L., four woodcuts, four columns.

Francis Grove registered this ballad on July 16, 1632 (Arber's *Transcript*, IV, 281). In it Martin Parker gives a mournful account of the evils of his time, but no doubt his disgust and cynicism were assumed for the occasion. Probably it was nothing but an answer to Laurence Price's "Honest Age" (No. 71). In the second stanza of part two, however, there are some bitter comments on persons who evade paying their scores in taverns and inns which may have been due to Parker's own experience. He is known to have been an ale-house keeper, and one of his lost ballads, licensed on July 19, 1636, had the significant title of "Certaine verses of Martin Parker against trusting to sett vp in Alehouses."

For the tune see Chappell's *Popular Music*, 1, 267.

𝔎𝔫𝔞𝔲𝔢𝔯𝔶 𝔦𝔫 𝔞𝔩𝔩 𝔗𝔯𝔞𝔡𝔢𝔰,

OR,

𝔥𝔢𝔯𝔢'𝔰 𝔞𝔫 𝔞𝔤𝔢 𝔴𝔬𝔲𝔩𝔡 𝔪𝔞𝔨𝔢 𝔞 𝔪𝔞𝔫 𝔪𝔞𝔡.

To the tune of, *Ragged and torne and true.*

1   AS I was walking of late,
         within the fields so faire,
    My minde to recreate,
         well nye orecome with care:
    I heard two men discourse,
         as I along did walke,
    It mou'd mee with remorse,
         to hearken to their talke,
    Full oftentimes they said,
         (to heare them I was sad)
    All honesty is decay'd,
         here's an age would make a man mad.

2 The one to the other did say,
    what course shall I take to liue,
For none can thriue at this day,
    but such as their mindes doe giue:
To ouer-reach and deceiue,
    and doing of others wrong,
All they that such courses leaue,
    may sing the Begger-Boyes Song.
A man can scarce thriue by his trade
    mens consciences are so bad,
All honesty is decay'd,
    here's an age will make a man mad.

3 Hee that is rich already,
    is like still to bee so,
And he that is poore and needy,
    his burthen must vndergoe;
Tis a Prouerb vs'd in our Towne,
    it hath beene and euer will,
That if a man be once downe,
    the world cryes downe with him still,
How shall a man finde a trade,
    whereby true meanes may be had,
All honesty is decay'd,
    here's an age would make a man mad.

4 If a poore man be wrong'd by a rich,
    as alas we daily see,
Without money to goe through stitch,
    in a pittifull case is hee:
He were better to pocket the wrong,
    than himselfe into trouble to draw,
For vnlesse his pockets be strong,
    tis but folly to meddle with Law,
This makes many men dismay'd,
    for the fee makes a case good for bad,
All honesty is decay'd,
    here's an age would make a man mad.

5 Betweene the Lawyer and
 the money-begetting Mizer,
Men lose both house and land,
 and afterwards wish they had bin wiser:
Although we haue plenty of Graine,
 yet the rich make among vs a dearth,
Which causeth the poore to complaine,
 as though little grew on the earth,
Ingrossing is growne such a trade,
 that the poore haue great cause to be sad,
All honesty is decay'd,
 here's an age would make a man mad.

6 One tradesman deceaueth another,
 and sellers will conycatch buyers,
For gaine one wil cheat his own brother,
 the world's full of swearers and lyars:
Men now make no conscience of oathes,
 and this I may boldly say,
Some Rorers doe were gallant clothes,
 for which they did neuer pay:
The rich shall a Saint be made,
 though his life be neuer so bad,
All honesty is decay'd,
 here's an age would make a man mad.

The second part. To the same tune:

7 THe Taylor can neuer liue well,
 as many men plainely perceiues,
Unlesse he haue gaines from hell,
 or liues vpon Cabidge leaues;
O is 't not a pittifull case,
 and a thing which few men beleeues?
A Taylor that will liue in grace,
 cuts out of one gowne three sleeues:
Thus they must vse their Trade,
 or else little meanes can be had,
All honesty is decay'd,
 here's an age would make a man mad.

8 The Victualers, Tapsters and Cookes,
    are hindered very sore,
With many sharking Rookes,
    that vse to encroch on their skore:
And when they are once in chalke,
    the house they will refraine,
And to other places they'l walke,
    but neuer come there againe.
This trusting without being paid,
    breakes many an honest Lad,
All honesty is decay'd,
    here's an age would make a man mad.

9 Plaine dealing now is dead,
    and truth is so rare to finde,
That most men now are led,
    contrary vnto kinde:
Where one man's iust and sound,
    whose words and deeds agree,
A dozen may be found,
    that will from their promise flee,
Such knaues makes men afraid,
    to beleeue a true hearted Lad,
For honesty is decay'd,
    here's an age would make a man mad.

10 Such horrible abuse,
    is practis'd in this Nation,
A fashion now in vse,
    next month is out of fashion:
Our men are effeminate,
    which all their manhood disgraces,
And makes our foes of late,
    to ieere vs to our faces,
They were of vs afraid,
    when English hearts wee had,
Our honour is much decay'd,
    here's an age would make a man mad.

KNAVERY IN ALL TRADES

11 A man I may rightly say,
      may be mad to note these times,
Since Vertue doth decay,
      and Vice to preferment climes:
Now couetousnesse and pride,
      is ore the Land bespread,
All charities laid aside,
      and conscience is quite dead:
The Master abuseth his Maid,
      which makes the Mistris sad,
Thus honesty is decay'd,
      here's an age would make a man mad.

12 Some men that haue wiues at home,
      both beautifull, vertuous, and chaste,
Abroad amongst whores doe rome,
      and with them their meanes they wast:
While the wife at home doth stay,
      the husband in Tauernes doth roare.
She thinkes he is busie all the day,
      indeed so he is with his whore:
In briefe no more need be said,
      all things doe appeare too bad,
For honesty is decay'd,
      here's an age would make a man mad.

Finis.

M.P.

London, Printed for F. Groue.

414

73

Gallants, to Bohemia

Pepys, I, 102, B.L., two woodcuts, four columns.

This musical ballad, dating about 1632, urges England to participate in the conquests and spoils of Gustavus Adolphus in Germany, and laments the apparent military decadence of England since the glorious days of Sir John Norris, George, Earl of Cumberland, Thomas Cavendish, Robert Devereux, Earl of Essex, Sir Humphrey Gilbert, Frobisher, Lord Grey de Wilton, and Lord Willoughby de Eresby. The writer's chief regret seems to be for the gold and precious stones in which, on account of her neutrality, England has no share; though he professes, also, an eagerness to help to defeat Popery. The ballad is valuable evidence of the feelings and the attitude of a man of the streets towards the German wars. Every important incident of the Thirty Years' War was, as soon as the news reached London, at once put into ballads for circulation. See, for example, Arber's *Transcript*, IV, 144, 268, 271, 274, 282, 299.

The "pleasant warlike tune" can be identified, thanks to a badly mutilated ballad in the Manchester Collection (I, 48) of "England's Monthly Predictions" to the tune of *Let us to the Wars Again; or, The Maying Time*; for the music of *Maying Time* was included by Chappell in his *Popular Music* (I, 377). Another ballad in the same collection (I, 2), "The Great Turk's Challenge, this Year 1640," is to be sung to *My bleeding heart* [a tune often referred to], *or, Lets to the wars again*. Martin Parker's own ballad of "News from Newcastle," 1640 (*ibid*. I, 1), is sung to *Lets to the wars again*.

Gallants, to Bohemia.
Or, let vs to the Warres againe: Shewing the forwardnesse of our English Souldiers, both in times past, and at this present.

To a pleasant new Warlike tune.

1 YE noble *Brittaines*, be no more
     possest with ease vpon the shore:
You that haue beene so bold and stout,
    sit not musing, but looke out:
Kings of England with their shields
    full oft haue fought in martiall fields,
And golden prizes did obtaine:
    Then let vs to the warres againe.

2 Ye noble Captaines of the Land,
    and Sea men of such braue command:
Bend all your forces to the Seas,
    and take on Land no longer ease:
For Drums and Trumpets are not mute,
    to call you forth with Fife and Flute,
To fleete your ships vpon the maine,
    Then let vs to the warres againe.

3 Now Sea-men Pylots leaue the Land,
    Card and Compasse take in hand:
And hye againe to *Neptune* Seas,
    where we'l haue riches when we please
Our Souldiers they are men of might,
    and will for gold and siluer fight:
Which doth vs brauely all maintaine,
    Then let vs to the warres againe.

4 *France* and *Flanders* makes no mone,
    they get riches, we get none,
Flemish Captaines sayle about,
    vnknowne Islands to find out:

GALLANTS, TO BOHEMIA

That *Indian* Pearles and Iewells store,
    may decke them brauely on the shore:
Away then Gallants, hence amaine,
    And let vs to the warres againe.

5 Some seeke in forraigne Lands to thriue,
    we like Bees do keepe our hiue:
Some get riches, Pearle and Gold,
    we sitting still grow faint and cold:
Once againe let it be said,
    we forraigne actions neuer fear'd,
The true Religion to maintaine,
    Come let vs to the warres againe.

6 In faire *Bohemia* now is sprung,
    a Seruice which we lookt for long:
Where Souldiers may their valour trie,
    when cowards from the field will flye:
It neuer shall of vs be said,
    that English Captaines stood afraide:
Or such aduentures would refraine,
    Then let vs to the warres againe.

7 Of late we had within our Land,
    a noble number of command:
Of gallant Leaders braue and bold,
    that almost all the world controld:
As *Essex*, *Cumberland* and *Drake*,
    which made both Sea & Land to shake,
The *Indian* siluer to obtaine,
    Then let vs to the warres againe.

The second Part. To the same tune.

8 THe *Norrisses*, and noble *Veeres*,
    and *Sidnies* famous many yeares:
The *Willoughby* and worthy *Gray*,
    that serued still for royall pay:

Made *England* famous euery where,
    to such as did their fortunes heare:
Then let vs not at home remaine,
    But Brauely to those warres againe.

9 *Gilbert, Hawkins, Forbisher,*
    and golden *Candish, Englands* starre:
With many a Knight of noble worth,
    that compass'd round the circled earth:
Haue left examples here behinde,
    the like aduentures forth to finde:
The which to follow and maintaine,
    Come, let vs to those warres againe.

10 Let vs no more sit musing then,
    but shew our selues true Englishmen,
Whose fames great *Mars* resounds from farre,
    to be the onely men of warre:
The bounds of *Europe* cannot yeeld,
    forth better Souldiers for the field:
Let bullets come as thicke as raine,
    Wee'l[1] brauely to those warres againe.

11 *Bohemian* Drums and Trumpets call,
    a Summons to vs Souldiers all:
Then who will from such seruice flye,
    when Princes beare vs company,
To armes, to armes all *Europe* sings,
    the cause is iust, we fight for Kings,
The which most brauely to maintaine,
    Come let vs to those warres againe.

12 The *Germane* States, and Netherlands,
    haue mustred vp their martiall bands:
The *Denmarke* King doth close combine,
    his forces to the *Palatine:*

[1] Text *We'el.*

With three hundred Princes more,
   'side Dukes, Earles and Barons store:
Then how can we at home remaine,
   But brauely to those warres againe.

13 The Seas with ships are richly spread,
   the Land with colours white and red
And euery Captaine ready prest,
   to rancke his squadrons with the rest:
The Martiall musickes ratling sound,
   sayes, Soldiers, stand & keep your ground
Though burning bullets flye amaine,
   Yet will we to those warres againe.

14 Our Leaders nobly minded are,
   for to maintaine so braue a warre
As this, for true Religions right,
   to spend their liues in bloudy fight:
For God and for his Gospell, then
   to armes, and fight it out like men,
The which most brauely to maintaine,
   Let vs go to the warres againe.

15 And let vs all that Souldiers be,
   both noble bloud and low degree:
Be true to him that takes in hand
   these popish kingdomes to withstand:
God guide him on with good successe,
   and all his noble army blesse:
And so we shall the right maintaine,
   And go vnto these warres againe.

Imprinted at London by G.E.

74

Charles Rickets' recantation

Pepys, 1, 172, B.L., three woodcuts, four columns.

Perhaps this was the ballad called "Long Runns that neere turnes" which was licensed to John Wright, July 8, 1633 (Arber's *Transcript*, IV, 299). "He runneth far that never turneth again" occurs among John Heywood's *Proverbs*, 1562 (*Works*, ed. J. S. Farmer, pp. 90, 182).

Charles Rickets may be a pseudonym of Charles Records, whose name is signed to a number of ballads of this type; as, "The Goodfellow's Advice" against drink and other vices (*Roxburghe Ballads*, III, 261; cf. the list given at p. 681). Possibly Charles was, as he professes, a roaring Oxfordshire trader; but certainly the exploits for which he grieves seem tame enough. The "crotchet" which he played on a tailor by spending his shilling hardly seems a matter for mention, much less for excessive repentance.

No information about the tune is available.

Charles Rickets 𝔥𝔦𝔰 𝔯𝔢𝔠𝔞𝔫𝔱𝔞𝔱𝔦𝔬𝔫.
𝔚𝔞𝔯𝔫𝔦𝔫𝔤 𝔞𝔩𝔩 𝔤𝔬𝔬𝔡 𝔉𝔢𝔩𝔩𝔬𝔴𝔢𝔰 𝔱𝔬 𝔰𝔱𝔯𝔦𝔲𝔢,
𝔗𝔬 𝔩𝔢𝔞𝔯𝔫𝔢 𝔴𝔦𝔱𝔥 𝔥𝔦𝔪 𝔱𝔥𝔢 𝔴𝔞𝔶 𝔱𝔬 𝔱𝔥𝔯𝔦𝔲𝔢.

To the Tune of his lamentation, or *Ile beat my wife no more*.

1 HE runs farre that ne'r returneth,
   is a Prouerbe still in vse:
And hee's vnhappy that ne'r mourneth,
   for his former times abuse.
     I therefore,
     who vs'd to rore,
Where-euer I did come or goe,
     do now repent,
     for time ill spent,
And vow Ile neuer more doe so.

2 All my folly now Ile banish,
 which before possest my minde:
All ill husbandry shall vanish,
 for I now begin to finde
  that mine owne good
  I haue withstood,
And brought my substance very low,
  but now Ile giue
  my mind to thriue,
Good heauens grant I may doe so.

3 I haue vs'd among the brauest,
 to keepe quarter like a gallant,
By which meanes my wealth is lauisht,
 for with the best I spent my talent:
  when to a Faire
  to sell my ware,
Or Market, I did vse to goe,
  there was but few
  but my name knew,
I vs'd to drinke and fuddle so.

4 Who but *Charles* the Lad of *Morton*[1],
 was denoted farre and neere?
But now alas they shall come short on,
 that which late I did appeare:
  for now I meane
  to abandon cleane,
Those humors which in me did flow,
  Ile bridle still
  my headstrong will,
Good heauens grant I may doe so.

5 Many times ith' towne of *Cambden*,
 where my businesse sometimes lay:
Among boone Lads, I haue been hemb'd in
 and inforced long to stay:
  both day and night
  for my delight,

[1] *I.e.* Moreton.

I tarri'd still, and would not goe
   to my owne home
   but lou'd to rome
Abroad, but Ile no more doe so.

6 At *Easam*[1] also, and at *Shipson*[2],
   I am for a rorer knowne,
Where many times mad *Charles* the gipson
   hath his merry humours showne,
     the stoutest there
     for wine and beere,
Me in expence could not outgoe,
     for all the day
     I'de call and pay:
But now I will no more doe so.

The second part. To the same tune.

7 MAny Crotchets haue I plaid,
   which in performance cost me deere,
Whereby my substance it decay'd,
   therefore Ile such tricks casheere:
     my mind was such
     it ioy'd me much,
When I such mad exploits did show,
     my time I lost,
     beside my cost,
But now I will no more doe so.

8 A Taylor once well sok't in Barley,
   profferd to lend me seuen pound,
About the same we two did parley,
   and when he my humour found,
     a shilling hee
     did giue to me
In earnest, his kinde loue to shew,
     and I in game
     did take the same,
Because he sware it should be so.

---

[1] *I.e.* Evesham.   [2] *I.e.* Shipton or Shipston, villages near Oxford.

9 Hauing tane the Taylors shilling,
    a Iugge of beere I cal'd for then:
I paid for that, and then was willing
    to giue him the rest agen:
        but he refus'd,
        and rather chus'd
To spend the rest ere he did goe,
        then I did call
        and paid for all,
The Taylor wil'd it should be so.

10 This and many more such actions
    haue I done to please my humour:
But now Ile leaue all drunken fashions,
    would to God I had done so sooner:
        in merryment
        my time I spent,
And mony too, which breeds my woe:
        now my mad pranks,
        I giue God thankes,
Are left, and Ile no more doe so.

11 I will follow my Vocation
    with industry and regard,
And maintaine my reputation,
    in this world thats growne so hard.
        Markets are naught,
        Ware is not bought,
As twas since I the Trade did know,
        tis time therefore
        now to giue ore
Such spending, and no more doe so.

12 My wife and children I will tender,
    more then heretofore I vs'd,
Ile be no more so vaine a spender,
    nor will I be with drinke abusde:
        Ile learne at last
        ere hope is past,

My selfe a ciuill man to shew,
    and banish quite
    my old delight:
Good heauens grant I may doe so.

13 You that heare my recantation,
    which I purpose to obserue:
When you see this alteration,
    from my rules doe you not swerue:
      through *Oxfordshire*,
      both farre and neere,
My resolution I will shew,
    that euery one
    which so hath done,
May mend with me. God grant it so.

Finis.

Charles Rickets.

Printed for *Iohn Wright.*

75

No natural mother

Manchester Free Reference Library Collection, II, 2, B.L., three wood-cuts, three columns.

The ballad was licensed for publication on July 16, 1634 (Arber's *Transcript*, IV, 323). A better example of a good-night, or last farewell, could hardly be found, though many of the stanzas have a *naïveté* that is a bit startling and that is somewhat unusual in so sophisticated a balladist as Parker. The first stanza is quoted in the *Roxburghe Ballads*, VIII, xviii***, with no indication of its source. For the tune see Chappell's *Popular Music*, I, 176. *Welladay* was the favourite tune for good-nights after it had been used in a ballad (1603) attributed to Robert, Earl of Essex. Other famous victims of the law whose woes were sung to it were Thomas Wentworth, Earl of Strafford (British Museum, C. 20. f. 2/8), and Charles I (*Roxburghe Ballads*, VIII, xc***). Cf. also Sir Walter Raleigh's lament (No. 15).

No naturall Mother, but a Monster.

Or, the exact relation of one, who for making away her owne new borne childe, about *Brainford* neere *London*, was hang'd at Teyborne, on Wednesday the 11. of December, 1633.

To the tune of, *Welladay*.

1 Like to a dying Swan
       pensiuely, pensiuely,
   (With mourning) I looke wan,
       for my life passed;
   I am exceeding sad,
   For my misdeeds too bad,
   O that before I had
       better fore-casted.

425

2 My Parents me vp brought,
      carefully, carefully,
   Little (God wot) they thought,
      that I should euer
   Haue run so bad a race,
   To dye in such a place,
   God grant all Maidens grace,
      to take example.

3 Dame Nature shew'd her art,
      skilfully, skilfully,
   For I in euery part,
      was made compleatly;
   But my vnbridled will
   Did put me forward still,
   From bad to further ill,
      as late appeared.

4 When my minority
      passed was, passed was,
   And some maturity,
      I had attained,
   I put to seruice was,
   With honest meanes to passe,
   My time which is alasse,
      too soone abridged.

5 My carriage was too wild,
      woe is me, woe is me,
   And I was got with child,
      take heed faire Maidens,
   The father on't was fled,
   And all my hopes were dead,
   This troubled sore my head,
      woe worth that folly.

6 How I my fault might hide,
      still I mus'd, still I mus'd,
   That I might not be spide,
      nor yet suspected,

To this bad thought of mine
The Deuill did incline,
To any ill designe,
   he lends assistance.

7 Not long before my date
   was expir'd, was expir'd,
To dwell it was my fate,
   in a good seruice,
With people of good note,
All thereabout doe know't,
Where this foule fact I wrought,
   to my destruction.

8 When the full time drew nigh,
   woe is me, woe is me,
Of my deliuery,
   unhappy labour,
Into the yard I ran,
Where sudden pangs began,
There was no woman than,
   neere to assist me.

The second part. To the same tune.

9 WIth little pain or smart,
   strange to think, strange to think
I with my child did part
   poore harmelesse Infant,
Being where none me saw,
Quite against natures law,
I hid it in the straw,
   where it was smother'd.

10 Then in againe I went,
   speedily, speedily,
Hoping thus to preuent
   any suspition,

But God that sits on high,
With his all-seeing eye,
Did see my cruelty,
    and wicked cunning.

11 And did detect the same,
    presently, presently,
Unto my open shame,
    and vilde discredit,
Forcing me to confesse,
My barbarous wickednesse,
That fouly did transgresse
    thus against nature.

12 My Mistresse to me said,
    earnestly, earnestly,
O *Besse* I am afraid,
    thou hast done euill,
Thy Belly that was high,
Is fallen suddenly,
This though[1] I did deny,
    she further vrged.

13 My conscience did me cast
    [woefully, woefully,][2]
So out I went in haste,
    she followed after,
And presently she saw,
Me run vnto the straw,
From whence I soone did draw,
    my strangled Infant.

14 Thus taken in the same,
    soone I was, soone I was,
With great disgrace and shame,
    carried to Newgate,

---

[1] *Text* theugh.   [2] Torn off.

> And at the Sessions last,
> For my offences past,
> I was condemned and cast,
>   and hangd at Teyborne.

15 Sweet Maidens all take heed,
>   heedfully, heedfully,
> Adde not vnto the deed
>   of fornication,
> Murder which of all things,
> The soule and conscience stings,
> Which God to light still brings,
>   though done in priuate.

16 Though the first fact be vilde,
>   yet be sure, yet be sure,
> If you be got with childe,
>   through lawlesse sporting,
> Be grieu'd for your offence,
> And with true penitence,
> Striue to make recompence,
>   for former vices.

17 Let not the feare of shame,
>   so preuaile, so preuaile,
> As to win you the name
>   of cruell M[other.]¹
> All those that God doe feare,
> Are frighted when they heare,
> That you more cruell are
>   than Sauage creatures.

18 Obserue the female Snake,
>   carefully, carefully,
> What speedy shift she'l make,
>   to saue her young ones,

¹ Torn off.

429

Being by any spide,
Her mouth she opens wide,
That they themselues may hide,
    within her belly.

19 The Tyger though by kind,
        truculent, truculent,
As nature doth her binde,
        is wondrous tender,
And louing to her young
Whom to secure from wrong,
Her selfe into the throng,
        shee boldly thrusteth.

20 And can a womans heart,
        bloodily, bloodily,
So willingly depart
        from her owne baby,
You that good women be,
Example take by me,
And striue your selfe to free,
        from shame and slander.

𝔉inis.

M.P.

London printed for F. Coule[s.]¹

¹ Torn.

76

Murder upon murder

Wood 401 (129), B.L., four woodcuts, five columns. The first column is badly mutilated: missing words and letters in stanzas 1–4 have been supplied in square brackets.

The melodious tears offered in this ballad to the memory of two notorious criminals may account for the references that were made to them for years after their execution. Thus in *Merlinus Anonymus*, for 1653, March 21 and March 29 are designated as "fest days" in honour of Canbury Bess and Country Tom; in *Montelion, 1660, Or, The Prophetical Almanack* (sig. B^v), January 3 and 4 are dedicated to them; and in *Montelion*, 1661 (sig. B^v), January 2 and 3.

In the *Obituary of Richard Smyth* (ed. Ellis, Camden Society, p. 10) occur the entries:

> 1635
>
> Apr[il]. 14. Tho. Sherwood hanged in chains in Grays Inne Fields for the murther of Mr Claxton and Holt.
>
> 17. Eliz. Evans hanged also there for ye same murther.

A full account of the two is given in H. G[oodcole]'s pamphlet called *Heavens Speedie Hue and Cry sent after Lust and Murther*, 1635 (British Museum, C. 27. c. 17). Goodcole tells that Canbury Bess and Country Tom killed (1) Rowland Holt, merchant, in Clerkenwell Fields, in January, 1635; (2) Lieutenant Thomas Claxton, of London, on April 1; and (3) Michael Lowe. Their arrest, trial, and execution came in rapid succession. Sherwood was hanged on April 14, and made a most edifying end. At the gallows he confessed and lamented his crimes, sang part of the fifty-first Psalm, "and after that by his request was sung the *Lamentation of a sinner*" [*i.e.* the ballad of "Fortune, my foe"]. Thereupon, he "ioyfully embraced" his death, while all the highly edified spectators prayed aloud for his soul. His body was hanged in chains at Battle-bridge, near Pancras Church, where such crowds of people swarmed to see it that fields and growing crops were trodden into slush and mire. The irate owners of the land surrounding the gibbet petitioned the King and Privy Council to remove the body. Shortly afterward, it was moved to the "Ring-Cross beyond Islington." After the execution of Elizabeth Evans, on April 17, her body "was conveied to Barber Surgions Hal for a *Skeleton*

431

having her bones reserved in a perfect forme of her body which is to be seene, and now remaines in the aforesaid Hall[1]."

The ballad is earlier in date than H. G.'s pamphlet[2]: it may have appeared on April 14, 1635 (cf. the title), and certainly was in print before the execution of Canbury Bess on April 17.

Murder upon Murder,

Committed by *Thomas Sherwood*, **alias,** *Countrey Tom* : **and** *Elizabeth Evans*, **alias,** *Canbrye Besse* : **The first upon M.** *Loe*, **The 2. of M.** *George Holt* **of** *Windzor*, **whom inhumanely they kild neare** *Islington* **on the 22. day of January 1635. The last upon M.** *Thomas Claxton* **of** *London*, **whom merci= lesly they murdered upon the second day of Aprill last past, neare unto Lambs Conduit on the back=side of Holborne, with many other robberies and mischiefes by them committed from time to time since Midsomer last past, now revealed and confest by them, and now according to Judgement he is hangd neare to Lambs Conduit this 14 of Aprill, 1635. to the terror of all such offenders.**

To the tune of *Bragandary downe, &c.*

1 [L]Ist Christians all vnto my song,
　　'twill moue your hearts to pitty,
　[W]hat bloody murders haue beene done,
　　[o]f late about the City:
　[W]ee daily see the brood of *Cain*,
　　[Am]ongst vs euer will remaine.
　　[*O m*]*urder, lust and murder,*
　　　[*is*] *the foule sinke of sin.*

2 [The]re's scarce a moneth within the yeare,
　　[bu]t murders vile are done,

---

[1] On the practice of preserving the skeletons of criminals at the Barber Surgeons Hall see Stow's *London*, ed. Strype, 1720, book v, p. 209.

[2] The pamphlet was registered for publication on April 22, 1635.

MURDER UPON MURDER

[The] Son, the Father murdereth,
   [th]e Father kills the Son,
[T]wixt man and man there's such debate,
[Wh]ich in the end brings mortall hate.
O murder, &c.

3 The mother loseth her owne life,
   cause she her child doth kill,
And some men in their drunkennesse,
   [the]ir deare friends blood doth spill,
[And] many more, through greedy gaine,
[The] brother hath the brother slaine.
[*O m*]*urder, &c.*

4 [But t]o the story now in hand,
   [the] truth I will declare,
[Whe]n God leaues man vnto himselfe,
   [of S]athan then beware,
[A]s doth *Sherwood* truely finde,
[Who] vnto murder bent his mind.
[*O mur*]*der, &c.*

5 A man of honest parentage,
   traind vp to husbandry,
But weary of that honest life,
   to London he did hye:
Where to his dismall wofull Fate,
He chose a Queane for his copesmate.
O murder, &c.

6 One Canbery *Besse* in Turnball-street,
   on him did cast an eye,
And prayd him to giue her some drinke,
   as he was passing by:
O too too soone he gaue consent,
And for the same doth now repent.
O murder, &c.

7 For by alluring tempting bates,
   she sotted so his minde,

That vnto any villany,
    fierce *Sherwood* was inclind,
His coyne all spent he must haue more,
For to content his filthy (Whoore).[1]
O murder, &c.

8 Much mischiefe then by them was done
    in and about the City,
But still they scape unpunished,
    (not knowne) more was the pitty,
To deadly sinnes they then did fall,
Not onely robbe but murder all.
O murder, lust and murder,
    is the foule sinke of sin.

9 The first was Master *William Loe*,
    a Gentleman of note,
And cruell *Sherwood* laid him low
    with an inhumane stroke:
Nor birth nor bloud they did regard,
Yet death for bloud is their reward.
O murder, &c.

10 One Master *Holt* of Winsor towne,
    a Norwich Factor he,
Walking abroad to take the ayre,
    felt next their buchery,
For *Sherwood* with a fatall blow,
This goodman kill'd, his quean wil so,
O murder, &c.

11 His cloak, hat, ruffe, from him they took
    eleuen groats also,
And were about his cloathes to stripe,
    his shirt, shooes, hose thereto,
But being scard, away they flye,
he hath confest this villany.
O murder, &c.

---

[1] No period in the text.

12 A vile loose life they still run on,
        regarding not their end,
    Their hearts still bent to cruelty,
        not minding to amend:
    They cannot see Sathan the deuill,
    That drags them vnto all this euill.
        O murder, lust and murder,
            is the foule sinke of sin.

Ⓣⓗⓔ second part Ⓣⓞ ⓣⓗⓔ same tune.

13 FOr being flusht with humane bloud,
        they thirsted still for more,
    The more from God O man thou runst
        the greater is thy score:
    Like rauening wolues they pry & watch,
    How they the innocent may catch.
        O murder, lust and murder,
            is the foule sinke of sin.

14 The last that fell into their hands,
        was Master *Claxton* he,
    A Gentleman of good descent,
        and well belou'd truely,
    Who walkt vnarm'd by breake of day,
    In holborne fields they did him slay.
        O murder, &c.

15 A scarlet coate from him they tooke,
        new suit from top to toe,
    His bootes, hat, shirt they tooke from him
        much money eke also,
    And left him in the fields so wide
    So fled away and not discride.
        O murder, &c.

16 But marke the goodnesse of the Lord,
        on the succeeding day,
    That *Sherwood* with his trull did think
        beyond sea take their way,

MURDER UPON MURDER

In Hounsdich were together tane,
Selling the coat in the same lane.
O murder, &c.

17 With the new suit vpon his back,
    and all things else beside,
The queane the hat of Master *Holt*,
    which they had murdered,
So vnto Newgate were they sent,
Confest all this, and doe repent.
O murder, &c.

18 Wishing all men when as they walke
    to haue a speciall care,
And not to go vnarm'd, or late,
    but sword or truncheon weare,
Had they done so *Sherwood* doth say,
He had not ventred them to slay.
O murder, &c.

19 Within three quarters of a yeare,
    these murders they haue done,
And maim'd and spoiled many a one,
    by their confession:
Such deadly blowes he did them giue,
Twas strange that after they should liue.
O murder, &c.

20 For these bad facts he now doth dye,
    iust iudgement for his meede,
All such ill liuers grant they may,
    no worse nor better speed,
So shall England from crying sinne,
Be euer freed, Gods mercy winne.
For murder lust and murder,
    is the foule sinke of sinne.

𝔉inis.

Printed at London for *T. Langley*,
and are to be sold by *Thomas Lambert*
in Smithfield, neare to the Hospitall
gate.

77

A description of a strange fish

Wood 401 (127), B.L., three woodcuts, four columns.

This ballad has been reprinted very inaccurately and with one whole stanza silently omitted in Halliwell-Phillipps's edition of *The Marriage of Wit and Wisdom*, Shakespeare Society, 1846, p. 95. Strange fishes, as Shakespeare himself bears witness, never failed to attract London crowds. In his *Annals* John Stow gravely recounts the most incredible marvels about fish: one mentioned there in the year 1606 is scornfully referred to in Ben Jonson's *Volpone*, II, i. In later days, too, the attraction held. Thus in June, 1658, Francis Grove printed a book called *London's Wonder. Being a most true and positive relation of the taking and killing of a great Whale neer to Greenwich; the said Whale being fifty eight foot in length, twelve foot high, fourteen foot broad, and two foot between the Eyes* (Bodleian, Wood 487).

Parker's ballad summarizes some pamphlet which I have not been able to locate, possibly the pamphlet licensed to Nicholas and John Okes on May 16, 1636, as *a wonder from the sea &c. of a fish*. It is evidently of about the same date as the licenses granted by Sir Henry Herbert to "James Seale to shew a strange fish for half a yeare, the 3d of September, 1632," and to "Francis Sherret, to shew a strange fish for a yeare, from the 10th of Marche, 1635" (Malone's *Shakespeare*, 1821, XIV, 368; XV, 95). For the tune cf. No. 49.

A DESCRIPTION OF A STRANGE FISH

𝔄 𝔡𝔢𝔰𝔠𝔯𝔦𝔭𝔱𝔦𝔬𝔫 𝔬𝔣 𝔞 𝔰𝔱𝔯𝔞𝔫𝔤𝔢 (𝔞𝔫𝔡 𝔪𝔦𝔯𝔞𝔠𝔲𝔩𝔬𝔲𝔰) 𝔉𝔦𝔰𝔥, 𝔠𝔞𝔰𝔱 𝔲𝔭𝔬𝔫 𝔱𝔥𝔢 𝔰𝔞𝔫𝔡𝔰 𝔦𝔫 𝔱𝔥𝔢 𝔪𝔢𝔞𝔡𝔰, 𝔦𝔫 𝔱𝔥𝔢 𝔥𝔲𝔫𝔡𝔯𝔢𝔡 𝔬𝔣 *Worwell*, 𝔦𝔫 𝔱𝔥𝔢 ℭ𝔬𝔲𝔫𝔱𝔶 𝔓𝔞𝔩𝔞𝔱𝔦𝔫𝔢 𝔬𝔣 *Chester*, (𝔬𝔯 *Chesshiere*. 𝔗𝔥𝔢 𝔠𝔢𝔯𝔱𝔞𝔦𝔫𝔱𝔶 𝔴𝔥𝔢𝔯𝔢𝔬𝔣 𝔦𝔰 𝔥𝔢𝔯𝔢 𝔯𝔢𝔩𝔞𝔱𝔢𝔡 𝔠𝔬𝔫𝔠𝔢𝔯𝔫𝔦𝔫𝔤 𝔱𝔥𝔢 𝔰𝔞𝔦𝔡 𝔪𝔬𝔰𝔱 𝔪𝔬𝔫𝔰𝔱𝔯𝔬𝔲𝔰 𝔉𝔦𝔰𝔥.

To the tune of *Bragandary*.

1   O F many maruels in my time
     I'ue heretofore,
  But here's a stranger now in prime
     that's lately come on shore,
  Inuites my pen to specifie
  What some (I doubt) will think a lie.
     O rare
     beyond compare,
  in England nere the like.

2 It is a fish, a monstrous fish,
    a fish that many dreads,

But now it is as we would wish,
    cast vp o'th sands i'th meads,
In *Chesshire;* and tis certaine true,
Describ'd by those who did it view.
    O rare
    beyond compare,
in England nere the like.

3 Full twenty one yards and one foot
    this fish extends in length,
With all things correspondent too't,
    for amplitude and strength:
Good people what I shall report,
Doe not account it fained sport.
    O rare
    beyond compare,
in England nere the like.

4 It is almost fiue yards in height,
    which is a wondrous thing,
O mark what maruels to our sight
    our Potent Lord can bring.
These secrets *Neptune* closely keeps
Within the bosome of the deeps.
    O rare
    beyond compare,
in England nere the like.

5 His lower jaw-bone's fiue yards long,
    the vpper thrice so much,
Twelue yoak of oxen stout and strong,
    (the weight of it is such)
Could not once stir it out o'th sands
Thus works the All-creating hands.
    O rare
    beyond compare,
in England nere the like.

6 Some haue a project now in hand,
    (which is a tedious taske)
When the Sea turnes, to bring to Land
    the same with empty cask:
But how I cannot well conceiue,
To each mans judgement that I leaue.
     O rare
     beyond compare,
   in England nere the like.

7 The lower jaw-bone nam'd of late,
    had teeth in't thirty foure,
Whereof some of them are in weight
    two pounds, or rather more:
There were no teeth i'th vpper jaw,
But holes, which many people saw.
     O rare
     beyond compare,
   in England nere the like.

The second part, To the same tune.

8 HIs Pissle is in length foure yards,
    big as a man i'th wast,
This monster he who well regards,
    from th' first vnto the last,
By euery part may motiues find,
To wonder at this wondrous kind.
     O rare
     beyond compare,
   in England nere the like.

9 His Cods are like two hogsheads great,
    this seemeth past beleefe,
But men of credit can relate
    what I describe in briefe:
Then let's with charity confesse
Gods works are more then man can guesse.
     O rare, &c.

10 The tongue on't is so mighty large,
     I will it not expresse,
    Lest I your credit ouer-charge,
     but you may easily guesse,
    That sith his shape so far excels,
    The tongue doth answer all parts else.
     O rare, &c.

11 A man on horseback as tis try'd
     may stand within his mouth,
    Let none that hears it this deride,
     for tis confirm'd for truth:
    By those who dare auouch the same,
    Then let the Writer beare no blame.
     O rare, &c.

12 His nerues or sinewes like Bulls pissles,
     for riding rods some vse:
    Of Spermaceti there's some vessels:
     if this be the worst newes,
    That of this monster we shall heare,
    All will be well I doe not feare.
     O rare, &c.

13 Already sixteene tuns of Oyle
     is from this fish extracted,
    And yet continually they boyle,
     no season is protracted:
    It cannot be imagin'd how much
    'Twill yeeld, the vastnesse on't is such.
     O rare, &c.

14 When he vpon the sands was cast
     aliue, which was awhile:
    He yell'd so loud, that many (agast)
     heard him aboue six mile:
    Tis said the Female fish likewise
    Was heard to mourne with horrid cryes:
     O rare, &c.

A DESCRIPTION OF A STRANGE FISH

15 The Mariners of *Chester* say
a Herring-hog tis nam'd:
Whatere it be, for certaine they
that are for knowledge fam'd,
Affirme, the like in ages past
Upon our Coast was neuer cast.
O rare
beyond compare,
in England nere the like.

M. P.

Printed at London for *Thomas Lambert*, at
the sign of the Hors-shoo in Smithfield.
There is a Book to satisfie such as desire a
larger description hereof.

78

Round, boys, indeed

Pepys, I, 442, B.L., four woodcuts, four columns.

A pretty, musical ditty by Laurence Price on the favourite topic of shoemakers. Evidently it was the ballad called "A Merry Round &c." which John Wright, Jr, registered on June 24, 1637 (Arber's *Transcript*, IV, 386). Price, the chief rival of Martin Parker, wrote very many ballads of equal merit to Parker's, but has left behind him almost no biographical record. There is a meagre sketch of his life in the *Dictionary of National Biography*, and a few other facts about him are given in my "Martin Parker, Ballad-Monger," *Modern Philology*, XVI (1919), 120. Of the friendly rivalry that, at least for a time, existed between Price and Parker many evidences remain (cf. No. 71); such as the habit each had of writing ballads to tunes named for a ballad by the other and of answering each other's productions. Price, furthermore, contributed complimentary verses to Parker's pamphlet, *Harry White's Humour* (1637), and mentions him by name in his *Map of Merry Conceits*, 1656, sig. A 2 (originally issued in 1639).

In striking contrast, however, to the numerous references to Parker, I have found,—after covering the period with some care,—only three allusions to Price. In a broadside in the Luttrell Collection (II, 22) called "On Bugbear Black-Monday, March 29. 1652. Or, The London-Fright at the Eclipse proceeding from a Natural cause," astrological pamphlets by him and by Will Lilly are thus sneered at:

> Was 't *Laurence Price's* Shepherd's Gnostication
> With cunning *Will's* wise Astrologization,
> That put ye in distemper, and such fits,
> As if their folly practis'd on your wits?

Mercurius Democritus for April 13–20, 1653 (p. 416), after a scurrilous tale, breaks off with the remark: "but more of this the next week; because you shall then have the true relation in a *Ballad*, to the Tune of the 7 *Champions* of the *Pens* in *Smithfield*, written by *Lawrenc[e] Price*." He is also classed as one of the "glorious three of poetry"—along with the equally prominent ballad-writers Samuel Smithson and Humphrey Crouch —in S. F.'s *Death in a New Dress, or Sportive Funeral Elegies* (1656), sig. A 2ᵛ. S. F., writing a comic elegy on Robin, the Annyseed-water seller, expresses his astonishment that this celebrated personage (an hermaphro-

dite) has been dead so long "without the meed of some melodious tear."
He exclaims:

*Samuel Smithson.	Ye glorious *three
	Who grasp the Poles of Star-crown'd Poesie;
Hum- phrey Crowch.	Has som Cask-piercing** Youth poison'd your wine
	With wicked *Læthe?* Did you ever dine
Lawrence Price.	On Turnep-tops, without or Salt, or Butter,
	That amongst all your Canzonets, or clutter
**Drawer Smalbeer.	You fail'd to mention this deceased *Robbin*,
	It seems you ne'r-quaft *Nectar* in his Noggin,
	As I have done.

The passage is all the more interesting in that allusions to Crouch and
Smithson are as rare as are allusions to Price.

Round boyes indeed.

Or

The Shoomakers Holy-day.

Being a very pleasant new Ditty,

To fit both Country, Towne and Citie,

Delightfull to peruse in every degree,

Come gallant Gentlemen, hansell from you let me see.[1]

To a pleasant new Tune:

1 HEre we are good fellowes all,
   round Boyes round:
Attendance giue when we doe call,
   round boyes indeed.
Since we are here good fellowes all,
   drinke we must and worke we shall.
And worke we will what ere befall,
   for money to serue our need.

2 We get our liuings by our hands,
   round boyes round,[2]
Then fill vs beare at our commands,
   round boyes indeed,

---

[1] Text has a comma.   [2] No comma in the text.

ROUND, BOYS, INDEED

Our liuings we get by our hands,
    as plainly you may vnderstand,
Whilst many gallants sell their land,
    for money to serue their need.

3 We set our stitches iust and straight,
    round boyes round,
  And doe our worke without deceite,
    round boyes indeed,
Tho Munday Sundayes fellow be,
    when tuesday comes to worke fall we
And fall to worke most merrily,
    for money to serue our need.

4 The titles which our trade adorne,
    round boyes round,
Shoemakers sonnes were princes borne,
    round boyes indeed,
For kind S Hughe and Crispins sake,
    a merry day we meane to make,
And after to our tooles betake,
    for money to serue our need.

5 And if our Master angry seeme,
    round boyes round,
We little doe of that esteeme,
    round boyes indeed,
S. Hughs bones vp we take in hast,
    both pinsers, punching alle and last,
The gentle Craft was neuer disgrast,
    they haue money to serue their need.

6 If we want cash ouer night,
    round boyes round,
We shall not long be in that plight,
    round boyes indeed,
Next day ere morne God will vs send,
    if wee to worke our humour bend,
And merry make each friend with friend
    with money to serue our need.

7 We scorne such cheating knaues and queanes,[1]
 round boyes round,
Which doe not liue by honest meanes,
 round boyes indeed,
When theues & whores to tyburne pack
 wele drink strong beere good ale and sack,
The gentle Craft did neuer lacke,
 for money to serue their need.

The second part. To the same tune.

8 O Fie vpon the cursed crew,
 round boyes round,
We doe defie the cursed crew,
 round boyes indeed,
The gallowes take that wicked crue,
 that will not keepe them iust and true,
And pay to euery man his due,
 and haue money to serue their need.

9 The shirking rooke and base decoy,
 round boyes round,
Our company shall not inioy,
 round boyes indeed,
But with those men of good report,
 that lead their liues in honest sort,
A Iugg or two will make vs sport,
 we haue money to serue our need.

10 The smith, the weauer, and the tayler,
 round boyes round,
The feriman and the iouiall sayler,
 round boyes indeed,
The mariner and souldier bold,
 are in the booke of fame inrold,[2]
That ventured haue their liues for gold
 and money to serue their need.

[1] No comma in the text.   [2] Text has a period.

ROUND, BOYS, INDEED

11 The carpenter we daily see,
    round boyes round,
The mason and bricklayers be,
    round boyes indeed,
The[1] Costerdmonger will not shrinke,
    he is noe niggard of his chincke,
But with boone blades will sit & drinke
    when he of it hath need.

12 The maltman and the baker stout,
    round boyes round,
Will with the brewer haue aboute,
    round boyes indeed,
The tapster may not loose his share,
    though barly broth be nere so deare,
Hele giue his friend a iugg of beare,
    if that he stand in need.

13 The butcher if he be a drie,
    round boyes round,
Hele keepe good fellowes company,
    round boyes indeed,
The tanner when he comes to towne,
    weighs not the spending of a crowne,
Amongst his chapmen up and downe,
    he hath money to serue his need.

14 All those good fellowes which are nam'd
    round boyes round,
Within this song I here haue fram'd,
    are round boyes indeed,
The gentle Craft doth beare good will,
    to all kind hearted tradesmen still,
That keepe the prouerbe to fullfill,
    a penny to serve their need.

[1] The *T* of this word was dropped in printing to the *he* of the following line.

ROUND, BOYS, INDEED

15 Now to conclude my harmlesse dittie,
   round boyes round,
I wish both countrie towne and Citie,
   round boyes indeed,
That euery man and woman kind,
   a faithfull friend may euer finde
So here my friends you know my mind,
   keepe money to serue your need.

16 I trust none of this company,
   round boyes, round,[1]
Will with this song offended bee,
   round boyes indeed,
therefore let some kind Creature heare
   giue hansell for to buy me beere,
To make my throat more shrill & cleere
   you see[2] *I haue great need.*

L. P.

Printed at London for *I. Wright.*

[1] No comma in the text. [2] *Text* sae.

448

79

A monstrous shape

Wood 401 (135), B.L., three woodcuts, four columns. One stanza is printed from this copy in the *Roxburghe Ballads*, VIII, 28.

In December, 1639, the "hog-faced gentlewoman" created great excitement in London journalistic circles. Ballads called "The Woman Monster," "A Maiden Monster," "A Strange Relation of a Female Monster," "A New Ballad of the Swines-faced Gentlewoman," and "A Wonder of These Times," registered on December 4–11, spread her fame abroad. Laurence Price's ballad was apparently not among these registrations. Along with the ballads appeared (on December 5) a book entitled *A certaine Relation of the Hog-faced Gentlewoman called Mistris Tannakin Skinker, who was borne at Wirkham a Neuter Towne betweene the Emperour and the Hollander, scituate on the river Rhyne. Who was bewitched in her mothers wombe in the yeare* 1618, *and hath lived ever since unknowne in this kind to any, but her Parents and a few other neighbours. And can never recover her true shape tell she be married &c. Also relating the cause, as it is since conceived, how her mother came so bewitched* (Ashbee's *Occasional Fac-Simile Reprints*, No. 16). According to the book, if any man will have the courage to marry this ugly but immensely wealthy woman he will find, as John Gower tells in the *Confessio Amantis* (book I, vv. 1407 ff.), that immediately her deformity will vanish and her beauty become ravishing. The same *motif* underlies Chaucer's *Wife of Bath's Tale* and the traditional ballad of "The Marriage of Sir Gawain" (F. J. Child's *English and Scottish Popular Ballads*, No. 31). See, further, Maynadier's *Wife of Bath's Tale, Its Sources and Analogues*, 1901.

"The Swines-fac't Lady" is the subject of an epigram in Robert Chamberlain's *Jocabella*, 1640. *Mercurius Democritus* for October 19–26, 1653, tells of a monstrous giant "taken by an English Merchant in a certain Iland in *America* called *Nera*," and remarks that "*The Hgogs-fac'd* [*sic*] *Gentle-Woman* is sent for out of *Holland* to be his godmother." (The same allusion is made in a separate tract on this subject printed by John Crouch in 1653.) *Mercurius Fumigosus*, August 9–16, 1654, p. 106, speaks of "the Signe of *Hoggs-fac'd* Gentlewoman in *Bartholmew Faire*." "The swine fac'd Lady" is mentioned also in *Ad Populum, or A Low-Country Lecture*, 1653, sig. A 2ᵛ. There is a wonderful lithographic facsimile of Miss Skinker, catalogued under her name, in the British Museum.

Swine-faced ladies of a much later period are frequently reported, though many of them were at the time disclosed as frauds. John Pitts, of 14, Great St Andrew Street, Seven Dials, London, printed about 1800 a ballad of "The Pig Faced Lady. Sung at Astley's Theatre, &c." (Douce Collection, III, 132.) The first stanza runs:

> Your zarvant all round and you zee I be here,
> And what I left plough for will soon make appear,
> For I's come to Lunnun an outlandish place,
> To marry the lady that's got the Pig's face!
> Tura, lura, lal lura, tura lura, lal la.

There is also a marvellous portrait of an Irish lady on a sheet in the British Museum called "The Pig-Faced Lady of Manchester-Square...Published by John Fairburn, 2, Broadway, Ludgate-Hill. (*Price One Shilling, coloured.*)," 1815 (2188(2)). A less satisfactory portrait is in 2188(3). James Caulfield's *Book of Wonderful Characters*, 1869, has an account of hog-faced ladies and an engraving of "the Wonderful Miss Atkinson," born in Ireland, worth £20,000, but fed from a silver trough. Cf. also Ebsworth's notes in the *Roxburghe Ballads*, VIII, 28.

The tune is given in Chappell's *Popular Music*, I, 240. It is worth noting, also, that a Douce (I, 52, 62ᵛ) ballad of "The Daughter's Complaint" is directed to be sung to "*The Spanish paving*, or *the Lovers Dream; or, Martin Parkers Medley*." Parker's "Medley" (*Roxburghe Ballads*, I, 52) is "to the Tune of *Tarlton's Medley*," which has hitherto been unknown but may now be identified with the *Spanish Pavin*.

A MONSTROUS SHAPE

𝕬 𝕸onstrous shape.
Or
𝕬 shapelesse 𝕸onster.
𝕬 𝕯escription of a female creature borne in 𝕳olland,
compleat in every part, save only a head like a swine,
who hath travailed into many parts, and is now to be
seene in 𝕷𝕺𝕹𝕯𝕺𝕹[1],
𝕾hees loving, courteous, and effeminate,
𝕬nd nere as yet could find a loving mate.

To the tune of *the Spanish Pavin*.

[1] *Wood added in MS.* 1640.

451

A MONSTROUS SHAPE

1 OF horned Vulcan I haue heard,
   His teeth were longer thē his beard,
Whose monstrous looks made all afeard
   which did that night behold him:
And of transformed Acteon,
Which like a Hart in Forest ran,
And how faire Lidia like a Swan
   transformed.

2 Of Robin Goodfellow also,
Which was a seruant long agoe,
The Queen of Fairies doth it know,
   and hindered him in fashion:
She knew not what she did her selfe,
She chang'd him like a Fairie elfe,
For all his money, goods, and pelfe,
   she gull'd him.

3 But yet be brisk you Yonkers bold,
And list to what I shall vnfold,
Such newes afore was neuer told,
   as I will now relate:
My subiect is of such a Girle,
That hath both siluer, gold, and pearle,
Yet neuer will be for an Earle
   right fitted.

4 This Urokin as I vnderstand,
Is now arriued from Dutchland,
And hath as much gold at command
   that she would wish or craue:
Her portion threescore thousand pound,
Both corn and cattell on her ground,
As good as any may be found
   in Holland.

5 Besides, a dainty Lasse is she,
A Boores daughter in the Low-country,
Her mother is in her degree
   a very proper Fro,

And all the Tribe from whence she came
Call her faire Pigs nye by her name,
You'l say they haue reason for the same
    hereafter.

6 To describe her from top to toe,
I purpose now for to doe so,
And shew how neatly she doth goe
    when young men come a wooing:
She shews her pretty heele and foot,
A dainty leg adioyning to't,
Her stockins silk, if that will do't
    she cares not.

The second part, To the same tune.

7 HEr person it is straight and tall,
  A lilly white hand, her fingers small
Makes her the handsomest wench of all
    that euer her father got:
In handsomnesse she doth excell
Both bouncing Kate, and bonny Nell,
In dancing she doth beare the bell
    of many.

8 So choice of face she is indeed,
As oft as she doth stand in need,
A siluer trough she hath to feed,
    when euer she wants victuall:
The siluer trough is straight brought out
Wherein she puts her dainty snout,
And sweetly sucks till all is out
    of action.

9 And to speak further for her grace,
She hath a dainty white swines face,
Which shews that she came of a race
    that loued fat porke and bacon:

A MONSTROUS SHAPE

Yet would I not her kindred wrong,
Her nose I think is two foot long,
Also her breath is very strong
    and fulsome.

10 Yet let no party her despise,
She is furnished with two pigs nies,
Though something of the largest size,
    they doe become her neatly,
Her ears hang lolling toward the ground
More fairer then a mastie hound,
Thus are her fortunes still renown'd
    by hearesay.

11 Great store of suters euery day,
Resort vnto her as they say,
But who shall get this girle away,
    as yet I doe not know:
But thus much I dare vndertake,
If any doe a wife her make,
It is onely for her moneyes sake
    he loues her.

12 If any young man long to see
This creature wheresoere she be,
I would haue him be rul'd by me,
    and not to be too forward,
Lest he at last should fare the worse,
Although she haue a golden purse,
She is not fit to be a nurse
    in England.

Finis.

L.P.

Printed by *M.F.* for *Tho: Lambert*, and
are to be sold at the signe of the
Horse shooe in Smithfield.

454

80

A new Spanish tragedy

Wood 401 (137), B.L., two woodcuts, four columns.

In a MS. note Wood dates the ballad "1640 or 41." It was, however, licensed to John Stafford as "a New Spanish Tragedy or the late fight betwixt the Spaniards and Hollanders" on October 15, 1639 (Arber's *Transcript*, IV, 484). Five other ballads on this event were entered on the same day: only one of them—Martin Parker's "A Lamentable Relation of a Fearful Fight at Sea, upon our English Coast, Between the Spaniard and the Hollander....To the Tune of *Let us to the Wars againe*" (cf. No. 73)—appears to be extant. It begins "In every place where men did meet," and is reprinted in *Ballads from the Collections of Sir James Balfour*, pp. 8–12. Ballads dealing with the first naval engagement of September 6 had been registered on September 16 and September 23 (Arber's *Transcript*, IV, 478, 480). Of the two ballads registered on the latter day, one is preserved. It is entitled "A famous Sea-fight: OR, [A Bloo]dy Battell, which was fought between the *Spaniard* [and th]e *Hollander*, beginning on the sixth day of this present month of *September*, 163[9] being Friday....To the Tune of *Brave Lord Willoughby*." It begins "Give ear you lusty gallants, my purpose is to tell," was printed by Francis Grove, is signed by John Lookes, and is preserved (though somewhat mutilated) in the Manchester Collection.

Price's spirited ballad is a good verse rendering of a news-pamphlet: it gives abundant information; and though this information came to him at second hand, his ballad is almost as satisfactory a document to a modern student of history as it was to a news-hungry throng of listeners in Charles I's time. The occasion for the ballad was this: Sir John Pennington, English Admiral guarding the Narrow Seas, was lying in the Downs when the Spanish fleet for Dunkirk, with troops on board, was driven into the Downs, on September 6, by the Dutch fleet under Trump. The latter fleet also anchored there. Pennington insisted that the neutrality of the roadstead be observed. On October 11, however, after receiving large reinforcements from Holland, Trump attacked and destroyed the Spanish fleet, while Pennington helplessly looked on. He had no instructions, indeed, to do anything else, though apparently he favoured Spain. The victory of the Dutch was received in England with joy, for some people there believed that the Spaniards had come, at the invitation of Charles I, to crush English liberty.

A NEW SPANISH TRAGEDY

The tune is derived from the ballad of "The Angel Gabriel: his Salutation to the blessed Virgin Mary. To the Tune of *The Blazing Torch is soon burnt out*" (*Roxburghe Ballads*, VII, 779), but the tune of *The Blazing Torch* is not known (cf. No. 37).

𝔄 new 𝔖panish 𝔗ragedy.

OR,

𝔐ore strange newes from the narrow seas, discovering two most dreadfull 𝔖ea fights betweene the 𝔖paniard and the ℌollander, the first happened on 𝔖eptember the 6, and the second upon 𝔉riday the 11 of 𝔒ctober last, in which were many 1000 slaine, and of the 𝔖paniards was 16 ships grounded, 28 fired, some sunke into the sea, and some taken.

To the tune of *the Angel Gabriel.*

1 ALL you that are brave Saylors,
    of courage stout and bold,
Give eare unto a fight at Sea,
    I purpose to unfold,
Newes of a famous battell,
    fought on the Ocean main,
Betweene the Hollander,
    and a mighty Fleet of Spaine.

2 The King of Spaines great Navy,
    for warre being ready bent,
About our coasts lay hovering,
    we know not their intent.
The Hollander perceiving this,
    went towards them amaine,
Not fearing of the force,
    of the mighty Fleet of Spaine.

3 The sixt of our September[1],
    began a dreadfull fight,

[1] *I.e.* September 17, new style.

A NEW SPANISH TRAGEDY

Not ceasing of the battell,
  by day, nor yet by night,[1]
Untill such time that thousands,
  on both sides there were slaine,
Both of the Hollanders,
  and the mighty Fleet of Spaine.

4 Much blood shed was amongst them,[1]
  and many harmes were done,
Untill that they were forc'd to part,
  by noble *Pennington,*
Who charg'd them to give over,[1]
  or else he told them plaine,
That he would sinke their ships,
  into the Ocean maine.

5 Whereby some of the Spaniards
  thought to escape by flight,
The Hollanders prepared,
  with them againe to fight,
And compass'd them about,
  their quarrell to maintaine,
Vowing to be revenged
  on the mighty Fleet of Spaine.

6 And so upon the eleventh day,
  in this moneth of October,
They had permission for to fight,
  neere *Deal* not farre from Dover,
The Dutchmen were resolved,
  to kill or to be slaine,
And bravely all prepared,
  against the Fleet of Spaine.

𝕿𝖍𝖊 𝖘𝖊𝖈𝖔𝖓𝖉 𝖕𝖆𝖗𝖙, 𝕿𝖔 𝖙𝖍𝖊 𝖘𝖆𝖒𝖊 𝖙𝖚𝖓𝖊.

7 SO giving the first onset
  unto this second Battell,

---

[1] Text has a period.

457

A NEW SPANISH TRAGEDY

Their Trumpets sound, their Ensigns spred,
    and their warlike Drums did rattle:
The thundring Canons roar'd,
    Bullets as thick as rain
Came from the Holland ships
    unto the Fleet of Spain.

8 No mercie 'mongst these Enemies
    could at that time be found,
Full 16 of the Spanish ships
    were forc'd to run o'th ground.
28 more at Sea were fired,
    thousands of men were slain
Both of the Hollander,
    and their enemies of Spaine.

9 The Spaniards in this conflict,
    was much with terrour fill'd,
For one man of the Hollanders,
    ten Spaniards then were kill'd,
Their Scooper-holes run down with blood,
    into the Ocean maine,
Which made them cry alas we shall
    never returne to Spaine.

10 Good Lord it was great griefe to see,
    dead men cast on the ground:
Some had their very braines dasht out,
    and others more were found
With mangled legs, and broken limbs,
    and most of them were slaine,
Which did belong to Dunkerk,
    and to the King of Spaine.

11 And as it was reported,
    the Spaniards wanting shot,
They let flye gold and silver store,
    out of their Ordinance hot.

458

And much there was thrown overboord,
   which will nere be found againe,
This misery was then
   amongst the ships of Spaine.

12 And being thus distressed,
   their men with fighting tired,
Some kil'd, some maim'd, some shot, som
      drown'd
   and some on ship-boord fired,[1]
The remnant that remained,
   no longer could maintaine,[1]
The fight wherefore I thinke,
   that they vvish themselves in Spaine.

13 But to conclude my Ditty,
   I thinke there have not beene,
Since eighty eight, the like sea fight,
   neere unto England seene,
The Lord preserve our gracious King,
   and send him long to raigne[2],
In health, and wealth, and peace,
   Gods Gospel to maintaine.

Finis.

L.P

London Printed for *Samuel Rand* on Holborne Bridge.

[1] Text has a period.   [2] *Text* ragine.

459

Index of
Titles, First Lines, and Tunes

Tunes are printed in italics. Titles and first lines are printed in roman type; the former are enclosed in quotation marks. An asterisk (*) indicates that the ballad in question is merely referred to in the notes.

461

INDEX OF TITLES,

FIRST LINES, AND TUNES

INDEX OF TITLES,

FIRST LINES, AND TUNES

INDEX OF TITLES,

FIRST LINES, AND TUNES

INDEX OF TITLES, ETC.

Glossarial Index

The references are to pages. Numbers in parentheses refer to stanzas.

469

GLOSSARIAL INDEX

GLOSSARIAL INDEX

GLOSSARIAL INDEX

soap, Turkish, 119 (18)
Sodom, 155, 187 (9 f.)
sole, soul, 168 (16)
Solomon, the judgment of, 350
something, somewhat, 74 (5)
somewhither, 242 (11)
sort of, a, company (used of high rank), 147 (7)
sotted, besotted, 433 (7)
sound, to, swoon, 359 (11)
souse, pickled pig, 142 (7)
Southwark, an apprentice murdered in, 223. *See* Bankside
Spain, naval battle of, with Holland, in 1639, 455; war of, with the Netherlands in 1621, 139
Spanish tragedy, a, in 1639, 455
sparks, gallants, 271 (2), 394 (1)
speed, to make, to have good fortune, 264 (3)
spells, the, of witches, 96
Spenser, John, of Chester, 256
spermaceti, 441 (12)
spight (spite), a, annoying matter, calamity, 86 (9), 363 (18)
spill, to, ruin, destroy, 321 (17)
Spinola, 139, 141
spittle, a, spital, specif. Bridewell, 41 (5), 245 (8), 318 (4)
spoiled (spoyled), despoiled, 46 (3); destroyed, 389 (10)
sport, amorous dalliance, 50 (2)
Sportive Wit, 60
sprats, 31 (2)
spread, to be, by racking one's body, 203 (7)
spurn, a, blow, kick, 225 (7)
spurn point, a game, 37 (25)
spurned, kicked, 227 (18)
standing, a, the station (of a pedlar's stall), 120 (26); stopping, delay, 388 (5)
stares, starlings, battles of, 150, 156
states, the, of France, the States General, 26 (4); personal condition, 28 (11)

stay, a, delay, 158 (13); condition or state, 184 (20)
stay, to, appease the appetite, 32 (7); delay, 26 (6), 159 (24); desist, cease, 106 (6); stop, 5 (11), 134 (6); stopped, seized, 27 (8), 142 (7); withhold, 23 (22)
stay in, to, remain unchanged (of a lamp-light), 52 (10)
stayed, to be, confined, 378 (16)
stealth, a, theft, 253 (12), 273 (6)
stiff, strong, stalwart, 169 (22); adv., 192 (4)
stil'd, distilled, 117 (7)
stile, style, title, 149 (13), where the title meant is "arrant knave"
stitch, to go through, to complete, to prosecute to the end, 411 (4)
stoates, European ermine, 62 (3)
stock, a, tree, 112 (8)
stocks, the, used for swearers, 189
Stoke, *alias* Francis, Katherine, 300
stool, *see* close-stool
store, abundance, abundantly, 1 (3), 4 (8), 37 (24), etc.
stoutness, rudeness, 15 (14)
Strafford, Earl of (Thomas Wentworth), 425
strangling twist, a, halter for hanging criminals, 103 (24)
street-cries of London, 30
street-walkers, tirade against, 376
strooke, struck, 87 (14)
Stourbridge (Sturbridge) Fair, Cambridgeshire, 65 (23)
suborned, 251 (4)
subtle-pated, 171 (2)
sugar-plum, a, 40 (3)
surfetes, surfeits, disorders due to excessive eating, 167 (11)
Susan and Simon, a jig of, 133
suspect, a, suspicion, 357 (3)
swarue, to, swerve, 68 (8)
sweale, to, swill, drink greedily, 193 (6)
swearing, statute against, 189
Sweauian, Swedish, 46 (6)

488

GLOSSARIAL INDEX

beheading at, 89; woman burned in, 284 (1), 289 (4)

Wetherall, John, 206

whale, the, and Jonah, 69 (12); a great, caught at Greenwich in 1658, 437

wheelbarrow, a scold carried in a, 76 (14)

when as, when, 73 (3), 285 (5), etc.

where as, where, 6 (14), 15 (12), 50 (3), 145 (1), 291 (9); whereupon, 87 (15)

whiff, a, draught of wine, 168 (16)

whipper, the, 40 (2)

whipping as a punishment, 204 (10), 222

whipping-cheer, ballad on, 39

white, the, bull's-eye of a target, 257 (3)

White Lion, the, 223 *n*.

Whitelocke, Sir Bulstrode, 276

white-pot, a, 346 (9)

whoot, variant of hoot, 192 (5)

wich, *see* witch

Wicked Will, his sauce to Turner, 31

widows, satires on, 229, 235, 239, 263

wife, a, Nobody on choosing, 263

Willoughby de Eresby, Lord, 417 (8)

Wiltshire, a father in, beguiles his son, 310 (2)

wimble, a, gimlet, 272 (4)

Windebank, Sir Francis, 248

Windham (Wymondham), Norfolk, burning of, 54

Windsor, Mr Holt of, murdered, 432; Woolner of, 342

winion, with a, 272 (5)

winters, sixteen (used of age), 312 (9)

Wise, John, 387

wisp, a, handful of straw, the sign of a scold or "a shameless callet" (cf. *3 Henry VI*, II, ii, 144) 76 (13)

wit, a countryman's attempt to buy, 244

witch, a, male conjurer, 279 (6)

witches, ballad and pamphlets on, 96

woe worth, interj., may woe come to, 55 (4), 303 (11), 426 (5)

Wood, Nicholas, 342

wooden horse, a, to ride, *i.e.* to ride a rail, 14 (9)

Woolner of Windsor, 342

words, to eat one's, 334 (9)

worser, 79 (4), 87 (13)

Worwell, Cheshire, 438

wrack, to, rack, torment, 371 (3)

wrackt, wrecked, 46 (3)

wrested (of laws), misapplied, falsely administered, 146 (3)

Wright, Jane, murder of, 249

Wright, Robert, 248

wrought, worked (like iron), 230 (2)

w^t, with, 346 (9)

Wymondham. *See* Windham

ye (yee), the, 106 (3), 167 (6), 381 (4), etc.

ympes, *see* imp

Yonge, Walter, diary of, 110, 150

yonkers, younkers, young people, 402 (7), 452 (3)

y^t, that, 241 (10), 301 (2), 345 (7), etc.

y^u, thou, 208 (1)